CADOGANguides

P9-CCL-471

PROVENCE

'A village in Provence' evokes rosy images, of sun-soaked stones and deep pastel colours and flowers spilling out of window boxes...'

Dana Facaros & Michael Pauls

About the Guide

The full-colour introduction gives visual highlights of the region, together with suggested itineraries and a regional 'where to go' map and feature to help you plan your trip.

Illuminating and entertaining cultural chapters on local history, culture, food, wine and everyday life give you a rich flavour of the region.

Planning Your Trip starts with the basics of when to go, getting there and getting around, coupled with other useful information, including a section for disabled travellers. The Practical A–Z deals with all the essential information and contact details that you may need while you are away.

The regional chapters are arranged in a loose touring order, with plenty of public transport and driving information. The authors' top 'Don't Miss' ⭐ sights are highlighted at the start of each chapter.

A language and pronunciation guide, a glossary of cultural terms, ideas for further reading and a comprehensive index can be found at the end of the book.

Although everything we list in this guide is personally recommended, our authors inevitably have their own favourite places to eat and stay. Whenever you see this Author's Choice ⭐ icon beside a listing, you will know that it is a little bit out of the ordinary.

Hotel Price Guide (*see also* p.76)

Luxury	€€€€€	€180 and above
Very Expensive	€€€€	€130–180
Expensive	€€€	€80–130
Moderate	€€	€50–80
Inexpensive	€	under €50

Restaurant Price Guide (*see also* p.83)

Expensive	€€€€	over €40
Moderate	€€	€20–40
Inexpensive	€	under €20

About the Authors

Dana Facaros and Michael Pauls have written over 30 books for Cadogan Guides. They have lived all over Europe with their son and daughter, and are currently ensconced in a old farmhouse in southwestern France with a large collection of tame and wild animals.

5th Edition published 2009

01 INTRODUCING PROVENCE

T he sun-drenched landscapes of Provence seduce like few others – the days shot through with the colour of silvery olives, purple mountains, yellow sunflowers, black cypresses and lavender, the nights thrilling, dry and clear and boiling with stars. Van Gogh, who saw more clearly into the heart of this extravagant world than anyone else, painted these landscapes, and especially those cypresses, as if they were churning and alive, with a lyrical and passionate intensity. Come to the hills around St-Rémy-de-Provence when the mistral is up, and you'll see nature imitating art.

We outsiders have had an on-off love affair with the south of France ever since the Romans colonized it and spent their decline here lounging around their heated pools. Even the medieval popes and cardinals in Avignon succumbed to its worldly temptations, its wines and the scents of the *maquis*, its roses and violets, the droning hum of the cicadas. The painters in the papal court, including some of the greatest artists of the 14th century, lent their radiant Madonnas something of the voluptuous Mediterranean light and colour that would one day inspire Van Gogh and Cézanne, Braque and Picasso – painters whose works have changed the way our eyes see not only the south of France, but the rest of our world as well.

These days, our world has decided on Provence as its possible paradise. Millions come here every year, hoping to catch a glimpse of it, wishing it didn't have so many second homes, holiday flats, trinket shops and traffic jams. To see the region at its best, the delicate question of *when* to go becomes as crucial as where: in August, the sacred month of French holidays, even the dullest

Above:delicious-smelling soaps in a Provençal market

Above: Palais des Papes, Avignon

Opposite: Garden, Arles

town in Provence can be as frantic as the monkey pit in a zoo. At other times, Provence's essentially classical spirit is easier to grasp – in the lovely countryside around Aix-en-Provence and Cézanne's fetish Montagne Sainte-Victoire, or the flame-like peaks of the Alpilles or Cubist tile-roofed *villages perchés* in the Luberon, the cliffs and fjord-like *calanques* off the coast of Marseille, the secret valleys in Mercantour national park in the Alps, the bullring of Arles and the Roman theatre of Orange, like molten gold in the last rays of the sun. Colourful markets, wild mountains, abandoned Brigadoons, beautifully restored art towns and restaurants that rival Paris' finest beckon, but perhaps best of all is doing as the Romans did and spending the day lounging around the pool, surrounded by perfumed gardens, idly dreaming about what's for lunch. No wonder that Pope Gregory XI, who returned the papacy to Rome in 1377, took one look at the Eternal City and immediately decided to pack his bags to return to the comforts and delights of Avignon. Much to the relief of the Italians, he died before he could go.

Provence's Top Ten Sights

1 **Avignon**: the Palais des Papes, museums and festival, pp.100–16

2 The majestic **Grand Canyon du Verdon**, pp.279–80

3 Cézanne's **Aix-en-Provence**, pp.201–13, and Montagne Sainte-Victoire, pp.213–14

4 Vibrant, buzzing **Marseille** and its *bouillabaisse*, pp.176–96

5 Wine touring in **Châteauneuf-du-Pape**, pp.96–8

6 Picture-postcard villages of the western **Luberon**, pp.234–6

7 **Arles** and its Roman and early Christian monuments, pp.144–57

8 The **Camargue** wetlands and beaches around **Saintes-Maries-de-la-Mer**, pp.161–5

9 The frescoed churches, prehistoric carvings and alpine scenery of the **Parc National du Mercantour**, pp.262–4

10 Van Gogh's **St-Rémy-en-Provence**, pp.132–6, and the magical Alpilles, pp.137–44

*Above: Roman Theatre,
Orange*

Below: Beach, La Ciotat

Where to Go

This guide covers the Provençal region excluding the coastal strip of the Côte d'Azur, and travels broadly west to east, from the Languedoc border and the river Rhône to the Alps and the border with Italy.

To start with, the first two chapters descend the Rhône to the coast, beginning in **Down the Rhône 1: Orange to Beaucaire**, which travels from Orange and its Roman theatre through the celebrated vineyards of Châteauneuf-du-Pape and Tavel to lively Avignon, the medieval city of the popes. As the Rhône continues south in **Down the Rhône 2: The Alpilles, Crau and Camargue**, it passes some of the south's most curious natural features: the jagged Alpilles, the rock-strewn plain of the Crau and the marshlands of the Camargue, where Provençal cowboys herd wild bulls and horses. Roman Provence is well represented in St-Rémy-de-Provence and Arles, and the Middle Ages in St-Gilles and Aigues-Mortes.

To the east, in **Metropolitan Provence**, lies Marseille, the metropolis of Provence, in a coastline of dramatic cliffs and *calanques*; here, too, are staid and elegant Aix-en-Provence, and the lovely countryside around Cézanne's Montagne Sainte-Victoire.

In **Northern Provence: The Vaucluse** comes the heartland of Provence: the Luberon and Mont Ventoux, and pockets of exquisite villages full of artists and refugees from the coast.

The Provençal Alps takes the inland route through the maritime Alps and their secret valleys, difficult of access but worth the trouble for the scenery – Mercantour National Park and the Grand Canyon of the Verdon – and for the art in their medieval chapels.

Finally, in **Beaches on the Côte d'Azur** we list the best beaches within reach of inland Provence.

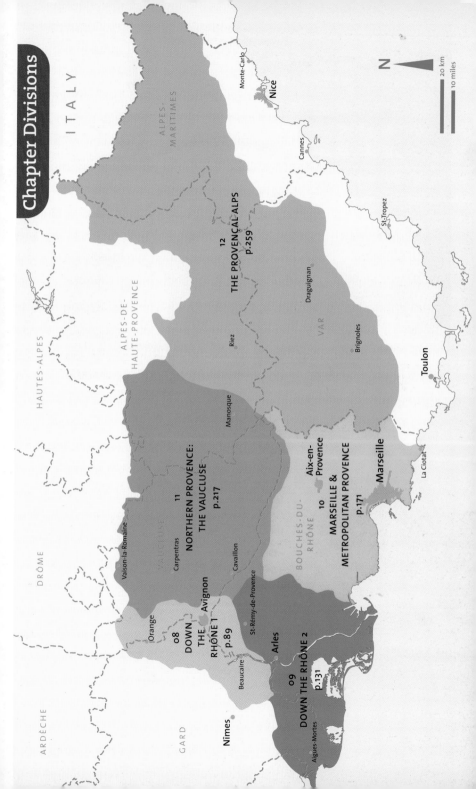

Chapter Divisions

ITALY

ARDÈCHE

GARD

DRÔME

HAUTES-ALPES

ALPES-DE-HAUTE-PROVENCE

ALPES-MARITIMES

VAUCLUSE

BOUCHES-DU-RHÔNE

VAR

Nîmes

Aigues-Mortes

Beaucaire

Orange

Vaison-la-Romaine

Carpentras

Avignon

St-Rémy-de-Provence

Cavaillon

Manosque

Riez

Draguignan

Brignoles

Aix-en-Provence

Marseille

La Ciotat

Toulon

St-Tropez

Cannes

Nice

Monte-Carlo

Arles

08
DOWN THE RHÔNE 1
p.89

09 DOWN THE RHÔNE 2
p.131

11
NORTHERN PROVENCE: THE VAUCLUSE
p.217

12
THE PROVENÇAL ALPS
p.259

10
MARSEILLE & METROPOLITAN PROVENCE
p.171

N

20 km
10 miles

Ancient Roots

The Roman empire had many provinces, but this was the province with a capital P, the one they loved most, where they felt the most at home with its sweet Mediterranean climate, olives and vines. Although you'll find a few traces of Provence's earlier Celto-Ligurian and Greek past, most of the region's surviving ancient monuments are Roman.

- **Orange**: the theatre and Triumphal Arch, pp.91–6
- **St-Rémy-de-Provence**: Les Antiques and ancient Glanum, pp.132–6 and p.135
- **Vaison-la-Romaine**: its Roman bridge, theatre and baths, pp.254–8
- **Arles**: the amphitheatre and cryptoporticus, pp.144–57
- **Marseille**: the Roman docks, p.184
- Near **Aix-en-Provence**: Celto-Ligurian Entremont, p.215

Top: Arc de Triumphe,
Orange; Above: Fountain,
Aix-en-Provence

Clockwise from left: Arles Theatre Antique; Theatre, Orange; Cloisters at Cathedral St Trophime, Arles

Itinerary 1: A Week in Ancient Provence

Day 1 Arrive in **Marseille**, pp.176–96, and visit the Musée des Docks Romains, the Musée d'Archéologie Méditerranéenne and the very early Christian Abbaye St-Victoire, then hire a car and drive to Aix-en-Provence and spend the night.

Day 2 In **Aix-en-Provence**, pp.210–13, visit the fascinating Celtic sanctuary in the Musée Granet and the Celto-Ligurian oppidum of **Entremont**, p.215. In the afternoon, head east to Riez.

Day 3 In **Riez**, p.280, visit the ruins of the temple of Apollo and the 6th-century Merovingian baptistry, made of Roman bits, and the nearby **Grand Canyon du Verdon**, p.279. Overnight in Apt.

Day 4 Visit the little archaeology museum of **Apt**, p.231, then drive to **Carpentras**, pp.245–8, for a look at its arch, and the Roman ruins and bridge at **Vaison-la-Romaine**, pp.254–8.

Day 5 **Orange** and its Roman monuments, pp.91–6 – the Théâtre Antique and the Arc de Triomphe, and the smaller treasures in the Musée Municipal.

Day 6 South to **St-Rémy-en-Provence**, pp.132–6, to see Les Antiques and ancient **Glanum**, p.135.

Day 7 A day in **Arles**, pp.144–57, for the Musée de l'Arles Antique, the Arènes, the Cryptoportiques and Thermes de Constantin.

Day 8 Back to **Marseille**.

Urban Provence

The cities of the south sparkle with that Mediterranean *joie de vivre* that comes from spending so much time out of doors.

- **Marseille**, France's busiest port and second city, with its colourful ethnic mix and sass, is full of surprises, pp.176–96

- Its great counterweight, elegant, arty, bourgeois **Aix-en-Provence**, keeps faith with tradition, although a lively posse of university students gives it a shot of adrenaline, pp.201–13

- **Avignon** is one of the France's great medieval cities, with plenty to show from its 14th-century heyday as the centre of Western Christendom, and with a summer festival that is one of the most prestigious in Europe, pp.100–16

- And then there's many-sided **Arles**, the capital of Camargue – a city of bullfights, of deep Roman and early Christan cultural roots, of Van Gogh, pp.144–7.

Opposite, top: Place de Albertas, Aix; Bottom: Place de Precheurs, Aix

This page, top: Marseille; Right: Arles

Above: Shops, Roussillon

Village Idylls

'A village in Provence' evokes rosy Marcel Pagnol images, of sun-soaked stones and deep pastel colours and flowers spilling out of window boxes. Shops are owned by characters straight out of central casting, and the dappled shade of the age-old plane trees dances over lazy cafés, where lazy people drink *pastis* while watching *boules*-players in berets clink and thud their metal balls. Yet no two are alike, as this short but hardly exhaustive list suggests:

- **Seillans**: all cobblestones and flowers, the last home of Max Ernst, p.284
- **Roussillon**: deep reds amid ochre quarries, p.233
- **Ansouis**: piled, picturesquely, under its castle, p.226
- **Pernes-les-Fontaines**: a tiny village mad for fountains, p.244
- **Moustiers-Ste-Marie**: hanging on the edge of the Grand Canyon du Verdun, pp.281–2
- **Lourmarin**: almost too pretty, but filled with exceptional restaurants, p.227
- **Coaraze**: arty mountain village, the 'cut tail' of the Devil, p.270
- **Forcalquier**: a sleepy hilltop town surrounded by lavender fields, p.221
- **Cassis**: sun-bleached houses tumbling down to the sea, pp.174–6

Above: Delicious food abounds in Provence, from fresh breads and delicate cheeses to fine patisserie

Food and Markets

The specialities of Provence, based on fresh, sun-ripened produce, olive oil and fresh herbs, prepared with a minimum of fuss and bother, make up one of France's healthiest and best-loved regional cuisines. Nearly every town has an outdoor market, offering a sensuous feast of fragrances, tastes and colours. Star-studded restaurants await to tickle your palate, but even a simple salad on a pavement café, dressed in the local olive oil, will taste ten times better than it does at home.

Some of the most colourful outdoor markets are well worth going out of your way to see:

- **Arles**: Wednesday and Saturday, p.155
- **Marseille**'s multi-cultural 'stomach', the Marché des Capucins : Monday–Saturday, p.188
- **Cavaillon**: Monday, p.237
- **Apt**: Saturday, p.231
- **Carpentras**: Friday, with truffles in winter, pp.246 and 248
- **Aix-en-Provence**: Tuesday, Thursday and Saturday, p.211
- **Tarascon**: Tuesday and Friday, p.125

World-class Wines

The ancient Greeks introduced vines and wine-making to Provence, and they've been making people happy ever since. The wide assortment of varietals, soils, and exposures to the sun and *mistral* makes for an exciting spectrum in eight main AOC regions: Les Coteaux d'Aix en Provence, p.215; Les Coteaux des Baux-en-Provence, p.139; Le Vignoble de Cassis; Les Côtes-du-Luberon, p.234; Les Côtes-de-Provence; Les Côtes-du-Rhône; Les Coteaux Varois; Les Côtes-du-Ventoux, p.250.

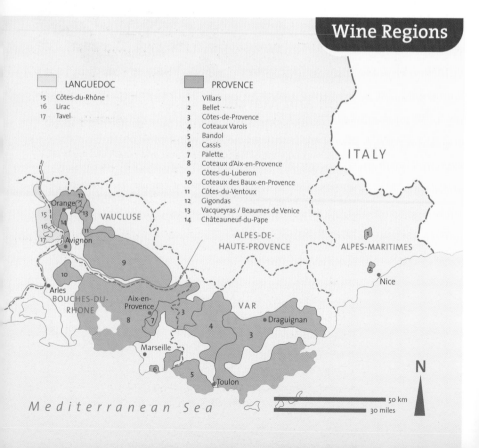

Wine Regions

LANGUEDOC

15 Côtes-du-Rhône
16 Lirac
17 Tavel

PROVENCE

1   Villars
2   Bellet
3   Côtes-de-Provence
4   Coteaux Varois
5   Bandol
6   Cassis
7   Palette
8   Coteaux d'Aix-en-Provence
9   Côtes-du-Luberon
10 Coteaux des Baux-en-Provence
11 Côtes-du-Ventoux
12 Gigondas
13 Vacqueyras / Beaumes de Venice
14 Châteauneuf-du-Pape

ITALY

VAUCLUSE

ALPES-DE-HAUTE-PROVENCE

ALPES-MARITIMES

Orange

Nice

Arles
BOUCHES-DU-RHONE

Aix-en-Provence

VAR

Draguignan

Marseille

Toulon

Avignon

Mediterranean Sea

N

50 km
30 miles

Itinerary 2

A Week on the Wine Roads

Day 1 Start in Marseille and head east along the coast to the beautiful seaside village of **Cassis**, centre of production for a tiny AOC white wine region (pp.174–5), where only 12 cellars produce their delicate, dry and fruity white nectar that 'dances in the glasses' and goes so well with the local *bouillabaisse*.

Day 2 Head briefly inland to the slopes around **Aix-en-Provence** (p.215) to taste the young red wines and rosés: Château de Fonscolombe in Le Puy Ste-Réparade is a good one to aim for. Provence's most rarefied wine, La Palette, first planted by the medieval Carmelites, grows on a mere 12 hectares on the north bank of the river Arc: visit the Château Simone at Meyreuil.

Day 3 Continue east in the **Côtes-de-Provence** (p.294), France's biggest wine region, and traditional source of its favourite summer tipple- a light, fruity rosé (75 per cent of the harvest) as well as good reds, especially from the **Coteaux Varois**, sandwiched in between **St-Maximin** and **Brignoles**. Many of the best wine estates are on either side of the A8 – villages to aim for are Puyloubier, Trets, Le Luc, Vidauban and Barjols.

Day 4 Next aim for **Pertuis** and the high-tech cellar of Château Val-Joanis, in the **Côtes-du-Luberon** (p.234) – not as well known but very pretty, noted for its young, delicate red wines. Overnight in **Bonnieux** (p.234), one of the main centres.

Day 5 Carry on to **Carpentras** (pp.245–8), centre of the **Côtes-du-Ventoux** area (p.250), also known for young red wines, sold at the Friday wine market in summer. In the afternoon, head into the big and diverse **Côtes-du-Rhône** area (p.253), with its fabled micro-labels – **Beaumes de Venise**, producing a lovely sweet white wine, and **Vacqueyras** and **Gigondas**, famous for their velvety reds.

Day 6 Explore the distinct pebbly vineyards of **Châteauneuf-du-Pape** (p.97); among the jewels are Château Rayas, Le Clos des Papes and Château La Nerthe.

Day 7 Head south to **Les Baux-en-Provence** (p.139), an AOC region since 1995 producing fine well-structured reds: one to try is the Domaine de la Vallongue in Eygalières. Return to Marseille.

Above: Vines ripening in the sun

Above: The pink flamingos of the Camargue

Landscapes Real and Imagined

Art changes the way we see things, and the paintings of Van Gogh and Cézanne certainly colour the way we see Provence. In our Van Gogh moments, the olives, cypresses and sky seemed to be filled with an inner life of their own; in our Cézanne moments, the landcapes dissolve, bordering on abstract planes of colour and geometry. Gorges, cliffs and jagged mountains, or sweet fields striped with lavender, sunflowers or vines – these are among the most dramatic Provençal landscapes:

- The white fjords of the *calanques*, pp.174–5
- The Grand Canyon du Verdun, pp.279–80
- The rugged alpine Parc National du Mercatour, pp.262–4
- The Garagai chasm on Montagne Sainte-Victoire, p.214
- Les Dentilles de Montmirail: mountains resembling lace, p.252
- A fairytale setting in Les Alpilles (pp.137–44) and Les Baux-de-Provence, p.137–40
- The Camargue and its white horses, black bulls and pink flamingos, pp.158–70
- Wild, windy Mont Ventoux, pp.249–51

CONTENTS

**01 Introducing
Provence 1**
Where to Go 7

02 History 19

**03 Art and
Architecture 31**

04 Topics 39
A Country Calendar 40
Mistral and the Félibrige 41
Hocus Pocus Popes 42
Marcel Pagnol and the
  Provençal Mystique 43
Troubadours 44
Up Your Nose 45
The Village Sociologist 46
Bullfights 48
Wide Open Spaces 49

05 Food and Drink 51
The Cuisine of Provence 52
Markets, Picnic Food
  and Snacks 54
Drink 66
Spirits and Apéritifs 55
Wine 55
Restaurant Basics 56
French Menu Reader 58

06 Planning Your Trip 63
When to Go 64
Climate 64
Festivals 64
Tourist Information 66
Embassies and Consulates 66
Entry Formalities 67
Disabled Travellers 67
Insurance and EHIC Cards 68
Money and Banks 68
Getting There 69
By Air 69
By Train 70
By Coach 71
By Car 72
Getting Around 73
By Train 73
By Bus 73
By Car 73

By Bicycle 74
On Foot 75
Where to Stay 75
Tour Operators 78

07 Practical A–Z 81
Conversion Tables 82
Children 83
Crime and the Police 83
Eating Out 83
Electricity 83
The Environment 83
Health and
  Emergencies 83
Internet 84
National Holidays 84
Opening Hours 85
Post Offices 85
Racism 85
Shopping 85
Sports and Activities 86
Telephones 87
Time 88
Tipping 88
Toilets 88

The Guide

**08 Down the Rhône 1:
Orange to Beaucaire 89**
From Orange to Avignon 91
Orange 91
South of Orange:
  Châteauneuf-du-Pape 96
The Left Bank of the
  Rhône 98
Avignon 100
Villeneuve lez Avignon 116
South of Avignon 119
Tarascon 122
Beaucaire 126

**09 Down the Rhône 2:
The Alpilles, Crau and
Camargue 131**
St-Rémy-de-Provence 132
The Chaîne des Alpilles 137
Arles 144
The Plaine de la Crau 157

The Camargue 158
Saintes-Maries-de-la-Mer 161
St-Gilles 166
Aigues-Mortes 169

**10 Metropolitan
Provence 171**
La Ciotat, Cassis and
  the *Calanques* 172
Marseille 176
West of Marseille: The Chaîne
  de l'Estaque and the Etang
  de Berre 196
Aix-en-Provence 201
Aix-urbia 213

**11 Northern Provence:
The Vaucluse 217**
Down the Durance 220
The Luberon 233
Apt 230

Maps and Plans

Provence *inside front*
Chapter Divisions 7
Wine Regions 14
Orange to Beaucaire 90
Avignon 102–103
South of Avignon 121
The Alpilles, Crau and
  Camargue 132
Arles 146
Metropolitan Provence 172
Marseille 178
Aix-en-Provence 202–203
Around Aix-en-Provence 213
Northern Provence:
  The Vaucluse 218–19
The Luberon 224–5
Plateau de Vaucluse and
  Mont Ventoux 238
The Provençal Alps 260–61
The Alpes-Maritimes 263
The Alpes de Haute-
  Provence South 284–5
Côtes-de-Provence Wine
  Villages 295
Touring maps *end of guide*

Contents

Contents

Red Villages North of Apt 232
Villages of the Petit
  Luberon 234
Cavaillon 236
The Vaucluse 237
The Plateau de Vaucluse 237
From Cavaillon to
  Carpentras 242
Carpentras 245
Between Carpentras and
  Mont Ventoux: The Gorges
  de la Nesque 248
Mont Ventoux and
  Around 249
Les Dentelles de
  Montmirail 252
Vaison-la-Romaine 254

**12 The Provençal
Alps 259**
The Alpes-Maritimes 262
The Parc National du
  Mercantour 262
La Vallée de la Roya 264
West of Sospel: The Paillon
  Valley 269
The Valleys of the Vésubie
  and Tinée 271
The Alpes de Haute-
  Provence North 275
The Alpes de Haute-
  Provence South 283
From Fayence to
  Draguignan 283

Villages of Central Var 287
Along the Motorway: From
  Draguignan to Aix 291

**13 Beaches on the
Côte d'Azur 297**

Reference

19 Language 299
20 Glossary 303
21 Chronology 305
22 Further Reading 308
23 Index 310

History

Prehistory 20
300 BC–AD 400 21
400–930 22
930–1000 23
1000–1213 24
1213–1542 25
1542–1789 26
1789–1860 27
1860– the Present 28

O2

The names of French regions can be maddeningly fluid, and one of the biggest problems with writing a history of Provence is that its boundaries change all the time. The Romans called Gaul's southern coast their dear 'province', their first conquest outside Italy. Specifically, this was the province of Gallia Narbonensis, stretching from Toulouse to Geneva, although its heartland was always the rich coast between Narbonne and Marseille. In the early Middle Ages, Gaul was evolving its linguistic north–south division between the *langue d'oïl* and the *langue d'oc* (two words for saying 'yes', from the Latin *ille* and *hoc*). Provence then came to mean the southern third of what is now France, stretching north to the Dordogne and Lyon.

At the same time, the political boundary of the Rhône river was redefining the terminology, between lands subject to the Holy Roman Emperors and those claimed by the kings of France. 'Provence' came to mean the semi-independent county to the east of the Rhône, while the rest, as far as Toulouse, came to be known as Languedoc. Today, southerners use the word Occitania (a word only invented in the 18th century) to describe all of the old *langue d'oc*. Old regional names fell out of official use during the Revolution, when France was divided into standardized *départements*. But with the regional autonomy laws passed by the Socialists in 1981, the five *départements* east of the Rhône were formed into the new region of Provence–Côte d'Azur. There, got it?

Prehistory
The First Million Years or So

It seems that Provence's charms were lost on the earliest inhabitants of the Mediterranean. On the Côte d'Azur, tools and traces of habitation around Monaco go back as far as 1,000,000 BC. To the west, in Languedoc, remains of 'Tautavel Man' date back to at least 450,000 BC and perhaps as far as 680,000. Someone may have been in Provence through all this, but evidence is rare. Neanderthals don't turn up till about 60,000 BC. The first evidence of the Neanderthals' nemesis, that quarrelsome and unlovable species *Homo sapiens*, appears some 20,000 years later.

Neolithic civilization arrived as early as 3500 BC, and endured throughout the region for the next 2,000 years. People knew agriculture and raised sheep, traded for scarce goods, and built dry-stone houses. The Neolithic era left few important monuments: there's an impressive but little-known temple complex at Castellet, near Arles, and some large dolmens in the Massif des Maures. Of succeeding ages we know more about technology than culture and changes in population: the use of copper began about 2000 BC, of iron *c*. 800 BC. In both cases the region was one of the last parts of the Mediterranean basin to catch on.

By this stage, at least, the inhabitants have got a name, even if it is a questionable one applied by later Greek and Roman writers: the people who occupied most of Provence in addition to northwestern Italy were now called the Ligurians. From about 800 BC they began building their first settled villages, today called by the Latin name *oppidum*, a word you will see often in the south; it even survives in village names (Oppedette). They were small, fortified villages, usually on a hilltop, built around a religious sanctuary or trading centre. Already, more advanced outsiders were coming to make deals with the natives: Phoenicians, Etruscans, and most importantly Greeks.

A major event of this era was the arrival of the Celts, Indo-European cousins of the Ligurians and Iberians from the north. Beginning in coastal Languedoc in the 8th century BC, they spread their conquests eastwards until the 4th century at the expense of the Ligurians. Meanwhile, Greek merchant activity was turning into full-scale colonization. The Ionian city-states of Asia Minor were overpopulated, agriculturally exhausted and politically precarious, and their citizens sought to reproduce them in new lands. The first was Massalia – Marseille, c. 600 BC. Soon Massalia was founding colonies of its own: Nice and Hyères were among the most important. Greek influence over the indigenous peoples was strong from the start; as with everywhere else they went, they brought the vine (wild stocks were already present, but the Celts hadn't worked out what to do with them) and the olive, and also their art. The Celts loved Greek vases, and had metals and other raw materials to offer in return. Increased trade turned some of the native *oppida* into genuine cities, such as Arles.

300 BC–AD 400
Roman Provincia

From the start, the Greeks were natural allies of the young city of Rome – if only because they had common enemies. Besides the strong Etruscan federation, occupying the lands in between the two, there was their trade rivals, the Phoenicians (later Carthaginians), and occasionally the Celts and Ligurians. As Rome gobbled up Etruria and the rest of Italy, the area became of increasing importance; a fact Hannibal demonstrated when he marched his armies along the coast towards Italy in 218 BC, with the full support of the Celts (historians still argue over how and where he got the elephants across the Rhône).

When the Romans took control of Spain in the Second Punic War (206 BC), the coasts of what they called Gaul became a logical next step. In 125, Roman troops saved Marseille from a Celtic attack. This time, though, they had come to stay. The reorganization of the new province – 'Provincia' – was quick and methodical. Domitius Ahenobarbus, the vanquisher of the Celts, began the great Italy–Spain highway that bears his name, the Via Domitia, in 121. New cities were founded, most importantly Aix (in 122). Dozens of other new foundations followed over the next century, many of them planned colonies with land grants for veterans of the legions.

The Celts were not through yet, though. Two northern tribes, the Cimbri and Teutones, mounted a serious invasion of Gaul and Italy in 115. They raided the areas continuously until 102, when they were destroyed by a Roman army under Marius near Montagne Sainte-Victoire. Marius, later populist dictator in Rome, became a folk hero and the subject of legends ever after (Provençal parents still name their children after him). Celtic-Ligurian resistance continued intermittently until 14 BC; the great monument at La Turbie, on the border of Gaul, commemorates the defeat of the last Alps holdouts.

The downfall of Marseille, still the metropolis of Provence and still thoroughly Greek in culture and sympathies, came in 49 BC. Though it had always been famed for its diplomacy, the city made the fatal mistake of supporting Pompey over Julius Caesar in the Roman civil wars. A vengeful Caesar crippled its trade and stripped nearly all its colonies and dependencies. Thereafter, the influence of Marseille gave way to newer, more Romanized towns: Aix, Arles and Fréjus.

Throughout all this, Provence had been easily assimilated into the Roman economy, supplying food and raw materials for the insatiable metropolis. With Caesar's conquest of the rest of Gaul, the Rhône trade route (which had always managed to bring down a little Baltic amber and tin from Cornwall) became a busy river highway and military route. Under the good government and peace bestowed by Augustus (27 BC–AD 14) and his successors, Provence blossomed into an opulence never before seen. The cities, especially those of the Rhône valley, acquired theatres, amphitheatres for the games, aqueducts, bridges and temples. Provence participated in the political and cultural life of the empire, even contributing one of the better emperors, Antoninus Pius (from Nîmes, AD 138–61), who is only obscure because his reign was so peaceful and prosperous.

Large areas of Roman towns have been excavated at Glanum and Vaison-la-Romaine, and both have turned up a preponderance of wealthy villas. This is the dark side of Roman Provence; from the beginning of Roman rule, wealthy Romans were able to grab much of the land, forming large estates and exploiting the indigenous population. This trend was magnified in the decadent, totalitarian and economically chaotic late empire, when, throughout Roman territory, the few remaining free farmers were forced to sell themselves into virtual serfdom to escape crushing taxes. After AD 200, in fact, everything was going wrong: trade and the cities stagnated while art and culture decayed; and the first of the barbarian raids brought Germans into Provence in the 250s, when they destroyed Glanum.

Constantine, while as yet emperor of only the western half of the empire (312–23), often resided at Arles and favoured the city; his baths there were probably the last big Roman building project in Provence. His pro-Christian policy gave the cult its first real influence in Gaul, at least in the cities; under his auspices, the first state-sponsored Church council was held at Arles in 314. Before that Christianity does not seem to have made much of an impression (later, to make up for this, elaborate mythologies were constructed to place Mary Magdalene and other early saints in Provence; see the towns of Saintes-Maries-de-la-Mer and St-Maximin-la-Ste-Baume).

400–930
600 Years of Uninvited Guests

French historians always blame the barbarian invaders of the 5th century for destroying the cities of Provence, as if Teutonic warriors enjoyed pulling down temple colonnades on their days off. In fact, few armies passed through Provence; the Visigoths, in the early 400s, were the most notable. Though government collapsed in chaos, business went on much as usual, with the Roman landowners (and their new German colleagues) gradually making the transition to feudal nobles. Arles, untouched by the troubles, became the most important city of the west, and briefly the capital, under Constantius III in 412. The weakness of the central power brought some long-due upheavals in the countryside, with guerrillas and vigilante justice against the landlords. The old and new rulers soon found common cause and, for a while, a clique of 100 of the biggest landowners took over administration in Gaul, even declaring one of their own as 'emperor' in Arles (455), with the support of the Visigoths.

The Visigoths soon tired of such games, and assumed total control in 476, the year the Western Empire formally expired. They had to share it, however, with the Ostrogoths, who had established a strong kingdom in Italy and seized all of Provence east of the Rhône – it was the beginnings of a political boundary that would last in various forms for 1,000 years. When the Eastern Empire under Justinian invaded Italy, the Franks were able to snatch the Ostrogoths' half (535). They were never able to hold it effectively, and the area gradually slipped into virtual independence.

The Visigoths kept the western half (now Languedoc), a distant zone of their Spanish kingdom, until the Arab invasion of the early 700s rolled over the Pyrenees. In 719 the Arabs took Narbonne. The next two centuries are as wonderfully confused as anything in prehistory. It's hard to separate fact from legend in, for example, the story of the great Spanish Caliph Abd ar-Rahman, defeated in battle and leaving a magnificent treasure buried somewhere in the Alpilles. Charles Martel, the celebrated Frankish *generalissimo* who stopped the Arab wave at Poitiers in 732, made an expedition to the southern coast in 737–9, brutally sacking Marseille, Avignon and Aix. His mission was hardly a religious crusade – rather a taking advantage of the Visigothic defeat to increase Frankish hegemony in the south; the cities of Provence are recorded as petitioning the Arabs at Córdoba to help them keep the Franks out.

The Arabs couldn't help; the climate was too eccentric and the pickings too slim for them to mount a serious effort in Gaul. The nascent Franks gained control everywhere, and the entire coast was absorbed by Charlemagne's father, Pépin the Short, in 759. Under Charlemagne (768–814), Occitania seems to have shared little in the Carolingian revival of trade and culture, and after the break-up of the empire (at the Treaty of Verdun in 843) its misery was complete. The 9th- and 10th-century invasions were the real Dark Age in many parts of Europe. Provence suffered constant and destructive raids by the Normans, the Arabs again (who held the Massif des Maures and St-Tropez until the 970s), and even the Hungarians, who sacked what was left of Nîmes in 924.

930–1000
The Beginnings of the Middle Ages

Even in this sorry period, the foundations were being laid for recovery. Monastic reformers in Charlemagne's time, men such as Benedict of Aniane (in the Hérault), helped start a huge expansion of Church institutions. The Abbaye St-Victor in

Marseille took the lead in this, founding hundreds of new monasteries around Occitania; hard-working monks reclaimed land from forests and swamps – later they sat back and enjoyed the rents, while always keeping up the holy work of education and copying books. Pilgrimages became an important activity, especially to Arles (St-Trophime), getting a sleepy and locally bound society moving again and providing an impetus to trade.

The Treaty of Verdun (*see* p.23) had confirmed the Rhône as a boundary, and politically Provence and Languedoc went their separate ways. The Kingdom of Provence (or 'Kingdom of Arles'), proclaimed by a great-grandson of Charlemagne in 879, was little more than a façade for a feudal anarchy. Though Provence was united with the Kingdom of Burgundy in 949, and formally passed to the Holy Roman Empire in 1032, the tapestry of battling barons and shifting local alliances continued without interference from the overlords.

1000–1213
Provençal Medieval Civilization

As elsewhere in Europe, the year 1000 is the rough milestone for the sudden and spectacular development of the medieval world. Towns and villages found the money and energy to build impressive new churches. The end of the foreign raiders made the seas safe for merchants, from Genoa, Pisa and Barcelona mostly, but also a few from Marseille. In 1002, the first written document in Occitan appears. The great pilgrimage to Santiago de Compostela, in Spain, made what was left of the old Roman roads into busy highways once more; along the main southern route the first of the medieval trade fairs appeared, at the new town of St-Gilles.

Things were on the upswing throughout the 11th century, and the trend was given another boost by the Crusades, which began in 1095. Increased prosperity and contact with a wider world brought in their wake better manners and the rudiments of personal hygiene. Feudal anarchy began to look quite genteel; a delicate balance of power was maintained, with feudal ties and blood relations keeping the political appetites of rulers from ever really getting out of hand.

From the more civilized east, and from nearby Muslim Spain, came new ideas, new technologies and a taste for luxury and art. As an indication of how far Occitania had come, there were the troubadours (*see* p.44), with modern Europe's first lyric poetry. Almost every court of the south was refined enough to welcome and patronize them.

The growing cities began to assert themselves in the 12th century, often achieving a substantial independence in *communes* governed by consuls: Avignon in 1129, Arles in 1132. In the countryside, successive waves of monastic reform spawned a huge number of new institutions: first the movement from Cluny in the 11th century, and in the 12th the Cistercians, who started a score of important monasteries. Efficiently exploiting the lands bequeathed by noblemen made the religious houses rich, and also did much to improve the agricultural economy.

By 1125 the counts of Barcelona controlled much of Provence south of the Durance. The other leading power in the region, Toulouse, contended with the

Catalans for Provence while being overlords of all Languedoc, excepting
Carcassonne and Béziers, ruled by the Trencavel family, and Narbonne, with its
independent viscounts. It was a great age for culture, producing not only the
troubadours but an impressive display of Romanesque architecture, and an original
school of sculpture at Arles. Perhaps the most remarkable phenomenon of the
times was a widespread religious tolerance, shared by rulers, the common people
and even many among the clergy. Religious dissenters of various persuasions
sprang up everywhere. Most of the new sects soon died out, and are little known
today – including the extremist 'Petrobrusians' of St-Gilles, who didn't fancy
churches, sacraments, relics or priests, and who even had their doubts about the
crucifixion of Jesus.

One sect, however, made startling inroads into every sector of society in 11th- and
12th-century Languedoc – the Cathars, or Albigensians. This Manichaean doctrine,
obsessed with Good and Evil, had in its upright simplicity a powerful attraction for
industrious townspeople and peasants. The Cathars were never a majority in any
part of the south; in most places they never made up more than 10 per cent of the
population. They might have passed on as only a curious footnote to history, had
they not provided the excuse for the biggest and most flagrant land grab of the
Middle Ages. The 'Albigensian Crusade', arranged after the 1208 murder of a papal
legate, was a cynical marriage of convenience between two old piratical enemies,
the papacy and the Crown of France. Diplomacy forced King Philip Augustus to
disclaim any part in the affair, but nevertheless a big army of knights from the Ile-
de-France, led by the redoubtable Simon de Montfort, occupied most of Languedoc,
while committing vicious massacres of the heretics everywhere. Montfort won
battle after battle and took every town he attacked, save Beaucaire.

In a last attempt to save their fortunes, Count Raymond VI of Toulouse and King
Peter II of Aragon combined to meet the northerners. With an overwhelmingly
superior force, they blundered their way to crushing defeat at the Battle of Muret
in 1213. Four centuries after the fall of the Carolingian empire, the French once again
had a foothold in the south. Languedoc was finished, its distinctive culture quickly
snuffed out.

1213–1542
The Coming of French Rule

Provence was still free, enjoying a prosperous era under its Catalan counts,
though still troubled by feudal struggles. Count Raymond Bérenger V (1209–45)
was usually strong enough to keep them in check; under him Provence did very
well, and developed a constitutional government on the Catalan model. It also
managed temporarily to avert French aggression in a roundabout way. In 1246,
Raymond Bérenger's daughter and heir married Charles of Anjou, Saint Louis'
brother. The ambitious Angevin used Provence as a springboard to create an
empire that at its height, in the 1280s, included southern Italy and parts of Greece.

The city of Avignon and its hinterlands, the Comtat Venaissin, loyal possessions of
Toulouse, had suffered greatly at the hands of Louis VIII after the Albigensian

Crusade. In 1274, Charles and Louis arranged to give the Comtat to the papacy, as its discreetly delayed share of the Albigensian booty. In 1309, Pope Clement V, fleeing anarchy in Rome, installed himself at Carpentras in the Comtat. Politically, the popes found Provence a convenient new home and decided to stay – this was the 'Babylonian Captivity' (as jealous Italians called it) that would last over a century. They soon moved to Avignon, purchasing the city in 1348 and conducting a worldly court that to many seemed a Babylon indeed.

The late 14th century brought hard times to Provence: first with the Black Death in 1348, and then in the guise of political instability under the hapless Queen Jeanne (1343–82). Once more the seigneurs of Les Baux and their imitators raged over the land, with bands of unscrupulous mercenaries (the *Grandes Compagnies*) to help them ravage town and country. The popes returned to Rome in 1377; they kept control of Avignon and the Comtat, though French-supported anti-popes held Avignon as late as 1403. After 1434 peace had returned and Provence was ruled by the Bon Roi René (count of Provence, and only 'king' from his claim to Sicily, where the Angevins had been replaced by the Aragonese after the 'Sicilian Vespers' revolution of 1282). The 'Good' is equally spurious. René was open-handed to courtiers, and a patron of artists, but his futile dream of recapturing Sicily and Naples led him to wring the last penny out of everyone else.

René's successor, Charles III, lasted only a year and died without an heir (in 1481), bequeathing Provence to the French crown. It was intended to be a union of equals, maintaining Provençal liberties and institutions. Accepting it as such, the Provençal estates-general ratified the agreement. The French immediately went back on their word, attempting to govern through royal commissioners. Their attempts to swallow Provence whole had to wait, however, though they were never to cease. Louis XI and Charles XII needed a peaceful Provence as a bridge for their invasions of Italy; the region paid for this dearly, with two destructive invasions in the 1520s and 30s by France's arch-enemy Charles V, Holy Roman Emperor and King of Spain.

This era also saw a landmark in the cultural effacement of Occitania, the 1539 Edict of Villers-Cotterêts that decreed French to be the official language throughout the kingdom.

1542–1789
The Wars of Religion

Meanwhile, the new Protestant heresy was floating down the Rhône from Calvin's Geneva. The Occitans received it warmly, and soon there were large Protestant communities in all towns. Though this seems a repeat of the Cathar story, the geographical distribution is fascinating – the old Cathar areas in Languedoc were now loyally Catholic, while the orthodox regions of the 1300s came out strongly for the dissenters. Tolerance was still out of fashion, and the opening round of a pointless half-century of religious wars came with the 1542 massacres in the Luberon mountains. The perpetrator was the Aix *Parlement* (pre-Revolution *parlements* were not parliaments, but powerful judicial bodies appointed by and responsible to the king); the victims mostly Waldensians

(Vaudois), pre-Reformation heretics who had migrated to Provence before the union with France, to escape oppression there.

In the open warfare that followed across the south, there were massacres and atrocities enough on both sides. Protestants distinguished themselves by the wholesale destruction of churches and their art (as at St-Gilles); churches were often converted into fortresses. Henry IV's 1598 Edict of Nantes acknowledged Protestant control of certain areas (Orange and Lourmarin in Provence).

The French monarchy had been weakened by the wars, but, as soon as it recovered, new measures were introduced to keep the south in line. Under Cardinal Richelieu in the 1630s, the laws and traditions of local autonomy were swept away; after 1639 the Etats-Généraux de Provence was not allowed to meet until the eve of the Revolution. As insurance, scores of feudal castles (such as Beaucaire and Les Baux-de-Provence) were demolished to eliminate possible points of resistance.

Louis XIV's revocation of the Edict in 1685 caused more troubles. Thousands of Protestants, the south's most productive citizens, simply left; most of the community in Orange went off to colonize new lands in Prussia. Louis' long and oppressive reign continued the impoverishment of the south, despite well-intentioned economic measures by his brilliant minister Colbert. The 18th century witnessed the beginnings of an important textile industry (usually promoted by the remaining Protestants): silk around Nîmes and parts of Provence (where farmers gave up their bedrooms to raise the delicate silkworms in them), and linen and cotton goods in Orange. In the rest of Provence, though, the century told a miserable tale: economic stagnation, deforestation of mountain areas that has still not been entirely repaired today, and plagues. The biggest plague, in 1720, carried off almost half the population of Marseille.

1789–1860
An Unwanted Revolution

The French Revolution was largely a Parisian affair, though southerners often played important roles (the Abbé Sieyès and Mirabeau), while bourgeois delegates from the manufacturing towns fought along with the Girondins in the national assembly for a respectable, liberal republic. Unfortunately, the winning Jacobin ideology was more centralist and more dedicated to destroying any taint of regional difference than the *ancien régime* had ever dreamed of being. Whatever was left of local rights and privileges was soon decreed out of existence, and when the Revolution divided France into homogenous *départements* in 1790, terms such as 'Provence' and 'Languedoc' ceased to have any political meaning.

In 1792 volunteers from Marseille had brought the *Marseillaise* to Paris, while local mobs wrecked hundreds of southern churches and châteaux. Soon, however, the betrayed south became counter-revolutionary. Incidents such as the one in Bédoin, near Carpentras, in 1793, occurred: when someone cut down the 'liberty tree', French soldiers burned the town and shot 63 villagers to 'set an example'. The Catalans raised regiments of volunteers against the Revolution. The royalists and the English occupied Toulon after a popular revolt, and were only dislodged by the brilliant tactics of a young commander named Bonaparte in 1793.

The south managed little enthusiasm for Napoleon or his wars. The emperor called the Provençaux cowards, and said theirs was the only part of France that never gave him a decent regiment. Today the tourist offices promote the 'Route Napoléon', where Napoleon passed through from Elba in 1815 to start the Hundred Days – but he had to sneak along those roads in an Austrian uniform to protect himself from the Provençaux.

After Waterloo, the restored monarchy started off with a grisly White Terror and tried to turn the clock back to 1789. After the Revolution of 1830, the 'July Monarchy' of King Louis-Philippe brought significant changes. The old industrious Protestant strain of the south finally got its chance with a Protestant prime minister from Nîmes, François Guizot (1840–8); his liberal policies and his slogan – *enrichissez-vous!* – opened an age where there would be a little Protestant in every Frenchman. Guizot's countrymen were rapidly demanding more; radicalism and anti-clericalism (except in the lower Rhône and Vaucluse) increased throughout the century.

Southerners supported the Revolution of 1848 and the Second Republic, and many areas, especially in the Provençal Alps, put up armed resistance to Louis-Napoleon's 1851 coup. Under the Second Empire (1852–70), France picked up yet another territory: Nice and its hinterlands (now the *département* of Alpes-Maritimes), with a mixed population of Provençaux and Italians. This was the price exacted by Napoléon III in 1860 for French aid to Vittorio Emanuele II in Italy's War of Independence.

1860–the Present
Rural Decay and Recovery

The second half of the century saw the beginnings of a national revival in Occitania. While in Languedoc it was political, largely involved with modern France's first agricultural movements, in Provence it tended to be all cultural and apolitical: a linguistic and literary revival bound up with Nobel Prize-winning poet Frédéric Mistral and the cultural group called the Félibrige (*see* pp.41–2), founded in 1854. To counter these advances, the post-1870 Third Republic pursued French cultural oppression to its wildest extremes. History was rewritten to make Occitania seem an eternal part of the 'French nation'. The Occitan languages were lyingly derided as mere patois, bastard 'dialects' of French; children were punished for speaking their own language in school – a practice that lasted until the 1970s.

After 1910, economic factors conspired to defeat both the political and cultural aspirations of the Midi; rural depopulation, which was caused by the break-up of the pre-industrial agricultural society, drained the life out of the villages – and decreased the percentage of people speaking the native languages. The First World War decimated a generation – go into any village church in the south and look at the war memorial plaques; from a total population of a few hundred, you'll see maybe 30 names of villagers who died for the 'Glory of France'. By 1950, most villages had lost at least half their population; some died out altogether.

After the French débâcle of 1940, Provence found itself under the Vichy government. German occupation came in November 1942, after the American landings in North Africa, provoking the scuttling of the French fleet in Toulon to keep it out of German hands. After 1942, the Résistance was active and effective in the Provençal Alps and the Vaucluse – not to mention Marseille, where the Germans felt constrained to blow up the entire Vieux Port area. Liberation began two months after D-Day, in August 1944. American and French troops hit the beaches around St-Tropez, and in a remarkably successful (and little-noticed) operation they had most of Provence liberated within the following two weeks. In the rugged mountains behind Nice, some bypassed German outposts held out until the end of the war.

The post-war era has brought momentous changes. The overdeveloped, ever-more schizophrenic Côte d'Azur has become the tail that wags the dog of Provence. Besides its resorts, it has the likes of IBM and the techno-paradise of Sophia-Antipolis. Above all, the self-proclaimed 'California of Europe' has money, and will acquire more; in two or three decades it will be the first province in centuries to start telling Paris where to get off. In rural Provence waves of Parisians and foreigners (mostly British) have come looking for the good life and a cheap stone house to fix up. They have brought life to many areas, though the traditional rural side suffers a bit. The increasingly posh Vaucluse has the highest rural crime and suicide rates in France.

The greatest political event of the modern era was the election of the Socialist Mitterrand government in 1981, followed by the creation of regional governments across France. Though their powers and budgets are extremely limited, this represents a major turning point – the first reversal of 1,000 years of increasing Parisian centralism. Its lasting effects will not be known for decades, perhaps centuries. Already the revival of Occitan language and culture is resuming; indicators include such things as new school courses in the language, and some towns and villages changing the street signs to Provençal.

Until quite recently politics could still be primeval in Provence. Jean-Marie Le Pen and his tawdry pack of bigots found their biggest following here, riding a wave of resentment against immigrants that Le Pen himself worked hard to create (although this is a Provençal tradition: there were anti-Italian pogroms in Marseille and other towns in the 1890s). Le Pen's National Front scared the daylights out of the French political class in the 1990s by winning control of four Provençal cities: Toulon, Orange and the gruesome Marseille suburbs of Marignane and Vitrolles. They scored up to 15 per cent of the vote in the mid-1990s and achieved one of their greatest successes in 1998, winning 275 council seats. Since then the party has split and split again, though Le Pen made a spectacular comeback by reaching the second round of the 2002 presidential elections. After that it's been a downhill ride; the Front's hopes of scoring a big hit in the regional elections of 2004 turned out a big disappointment and in the 2007 presidential election, Le Pen came in a distinct fourth place with only 11 per cent of the vote. Since then the party has fallen into such economic straits that Le Pen has been forced to sell their château head-quarters and his armoured Peugeot. To add insult to injury, even the party's attempt to set up a virtual headquarters in the internet game Second Life was doomed by a united virtual Socialist reaction. The Front's favourite issue, immigration, still gets a ready hearing in Provence, but the party's never-ending splitting into factions and interior quarrels do their bit in keeping it from having any real strength. The two surviving FN mayors, in Orange and Marignane have joined splinter parties.

The other notable Provençal figure in recent years has been Le Pen's arch-enemy, the liberal Marseille industrialist, film star, novelist, rapper, politician, playboy, football club owner and jailbird Bernard Tapie. Tapie became embroiled in scandals involving asset-stripping, tax evasion and game-fixing for his soccer club, L'Olympique de Marseille, the last of which landed him in prison and ended his business career. From being chairman of Adidas and minister for urban affairs, he spent eight months in France's most notorious prison. But the 'Trampoline Man' bounced back: in 2001 he returned to his old club as sporting director (he left again in 2002), and he was the subject of a curious 2001 documentary called *Who is Bernard Tapie?* by American film maker Marina Zenovich, who stalked him for three and a half years.

And Provence today? The three-hour TGV from Paris to Marseille, inaugurated in 2001, has been a roaring success. Marseille's beloved football team keeps winning, and Peter Mayle has made writing about Provence, both fiction and non, a cosy little industry, even if the 2008 economic downturn has dramatically slowed down the influx of expats in search of the good life. There are bright spots on the horizon however; Marseille-Provence is bidding to become the 2013 European Capital of Culture, while President Sarkozy's recently minted union of Mediterranean countries will naturally put more focus on Marseille as France's biggest and most international city in the region.

Art and Architecture

Prehistoric and Pre-Roman 32
Gallo-Roman: 3rd Century BC–4th
  Century AD 32
Early Christian and Dark Ages:
  5th–10th Centuries 33
Romanesque: 11th–14th Centuries 33
Gothic and Renaissance:
  14th–16th Centuries 34
The Age of Bad Taste:
  17th–18th Centuries 34
France's Little Ice Age:
  Late 18th–mid-19th Centuries 35
Revolutions in Seeing:
  1850–the Present 36

03

Great art and architecture in Provence coincides neatly with its three periods of prosperity: the Roman, the Middle Ages, and the mid-19th and early 20th centuries, when railways opened up the coast not only to aristocrats but to artists as well.

Prehistoric and Pre-Roman

Back in the Upper Palaeolithic era, the first known inhabitants of Provence decorated at least one cave, the recently discovered Grotte Cosquer; its awkward submerged entrance in the *calanques* near Marseille suggests that others may have been lost in rising sea levels. Their Neolithic descendants left few but tantalizing traces of their passing: dolmens (there's a good one near **Draguignan**), a few menhirs and a tomb-temple complex at **Castellet**, near Arles. The first shepherds may well have put up the dry-stone, corbel-roofed huts called *bories*, rebuilt countless times since and still a feature of the landscape (especially at the 18th-century Village des Bories outside **Gordes**). In the Iron Age (1800–1500 BC), the Ligurians or their predecessors covered the Vallée des Merveilles, under Mont Bégo, with extraordinary rock incisions of warriors, bulls, masked figures and inexplicable symbols.

The arrival of the Celts around 800 BC coincided with an increase in trade; Greek, Etruscan and Celtic influences can be seen in the artefacts of this age. The Celts had talents for jewellery and ironwork – and a bizarre habit of decapitating enemies and making images of the heads (atavistically surviving in the little grotesque heads that pop up all over Romanesque buildings). The best of the original images and sculptures are in the Musée Granet in **Aix-en-Provence**, the Musée d'Archéologie Méditerranéenne in **Marseille** and the Musée Lapidaire of **Avignon**.

Gallo–Roman: 3rd Century BC–4th Century AD

Archaeologically the Greeks are the big disappointment of Provence – the only remains of their towns are bits of wall at **Marseille** and at **St-Blaise** on the Etang de Berre. But what the Romans left behind in their beloved Provincia makes up for the Greeks: the theatre of **Orange**, with the only intact stage building in the west; the amphitheatre and cryptoporticus in **Arles**; the elegant 'Antiques' of **St-Rémy**; the Pont Flavien at **St-Chamas**; the excavated towns at **Vaison-la-Romaine** and **Glanum** (St-Rémy-de-Provence).

Thanks to a lingering Celtic influence, Provence was the one province of the Western Roman Empire that developed a definite style of its own, characterized by vigorous barbaric reliefs emboldened by deeply incised outlines. Battle scenes were the most popular subject, or shields and trophies arranged in the exotic, uncouth style you see on the triumphal arches of **Orange** and **Carpentras**, or in the Musée de l'Arles et de la Provence Antiques in **Arles**.

Roman landowners lived in two-storey stone houses, with their farm buildings forming an enclosed rectangular courtyard known as a *mansio*, the ancestor of the modern Provençal farmhouse, the *mas*.

Early Christian and Dark Ages: 5th–10th Centuries

Very few places had the resources to create any art at all during this period; the meagre attempts were nearly always rebuilt later. The oldest Christian relics are a remarkable 2nd-century sarcophagus in **Brignoles**, and a large collection of 4th-century sarcophagi in the Musée de l'Arles et de la Provence Antiques at **Arles**, close to Roman pagan models.

Octagonal baptistries from the 5th and 6th centuries survive in **Aix-en-Provence** and **Riez**. Many church crypts are really the foundations of original Dark Age churches.

Romanesque: 11th–14th Centuries

When good times returned in the 11th century, people began to build again, inspired by the ancient buildings they saw around them. There is a great stylistic continuity not only from Roman to Romanesque (rounded arches, barrel vaults, rounded apses), but also in the vigorous, Celtic-inspired decoration of Roman Provence. At the same time, the enduring charm of Romanesque is in its very lack of restrictions and codes, giving architects the freedom to improvise and solve problems in highly original and sophisticated ways. Although parish and monastic churches were usually in the basilican form (invented for Roman law courts, and used in Rome's first churches), masons also created extremely esoteric works, often built as funeral chapels on pre-Christian holy sites: **Notre-Dame-du-Groseau** and **Montmajour** are two.

Of the four distinct styles of Romanesque that emerged in southern France, the **Provençal** is the most austere and heavy, characterized by simple floor plans, thick-set proportions, few if any windows, minimal if any decoration, and façades that are often blank. Churches that could double as fortresses were built along the pirate-plagued coast, most notably the church of **Saintes-Maries-de-la-Mer**. In the mid-12th century, the Cistercians founded three important new abbeys in a sombre and austere style, known as the 'Three Sisters': **Le Thoronet**, **Sénanque** and **Silvacane**. An octagonal dome at the transept crossing is a common feature of more elaborate churches, especially **Avignon** cathedral, the Ancienne-Major in **Marseille**, **Vaison-la-Romaine**, **Le Thor** and **Carpentras** (the ruined original). The finest of the few paintings that survive from this epoch is the 13th-century fresco cycle at the Tour Ferrande, in **Pernes-les-Fontaines**. **Ganagobie** has the only floor mosaics from the period, as well as good sculpture.

In general, churches in the Rhône valley are more ornate, thanks to a talented group of sculptors known as the **School of Arles**. The wealth of ruins inspired them to adapt Roman forms and decorations to the new religion, complete with triumphal arches, gabled pediments, and Corinthian columns. The saints on the façade of St-Trophime in **Arles** seem direct descendants of Gallo-Roman warriors. Arlésien artists also created the remarkable façade of **St-Gilles**, portraying the New Testament – the true dogma in stone for all to see, perhaps meant as a refutation of the Cathar and other current heresies. Yet other Romanesque sculpture in the area, such as that at **Vaison-la-Romaine**, seems nothing but heretical.

Gothic and Renaissance: 14th–16th Centuries

Although Gothic elements first appear in Provence in 1150 (the façade of St-Victor in **Marseille**), the style's ogival vaulting and pointy arches belonged to a foreign, northern style that failed to touch southern hearts. The only place where it really found a home was in **Avignon**, when the 14th-century popes summoned architects from the north to design the flamboyant papal palace, St-Pierre, and St-Didier (other isolated examples include the basilica of **St-Maximin-la-Ste-Baume**).

Painting in the south of France took a giant leap forward when the papal court in **Avignon** hired some of Italy's finest *trecento* artists, especially **Simone Martini** of Siena and **Matteo Giovannetti** of Viterbo. Their frescoes combined the new Italian naturalism with the courtly, elongated grace of medieval French art to create the fairytale style known as **International Gothic** (*see* **Avignon** and its Petit Palais museum). From International Gothic, and from the precise techniques of the Flemish painters favoured by the last popes, a new local style developed in the early 15th century, the **School of Avignon**. The school's greatest masters were from the north: the exquisite **Enguerrand Quarton** (or Charton, *c.* 1415–66) from Laon (**Villeneuve lez Avignon**), and **Nicolas Froment** (cathedral, **Aix-en-Provence**); also *see* Aix's church of the Madeleine and the Petit Palais museum in **Avignon**. Their most interesting native contemporaries were a pair of Piedmontese painters, **Giovanni Canavesio** (*c.* 1430–1500) and **Giovanni Baleison** (*c.* 1425–95), who would be better known had they not left their charming fresco cycles in remote, out-of-the-way churches up in Provence's alpine valleys, most notably **Notre-Dame-des-Fontaines** in the Roya valley, and others in the valleys of the Vésubie and Tinée.

This was also the time when the Bon Roi René, the great patron of the artists, had himself built a fine chivalric castle in **Tarascon** and had a hand in the evolution of French sculpture when he invited the Italian Renaissance master **Francesco Laurana** (*c.* 1430–1502) to Provence. Laurana, a Dalmatian who was trained in Tuscany, is best known for his precocious geometrical softening of features and forms, especially in his portrait busts (in St-Didier, **Avignon**; Ancienne-Major, **Marseille**; and cathedral, **Aix-en-Provence**).

Despite this promising start, subjugation by the French and the Wars of Religion made the Renaissance a non-event in Provence. The few buildings of the day are imitative, mostly of the heavy, classicizing Roman style, as in the Petit Palais of the Cardinal Legate in **Avignon**. The best Renaissance building, the once-delightful Château de la Tour d'Aigues in the **Luberon**, is a burnt-out shell today.

The Age of Bad Taste: 17th–18th Centuries

The French prefer to call this their *époque classique*, and, admittedly, even in the poor, benighted south many fine things were done. Towns laid out elegant squares, fountains and promenades, as in **Pernes-les-Fontaines**, **Aix-en-Provence** and

Barjols; trees were planted on a grand scale, on market squares and along roads – many (mostly out-of-the-way ones) are still lined with majestic 18th-century avenues of plane trees. **Moustiers** has a collection from its thriving faïence industry of the day (as does **Marseille**'s Musée Cantini). Southerners went ape for organs, gargantuan works sheathed in ornate carved wood.

But nearly everything else is all wrong. People took the lovely churches left to them by their ancestors and tricked them out like cat-houses in pink and purple, and tinkered so much with the architecture that it's often difficult to tell the real age of anything. **Aix**, the capital of Provence and self-proclaimed arbiter of taste, knocked over its magnificently preserved Roman mausoleum and medieval palace of the counts of Provence just before the Revolution. Although the 17th- and 18th-century palaces that replaced them lend Aix a distinctive urbanity and ostentation, they are rarely first-rate works of architecture in their own right, but rather eclectic jumbles with touches from Gothic, Renaissance and Baroque stylebooks.

The one great Baroque sculptor and architect Provence produced, **Pierre Puget** (1620–94), suffered the usual fate of a prophet in his own land. Puget began his career painting ships' figureheads before he went on to study in Rome under Bernini; snubbed at home, he spent much of his career sculpting enormous saints in Genoa, but left his native **Marseille** the striking Vieille-Charité and a handful of sculptures in its Musée des Beaux-Arts. In painting, the south produced two virtuoso court painters, **Hyacinthe Rigaud** and **Jean-Honoré Fragonard**, whose portrayals of happily spoiled, rosy-cheeked aristocrats were enough in themselves to provoke a Revolution. The most sincere paintings of the age are the naïve *ex votos* in many churches (some of the best are from sailors, as at Notre-Dame-de-la-Garde in **Marseille**). Then there are the works of Avignon native **Claude-Joseph Vernet** (1714–89), a landscape painter best known for his seascapes and ports, in which he showed himself to be one of the first French artists interested in the play of light and water, if in a picturesque manner (Musée Calvet, **Avignon**; Musée des Beaux-Arts, **Marseille**).

France's Little Ice Age: Late 18th–mid-19th Centuries

If the last era lacked vision, taste in the neoclassical/Napoleonic era had all the charm of embalming fluid. The Revolution destroyed more than it built; the wanton devastation of the region's greatest Romanesque art begun during the Wars of Religion was a loss matched only by the mania for selling it off in the next century to the Americans. The greatest monuments of the Napoleonic era include the paintings in many museums by David, Ingres and **Hubert Robert**, the latter of whom specialized in scenes of melancholy Roman ruins in Provence and Italy, capturing the taste of the day (it was also a great age for cemeteries). **Jacques-Louis David** (1748–1825) deserves special mention as Napoleon's favourite painter, as cold and perfect as ice, who portrayed the Frenchies of his day in kitsch-Roman heroic attitudes and costumes (Musée Granet, **Aix-en-Provence**; Musée Calvet, **Avignon**). David's pupil, **François-Marius Granet** (1775–1849), was a native of Aix; although his canvases are run-of-the-mill academic, his watercolours and sketches bear witness to a poetic observation of nature that became the hallmark of the Provençal school (Musée Granet, **Aix-en-Provence**).

Another current in French painting at the time is represented by **Camille Corot** (1796–1875), a landscape painter of ineffable charm, who made the typical French sojourn in Rome to discover the calm and tranquillity of classical landscapes. Although not a southerner, he spent time in Provence, and his smaller, spontaneous sketches and private portraits that remain here show him off as a precursor of the Impressionists (Musée Calvet, **Avignon**; Musée des Beaux-Arts, **Marseille**). In his lifetime, Corot was known for his kindness, and one who benefited the most was **Honoré Daumier** (1808–79), whom Corot supported in his impoverished blind old age. Born in Marseille, Daumier began his career risking jail terms as a political caricaturist for a magazine. But he was also a highly original pre-Expressionist painter in the Goya mould, best known for his hypnotic, violently lit scenes based on the inherent tragedy of the human condition – he was a precursor of Toulouse-Lautrec, Degas and Picasso (Musée des Beaux-Arts, **Marseille**).

For the first time, however, there was a reaction to purposeful destruction of the past. Ruskin's contemporary **Viollet-le-Duc** (1814–79) restored architecture, rather than just writing about it (the walls of **Avignon**). Thanks to the Suez Canal, **Marseille** suddenly had money to burn and tried to revive the past in its own way, with monstrous neo-Byzantine basilicas and the overripe Baroque Palais Longchamp. It also produced **Adolphe Monticelli** (1824–86), perhaps Van Gogh's most important precursor, especially in his technique. Obsessed with light (*'La lumière, c'est le ténor,'* he claimed), Monticelli conveyed its effects with pure unmixed colour applied with hard brushes; subjects dissolve into strokes and blobs of paint (Musée des Beaux-Arts and Musée Cantini, **Marseille**).

Revolutions in Seeing: 1850–the Present

A lady once came to look at Matisse's paintings and was horrified to see a woman with a green face. 'Wouldn't it be horrible to see a woman walking down the street with a green face?' she asked him. 'It certainly would!' Matisse agreed. 'Thank God it's only a painting!'

In the 1850 Paris Salon, hanging amongst the stilted historical, religious and mythological academic paintings were three large canvases of everyday scenes by **Gustave Courbet** (1819–77). Today it's hard to imagine how audacious his contemporaries found Courbet's new style, which came to be called realism – almost as if it took the invention of photography by Louis Daguerre (in 1837) to make the eye see what was 'really' there. 'Do what you see, what you want, what you feel,' was Courbet's advice to his pupils. A keen student of luminosity in nature, Courbet felt like painting in the south, where his art revelled in the bright colour and light; his seascapes are awash in atmosphere (Musée des Beaux-Arts, **Marseille**).

Courbet's visit and fresh luminous style was a major influence on the 19th-century painters of Provence, especially **Paul Guigou** (1834–71). Born in Villars in the Vaucluse, Guigou sought out the most arid parts of Provence, especially the banks of the Durance, for his subjects, illuminating them with scintillating light and colour. Unable to make a living in the south, he took teaching jobs in the north, where he died at the age of 37, just as his career began to take off (Musée des Beaux-Arts, **Marseille**; Musée Granet, **Aix-en-Provence**).

In the 1860s, physicists made the discovery that colour derives from light, not from form. The idea inspired a new kind of art known as **Impressionism**. **Camille Pissarro**, **Pierre-Auguste Renoir**, **Edouard Manet** and company made it their aim to strip Courbet's newfound visual reality of all subjectivity and to simply record on canvas the atmosphere, light and colour the eye saw, all according to the latest scientific theories. The crucial role Provence was to play in modern art came later, in the 1880s, thanks to the careers of the two great post-Impressionist painters: Vincent Van Gogh and Paul Cézanne. Not only did they change the history of art, but they produced, albeit in wildly different styles, the most loved images that the outside world has of Provence.

A failed Dutch minister, **Vincent Van Gogh** (1853–90) was inspired by the Impressionists and Japanese prints in Paris, but the most astonishing revolution in his art occurred when he moved to Arles in 1888 in search of 'a different light, in the belief that to look at nature under a clearer sky could give us a better idea of the way the Japanese see and draw; finally, I seek a stronger sun'. He responded to the heightened colour and light on such an emotional level that colour came less and less to represent form in his art (as it did for the Impressionists), but instead took on a symbolic value as the only medium Van Gogh found powerful enough to contain his extraordinary moods and visions: 'Instead of trying to reproduce exactly what I have before my eyes, I use colour more arbitrarily so as to express myself more forcibly.' The result was an intense lyricism that has never been equalled, a 'research into the infinite' that ended with suicide. He sold only one painting in his 37 years, and ironically not a single one of the 800 or so canvases he painted around Arles remains in Provence.

Van Gogh's revolutionary liberation of colour from form was taken to an extreme by a group of painters that the critic Louis Vauxcelles nicknamed the **Fauves** ('wild beasts') for the violence of their colours. The Fauves used colour to express moods and rhythms to the detriment of detail and recognizable subject matter. As a movement they lasted from 1904 until 1908, but in those few years they revolutionized European art. Nearly all the Fauves – **André Derain**, **Henri Matisse**, **Maurice Vlaminck**, **Raoul Dufy**, **Kees Van Dongen** – painted in the south, along the Riviera and at La Ciotat, Cassis and L'Estaque. Their work paved the way for **Expressionism**, **Cubism** and **Abstractionism** – avenues few of the Fauvists themselves ever explored. For after 1908 the collective new vision these young men had shared in the south of France vanished as if they had awoken from a mass hypnosis; all went their separate ways, leaving others to carry their ideas on to their logical conclusions. 'Fauve painting is not everything,' Matisse explained. 'But it is the foundation of everything.'

Unlike Van Gogh, **Paul Cézanne** (1839–1906) was a native of Provence, born in Aix-en-Provence, where fellow schoolmate Emile Zola was his best friend, until Zola published his autobiographical *L'Œuvre*, which thinly disguised Cézanne as the failed painter Claude Lantier. Cézanne never forgave him, and anyway, compared to poor Van Gogh, Cézanne enjoyed a certain amount of success in his lifetime. His response to Provence was analytical rather than emotional, his interest not so much in depicting what he saw, but in the contradiction between the eye and mind, between the permanence of nature and the ephemeral qualities of light and movement. 'Nature is always the same, but none of it lasts beyond what we perceive,' he wrote. His goal was 'to make Impressionism solid and enduring, like the art of the museums'. His painting went through several distinct periods: a sombre romantic stage (1861–71); an Impressionistic manner, inspired by Pissarro (1872–82); a period of synthesis (1883–95), combining elements of Impressionism with an interest in volume, surface planes and the desire to represent perspective by nuances of colour and tonality only; and lastly, his lyric period (1896–1906), where singing rhythms of colour and form are intellectually supported by the basic tenets of Cubism, splitting planes and volumes into prisms to express the tension between seeing and knowing. A handful of his paintings are on display in the Musée Granet in **Aix**.

In 1908, Georges Braque and the Fauvist Raoul Dufy went to paint together at L'Estaque in homage to Cézanne. The beginnings of the prismatic splitting of forms are in their respective works, and when the same critic Vauxcelles saw Braque's paintings, he came up with a new name: **Cubism**. In 1912, Braque and Picasso worked together in **Sorgues**, near Avignon, where they produced canvases that verge on abstraction. **Pablo Picasso** (1881–1973), the 20th century's most endlessly inventive and prolific artist, returned to the south of France for good in 1948. Living there heightened the Mediterranean and pagan aspects of his extraordinarily wide-ranging work; when he felt nostalgic for his native Spain he would attend the bullfights at **Arles**, and he left a collection of drawings to the town's Musée Réattu.

Although a long list of other 20th-century artists, including Renoir and Chagall, settled in the south, like Picasso they usually chose to live on the Côte d'Azur. One exception in Provence is Hungarian-born founder of **Op Art** and experimenter in kinetic art **Victor Vasarély** (1908–97), whose foundation in **Aix-en-Provence** waits to make your eyeballs squirm. Modern architecture has also left most of Provence alone: the one notable exception is **Le Corbusier**'s idealistic *unité d'habitation* in **Marseille** (1952), part of a large housing project that was to consist of a row of rectangular slabs built on stilts. The rest were cancelled by the horrified Marseillais after the first building was finished. Other architects thought it was the future, however, and it's hard to think of any city in the world that has escaped a copy since.

Topics

A Country Calendar 40
Mistral and the Félibrige 41
Hocus Pocus Popes 42
Marcel Pagnol and the Provençal
  Mystique 43
Troubadours 44
Up Your Nose 45
The Village Sociologist 46
Bullfights 48
Wide Open Spaces 49

FRANCE

ITALY

SPAIN

04

A Country Calendar

Beyond the glamorous life in the villas and *résidences secondaires*, the cycle of the seasons goes on in the south of France as it has since Hector was a pup. A few crops have changed – silk, madder and a dozen different varieties of wheat have vanished, while flowers and early garden vegetables have become more important. Some corners are warm enough to produce three crops a year.

The calendar begins with two months of repose: *l'ivèr a ges d'ouro* ('winter has no hours') is an old saying in the country. The mistral howls away, and it snows, sometimes even in Nice. In **January** the Three Kings are fêted with crown-shaped brioches studded with candied fruit. Fattened geese and ducks are turned into *confits* and pigs into sausages and raw ham. In early **February** the mimosas bloom and olives are squeezed into oil; traditional presses are still used in many villages. Flaky tarts filled with jam or cream are baked for Carnival. By the end of February the almonds burst into lacy bloom.

The real work begins in **March**, when farmers prune their olives and vines and sow their wheat and oats, and plant potatoes and melons. In **April** two things have to be cut, hay and fleece; much of the latter is done by itinerant sheep-shearers who travel from farm to farm. Plums, apricots, cherries and pears spring into blossom, and everyone prays that the mistral doesn't blow the flowers and buds off the trees. Good Friday is traditionally celebrated with an *aïoli*, or dried cod and garlic mayonnaise feast; for Easter the first roast lamb of the year is accompanied by with a salad of romaine lettuce, fresh onions and hard-boiled eggs.

In **May** the flocks are driven to the greener pastures in the hills, following transhumance trails that date back as far as the Neolithic era. Early vegetables are abundant in the markets – the little green artichokes called *mourre de gat* for omelettes, *fèves* (broad beans), garlic, spring onions and peas.

June brings the wheat harvest, once the most colourful event on the calendar as mountaineers descended by the thousands to provide the labour, fuelled on five meals and a barrel of wine a day. Asparagus, cherries and apricots ripen, and gourmets poke around in the woods for delectable morel mushrooms. The summer solstice and end of the harvest (*Fête de la St-Jean*) are given a good old-fashioned Celtic send-off with bonfires and fireworks; the sun itself is said to dance and jump three times over the Alpilles. Almonds are ready to be picked in **July**, but now and throughout **August** it's too hot to work except in the early morning. Melons and peaches are everywhere, and the lavender is ready to be cut. The evenings are alive with village fêtes, for this has always been the time to eat, drink and make merry, to hoard strength for the hard tasks ahead.

September brings fresh figs, and the rice is ready to be harvested in the Camargue. With the first rains mushrooms begin to poke up in the woods, especially the fragrant *cèpes*; these are tracked down with a relentlessness matched only by the hunters, whose blasting advent is marked by a noticeable decline in birdsong. But the most important event of the month is the *vendange*, or grape harvest. **October**, too, is very much occupied with winemaking. The stripped vines turn red, wild boar meat appears in the markets, walnuts and chestnuts are gathered in the hills.

November marks the beginning of a new agricultural year, with the planting of wheat. Cold weather forces the shepherds and their flocks down from the mountains. Olives wait to be picked, and truffle hounds (the picturesque but uncontrollably greedy pigs have been retired) seek out the elusive *rabasso*, the black gold of the Vaucluse.

December brings Christmas, or *Calendo* in Provençal – a word resulting from an early confusion of Christ's birth with the Roman Calends. On Christmas Eve, *le réveillon*, the grandfather of each family blesses the *cacho-fiô* (a Yule log from a fruit tree) and the youngest person in the family lays it in the hearth; a lavish meal of fish and vegetables traditionally followed by 13 desserts precedes midnight Mass. This being France, the stomach dominates Christmas Day as well: a feast of oysters, foie gras, black truffles, stuffed capon, goose with pears and champagne is by necessity punctuated by frequent *trous provençaux* – snorts of frozen *marc* that magically make it possible to eat as much as Gargantua. And by New Year's Eve (St-Sylvestre) everyone's digestion has sufficiently recovered to eat it all again.

Mistral and the Félibrige

The attitude of the French to their language was best expressed by Paul Morand's speech upon being admitted to the Académie Française: 'To write in French is to see flowing the waters of a mountain stream, next to which all languages are muddy rivers; it is to live in a crystal palace.' To someone like Morand, master of *pointu*, or 'proper' French, with all its mushy slushy vowel sounds, one of the muddiest rivers was *langue d'oc*. Its demise became a priority in the 19th century; after subjugating the south politically and religiously, Paris decided to finish off the job linguistically and decreed French the sole legal language in the schools, military, government and press.

One of the strategies of the *Franchimands* (as the southerners call French-speakers) was to divide and conquer: *langue d'oc*, claimed the central Frenchifiers, was actually thousands of dialects and could never constitute a language. Even the southerners admit to seven 'grand dialects' of Occitan, two of which fall into the confines of this book: the Dauphinois of the Alpine valleys and Provençal. But it was in Provence that the reaction to the *Franchimands'* linguistic imperialism took its most curious form – in a sentimental, artificially contrived literary movement called the Félibrige.

According to legend, the idea for the Félibres was 'born of a mother's tear' when the mother of the poet Joseph Roumanille wept because she couldn't understand the French verses of her son. Not long afterwards, on 21 May 1854, at the Château de Font-Ségugne near Avignon, Roumanille, Frédéric Mistral and five other poets proclaimed the formation of a literary school to 'safeguard indefinitely for Provence its language, its colour, its easy liberty, its national honour, and its fine level of intelligence, for such as it is, we like Provence'.

It was the 24-year-old Mistral who came up with the name for the school when he quoted a folk rhyme on the Seven Sorrows of Mary from his native village Maillane: *li sètt felibre de la Lèi* – the seven doctors or sages of the law. As 21 May (the day when the sun is in the constellation of the Pleiades, or Seven Sisters) was the feast day of Santo Estello, the seven-pointed star of the Cathars was adopted as one of the Félibres' symbols. In later years, after Mistral's epic *Miréio* gave the movement its lustre, 21 May would be celebrated with a Grand Félibre Banquet, when all 50 members or *majoraux* and their leader, the *capoulié* (Mistral, naturally), would pass around the *Coupo Santo*, the Félibres' Holy Grail.

The Félibres' greatest moment came in 1904, when Mistral won the Nobel Prize for Literature – he was the only writer in a minority language ever to be awarded a Nobel Prize. Thanks to him and the other Félibres, Provence became conscious and proud of its separate identity; the richness of the language charmed even foreigners such as Ezra Pound, who wrote and translated Provençal. But in spite of these successes, the Félibrige best serves as a lesson on how not to revive a language. Today only a few people in their eighties in remote areas still use Provençal as a daily tool – a sorry record compared to the subsequent revivals of Irish, Catalan, Basque, Welsh, and most successful of all, Hebrew.

Where did the Félibres go wrong? Well, it certainly wasn't for lack of trying: unlike the courtly troubadours, they purposely wrote in a simple style in order to appeal to the *paysans*. Slipshod grammar and spelling were codified in Mistral's labour of love, the *Trésor du Félibrige* (a work that was accused by some of passing off the rustic dialect of Maillane as the last word in Provençal). But the Félibres' biggest mistake was in confusing language and time, in associating Provençal with folklore and the past, and in shunning the necessary political fight with Paris in a romantic illusion that their poetry was powerful enough in itself to revive a dying tongue. Mistral's powerful, mystical evocation of western Provence (the real hero of all his epics) was more of a swansong to a dying culture, not the foundation stone for a Renaissance of a new troubadour movement.

For nearly everything that Frédéric Mistral celebrated in his poetry was undergoing a sea change – Italians, Corsicans and Spaniards were moving in to the region by the thousands, and helping to construct new roads and railway lines, while old farming practices, rural customs, traditions, and even villages were rapidly being abandoned altogether. Mistral, for all his art, energy, charm and influence, could not turn the clock back. He had the unique honour of attending the unveiling of his own statue in Arles, forcing upon him a melancholy recognition that he was dead in his own lifetime.

Hocus Pocus Popes

Filling the lifeless shell of the papal palace in Avignon with the lost trappings of the medieval popes is not an easy task for the imagination. And the more you learn, the harder it gets, for besides all the harlots, speculators, gluttons and cheats that Petrarch railed against, there seems to have been a shocking amount of voodoo. Accusations of sorcery had already sullied the name of one Occitan pope, Sylvester II (Gerbert of the Auvergne), who reigned from 999 to 1003 after studying in the Islamic schools in Toledo, where he acquired a prophetic bronze head that advised him in sticky moments. Even today, his tombstone in St John Lateran is said to sweat and rattle before the death of each pope.

In 1309 the French pope Clement V moved the Papacy from Rome to Avignon, then died from eating a plate of ground emeralds (prescribed by his doctor for a stomach ache). He was succeeded by John XXII, a native of Cahors, who owed his election to a magic knife that enchanted the conclave of cardinals. This John was also a famous alchemist, and he filled the papal treasury with gold, while King Philip V gave him a pair of *languiers*, or amulets shaped like serpents' tongues, encrusted with gems that changed colour on contact with poison. They served the pope in good stead, as plenty of rivals in the Church were trying to do him in. The most notable culprits were Clement V's doctor, caught manufacturing a diabolical homunculus, and Hugues Géraud, Bishop of Cahors, who confessed in 1317 that he had tried to assassinate the pope 'by poison and by sorcery with wax images, ashes of spiders and toads, the gall of a pig, and the like substances'. John XXII ordered him burnt at the stake.

The next pope, Benedict XII, spent hundreds of thousands of florins on a new palace, and still had enough gold and precious stones left over to top up his treasury – thanks, it is said, to an elderly woman residing in Avignon's ghetto, who told him where to find the 'treasure of the Jews' buried under her hovel. And in the bitter end, just before the antipope Benedict XIII was forced to flee Avignon, he sealed up a secret room in the palace with a cache of solid gold statues, confiding the secret to his friend, the Venetian ambassador. They were never found, although in Mistral's epic *Poème du Rhône*, three Venetian ladies who inherited the secret come to the palace and remove the flagstones that cover up the secret room – only to discover a bottomless abyss.

Marcel Pagnol and the Provençal Mystique

A certain part of Provence's current mystique derives from two of the best-loved French movies in recent decades, *Jean de Florette* and *Manon des Sources*, directed by Claude Berri. Not only are both beautifully set in the heart of Provence, but more than that, they stick in the mind like glue – these are tales of mythic simplicity, of water, of a conspiracy of silence, of revenge. The stories, from *L'Eau des Collines*, were written by Marcel Pagnol and are based, according to him, on true stories that he heard as a child. The even more recent films, *La Gloire de mon père* and *Le Château de ma mère*, were based on Pagnol's childhood memories. They evoke a Provençal idyll from the beginning of the century; from the photography alone you can almost smell the wild herbs of the *garrigue* baking in the sun.

Yet Marcel Pagnol's role in creating a universal mental image of Provence goes back to the 1930s, when he himself was a pioneer in the then new medium of 'talkies' – in fact, it's impossible to imagine a Pagnol film without sound because most of the time his characters are jawing away non-stop. Now relegated to *cinémathèques* and the occasional late-night movie slot on television, his films, all made on location in Provence's villages, are often difficult to watch for modern viewers weaned on colour, constantly changing camera angles and scenes, fast-paced dialogue and action. Many families shoot better home videos. Pagnol's photography is bad, the camera angles are boring, and he never uses the slightest cinemagraphic trick, always preferring to 'say' rather than 'show' – it often seems that no one is directing the film at all (many of Pagnol's ideas were adopted by the Nouvelle Vague directors in the 1960s).

Pagnol was a fervent believer in the power of human speech: for him the word was sacred. He was one of the first playwrights to move on to film because he was delighted to have his actors express themselves in conversational tones – with rich Provençal accents, naturally, and without using the exaggerated voices, gestures and make-up necessary in the theatre or in silent movies. No director before him gave his actors so much freedom. When filming his favourite actor, Raimu, star of *Marius*, *César* and *La Femme du boulanger*, Pagnol said: 'He's so good that I just let him go on until he's tired of talking or we've run out of film.'

Most importantly, where Mistral and the Félibres failed to reach the masses through atavistic artiness (*see* p.42), Pagnol succeeded. There is nothing folkloric, stilted or affected in his Provence, but instead a sunny, attractive vision on a human scale and measured to a moral order, where life, as in all Mediterranean lands, revolves around the family. His stories are invariably simple – eternal fables of the human condition, planted in the fragrant soil of the Midi. An often wry sense of humour is never far, even when everything is going wrong. In 1967, French critic Jacques Lourcelles summed up the effect of Pagnol:

Seeing his films today, one realizes that they are a kind of classic, for which the scenario and creation of characters counted more than anything... His Provence is an immemorial Provence, static, hardly referred to [in the films] but profoundly linked to the destiny of his characters, underemphasized, and yet as present as the landscapes in the best westerns, with which the films of Pagnol are not without affinity. This vanished, non-touristy Provence is without doubt the most interesting feature of Pagnol's classicism.

Troubadours

Lyric poetry in the modern western world was born around the year 1095 with the rhymes of Count William (1071–1127), grandfather of Eleanor of Aquitaine. William wrote in the courtly language called Old Provençal (or Occitan), although his subject matter was hardly courtly:

Do you know how many times I screwed them?
One hundred and eighty-eight to be precise;
so much so that I almost broke my girth and harness...

A descendant of the royal house of Aragon, William had Spanish-Arab blood in his lusty veins and had battled against the Moors in Spain on several occasions, but at the same time he found inspiration (for his form, if not his content) from a civilization that was centuries ahead of Christian Europe in culture.

The word *troubadour* may be derived from the Arabic root for lutenist (*trb*), and indeed, the ideal of courtly love makes its first appearance in the writings of the spiritual Islamic Sufis. The Sufis believed that true understanding could not be expressed in doctrines, but could be suggested obliquely in poetry and fables. Much of what they wrote was love poetry addressed to an ideal if unkind and irrational muse, whom the poet hopes will reward his merit and devotion with enlightenment and inspiration.

Christians who encountered this poetry in the Crusades converted this ideal muse into the Virgin, giving birth to the great 12th-century cult of Mary. But in Occitania this mystic strain was reinterpreted in a more worldly fashion by troubadours, whose muses became flesh and blood women, although these darlings were equally unattainable in the literary conventions of courtly love. The lady in question could only be addressed by a pseudonym. She had to be married to someone else. The poet's hopeless suit to her hinged, not on his rank, but on his virtue and worthiness. The greatest novelty of all was that this love had to go unrequited.

Art songs of courtly love were known as *cansos*, and rarely translate well, as their merit was in the poet's skill in inventing new forms in his rhyming schemes, metres, melodies and images. But the troubadours wrote other songs as well, called *sirventes*, which followed established forms but took for their subjects politics, war, miserly patrons and even satires on courtly love itself.

The golden age of the troubadours began in the 1150s, when the feudal lords of Occitania warred amongst each other with so little success that behind the sound and fury the land enjoyed a rare political stability. Courts indulged in new luxuries and the arts flourished, and troubadours found ready audiences, travelling from castle to castle. One of their great patrons was En Barral, viscount of Marseille, who was especially fond of the reputedly mad but charming Peire Vidal. Vidal not only wrote of his love for En Barral's beautiful wife, but in a famous incident even went beyond the bounds of convention by stealing a kiss from her while she slept (her husband, who thought it was funny, had to plead with her to forgive him). Vidal travelled widely, especially after the death of En Barral in 1192, and wrote a rare nostalgic poem for the homeland of his lady fair:

> With each breath I draw in the air
> I feel coming from Provence;
> I so love everything from there
> that when people speak well of it,
> I listen smiling, and with each
> word ask for a hundred more,
> so much does the hearing please me.
>
> (trans. by Anthony Bonner, in *Songs of the Troubadours*)

Up Your Nose

If nothing else, Provence will make you more aware of that sense we all too often only remember when something stinks. Every *village perché* has shops overflowing with scented soaps, pot-pourris and bundles of *herbes de Provence*; every kitchen emits intoxicating scents of garlic and thyme; every cellar wants you to breathe in the bouquets of its wines. And when you begin to almost crave the more usual French smells of Gauloise butts, *pipi* and *pommes frites*, you discover that this nasal obsession is not only profitable to some, but healthy for all.

Aromathérapie, a name coined in the 1920s for the method of natural healing through fragrances, is taken very seriously in the land where one word, *sentir*, does double duty for 'feel' and 'smell'. French medical students study it, and its prescriptions are covered by the national social security. For, as an aromatherapist will tell you, smells play games with your psyche; the nose is hooked up not only to primitive drives such as sex and hunger, but also to your emotions and memory. The consequences can be monumental. Just the scent of a madeleine cake dipped in tea was enough to set Proust off writing *Remembrance of Things Past*.

Essential oils are created by the sun, and the most useful aromatic plants grow in hot and dry climates – as in the south of France, the spiritual heartland of aromatherapy. Lavender, the totem plant of the Midi, has been in high demand for its mellow soothing qualities ever since the Romans used it to scent their baths (hence its name from the Latin *lavare*, to wash). Up until the 1900s, nearly every farm in Provence had a small lavender distillery, and you can still find a few kicking about today. Most precious of all is the oil of *lavande fine*, a species that grows only above 3,000 feet on the sunny side of the Alps; 150 pounds of flowers are needed for every pound of oil.

Aromatherapy is really just a fashionable name for old medicine. The Romans had a saying, *Cur moriatur homo, cui salvia crescit in horto?* (Why should he die, who grows sage in his garden?), about a herb still heralded for its youth-giving properties. Essential oils distilled from plants were the secret of Egyptian healing and embalming, and were so powerful that there was a bullish market in 17th-century Europe for mummies, which were boiled down to make medicine.

For centuries in Provence, shepherds were regarded as magicians for their plant cures, which involved the picking of herbs in certain places and certain times. It sounds like a load of mumbo jumbo, but in fact modern analysis has shown that the chemical composition of a herb such as thyme varies widely, depending on where it grows and when it's picked. When the sun is in Leo, shepherds make *millepertuis*, or red oil (a sovereign anaesthetic and remedy for burns and wounds), by soaking the flowers of St John's wort in a mixture of white wine and olive oil that has been exposed to the hottest sun. After three days, they boil the wine off and let the flowers distil for another month; the oil is then sealed into tiny bottles, good for one dose each, to maintain its healing properties.

Still awaiting a fashionable revival are other traditional Provençal cures: baked ground magpie brains for epilepsy, marmot fat for rheumatism, dried fox testicles rubbed on the chest for uterine disease, and mouse excrement for bedwetting.

The Village Sociologist

Look up from the lavender fields for a minute, towards the typically picturesque *village perché* on the hills above. It seems a timeless place, where generation after generation of peasants have tilled the soil and lived their simple lives, until modern times came in with tractors, cars and store-bought clothes to spoil the effect. Writers such as Alphonse Daudet and Jean Giono, living in a time when rapid change was transforming villages and village life, made their careers chronicling the loss of old country ways with a sort of romantic melancholy. City people weren't discouraged, of course. The fantasy that attaches to places such as Bonnieux, Les Arcs or Lacoste has a lot to do with this image of a lost rustic paradise. Along with the lavender, it's what draws the tourists, the second-home buyers and the art schools.

This picture isn't entirely false – only nearly so. The romantic point of view can often lead to gross over-simplifications that do the little rural communities of Provence scant justice. If you look closely at a village and its past, you'll most likely find a fascinating story, with as much change and troubles as any big city. One way to do this is to read a lovely book called *Village in the Vaucluse*, written by an American sociologist named Laurence Wylie. In the 1950s, Wylie wangled one of the all-time sweet study grants, allowing him and his family to spend a year in Roussillon (disguised in the book as 'Peyrane') to examine the structure of village society. *Village in the Vaucluse* is hardly a dry sociological text: Wylie poked into every aspect of village life, sitting in at the local school, sifting through the archives (a bag of old papers in the mayor's closet) and gossiping with the old farmers. The result was a book written with considerable understanding and affection, one more like Marcel Pagnol than sociology.

Wylie also took the trouble to explore Roussillon's history – a tale full of ups and downs that serve as a perfect illustration of the complexity of village life. In the early 19th century, as Roussillon entered the modern world, it began changing from a largely self-sufficient farming economy. Village women found good money in the exacting work of raising silkworms, while the men raised a new cash crop: madder, used in dying cloth. The Roussillonnais did just fine until the disaster of the 1860s and 70s, with their silkworm diseases, a terrible winter that destroyed the olive trees, and the phylloxera epidemic that did in the vines. Things picked up again in the 1890s, when the ochre mines came back into production; depending on the market, these have been exploited on and off since Roman times. The First World War shut the mines off from their market in Russia, and carried away all too many of the village's sons, resulting in a steep decline not reversed until the 1950s, when modern farming methods and tourism brought prosperity gradually back.

Along with the changes in the economy there have been correspondingly extreme swings in population. Roussillon has been a boom town many times over the centuries – and bust just as often, as it was in the 1950s with half its houses empty and mostly old folks in the rest of them. In the first half of the 19th century, the population increased from 1,195 to 1,568. By 1886 it was back down to 1,213. After the First World War it reached a low point of about 900, and the village has been inching its way back since. Today the population is 1,300 and growing.

This population has always been more complex than just a simple collection of Provençal farmers. Even back in 1896, more than 10 per cent of Roussillon's population was made up of people from elsewhere. In the past, whenever the business cycle favoured a village new people would come from somewhere, and the natives would undoubtedly call them *étrangers*, even if they came from Marseille. In the 1890s Italian immigrants came to try their fortune. More recently it has been the Spanish, many of them Republicans exiled by the Civil War, as well as some Portuguese and a large number of *pieds noirs*, French settlers chased out of Algeria when that country won its independence. Lately the 'immigrants' have been Parisian, British and American refugees from the rat race.

Another surprising fact revealed by Wylie is how much internal politics, conflict and mutual dislike a village of 1,000 people or so can generate. But it's no surprise, really, to anyone who has ever spent time in such a village. Under a seamless veneer of French politeness, you'll always find that most of the inhabitants don't really much care for each other; life can be as intense as any soap opera, though without the glitter. To each, there's always the division between a few families whom one knows and who can be trusted, and *les autres* – those neighbours who are always peeking from behind their curtains, and who might report you to the tax man. Feuds of one sort or another are common – they may be the village's main source of entertainment. In our times these are usually expressed in politics; any French village could provide enough political news and opinions to fill a daily newspaper, if only there were enough people to read it.

Amidst all the change, these feuds sometimes provide the biggest element of stability. Wylie knew of two families in Roussillon that didn't get along, the Jouvauds and the Favres; the family heads were also among the leaders of two rival political parties in the village. Looking through the old records, he found that a Jouvaud had killed a Favre back in 1740, in a dispute that started when the victim led a band dancing the *farandole* (*see* p.64) across a square where Jouvaud had been playing an intense game of boules.

In Roussillon, or any other village for that matter, you will never been in danger of running out of something to talk about. In the anomie of modern life, it is easy to forget just how complex a community of 1,000 or so souls can be. A village really does constitute a world in itself, with enough interest and incident to satisfy all but the most jaded. Once they come to know what a rich and intricate place they have moved to, many of the city folk who seek refuge in the village find that this is the biggest attraction of all.

Bullfights

The Roman amphitheatres at Nîmes and Arles had hardly been restored in the early 1800s when they once again became venues for *tauromachie*. Attempts to abolish the sport in the 1900s fell flat when poet Frédéric Mistral, the self-appointed watchdog of all things Provençal, intervened; and if anything, bullfights are now more popular than ever.

Provence is so long in the tooth that not only does it put on regular bullfights with picadors and matadors, ultimately derived from the amphitheatres of ancient Rome, but also *courses provençales* (or *courses libres*), which can be traced back to the bull games described by Heliodorus in ancient Thessaly. Played by daring young men dressed in white called *razeteurs*, the sport demands grace, daring and dexterity, especially in leaping over the barriers before a charging bull.

Most bullfights in Provence are not bloody: the object is to remove a round cockade from between the horns of the bull (or cow) by cutting its ribbons with a blunt razor comb – a sport far more dangerous to the human players than the animals. The animals used for the *courses provençales* are the small, lithe, high-horned breed from the Camargue; good sporty ones retire with fat pensions.

You will see three other types of bullfight advertised. The *corrida*, or traditional Spanish bullfight, is where the bull is put to death. The bullfighters are usually Spanish as well, and the major festivals, or *ferias*, bring some of the top *toreros* to France, although beware that the already expensive tickets tend to be snapped up by touts. A *novillada*, pitting younger bulls against apprentice *toreros* (*novilleros*), is less expensive, but much more likely to be a butchery devoid of *arte*. In a *corrida portugaise* the bullfighter (*rejoneador*) fights from horseback but doesn't kill the bull.

Wide Open Spaces

The writer Gertrude Stein, a great fan of Provence who spent a good deal of time in St-Rémy-de-Provence thinking inscrutable thoughts, once dropped a famous line about Oakland, California: 'There's no there there,' she concluded after a brief visit. Take an equally inscrutable modern-day rapper from Oakland out to the exact centre of Provence, around the Lac de Castillon, and you will get a neatly symmetrical opinion. Lac de Castillon, a big artificial lake situated behind a concrete dam, is a special place, surrounded by wrinkled hills of a grey so immaculate that it is hard to see them at all. Outside of a few dam workers and an occasional trendy hang-glider, the whole gigantic grey place will be eerily deserted. The Lac de Castillon is nowhere, and all the towns and villages for 50km or more in any direction are only variations on the theme. We like to imagine an advert in a London paper: 'Delightful farmhouse half-restored in the heart of the Provençal mountains, near mountain lake; 1½hr from Cannes. Must sell.'

When you visit, take a look at the sort of Frenchman who lives in such a place: no poodles, no shades, no attitudes; even in summer, he may well be wearing a flannel shirt, which under the big moustaches will make him look entirely like one of the jolly Gaulish villagers in *Astérix*. Some of these are real frontiersmen, rough-edged, self-sufficient types whose lives revolve around hunting, gathering mushrooms and getting in wood for the winter; they grumble laconically in a tongue that is still more Provençal than French. We once met a picture-perfect example on the way to Draguignan. He was the baker in a village near the lake, hitch-hiking to the city with a jerry can of petrol to buy a used car (in France one never expects a used car to have any in the tank). His brother had gone off to the Harvard Business School and made it big. The baker, with his degree in cultural anthropology, preferred less stress and yeastier dough; having an assistant allowed him enough time for long scholarly vacations in the darker corners of South America and Asia.

The moral seems to be that rural France provides some of the world's most interesting hitch-hikers. And indeed it does. But the real point is that the English shibboleth 'the South of France' is not always what one might expect. The toadstool growth of the Côte d'Azur in the last century has entirely eclipsed the real Provence: lonely expanses of mountain and introverted villages, shepherds who still drive their flocks up to the mountains in summer on the old transhumance paths, and a traditional rural culture that, despite a great loss of population in the 20th century, is not yet prepared to compromise entirely with the modern world.

One wild snapshot among many sticks in the mind: two Indian chiefs, Iron Tail and Lone Bear, sipping champagne with the Marquis de Baroncelli-Javon in 1889, while watching Camargue *gardians* and the cowboys of Buffalo Bill's Wild West Show compare their skills at a Provençal rodeo. The men of two worlds had a great time together, and seemed to understand one another perfectly. One young Sioux, whom the French called Pain Perdu, even chose to stay behind in Provence; Frédéric Mistral met him, and thought he might be the reincarnated soul of a troubadour.

Food and Drink

The Cuisine of Provence 52
  Markets, Picnic Food and Snacks 54
Drink 54
  Spirits and Apéritifs 55
  Wine 55
Restaurant Basics 56
French Menu Reader 58

05

...and south of Valence, Provincia Romana, the Roman Provence, lies beneath the sun. There there is no more any evil, for there the apple will not flourish and the Brussels sprout will not grow at all.

Ford Madox Ford, *Provence*

Eating is a true pleasure in the south, where seafood, herbs, fruit and vegetables are often within plucking distance of the kitchen and table. The high quality of these fresh native ingredients demands minimal preparation – Provençal cooking is perhaps the least fussy of any regional French cuisine, and as an added plus neatly fits the modern definition of a healthy diet. The artery-hardening delights of the north – the rich creamy sauces, the butter, cheese and egg dishes, and the calorific desserts – are rare birds in this land brimming with olives, fresh vegetables, apricots and almonds.

Some of the most celebrated restaurants in the world grace the south of France, but there are plenty of stinkers too. The most tolerable are humble in their mediocrity, while others are oily with pretensions, staffed by folks posing as grand dukes and duchesses fallen on hard times, whose exalted airs are somehow supposed to make their clients feel better about paying an obscene amount of money for the eight *petits pois à la graisse de yak* that the chef has so beautifully arranged on a plate.

Just as intimidating for the hungry traveller are France's much ballyhooed gourmet bibles, whose annual awarding or removing of a star here, a chef's hat there, grade food the way a French teacher grades a *dictée* in school. Woe to the chef who leaves a lump in the sauce when those incognito pedants of the perfect palate are dining, and whose guillotine pens will ruthlessly chop off percentage points from the restaurant's final score. The less attention you pay them, the more you'll enjoy your dinner.

The Cuisine of Provence

Thanks to the trailblazing work of writers and chefs such as Elizabeth David and Roger Vergé, Provençal cooking no longer sends the average Anglo-Saxon into paroxysms of garlic paranoia as it did 100 years ago. Many traditional dishes actually presage *nouvelle cuisine*, and their success hangs on the quality of the ingredients and fragrant olive oil, including the well-known ratatouille – aubergines (eggplant), tomatoes, garlic and courgettes (zucchini) cooked separately in order to preserve their individual flavour, before being mixed together in olive oil – and *bagna cauda*, a dish of the southern Alps, consisting of raw vegetables dipped in a hot fondue of garlic, anchovies and olive oil.

Many a Provençal dinner starts with an apéritif and *tapenade*, a purée of olives, anchovies, olive oil and capers served on toast. The heraldic starter on a thousand menus, the *salade niçoise*, is interpreted in a hundred different ways even in Nice, but in general it contains most of the following: tomatoes, cucumbers, hard-boiled eggs, black olives, onions, anchovies, artichokes, green peppers, croûtons, green beans, tuna and even potatoes. Another lighter speciality is *omelette de putine*, an

Aïoli Recipe

This typical Provençal mayonnaise is best served with white fish such as bourride, *or with snails, potatoes or soup.*

Ingredients (per person)
1 clove of garlic (more if you're a garlic fiend)
1 egg yolk
extra virgin olive oil

Using a mortar and pestle, crush the garlic to a paste and add the egg yolk(s).

Begin whipping the mixture with a fork or small whisk while adding good quality (extra virgin) olive oil, first drop by drop, then in a thin stream as the mayonnaise begins to set.

Add salt only once all the oil has been incorporated and the mayonnaise has formed.

Should the aïoli lack substance or the oil separate from the mixture, you can still 'save' your mayonnaise: remove the mixture and add another egg yolk to the clean mortar. Whipping constantly, reintegrate the old aïoli mixture and any remaining oil. This operation is called 'reconstituting' the aïoli.

omelette with tiny fish. Another dish that tastes best in the summer, *soupe au pistou*, is a thick minestrone served with a fresh basil, garlic, and pine-nut sauce similar to Italian pesto.

Aïoli, a mayonnaise made from garlic, olive oil, lemon juice and egg yolks, served with cod, snails, potatoes or soup, is for many the essence of Provence; Frédéric Mistral even named his nationalist Provençal magazine after it. In the same spirit Marseille named its magazine *Bouillabaisse*, for its world-famous soup of five to twelve kinds of Mediterranean **fish**, flavoured with saffron; the fish is removed and served with *aïoli* or *rouille*, a sauce of fresh red chilli peppers crushed with garlic, olive oil, and the soup broth. Because good saffron costs money and the fish, especially the gruesome *rascasse* (scorpion fish) are rare, a proper *bouillabaisse* will cost at least €30.

A less expensive but delicious alternative is *bourride*, a soup made from white-fleshed fish served with aïoli. Down a gastronomical notch is *baudroie*, a fish soup with vegetables and garlic. A very different kettle of fish is the indigestible favourite *estocaficada* – salt cod stewed with tomatoes, olives, garlic and eau de vie. Less adventurous, yet an absolutely delicious dish, is *loup au fenouil*, sea bass grilled over fennel stalks.

Lamb is the most common meat dish; real Provençal lamb (increasingly scarce) grazes on herbs and on special salt-marsh grasses from the Camargue and Crau. **Beef** usually comes in the form of a *daube*, slowly stewed in red wine and often served with ravioli. A Provençal cook's prize possession is the *daube* pan, which is never washed, but wiped clean and baked to form a crust that flavours subsequent stews. **Rabbit** is simmered in white wine with garlic, mustard, tomatoes and herbs, to make *lapin à la provençale*.

The more daunting *pieds et paquets* are **tripe** packages stuffed with garlic, onions and salt pork, traditionally (although rarely) served with calf's or sheep's trotters. Also look for *capoun fassum*, cabbage stuffed with sausage and rice, and *artichauts à la barigoule*, artichokes filled with pork and mushrooms.

Purely **vegetable** dishes, besides ratatouille, include *tian*, a casserole of rice, spring vegetables (usually courgettes) and grated cheese baked in the oven; *tourta de blea*, a sweet-savoury Swiss chard pie; stuffed courgette (zucchini) flowers; grilled tomatoes with garlic and breadcrumbs (*à la provençale*); and *mesclun*, a salad of dandelion and other green leaves.

There aren't many Provençal **cheeses**: *banon*, nutty discs made from goat, sheep, or cow's milk, wrapped in chestnut leaves, is perhaps the best known; *poivre d'Ain* is *banon* flavoured with savory; thyme and bay add a nuance to creamy sheep's milk *tomme arlésienne*.

Markets, Picnic Food and Snacks

The markets in the south of France are justly celebrated for the colour and perfumes of their produce and flowers. They are fun to visit, and become even more interesting if you're cooking or gathering the ingredients for a picnic. In the larger cities food markets take place every day, while smaller towns and villages have markets on one day a week (we've listed all the ones we know in the text), which double as social occasions for the locals. Most markets finish around noon.

Other good sources for picnic food are the *charcuteries* or *traiteurs*, both of which sell prepared dishes sold by weight in cartons or tubs. You can also find deli counters at larger supermarkets. Cities are snack-food wonderlands, with outdoor counters selling pastries, crêpes, pizza slices, *frites*, *croque-monsieur* (toasted ham and cheese sandwiches) and a wide variety of sandwiches made from baguettes (long, thin loaves of bread).

Drink

You can order any kind of drink at any bar or café – except cocktails, unless it has a certain cosmopolitan savoir-faire or stays open into the night. Cafés are also a home from home, places to read the papers, meet friends and watch the world go by. You can spend hours over a coffee and no one will hurry you. Prices are listed on the *tarif des consommations*: note they are progressively more expensive depending on whether you're served at the bar *(comptoir)*, at a table (*la salle*) or outside (*la terrasse*).

French **coffee** is strong and black, but lacklustre next to the aromatic brews of Italy or Spain (you'll notice an improvement in the coffee near their respective frontiers). If you order *un café* you'll get a small black *express* (espresso); if you want milk, order *un crème*. If you want more than a few drops of caffeine, ask them to make it *grand*. For decaffeinated, the word is *déca*. Some bars offer cappuccinos, but again they're only really good near the Italian border; in the summer try a *frappé* (iced coffee). The French only order *café au lait* (a small coffee topped off with lots of hot milk) when they stop in for breakfast, and if what your hotel offers is expensive or boring, consider joining them. There are baskets of croissants and pastries, and some bars will make you a baguette with butter, jam or honey. *Chocolat chaud* (**hot chocolate**) is usually good; if you order *thé* (**tea**), you'll get a nasty ordinary bag and the water will be hot rather than boiling. An *infusion* is a **herbal tea** – *camomille, menthe* (mint), *tilleul* (lime or linden blossom), or *verveine* (verbena). These are kind to the all-precious *foie*, or liver, after you've over-indulged at the table.

Mineral water (*eau minérale*) can be addictive, and comes either sparkling (*gazeuse* or *pétillante*) or still (*non-gazeuse* or *plate*). If you feel run down, Badoit has lots of peppy magnesium in it – it's the current trendy favourite, even though Perrier comes from the Languedoc next door. The usual international corporate **soft drinks** are available, and all kinds of bottled fruit juices (*jus de fruits*) including delicious apricot (*abricot*). Some bars also do fresh lemon and orange juices (*citron pressé* or *orange pressée*, served with a separate *carafe d'eau* to dilute to taste). The French are also fond of fruit syrups – red *grenadine* and ghastly green *menthe*, which are mixed with lemonade to form a *diabolo* (e.g. *diabolo menthe*). If you like mint but not so sweet, try a refreshing clear sparkling Riqlès.

Beer (*bière*) in most bars and cafés is run-of-the-mill big brands from Alsace, Germany and Belgium. Draft (*à la pression*) is cheaper than bottled beer. Nearly all resorts have bars or pubs offering wider selections of drafts and bottles.

Spirits and Apéritifs

The strong spirit of the Midi comes in a liquid form called *pastis*, first made popular in Marseille as a plague remedy; its name comes from the Latin *passe-sitis*, or thirst-quencher. A pale yellow 90 per cent nectar flavoured with anise, vanilla and cinnamon, *pastis* is drunk as an apéritif before lunch and in rounds after work. The three major brands, Ricard, Pernod and Pastis 51, all taste slightly different; most people drink their '*pastaga*' with lots of water and ice (*glaçons*), which makes it almost palatable. A thimble-sized *pastis* is a *momie*; mixed with grenadine it becomes a *tomate*; with *orgeat* (almond and orange flower syrup) it's a *mauresque*, and a *perroquet* is mint.

Other popular apéritifs come from Languedoc-Roussillon, including Byrrh 'from the world's largest barrel', a sweet wine mixed with quinine and orange peel, similar to Dubonnet. Spirits include the familiar cognac and armagnac brandies, liqueurs and *digestifs* made from walnuts, cherries, pears and herbs (these are a speciality of the Alps), and fiery *marc*, the grape spirit that is the same as Italian *grappa* (but usually better). Many Provençal villages have a special *marc* of their own; the *marc des orangers*, made in spring with orange flowers, is one of the nicest you'll come across.

Wine

One of the pleasures of travelling in France is drinking great wines for a fraction of what you pay at home, and discovering new ones you've never seen. The south holds a special place in the saga of French wines, with a tradition dating back to the Greeks, who are said to have introduced an essential Côtes-du-Rhône grape variety called syrah, originally grown in Shiraz, Persia. Nurtured in the Dark and Middle

Ages by popes and kings, the vineyards of Provence and Languedoc-Roussillon still produce most of France's wine – some graded only by its alcohol content.

If a wine is labelled AOC (*Appellation d'Origine Contrôlée*) it means that the wine comes from a certain defined area and is made from certain varieties of grapes, guaranteeing a standard of quality. *Cru* on the label means vintage; a *grand cru* is a great, noble vintage. Down the list in the vinous hierarchy are those labelled VDQS (*Vin de Qualité Supérieure*), followed by *Vin de Pays* (guaranteed at least to originate in a certain region), with *Vin Ordinaire* (or *Vin de Table*) at the bottom, which is usually drinkable and cheap. In a restaurant if you order a *rouge* (red), *blanc* (white) or *rosé* (pink), this is what you'll get, either by the glass (*un verre*), by the quarter-litre (*un pichet*) or bottle (*une bouteille*). *Brut* is very dry, *sec* dry, *demi-sec* and *moelleux* are sweetish, *doux* sweet, and *méthode champenoise*, sparkling.

Some of Provence's best-known wines grow in the ancient places near the coast, especially its quartet of tiny AOC districts Bellet, Bandol, Cassis and Palette. But the best-known wines of the region come from the Rhône valley, under the general heading of Côtes-du-Rhône, including Châteauneuf-du-Pape, Gigondas, the famous rosé Tavel and the sweet muscat apéritif wine, Beaumes-de-Venise. Elsewhere, winemakers have made great strides in boosting quality in the past 30 years, recognized in new AOC districts.

Note that restaurants make a good portion of their income from marking up wines to triple or quadruple the retail price. Save money by buying direct from the producers, or *vignerons* (or a wine co-operative, or *syndicat*, a group of producers). In the text we've included a few addresses for each wine to get you started. Note that when you go tasting, each wine you are offered will be older than the previous one until you are feeling quite jolly and ready to buy the oldest (and most expensive) vintage. On the other hand, some sell loose wine *à la* petrol pump; many *caves* even sell the little plastic barrels to put it in, so you can either bottle it yourself or take home to quaff as is (just don't leave it more than a couple of weeks, especially in the summer, or it will go off).

Restaurant Basics

Restaurants generally serve between 12 noon and 2pm and in the evening from 7 to 10pm, with later summer hours; brasseries in the cities generally stay open continuously. Most post menus outside the door so you know what to expect, and offer a choice of **set-price menus**; if prices aren't listed, you can bet it's not because they're a bargain.

If you summon up the appetite to eat the biggest meal of the day at noon, you'll spend a lot less money, as many restaurants offer special **lunch menus** – an economical way to experience some of the finer gourmet temples. Some of these offer a set-price gourmet *menu dégustation* – a selection of chef's specialities, which can be a great treat. At the humbler end of the scale, bars and brasseries often serve a simple *plat du jour* (daily special) and the no-choice *formule*, which is more often than not steak and *frites*. Eating *à la carte* anywhere will always be more expensive, in many cases twice as much.

Menus sometimes include the house wine (*vin compris*). If you choose a better wine anywhere, expect a scandalous mark-up; the French wouldn't dream of a meal without wine, and the arrangement is a simple device to make food prices seem lower. If **service** is included it will say *service compris* or *s.c.*, if not *service non compris* or *s.n.c.*

French restaurants, especially the cheaper ones, presume everyone has the appetite of Gargantua. A full meal consists of: an apéritif (*pastis*, the national drink of the south, is famous for its hunger-inducing qualities), hors-d'œuvre or a starter (typically, soup, pâté or *charcuterie*), an *entrée* (usually fish, or an omelette), a main course (usually meat, poultry, game or offal, *garni* with vegetables, rice or potatoes), often followed by a green salad (to 'lighten' the stomach), then cheese, dessert, coffee, chocolates and *mignardises* (or *petits fours*) and perhaps a *digestif* to round things off. Most people only devour the whole whack on Sunday afternoons, and at other times condense this feast to a starter, *entrée* or main course, and cheese or dessert. Vegetarians usually have a hard time in France, especially if they don't eat fish or eggs, but most establishments will try to accommodate them.

When looking for a restaurant, homing in on the one place crowded with locals is as sound a policy in France as anywhere. Don't overlook hotel restaurants, some of which are absolutely top notch even if a certain red book refuses on some obscure principle to give them more than two stars. To avoid disappointment, call ahead in the morning to reserve a table, especially at the smarter restaurants, and especially in the summer.

You'll soon notice that the big cities have a wide choice of regional and ethnic restaurants: Breton crêperies or *galetteries* (with wholewheat pancakes), restaurants from Alsace serving *choucroute* (sauerkraut) and sausage, Périgord restaurants featuring *foie gras* and truffles, Lyonnaise *haute cuisine*, and *les fast foods* offering *basse cuisine* of chips, hot dogs and cheese sandwiches. North African restaurants are a favourite for their economical couscous – spicy meat and vegetables served on a bed of steamed semolina with a side dish of *harissa*, a hot red pepper sauce; Asian (usually Vietnamese, sometimes Chinese, Cambodian, or Thai) and Italian are popular as well, the latter often combined with a pizzeria, although quality very much depends on its geographical proximity to Italy.

There are still a few traditional French restaurants that would meet the approval of Auguste Escoffier, the legendary chef; quite a few serve regional specialities and many feature *nouvelle cuisine*, which isn't so *nouvelle* any more, and has come under attack by foodies for its expense (only the finest, freshest, rarest ingredients are used), portions (minute, because the object is to feel good, not full), and sheer quackery. For *nouvelle cuisine* is a subtle art, emphasizing the natural flavour and goodness of a carrot by contrasting or complementing it with other flavours and scents; disappointments are inevitable when a chef is more concerned with appearance than taste, or combines oysters, kiwis and cashews or some other abomination. But *nouvelle cuisine* has had a strong influence on attitudes to food in France, and it's hard to imagine anyone going back to smothering everything in a béchamel sauce. On the whole, though, regional *cuisine de terroir*, modern Mediterranean and fusion are the rule.

French Menu Reader

Hors-d'œuvre et Soupes
(Starters and Soups)
amuse-gueule appetizers
assiette assortie mixed cold hors-d'œuvre
bisque shellfish soup
bouchées mini vol-au-vents
bouillabaisse famous fish soup of Marseille
bouillon broth
charcuterie mixed cold meats, salami, ham, etc.
consommé clear soup
coulis thick sieved sauce
crudités raw vegetable platter
potage thick vegetable soup
tourrain garlic and bread soup
velouté thick smooth soup, often fish or chicken
vol-au-vent puff-pastry case with savoury filling

Poissons et Coquillages (Crustacés)
(Fish and Shellfish)
aiglefin little haddock
alose shad
anchois anchovies
anguille eel
bar sea bass
barbue brill
baudroie angler fish
belons flat oysters
bigorneau winkle
blanchailles whitebait
brème bream
brochet pike
bulot whelk
cabillaud cod
calmar squid
carrelet plaice
colin hake
congre conger eel
coques cockles
coquillages shellfish
coquilles St-Jacques scallops
crabe crab
crevettes grises shrimps
crevettes roses prawns
cuisses de grenouilles frogs' legs
darne slice or steak of fish
daurade sea bream
écrevisse freshwater crayfish
éperlan smelt
escabèche fish fried, marinated and
   served cold
escargots snails
espadon swordfish
esturgeon sturgeon
flétan halibut
friture deep-fried fish
fruits de mer seafood

gambas giant prawns
gigot de mer a large fish cooked whole
grondin red gurnard
hareng herring
homard Atlantic (Norway) lobster
huîtres oysters
lamproie lamprey
langouste spiny Mediterranean lobster
langoustines Norway lobster (often called
   Dublin Bay prawns)
limande lemon sole
lotte monkfish
loup (de mer) sea bass
louvine sea bass (in Aquitaine)
maquereau mackerel
merlan whiting
morue salt cod
moules mussels
oursin sea urchin
pagel sea bream
palourdes clams
poulpe octopus
praires small clams
raie skate
rascasse scorpion fish
rouget red mullet
St-Pierre John Dory
saumon salmon
sole (meunière) sole (with butter, lemon and
   parsley)
stockfisch stockfish (wind-dried cod)
telline tiny clam
thon tuna
truite trout
truite saumonée salmon trout

Viandes et Volailles
(Meat and Poultry)
agneau (de pré-salé) lamb (grazed in fields
   by the sea)
ailerons chicken wings
aloyau sirloin
andouillette chitterling (tripe) sausage
autruche ostrich
biftek beefsteak
blanc breast or white meat
blanquette stew of white meat, thickened with
   egg yolk
bœuf beef
boudin blanc sausage of white meat
boudin noir black pudding
brochette meat (or fish) on a skewer
caille quail
canard, caneton duck, duckling
carré crown roast
cassoulet haricot bean stew with sausage, duck,
   goose, etc.
cervelle brains

chair flesh, meat
chapon capon
châteaubriand porterhouse steak
cheval horsemeat
chevreau kid
chorizo spicy Spanish sausage
civet meat (usually game) stew, in wine and
  blood sauce
cœur heart
confit meat cooked and preserved in its
  own fat
côte, côtelette chop, cutlet
cou d'oie farci goose neck stuffed with pork,
  foie gras and truffles
crépinette small sausage
cuisse thigh or leg
dinde, dindon turkey
entrecôte ribsteak
épaule shoulder
estouffade a meat stew marinated, fried
  and then braised
faisan pheasant
faux-filet sirloin
foie liver
frais de veau veal testicles
fricadelle meatball
gésier gizzard
gibier game
gigot leg of lamb
graisse, gras fat
grillade grilled meat, often a mixed grill
grive thrush
jambon ham
jarret knuckle
langue tongue
lapereau young rabbit
lapin rabbit
lard, lardons bacon, diced bacon
lièvre hare
maigret, magret de canard breast of duck
manchons duck or goose wings
marcassin young wild boar
merguez spicy red sausage
moelle bone marrow
mouton mutton
museau muzzle
navarin lamb stew with root vegetables
noix de veau topside of veal
oie goose
os bone
perdreau, perdrix partridge
petit salé salt pork
pieds trotters
pintade guinea fowl
plat-de-côtes short ribs or rib chops
porc pork
pot au feu meat and vegetables cooked in stock
poulet chicken

poussin baby chicken
quenelles poached dumplings made of fish,
  fowl or meat
queue de bœuf oxtail
ris (de veau) sweetbreads (veal)
rognons kidneys
rosbif roast beef
rôti roast
sanglier wild boar
saucisses sausages
saucisson dry sausage, like salami
selle (d'agneau) saddle (of lamb)
steak tartare raw minced beef, often topped
  with a raw egg yolk
suprême de volaille fillet of chicken breast
  and wing
taureau bull meat
tête (de veau) calf's head, fatty and usually
  served with a mustardy vinaigrette
tortue turtle
tournedos thick round slices of beef fillet
travers de porc spare ribs
tripes tripe
veau veal
venaison venison

Légumes, Herbes, etc.
(Vegetables, Herbs, etc.)

ail garlic
aïoli garlic mayonnaise
algue seaweed
aneth dill
anis anis
artichaut artichoke
asperges asparagus
aubergine aubergine (US eggplant)
avocat avocado
basilic basil
betterave beetroot (US red beet)
blette Swiss chard
bouquet garni mixed herbs in a little bag
cannelle cinnamon
céleri celery
céleri-rave celeriac
cèpes ceps, wild boletus mushrooms
champignons mushrooms
chanterelles wild yellow mushrooms
chicorée curly endive (US chicory)
chou cabbage
choucroute sauerkraut
chou-fleur cauliflower
choux de bruxelles Brussels sprouts
ciboulette chives
citrouille pumpkin
clou de girofle clove
cœur de palmier heart of palm
concombre cucumber
cornichons gherkins
courgettes courgettes (zucchini)

cresson watercress
échalote shallot
endive chicory (US endive)
épinards spinach
épis de maïs sweetcorn (on the cob)
estragon tarragon
fenouil fennel
fèves broad (fava) beans
flageolets white beans
fleurs de courgette courgette blossoms
frites chips (French fries)
genièvre juniper
gingembre ginger
haricots blancs white beans
haricots rouges kidney beans
haricots verts green (French) beans
jardinière with diced garden vegetables
laitue lettuce
laurier bay leaf
lavande lavender
lentilles lentils
marjolaine marjoram
menthe mint
mesclun herb salad
morilles morel mushrooms
moutarde mustard
navet turnip
oignons onions
oseille sorrel
panais parsnip
persil parsley
petits pois peas
piment pimento
pissenlits dandelion greens
poireaux leeks
pois chiches chickpeas (US garbanzo beans)
pois mange-tout sugar peas, mangetout
poivron sweet pepper (US capsicum)
pomme de terre potato
potiron pumpkin
primeurs young vegetables
radis radishes
raifort horseradish
riz rice
romarin rosemary
roquette rocket
safran saffron
salade verte green salad
salsifis salsify
sarrasin buckwheat
sarriette savory
sauge sage
seigle rye
serpolet wild thyme
thym thyme
truffes truffles

Fruits et Noix (Fruit and Nuts)
abricot apricot

amandes almonds
ananas pineapple
banane banana
bigarreaux black cherries
brugnon nectarine
cacahouètes peanuts
cassis blackcurrant
cerise cherry
citron lemon
citron vert lime
coing quince
dattes dates
figues (de Barbarie) figs (prickly pear)
fraises (des bois) strawberries (wild)
framboises raspberries
fruit de la passion passion fruit
grenade pomegranate
groseilles redcurrants
mandarine tangerine
mangue mango
marrons chestnuts
mirabelles mirabelle plums
mûre (sauvage) mulberry, blackberry
myrtilles bilberries
noisette hazelnut
noix walnuts
noix de cajou cashews
noix de coco coconut
pamplemousse grapefruit
pastèque watermelon
pêche, pêche blanche peach, white peach
pignons pine nuts
pistache pistachio
poire pear
pomme apple
prune plum
pruneau prune
raisins, raisins secs grapes, raisins
reine-claude greengage plums

Desserts
Bavarois mousse or custard in a mould
biscuit biscuit; cracker; cake
bombe ice-cream dessert in a round mould
bonbons sweets (US candy)
brioche light sweet yeast bread
charlotte sponge fingers and custard cream dessert
chausson turnover
clafoutis baked batter pudding with fruit
compote stewed fruit
corbeille de fruits basket of fruit
coulis thick fruit sauce
coupe ice cream: a scoop or in cup
crème anglaise egg custard
crème caramel vanilla custard mould with caramel sauce
crème Chantilly sweet whipped cream
crème fraîche slightly sour cream

crème pâtissière thick pastry cream filling made with eggs
gâteau cake
gaufre waffle
génoise rich sponge cake
glace ice cream
macarons macaroons
madeleine small sponge cake
miel honey
mignardise same as *petits fours*
mousse 'foam': frothy dessert
œufs à la neige floating islands/meringues on a bed of custard
pain d'épice gingerbread
parfait frozen mousse
petits fours sweetmeats; tiny cakes and pastries
profiteroles choux pastry balls, often filled with chocolate or ice cream
sablé shortbread
savarin a filled cake, shaped like a ring
tarte, tartelette tart, little tart
tarte tropézienne sponge cake filled with custard and topped with nuts
truffes chocolate truffles
yaourt yoghurt

Fromage (Cheese)
cabécou sharp local goat's cheese
chèvre goat's cheese
doux/fort mild/strong
fromage blanc yoghurty cream cheese
fromage de brebis sheep's cheese
fromage frais a bit like sour cream
fromage sec general name for solid cheeses
plateau de fromage cheese (board)

Cooking Terms and Sauces
bien cuit well-done steak
à point medium steak
saignant rare steak
bleu very rare steak
aigre-doux sweet and sour
aiguillette thin slice
à l'anglaise boiled
à la bordelaise cooked in wine and diced vegetables
à la châtelaine with chestnut purée and artichoke hearts
à la diable in spicy mustard sauce
à la grecque cooked in olive oil and lemon
à la jardinière with garden vegetables
à la périgourdine in a truffle and foie gras sauce
à la provençale cooked with tomatoes, garlic and olive oil
allumettes strips of puff pastry
au feu de bois cooked over a wood fire
au four baked
auvergnat with sausage, bacon and cabbage
barquette pastry boat

beignets fritters
béarnaise sauce of egg yolks, shallots and white wine
broche roasted on a spit
chasseur mushrooms and shallots in white wine
chaud hot
cru raw
cuit cooked
diable sauce of spicy mustard or green pepper
émincé thinly sliced
en croûte cooked in a pastry crust
en papillote baked in buttered paper
épices spices
farci stuffed
feuilleté flaky pastry
flambé set aflame with alcohol
forestière with bacon and mushrooms
fourré stuffed
frais, fraîche fresh
frappé with crushed ice
frit fried
froid cold
fumé smoked
galantine cooked food served in cold jelly
galette puff pastry case or pancake
garni with vegetables
(au) gratin topped with cheese and breadcrumbs and browned
grillé grilled
haché minced (US ground)
hollandaise a sauce of egg yolks, butter and vinegar
marmite casserole
médaillon round piece
mijoté simmered
mornay cheese sauce
pané breaded
parmentier with potatoes
pâte pastry; pasta
pâte brisée shortcrust pastry
pâte à chou choux pastry
pâte feuilletée puff pastry
paupiette thin slices of fish or meat, filled and rolled
pavé slab
piquant spicy hot
poché poached
pommes allumettes thin chips (fries)
raclette melted cheese with potatoes, onions and pickles
salé salted; spicy
sucré sweet
timbale pie cooked in a dome-shaped mould
tranche slice
vapeur steamed
véronique grape, wine and cream sauce
vinaigrette oil and vinegar dressing

Miscellaneous

addition bill (US check)
baguette long loaf of bread
beurre butter
carte non-set menu
confiture jam
couteau knife
crème cream
cuillère spoon
formule set menu
fourchette fork
fromage cheese
huile (d'olive) (olive) oil
menu set menu
nouilles noodles
œufs eggs
pain bread
poivre pepper
sel salt
service compris/non compris service
   included/not included
sucre sugar
vinaigre vinegar

Snacks

chips crisps (US potato chips)
crêpe thin pancake
croque-madame toasted ham and cheese
   sandwich with fried egg
croque-monsieur toasted ham and
   cheese sandwich
croustade small savoury pastry
frites chips (US French fries)
gaufre waffle
pissaladière a kind of pizza with onions,
   anchovies, etc.
sandwich canapé open sandwich

Boissons (Drinks)

bière (pression) (draught) beer
bouteille (demi) bottle (half-bottle)
brut very dry
café coffee
café au lait white coffee
café express espresso coffee
café turc Turkish coffee
chocolat chaud hot chocolate
citron pressé fresh lemon juice
demi a third of a litre
doux sweet (wine)
eau (minérale, non-gazeuse ou gazeuse) water
   (mineral, still or sparkling)
eau-de-vie brandy
eau potable drinking water
gazeuse sparkling
glaçons ice cubes
infusion or *tisane (camomille, verveine, tilleul,
   menthe)* herbal tea (camomile, verbena, lime
   flower, mint)
jus juice
lait milk
menthe à l'eau peppermint cordial
moelleux semi-dry
mousseux sparkling (wine)
orange pressée fresh orange juice
pastis anis liqueur
pichet carafe
pression draught
ratafia home-made liqueur made by steeping
   fruit or green walnuts in alcohol or wine
sec dry
sirop d'orange/de citron orange/lemon squash
thé tea
verre glass
vin blanc/rosé/rouge white/rosé/red wine

Planning
Your Trip

When to Go 64
  Climate 64
  Festivals 64
Tourist Information 66
Embassies and Consulates 66
Entry Formalities 67
Disabled Travellers 67
Insurance and EHIC Cards 68
Money and Banks 68
Getting There 69
  By Air 69
  By Train 70
  By Coach 71
  By Car 72
Getting Around 73
  By Train 73
  By Bus 73
  By Car 73
  By Bicycle 74
  On Foot 75
Where to Stay 75
Tour Operators 78

06

When to Go

Climate

Provence has a basically Mediterranean climate, one wafted by **winds** that give it a special character. The most notorious is the *mistral* (from the Provençal *mistrau*, or master – supposedly sent by northerners jealous of the south's climate), rushing down the Rhône and gusting east as far as Toulon and west to Narbonne. On average the *mistral* blows 100–150 days a year, nearly always in multiples of three, except when it begins at night. It is responsible for the dryness in the air and soil (hence its nickname, *mangio fango*, or mud-eater). Houses in its line of fire are built *pointes en avant*, at an angle, the north side blank and in the shade, protected by cypresses, while on the south side plane trees protect the house from the strong sun. It blows so hard that it can drive people mad: an old law in Provence acquitted a murderer if it could be proved that he killed his victim while the *mistral* was blowing. But the *mistral* has its good points: it blows away harmful miasmas and pollution from the Rhône and makes the stars radiantly clear.

Besides the Master, there are 22 other winds, most importantly: the *levant*, the east or southeasterly 'Greek' wind which brings the much desired rain; the *pounent*, or west wind; and the suffocatingly hot sirocco from Africa.

Rainfall varies widely across the south. The Camargue barely gets 500mm a year, the least rainfall in France. In the average year, it rains more in Marseille than in Paris. In the heart of Provence it rains much less frequently – not at all in the summer, and violently in spring and autumn (up to 135mm in an hour) – hence the *restanques*, or terraces carved in the hills by the farmers to prevent erosion.

Each **season** has its pros and cons. In **January** all the tourists are in the Alps; in **February and March** the mimosa and almonds bloom. In **April** and **May** you can sit outside at restaurants and swim, and within an hour's drive ski at Auron or Isola 2000. By **June**, the *mistral* is slowing down and the resorts begin to fill up; walking is safe in the highest mountains. **July** and **August** are bad months, when everything is crowded, temperatures and prices soar and tempers flare, but it's also the season of the great festivals in Avignon and Aix. Once French school holidays end in early **September**, prices and crowds decrease with the temperature. In **October** the weather is traditionally mild on the coast, although torrential downpours and floods are not unknown; the first snows fall in the Alps. **November** is another bad month; it rains and many museums, hotels and restaurants close down. **December** brings Christmas tourists and the first skiers.

Festivals

The south of France offers everything from the Cannes Film Festival to the village fête, with a pilgrimage or religious procession, bumper cars, a *pétanque* tournament, a feast and an all-night dance, sometimes with a local band but often a travelling troupe playing 'Hot Music' or some other electrified cacophony. Bullfights (*see* p.86) play a part in many fêtes west of the Rhône. A *bravade* entails pistol or musket-shots; a *corso* is a parade with carts or floats. St John's Day (24 June) is a big favourite and often features bonfires and fireworks.

In the southern Rhône valley, people still like to celebrate with a *farandole*, a dance in 6/8 time with held hands or a handkerchief, which may be as old as the ancient Greeks. One-man musical accompaniment is provided by a little three-holed flute called a *galoubet*, played with the left hand, and a *tambourin*, a drum played with the right. Both *farandoles* and flamenco enliven the proceedings of the 24 May pilgrimage at Saintes-Maries-de-la-Mer, by far the best attended of all popular festivities in the south.

Average Temperatures in °C (°F)

Jan	Feb	Mar	April	May	June	July	Aug	Sept	Oct	Nov	Dec
7 (44)	7 (44)	11 (52)	15 (59)	17 (62)	21 (70)	23 (73)	25 (77)	23 (73)	16 (61)	10 (50)	8 (45)

Calendar of Events

Note that dates change every year; for complete listings and precise dates of events, pick up a copy of the annual lists, available in most tourist offices, consult the regional tourist office websites (see p.66), or see www.francefestivals.com, www.franceguide.com, www.culture.fr or www.whatsonwhen.com.

January

Sun nearest 17th *Fête de St-Marcel*, folk dancing and singing at **Barjols**; every four years (next 2010) Barjols does an ox roast

Third Sun *Fête des Vanniers*, basket-makers' festival, **Cadenet**

End of month Truffle festival, **Aups**

February

Hivernales d'Avignon, contemporary dance events, **Avignon**

Every Sun *Oursinades*, sea urchin festival, **Carry-le-Rouet**

First week *Fête de la Chandeleur*, religious pilgrimage, **Marseille**

Carnival traditional celebrations during the school break in many towns including **Aix-en-Provence, Arles, Aups, La Ciotat** and **Marseille**

15 days at Carnival *Fête du Citron*, **Menton**

April

Good Fri–Easter (may be in March) Bullfights, **Arles**

25 *Fête Votive de la St-Marc*, **Villeneuve lez Avignon**

Last Sun *Fête des Gardians*, traditional rodeo in **Arles**

Last week Wine festival, **Châteauneuf-du-Pape**

May

Third Sun Cherry Festival, **Le Luc-en-Provence**

Ascension weekend Festival of Ochre and Colour, **Roussillon**

24–25 Gypsy pilgrimage, **Saintes-Maries-de-la-Mer**

10 days at Pentecost *Cavalcade*, music festival, **Apt**

June

Fête de la Musique, with outdoor concerts, celebrated all over France

1 *Cérémonie du St-Vinage*, **Boulbon**

Around 23–24 *Fête de la St-Jean*, with processions in **Entrevaux, Arles, Les Baux-de-Provence** and elsewhere

Last Sun *Fête de la Tarasque*, **Tarascon**; *Fête Provençale*, with blessings of animals, **Allauch** (near Marseille)

Late June *Fête du Panier*, neighbourhood parties, **Marseille**

Last half of June Jazz and chamber music in **Aix-en-Provence**

July

All month *Cocarde d'Or* festival of music, dance and drama, **Arles**; *Festival de la Sorgue*, music, theatre and dance at **Fontaine-de-Vaucluse** and around; *Festival de Marseille*, the city's largest party, **Marseille**

First 2 weeks International Folklore Festival, **Marseille**

Mid-month *Fête de St-Eloi*, bullfights and a decorated cart pulled by 40 horses, **Châteaurenard**

Mid-month *Corso de Nuit* for Notre-Dame-de-Santé, **Carpentras**; *Soirées Musicales*, **St-Maximin-la-Ste-Baume**; Film Festival, **La Ciotat**

14 Fireworks, parties, *batailles des fleurs* and big celebrations in many places for Bastille Day; superb shows in **Avignon**

Last 3 weeks Music Festival, **Aix**

Last 2 weeks music festival, **Orange**; fête in **Martigues**, with theatre, seafood, music

Late July *Estivals*, week-long re-creation of medieval market, **Beaucaire**

Last Sun Donkey races and village fête, **Lacoste**

July–Aug

Festival of Early Music, **Entrevaux**; *Nuits de l'Empéri*, theatre festival in **Salon-de-Provence**; Festival of Dance, Music and Theatre, **Vaison-la-Romaine**; *Rencontres Internationales d'Eté à la Chartreuse*, concerts, dance and theatre, **Villeneuve lez Avignon**

Mid-July–mid-Aug International Theatre Festival, **Avignon**; *Festival Passion*, operettas, ballet and music, **Carpentras**

August

All month Music and Dance Festival, **Arles**

First Sun *Fête de la Madeleine*, with parade of flowered carts, **Châteaurenard**; Lavender Festival, **Digne-les-Bains**

9 and 11 *Fête de St-Laurent*, with bullfights, **Eygalières**

15 Village fête and operettas, **Le Thor**

Third week Provençal Festival, with wine, processions, *bravades* and drama, **Séguret**

First Sun after 20th *Fête du Traou*, dancing and polenta feasts, **Tende**

End of month *Fête de Saint-Louis*, with historical re-enactment, **Aigues-Mortes**

September
Second Sun Last bullfights of year, coinciding with *premices du riz* (rice harvest), **Arles**

Third weekend *Journées du Patrimoine*, special events across the region to showcase national treasures plus free entry to museums

October
Early Oct *Fête des Vendanges* to celebrate grape harvest, various locations

Mid-Oct *Fête-Votive*, with Provençal bullfights, in **Aigues-Mortes**

November
Last Fri *Foire St-Siffrein*, with truffle market, **Carpentras**

Last Sun *Foire des Santons*, until Epiphany, **Marseille**

December
All month Music Festival, **Marseille**

24 Midnight Mass in **St-Maximin-la-Ste-Baume**, **Séguret** and **Fontvieille**, with shepherds at **Allauch**, near Marseille; *Fête des Bergers* and midnight Mass, **Les Baux**; torchlight vigil, **Séguret**

Tourist Information

Every city and town, and most villages, have a tourist information office, usually called an *Office de Tourisme* (sometimes a *Maison de Tourisme*). In smaller villages this service is provided by the town hall (*mairie*). Most offices, even in the small villages, have a website nowadays. If you plan to stay in one area, look on the websites of the local tourist offices listed in the text or write to them for complete lists of accommodation.

Regional tourist offices known as CRTs (Comités Régionaux de Tourisme) offer useful information: *www.decouverte-paca.fr* (for Provence), *www.alpes-haute-provence.com* (for the Alpes de Haute-Provence), *www.provenceguide.com* (for the Vaucluse), *www.visitprovence.com* (for Bouches-du-Rhône), *www.tourismevar.com* (for the Var).

For more general information and a complete list of tour operators, get in touch with a French Government Tourist Office, or check the **Maison de la France** website (*www.franceguide.com*).

French Tourist Offices Abroad
UK: Lincoln House, 300 High Holborn, London WC1V 7JH, **t** 09068 244 123, *www.franceguide.com*.

Ireland: 10 Suffolk St, Dublin 1, **t** (01) 635 1008.

USA: 825 Third Avenue, 29th floor, New York, NY 10022, **t** (514) 288 1904; 676 N. Michigan Avenue, Suite 3770, Chicago, IL 6061, **t** (312) 327 0290; 9454 Wilshire Bd, Suite 210, Beverly Hills, CA 90212, **t** (310) 271 6695.

Canada: 1800 Avenue McGill College, Suite 1010, Montréal, Québec H3A 3J6, **t** (514) 288 2026.

Australia: Level 20, 25 Bligh Street, Sydney, NSW 2000, **t** (02) 9231 5244.

Useful Web Addresses
www.tourisme.fr
www.france.com (for hotels and tours)
www.avignon-et-provence.com
www.provencetourism.com
www.provenceweb.fr
www.visit-riviera.com (for hotels)
www.francekeys.com
www.frenchconnections.co.uk

Embassies and Consulates

Foreign Embassies, etc. in France
UK: Marseille: 24 Av du Prado, **t** 04 91 15 72 10; Nice: by appointment only, **t** 04 91 15 72 10; *http://ukinfrance.fco.gov.uk*.

Ireland: Paris: 4 Rue Rude, 75016, **t** 01 44 17 67 00, *www.irlgov.ie/irishembassy/ France.htm*.

USA: Marseille: Place Varian Fry, **t** 04 91 54 92 00; Nice: 7 Av Gustave V, **t** 04 93 88 89 55, *www.amb-usa.fr*.

Canada: Nice: 10 Rue Lamartine, **t** 04 93 92 93 22, *www.dfait-maeci.gc.ca*.

Australia: Paris: 4 Rue Jean Rey, 75724 Paris Cedex, **t** 01 40 59 33 00, *www.austgov.fr*.

New Zealand: Paris: 7 Rue Léonard da Vinci, 75116 Paris, **t** 01 45 01 43 43, *www.nzembassy.com*.

French Embassies, etc. Abroad

UK: 58 Knightsbridge, London SW1X 7JT,
t (020) 7073 1000, *www.ambafrance-uk.org*;
21 Cromwell Rd, London SW7 2EN, **t** (020) 7073
1200, *www.consulfrance-londres.org* (*for
visas*); 11 Randolph Crescent, Edinburgh
EH3 7TT, **t** (0131) 225 7954, *www.consulfrance-edimbourg.org*.

Ireland: 36 Ailesbury Rd, Ballsbridge, Dublin 4,
t (01) 277 5000, *www.ambafrance.ie*.

USA: 4101 Reservoir Rd NW, Washington,
DC 20007-2185, **t** (202) 944 6195, *www.ambafrance-us.org*; 205 North Michigan
Avenue, Suite 3700, Chicago, IL 60601, **t** (312)
327 5200, *www.consulfrance-chicago.org*;
10990 Wilshire Bd, Suite 300, Los Angeles, CA
90024, **t** (310) 235 3200, *www.consulfrance-losangeles.org*; 934 Fifth Av, New York, NY
10021, **t** (212) 606 3600, *www.consulfrance-newyork.org*. There are also French consulates
in Atlanta, Boston, Houston, Miami, New
Orleans and San Francisco.

Entry Formalities

Passports and Visas

Holders of **EU, US, Canadian, Australian,
New Zealand** and **Israeli** passports do not
need a visa to enter France for stays of up to
three months; most other nationals do. Apply
at your nearest French consulate or embassy.
The most convenient visa is the *visa de
circulation*, allowing for multiple stays of
three months over a five-year period. If you
intend to stay for longer, the law says that
non-EU citizens need a *carte de séjour*.

The creeping rise of xenophobic legislation
in France means that non-EU citizens had
best apply for an extended visa prior to
leaving home – a complicated procedure
requiring proof of income, etc. You can't get a
carte de séjour without the visa.

Customs

EU citizens over the age of 17 do not have to
declare goods imported into France for
personal use if they have paid duty on them
in the country of origin. In theory, you can buy
as much as you like, provided you can prove
the purchase is for your own use. In practice,
customs will be more likely to ask questions

if you buy in bulk, e.g. more than 3,200
cigarettes or 400 cigarillos, 200 cigars or 3kg
of tobacco; plus 10 litres of spirits, 90 litres of
wine and 110 litres of beer. Travellers caught
importing any of the above for resale will
have the goods seized along with the vehicle
they travelled in, and could face imprison-
ment for up to seven years.

Travellers from **outside the EU** must pay
duty on goods worth more than €175 that
they import into France.

Travellers from the USA are allowed to
bring home, duty-free, goods to the value of
$400, including 200 cigarettes or 100 cigars;
plus one litre of alcohol. For more information, call the US Customs Service. You're not
allowed to bring back certain brands of
absinthe or Cuban cigars. Canadians can
bring home $300 worth of goods in a year,
plus their tobacco and alcohol allowances.

French Customs, *www.douane.gouv.fr*.

UK Customs, **t** 0845 010 9000,
www.hmrc.gov.uk.

US Customs, **t** (202) 354 1000,
www.customs.gov.

Canadian Customs, *www.cbsa.gc.ca*.

Disabled Travellers

When it comes to providing access for all,
France isn't exactly in the vanguard, but
things are beginning to change, especially in
newer buildings, and national organizations
are becoming more helpful too. All TGVs
are equipped for wheelchair passengers –
contact Rail Europe in the UK or USA (*see* p.71)
or the SNCF in France (*see* p.73) for details;
alternatively you can ask for an assistant to
accompany you on your journey (although
you will have to pay for the
assistant). For more information contact the
French Railways office in your country.

The Channel Tunnel is a good way to travel
by car; on Eurotunnel trains passengers stay
in their vehicles, while Eurostar has a special
area reserved for wheelchair users and their
assistants (who can travel at reduced rates,
t 08705 186 186 for more information).

Ferry companies offer special assistance if
contacted beforehand. Vehicles modified for
disabled people are charged reduced tolls on
autoroutes. For more information contact the

Disability Organizations

In France

Association des Paralysés de France, 17 Bd Auguste Blanqui, Paris, **t** 01 40 78 69 00, *www.apf.asso.fr*. A national organization with offices in all *départements*.

In the UK

Can Be Done, t (020) 8907 2400, *www. canbedone.co.uk*. Specialist holidays.

Holiday Care Service, The Hawkins Suite, Enham Place, Enham, Alamein, Andover SP11 6JS, **t** 0845 124 9974, *www.holidaycare.org.uk*. Publishes an information sheet on holidays for disabled and older people (£5).

RADAR (Royal Association for Disability and Rehabilitation), 12 City Forum, 250 City Rd, London EC1V 8AF, **t** (020) 7250 3222, *www.radar. org.uk*. Some travel information.

In the USA

Alternative Leisure Co., 165 Middlesex Turnpike, Suite 206, Bedford, MA 01730, **t** (718) 275 0023, *www.alctrips.com*. Organizes vacations abroad for disabled people.

Mobility International USA, 132 E. Broadway, Suite 343, Eugene, Oregon, 97401, **t/TTY** (541) 343 1284, *www.miusa.org*. Information on international educational exchange programmes and volunteer service overseas for the disabled.

SATH (Society for Accessible Travel and Hospitality), 347 5th Ave, Suite 610, New York, NY 10016, **t** (212) 447 7284, *www.sath.org*. Travel and access information.

Other Useful Contacts

Access Ability, *www.access-ability.co.uk*. Info on travel agencies catering to the disabled.

Access-Able Travel Source, *www.access-able. com*. A database of information, travel operators, cruise lines, hotels, etc.

Emerging Horizons, *www.emerginghorizons. com*. An international subscription-based online (or mailed) quarterly travel newsletter.

Ministère des Transports, 246 Boulevard St Germain, 75700 Paris, **t** 01 40 81 21 22, *www.transports.equipement.gouv.fr*.

The *Gîtes accessibles aux personnes handicapées*, published by Gîtes de France, lists self-catering possibilities (*see* p.77 and *www.gites-de-france.fr*). Hotels with facilities for the disabled are listed in Michelin's *Red Guide to France*.

Insurance and EHIC Cards

Citizens of the EU who bring along their **European Health Insurance Card** (EHIC – apply online at *www.ehic.org.uk*, or pick up a form from a post office) are entitled to the same health services as French citizens. This means paying upfront for medical care and prescriptions, of which costs 75–80 per cent are reimbursed later – a complex procedure for the non-French. The website *www. nhs.uk/healthcarefrance* is useful.

As an alternative, consider a **travel insurance** policy, covering theft and losses and offering 100 per cent medical refund; check to see if it covers extra expenses if you get bogged down in airport or train strikes. Beware that accidents resulting from sports are rarely covered by ordinary insurance.

Canadians are usually covered in France by their provincial health coverage; Americans and others should check their individual policies. Many larger credit card companies offer free travel insurance when you use them to book a package holiday or aeroplane/train tickets, but read the small print very carefully, especially if you're travelling with expensive equipment.

Money and Banks

Euros come in denominations of €500, 200, 100, 50, 20, 10 and 5 (banknotes) and €2, €1, 50 cents, 20 cents, 10 cents, 5 cents, 2 cents and 1 cent (coins). For the latest **exchange rates**, see *www.xe.com/ucc*.

Under the Cirrus system, withdrawals in euros can be made from bank and post office automatic cash machines (**ATMs**; *distributeurs de billets*) using your usual debit or credit card and PIN number. The specific cards accepted are marked on each machine, and most give instructions in English. The wide acceptance of **credit cards** in ATM machines for withdrawing cash make them by far the most convenient way of carrying cash for the traveller, although there are a few things to note. Although it is always wise to have some euros in cash on hand, note that you'll often come out better by using your card to pay when you can rather than taking out loads of cash from the machine and paying the fee for cash advances.

Visa (Carte Bleue) is by far the most widely recognized credit card, followed by **MasterCard** and **American Express**. It must also be said that smaller establishments (especially *chambres d'hôtes* and *fermes-auberges*) tend to accept only cash, and that ATMs are few outside the main towns.

Banks are generally open 8.30am–12.30pm and 1.30–4pm; they close on Sunday, and most close either on Saturday or Monday as well. Exchange rates vary, and nearly all take a commission of varying proportions. *Bureaux de change* that do nothing but exchange money usually have the worst rates or take the heftiest commissions.

Getting There

By Air

The main international airports in the area are at Marseille, Nice and Montpellier. Thanks to deregulation, budget airlines and the disintegration of state monopolies, prices of scheduled flights are hugely competitive; to ensure a seat and save money, be sure to shop around and book ahead – especially during the summer and Easter holidays. Quoted prices usually exclude airport taxes.

Check with your travel agent or in major Sunday newspapers for bargains. There is often a discount for booking online, even with the major national airlines.

There are a number of charters and budget flights from London to Nice and Marseille and a good selection of both scheduled and low-cost flights from UK regional airports, but from most other points of departure – North America, Australia, etc. – it is often cheaper to fly to Paris, and from there catch a cheap flight or train to the south. There are domestic flights on Air France from Orly in Paris to Marseille and Nice. Services may be less frequent in winter.

Students who equip themselves with the relevant ID cards are eligible for considerable reductions, not only on flights, but also on trains and admission fees to museums, concerts, and more. Agencies (*see* box, overleaf) specializing in student and youth travel can help in applying for the cards, as well as filling you in on the best deals.

Airline Carriers

UK and Ireland

Aer Lingus, t 0818 365 000, UK t 0870 876 5000, *www.aerlingus.com*. To Marseille and Nice from Dublin, and to Nice from Cork.

Air France, t 0870 142 4343, *www.airfrance. co.uk*. Direct from London City to Nice, and from London Heathrow via Paris to Marseille.

British Airways, t 0844 493 0787, *www.ba.com*; France t 0825 825 400. To Nice from London City and Heathrow, and Marseille from Gatwick.

easyJet, t 0905 821 0905 (65p/min), *www.easyjet.com*. To Nice from many cities, Marseille from London Gatwick and Bristol.

Flyglobespan.com, t 0871 971 1440, *www.flyglobespan.com*. To Nice from Edinburgh, summer only.

Jet 2, t 0871 2261 737, *www.jet2.com*. To Nice from Leeds-Bradford and Manchester.

Ryanair, t 0906 270 5656, *www.ryanair.com*. To Marseille from Birmingham, Bournemouth, Dublin, Edinburgh, Glasgow, London Stansted and Manchester.

USA and Canada

For services to Paris and London, from where you can catch a domestic flight or train down to the south.

Air Canada, Canada/USA t 888 247 2262, *www.aircanada.com*.

Air France, USA t 800 237 2747, Canada t 800 667 2747, *www.airfrance.us*.

American Airlines, t 800 433 7300, *www.aa.com*.

British Airways, t 800 247 9297, *www.ba.com*.

Continental, USA/Canada t 800 231 0856, t 800 343 9195 (hearing-impaired), *www.continental.com*.

Delta, USA/Canada t 800 221 1212, *www.delta.com*. To Paris, but also a direct flight to Nice from New York.

KLM, USA represented by Northwest Airlines, t 800 225 2525, *www.nwa.com*.

Lufthansa, USA t 800 645 3880, Canada t 800 563 5954, *www.lufthansa.com*

United Airlines, t 800 538 2929, *www.united.com*.

Charters, Discounts, Students and Special Deals

UK and Ireland

Budget Travel, 134 Lower Baggot St, Dublin 2, **t** (01) 631 1100, *www.budgettravel.ie.*

Club Travel, 30 Lower Abbey St, Dublin 1, **t** (01) 570 719 880 (€1.75 per minute) within Eire, *www.clubtravel.ie.*

Europe Student Travel, 6 Campden St, London W8, **t** (020) 7727 7647. A small travel agent catering to non-students too.

STA Travel, 52 Grosvenor Gardens, London SW1W, **t** 0871 468 0649, *www.statravel.co.uk.* Many other branches in the UK, including: Bristol **t** 0870 166 2609; Leeds **t** 0870 168 6878; Manchester **t** 0870 166 2622; Oxford **t** (01865) 262 300; Cambridge **t** 0870 166 2591.

Trailfinders, 194 Kensington High St, London W8, **t** (020) 7938 3939, *www.trailfinders.com.*

United Travel, 12 Clonkeen Road, Deansgrange, Blackrock, County Dublin, **t** (01) 219 0600, *www.unitedtravel.ie.*

USIT Now, 19–21 Aston Quay, Dublin 2, **t** (01) 602 1906, and other branches in Ireland, *www.usitnow.ie.*

Websites (UK and Ireland)

www.aboutflights.co.uk (**t** 0870 330 7311; for price comparisons)
www.attitudetravel.com/france/lowcostairlines
www.cheapflights.co.uk
www.ebookers.co.uk
www.expedia.co.uk
www.flightcentre.com
www.icelolly.com
www.lastminute.com
www.majortravel.co.uk
www.opodo.co.uk
www.sky-tours.co.uk
www.travelocity.com
www.whichbudget.com

USA and Canada

For discounted flights, try the small ads in newspaper travel pages (for example, *New York Times, Chicago Tribune,* and *Toronto Globe and Mail*). Numerous travel clubs and agencies also specialize in discount fares, but they may require you to pay an annual membership fee.

Airhitch, 481 Eighth Avenue Suite 1771, New York NY, 10001-1820, *www.airhitch.org.* Last-minute discount tickets to Europe.

Last Minute Travel Club, USA **t** 800 442 0568, *www.lastminuteclub.com.* An annual membership fee entitles you to cheap stand-by deals and to special rates for some of the major car rental companies in Europe, plus deals on rail passes.

Now Voyager, 74 Varick St, Suite 307, New York, NY 10013, **t** (212) 431 1616, *www.nowvoyager.com.* For courier flights, plus gay and lesbian travel.

STA Travel, 2871 Broadway, New York, NY 10017, **t** (212) 865 2700 or **t** 800 781 4040; or 920 Westwood Boulevard, Los Angeles, CA 90024, **t** (310) 824 1574, *www.statravel.com.*

TFI, 1270 Broadway, Suite 409, New York, NY 10001, **t** (212) 736 1140, **t** 800 745 8000, *http://tfitours.com.* Low-cost negotiated fares, with discounts of up to 80% on Air France, Continental, Virgin Atlantic, Northwest Airlines and US Airways.

Travel Cuts, 187 College St, Toronto, Ontario M5T 1P7, **t** (416) 979 2406, *www.travelcuts.com.* Canada's largest student travel specialists; branches in most provinces. In the USA, call **t** 1-800 592 2887, *www.travelcuts.com/us*

www.traveldiscounts.com, USA **t** (408) 813 1111. Members get special rates on flights, hotels and tours.

Websites (USA and Canada)

You could also try some of the US cheap flight websites, which include:
www.eurovacations.com
www.expedia.com
www.flights.com
www.orbitz.com
www.priceline.com (bid for tickets)
www.smartertravel.com
www.travelocity.com
www.traveldiscounts.com

By Train

Airport awfulness makes France's high-speed **TGVs** (*trains à grande vitesse*) an attractive (but not necessarily cheaper) alternative. **Eurostar** trains leave from London St Pancras/Ashford International in Kent, and there are direct connections to Paris Gare du Nord (2hrs 15mins) and Lille (1hr 20mins). In summer (July–Sept) there are also direct Eurostar journeys from London to Avignon. The journey takes 6½hrs; fares are non-refundable and non-changeable; be sure to book ahead. As a general rule of thumb, fares on the Eurostar are cheaper if booked at least 7 or 14 days in advance, best at 21 days' notice and if you include a Saturday night away. Check in at least 30mins before departure or you will not be allowed on the train.

In Paris, go to the Gare de Lyon for a **TGV** to the south. France's TGVs shoot along at the average of 180mph when they're not breaking world records, and the journey from Paris' Gare de Lyon to Marseille or Montpellier takes only 4½ hours; 3½ hours to Avignon; 6½ hours to Nice. Costs are only minimally higher on a TGV. Some weekday departures require a very small supplement; all require a seat reservation, which you make when you buy your ticket or at the station before departure. People under 26 are eligible for a 30% discount on fares if they have an ISIC or other student ID card, and there are also discounts if you're 60 or over, available from major travel agents.

Another pleasant, if slower, way of getting south is by overnight sleeper (from Gare d'Austerlitz) after dinner in Paris.

If you plan to take some long train trips, it may be worth investing in a **rail pass** (*see www.raileurope.co.uk/railpasses*). An **Inter-Rail** standard one-country pass for France (for **European residents** of at least 6 months) costs £161 for three days' travel in one month, rising to £254 for eight days. For young people aged 12–25, prices start at £106 for three days' travel in a month rising to £165 for eight days. If you want to travel through several countries, ask about the Global Pass. You cannot buy a pass valid for the country in which you live.

Passes for **North Americans** include the **France Railpass**, giving three days' unlimited travel throughout the country in any one month for around $278–328 (less if 2 people are travelling together) including special rates on Eurostar and an option to purchase 6 extra days if required. The equivalent **France Youthpass** for under-26s costs around $206–243. There's also the **France Rail 'n' Drive** pass, giving 2 days' unlimited 1st-class rail travel through France and 2 days' car rental from $336.

Also for non-Europeans, the **Eurail Global Pass** allows unlimited 1st-class travel through 20 European countries for 15, 21, 30, 60 or 90 days; it saves the hassle of buying numerous

tickets but will only pay for itself if you use it a lot; a 15-day Eurail Pass costs around $796, a 21-day pass $1,032, 30 days $1,281, 2 months $1,808, 3 months $2,232. A 15-day **Eurail Pass Youth** for under-26s costs around $517 but is for 2nd-class travel only. The **Eurail Pass Flexi** allows first-class travel for any 10 days or 15 days in a 2-month period for around $612 or $808 respectively. All fares include discounted fares on Eurostar plus free or discounted travel on selected ferries, lake steamers, boats and buses. Passes are not valid in the UK, Morocco or countries outside the EU.

There are other combinations of passes available, such as for couples travelling together. See the Rail Europe website for full details and up-to-date prices. **Rail Europe** handles bookings for all services, including Eurostar and Motorail, sells rail passes and acts for other continental rail companies. Note that the German railways website ***www.deutsche-bahn.co.uk*** has a useful English-language journey planner and ticket-booking service for all of Europe. You can book tickets online on the French railways website ***www.sncf.com***, available in French and English, and have them sent to addresses outside France.

Rail Europe (UK), 1 Lower Regent Street, London SW1Y 4XT, **t** 0844 8484 064, *www.raileurope.co.uk*.

Rail Europe (USA and Canada), **t** 888 382 7245 (USA), or **t** 800 361 7245 (Canada), *www.raileurope.com*.

Eurostar, **t** 08705 186 186, *www.eurostar.com*.

www.seat61.com. An incredibly useful independent train travel website.

By Coach

National Express Eurolines offers services from London to Avignon (17½hrs), Aix-en-Provence (20hrs) and Marseille (20½hrs). There are up to 4 services a week and tickets start at around £70 (book 30 days ahead), £80 (book 15 days ahead) or £90 (standard return) to Avignon.

National Express Eurolines, **t** 08717 818181, *www.nationalexpress.com/eurolines* or *www.eurolines.co.uk*.

Drivers' Clubs

For more information on driving in France, contact the AA, RAC, or, in the USA, the AAA:

AA, General enquiries, t 0870 600 0371, *www.theaa.com*.

RAC, General enquiries, t 0870 572 2722, *www.rac.co.uk*.

AAA (USA), t 800 222 4357, *www.aaa.com*.

By Car

A car entering France must have its **registration and insurance papers. Green cards** are no longer compulsory but are worth getting, as they give fully comprehensive cover – your home insurance may only provide minimum cover. Drivers with a valid licence from an EU country, Canada, the USA or Australia don't need an **international licence**.

If you're coming from the UK or Ireland, the dip of the car **headlights** must be adjusted to the right. Carrying a **warning triangle** and a **reflective jacket** are now mandatory and you will be fined if caught without it. The triangle should be placed 50m behind the car if you have a breakdown. You can pick them up from supermarkets in France if the port shops have run out.

If you're **driving down from the UK**, you can either go through or around Paris, or take the A26 via Reims and Troyes. The *autoroutes* will get you south the fastest, but be prepared to pay some €50–100 in **tolls**; the N7 south of Paris takes longer, but costs nothing. For **toll charges** and route information, see *www.autoroutes.fr*. For information on driving rules and regulations, *see* 'Getting Around'.

By Car and Train

A fairly comfortable option is to put your car on the train. It can be costly, but there is a sleeper service that is well priced if bought in advance and in conjunction with Eurotunnel. Taking your car on a **Eurotunnel train** is a convenient (if fairly costly) way of crossing the Channel between the UK and France. It takes only 35mins to get through the tunnel from Folkestone to Calais; you remain in the car, although you can get up to stretch your legs. Fares start from around £125 for a standard return in low season, rising substantially in summer and high seasons. The price for all tickets is per car less than 6.5m in length and 1.85m high, plus the driver and all passengers.

In mid-April–mid-Oct **Motorail** offers up to 6 departures a week from Calais to Avignon or Nice. Accommodation is compulsory, in a 4-berth (1st-class) or 6-berth (2nd-class) carriage. Linen is provided, along with washing facilities. Compartments are not segregated by sex.

Eurotunnel, t 08705 35 35 35, *www.eurotunnel.com*.

Motorail, contact Rail Europe on t 0844 8484 050, *www.raileurope.co.uk/frenchmotorail*.

By Car and Sea

If you prefer a dose of bracing sea air, you've plenty of choice, although changes and mergers are always on the horizon and crossing may cost significantly more than travelling by air or rail. The shortest ferry/ catamaran crossing from the UK is currently **Dover–Calais** with P&O Ferries or SeaFrance.

Brittany Ferries operates from Plymouth to Roscoff in Brittany, Cork to Roscoff, Portsmouth to Caen, Cherbourg and St-Malo. **Speed Ferries** operates Dover to Boulogne and is one of the cheapest routes across the Channel. **Norfolkline** goes from Dover to Dunkerque. **Condor Ferries** sail from Poole or Weymouth to St-Malo, and Portsmouth to Cherbourg from July–Sept. **Irish Ferries** sails Rosslare to Cherbourg and Roscoff.

Prices vary considerably according to season and demand, so shop around for the best deal.

Ferry Operators

See also *www.ferrybooker.com* and *www. transmanche.ferries.org* for ferry and Eurotunnel bookings.

Brittany Ferries, t 0871 244 0439, *www.brittanyferries.com*.

Condor Ferries, t 0845 609 1024 *www.condorferries.co.uk*.

Irish Ferries, t 0818 300 400, *www.irishferries.com*.

Norfolkline, t 0844 847 5007, *www.norfolkline.com*.

P&O Ferries, t 08716 645 645, *www.poferries.com*.

SeaFrance, t 08705 711 711, *www.seafrance.com*.

Speed Ferries, t 0870 222 7546, *www.speedferries.com*.

Getting Around

By Train

SNCF nationwide information number,
t 36 35 (€0.34/min), *www.sncf.com*.

The **SNCF** runs a decent and efficient network of trains through the major cities of the south, and prices are reasonable. The narrow-gauge **Train des Pignes** operated by the Chemin de Fer de Provence from Nice to Digne is worth taking for the mountain scenery (*http://cccp.traindespignes.free.fr*).

If you plan on making only a few long hauls, an **Inter-Rail** pass or **France Railpass** (*see* p.71) bought before you leave home will save you money. Other possible discounts can be obtained once in France and hinge on the exact time of your departure. The SNCF has divided the year into **blue** (off-peak; *bleue*) and **white** (peak; *blanche*) **periods**, based on demand: white periods run from Friday noon to midnight Saturday, and from Sunday 3pm to Monday 10am and during holidays (all stations give out little calendars).

There is then a complicated system of discounts aimed mainly at French residents but which may just fit your circumstances – annual *cartes* must be paid for but can sometimes save you money. Log on to *www.voyages-sncf.com* to check them out, or ask at a station for *Le Guide du Voyageur*.

Tickets must be stamped in the little orange machines by the entrance to the platforms that say *Compostez votre billet* (this puts the date on the ticket). Any time you interrupt a journey until another day, you have to revalidate your ticket.

Long-distance trains (*trains Corail*) have snack trolleys and bar/cafeteria cars; some have play areas.

Nearly every station has large computerized **lockers** (*consigne automatique*) which take a while to puzzle out the first time; note that any threat of terrorist activity in France tends to close them down across the board.

By Bus

Do not count on seeing much of rural France by public transport. The bus network is barely adequate between major cities and towns (places often already well served by rail) and rotten in rural areas, where the one bus a day fits the school schedule, leaving at the crack of dawn and returning in the afternoon; more remote villages are linked to civilization only once a week or not at all.

Buses are run either by the **SNCF** (replacing discontinued rail routes) or **private firms**. Rail passes are valid on SNCF lines, which generally meet trains. Private bus firms, especially when they have a monopoly, tend to be a bit more expensive than trains.

Some towns have a *gare routière* (coach station), usually near the train station, though many lines start from any place that catches their fancy.

By Car

Unless you plan to stick to the major cities, a car is unfortunately the only way to see most of Provence. This has its drawbacks: high car rental rates and petrol prices, and an accident rate higher than in the UK (and much higher than the USA).

Though **roads** are generally excellently maintained, anything of less status than a departmental route (D-road) may be uncomfortably narrow. Mountain roads are reasonable except in the vertical *département* of Alpes-Maritimes, where they inevitably follow old mule tracks. Shrines to St Eloi, patron of muleteers, are common here, and a quick prayer is a wise precaution.

Blue 'P' signs will infallibly direct you to a village or town's already full **car park**. Watch out for the tiny signs that indicate which streets are meant for pedestrians only (with complicated schedules in even tinier print); and for Byzantine street parking rules (which would take pages to explain – do as the natives do, and be especially careful about village centres on market days).

Petrol (*essence*) is relatively expensive in France. The cheapest place to buy petrol is at the big supermarkets; the most expensive is on motorways. Petrol stations keep shop hours (*most close Sun and/or Mon, plus lunchtimes*) and are rare in rural areas, so replenish your fuel supply before making any forays into the mountains. Unleaded is *sans plomb*; diesel is *gazole* or *gasoil*. Automated machines functioning outside these hours don't currently accept foreign debit/credit cards. If you come across a garage with attendants, they will expect a tip for oil, windscreen-cleaning and air.

Speed limits are 130km/80mph on the *autoroutes* (toll motorways); 110km/69mph on dual carriageways (divided highways); 90km/55mph on other roads; 50km/30mph in an 'urbanized area' – as soon as you pass a white sign with a town's name on it and until you pass another sign with the town's name barred. **Fines** for speeding, payable on the spot, are high (from €68), and can be astronomical (up to €4,500) if you fail a breathalyser test.

If you wind up in an **accident**, the procedure is to fill out and sign a *constat amiable*. If your French isn't sufficient to deal with this, hold off until you find someone to translate for you so you don't accidentally incriminate yourself. If you have a **breakdown**, it is best to telephone the police (**t** 17).

France used to have a rule of giving **priority to the right** at every intersection. This has largely disappeared, although there may still be intersections, usually in towns, where it applies – these will be marked. Watch out for the *Cédez le passage* (give way) signs and be careful. Generally, as you'd expect, drive on the right, give priority to the main road, and to the left on roundabouts. When you (inevitably) get lost in a town or city, the *toutes directions* or *autres directions* signs are like Get Out of Jail Free cards.

Europ Assistance, t 0870 737 5720, *www.europ-assistance.co.uk*. Help with car insurance for abroad.

Useful Websites

Route planners: *www.mappy.com*, *www.rac.co.uk*, *www.theaa.com*.

Autoroute information: *www.route. equipement.gouv.fr*.

Road and traffic information: *www.asf.fr*, *www.autoroutes.fr* (both also in English).

Car Hire

If you plan to stay for three weeks or more, consider leasing a car. Car hire in France can be an expensive proposition. To save money, look into air and holiday package deals, as well as combination 'Train & Auto' rates. Prices vary widely from firm to firm: beware the small print about service charges and

Car Hire

UK

Avis, t 0844 581 0147, *www.avis.co.uk*.

Budget, t 0844 444 0002, *www.budgetinternational.com*.

easyCar, t 0871 0500 444, *www.easycar.com*.

Europcar, t 0845 722 2525, *www.europcar.co.uk*.

Hertz, t 08708 44 88 44, *www.hertz.co.uk*.

Thrifty, t (01494) 751 500, *www.thrifty.co.uk*.

USA and Canada

Auto Europe, t 1 888 223 5555, *www.autoeurope.com*.

Avis, t 800 331 1212, **t** 800 331 2323 (hearing-impaired), *www.avis.com*.

Europcar, t 877 940 6900, *www.europcar.com*.

Europe by Car, t 800 223 1516, *www.europebycar.com*.

Hertz, t 800 654 3131 (USA), **t** 800 654 3001 (international toll free), *www.hertz.com*.

taxes. It's often cheaper to book through car hire companies in your own country before you go.

The minimum age for hiring a car in France is 18 under certain conditions, but often 21 or 23 – you need to check with the hire company. Some companies have no maximum age, some say 70. Car hire firms are also listed for the larger towns in this book. For an instant online price comparison, log on to *www.autosabroad. com*, or call **t** 0845 029 1945.

By Bicycle

Cycling spells more pain than pleasure in most French minds, and one of the hazards of driving in the Alps and Pyrenees is suddenly coming upon bands of cyclists pumping up the kinds of inclines that most people require escalators for. If you mean to cycle in the summer, start and stop early to avoid heat-stroke. French drivers, not always courteous to fellow motorists, usually give cyclists a wide berth; and yet on any given summer day, half the patients in a French hospital are from accidents on two-wheeled transport. Wear a helmet. Also beware that bike thefts are fairly common.

Getting your own bike to France is fairly easy: Air France and British Airways carry them free from Britain, for example. From the

USA or Australia, most airlines will carry them as long as they're boxed and are included in your total baggage weight. In all cases, telephone ahead to the relevant airline to check on terms and conditions. On Eurostar cross-Channel trains, passengers travelling direct to Paris/Brussels or direct to Avignon (summer only) may take a bike with them provided it can be folded and carried on board in a bicycle bag (front wheel removed, etc). The bike will count as one item of your baggage allowance; for further information see *www.eurostar.com*.

Certain French trains (*autotrains*, marked with a bicycle symbol in the timetable) carry bikes for free, in the luggage van. You can dismantle and pack your cycle (max size 120 by 90cm) and stow it in the luggage space on long-distance trains (*trains Corail*) and TGVs. Some of these trains can reserve space for your bike undismantled; check when booking your ticket. You can also send your bike ahead for a fee (t 36 35 and dial 41) – reservation obligatory.

For cycling holidays, *see* the list of special-interest holiday companies, pp.78–80.

Fédération Française de Cyclotourisme, t 01 56 20 88 88, *www.ffct.org*. Maps and cycling information in France.

Cyclists' Touring Club, t (01483) 238 337, *www.ctc.org.uk*. Information in Britain.

Bike Hire

If you haven't brought a bike, main towns and holiday centres always seem to have at least one shop that hires them out – local tourist offices have lists. A *vélo tout terrain* (abbreviated to VTT) is a mountain bike. You may want to enquire about theft insurance.

You can also hire bikes from most SNCF train stations in major towns; they vary in quality, so check them. The advantage of hiring from a station is that you can drop the bike back off at another, as long as you specify where when you hire it. Rates should be around €9 a day, with a deposit of up to €80 or the yielding of a credit card number. Avoid the busy N roads as far as possible.

On Foot

A network of long-distance paths or *Grandes Randonnées* (GRs; marked by red and white signs, or splodges of red and white paint; at path junctions, an 'X' denotes this is not the right one to take) take in some of the most beautiful scenery in the south of France. Each GR is described in a *Topoguide*, with maps and details about camping sites, *refuges* and so on, available in local bookshops or the **Fédération Française de la Randonnée Pédestre**, 14 Rue Riquet, 75019 Paris, t 01 44 89 93 93, *www.ffrp.asso.fr*. *Walking in Provence*, with over 40 walks in the Alpes-Maritimes, Var, Vaucluse and northern Provence, is available from Stanfords, Long Acre, London WC2E 9LP, t (020) 7836 1321. Otherwise, the best maps for local excursions, based on ordnance surveys, are by the Institut Géographique National (1:50,000 or 1:100,000) and are available in most French bookshops.

There are 5,000km of marked paths in the Alpes Maritimes alone. Of special interest are: **GR5** from Nice to Aspremont, the Gorges de la Vésubie and St-Dalmas-Valdeblore; **GR52** from Menton up to Sospel, the Vallée des Merveilles and St-Dalmas-Valdeblore; **GR52a** and **GR5** through Mercantour National Park, both of which are open only from the end of June to the beginning of October. The **GR9** begins in St-Tropez and crosses over the region's most famous mountains: Ste-Baume, Ste-Victoire, the Luberon and Ventoux. **GR4** crosses the Dentelles de Montmirail and Mont Ventoux *en route* to Grasse; and **GR6** crosses from the Alps through the Vaucluse and Alpilles, to Beaucaire and the Pont du Gard, before veering north up the river Gard on to its final destination by the Atlantic.

Most tourist information centres also have maps and leaflets on shorter walks in their area.

Where to Stay

Hotels

In the south of France you can find some of the most splendid hotels in Europe and some genuine scruffy fleabags of dubious clientele, with the majority of establishments falling somewhere between. As in most countries in Europe, the tourist authorities grade hotels by their facilities (not by charm or location) with **stars** from four (or four with an L for luxury – a bit confusing, so in our text luxury places are given five stars) to one, and there are even some cheap but adequate places undignified by any stars at all.

We would have liked to put the exact prices in the text, but almost every establishment has a wide range of rooms and prices – a very useful and logical way of doing things, once you're used to it. In some hotels, every single room has its own personality and the difference in quality and price can be enormous: a large room with antique furniture, a television or a balcony over the sea and a complete bathroom will cost much more than a poky back room in the same hotel, with a window overlooking a car park, no antiques and the WC down the hall. Some proprietors will drag out a sort of menu for you to choose the level of price and facilities you would like. Most two-star hotel rooms have their own showers and WCs; most one-stars offer rooms with or without. The guide in the box below will give you an idea of what prices to expect. Hotels with no stars are not necessarily dives; the owners probably never bothered filling out a form for the tourist authorities. Prices are usually the same as one-star places.

Standards vary so widely that it's impossible to be more precise, but we can add a few more generalizations. **Single rooms** are relatively rare, and usually two-thirds the price of a double; rarely will a hotelier give you a discount if only doubles are available (again, because each room has its own price). On the other hand, if there are three or four of you, triples or quads or adding extra beds to a double room is usually cheaper than staying in two rooms. Flowered wallpaper, usually beige, comes in all rooms with no extra charge – it's an essential part of the French experience.

Breakfast (usually coffee, a croissant, bread and jam for €6 or €7) is nearly always optional: you'll do as well for less in a bar. As usual, rates rise in the busy season (holidays and summer, and in the winter around ski resorts), when many hotels with restaurants will require that you take **half-board** (*demi-pension* – breakfast and a set lunch or dinner). Many hotel restaurants are superb and non-residents are welcome. At worst the food will be boring. In the off-season, board requirements vanish into thin air.

Your holiday will be much sweeter if you book ahead. July and August are the only really impossible months; otherwise it usually isn't too difficult to find something. Phoning a day or two ahead is always a good policy, although beware that many hotels will only confirm a room with the receipt of a cheque or credit card number to cover the first night. Tourist offices have complete lists of accommodation in their given areas or even *département*, which come in handy during the peak season; many will even call around and book a room for you on the spot for free or a nominal fee.

There are **chain hotels** (Sofitel, Formula One, etc.) in most cities, but these are always dreary and geared to the business traveller more than the tourist, so you won't find them in this book. Don't confuse chains with the various umbrella organizations like Logis de France (*www.logis-de-france.fr*), Relais du Silence (*www.silencehotel.com*) or the prestigious Relais et Châteaux (*www.relaischateaux.fr*), which promote and guarantee the quality of independently owned hotels and their restaurants. Many are recommended in the text. Larger tourist offices usually stock their booklets, or you can pick them up before you leave from the French National Tourist Office.

Bed and Breakfast

In rural areas, there are plenty of opportunities for a stay in a private home or farm. *Chambres d'hôtes* are listed separately from hotels in the tourist office brochures, along with the various *gîtes* (*see* below). Some are connected to *ferme-auberge* restaurants, others to wine estates or a château; prices

Hotel Price Categories

Note that prices listed here and elsewhere in this book are for a double room in high season.

luxury	€€€€€	€230 or more
very expensive	€€€€	€150–230
expensive	€€€	€100–150
moderate	€€	€60–100
inexpensive	€	under €60

tend to be moderate to inexpensive and payable in cash only.

Association Française BAB France, 23 Centre Commercial Les Vergers, 95350 St Brice Sous Forêt, **t** 01 34 19 90 00, *www.maisonsdhotes defrance.fr.*

Bedbreak, PO Box 47085, London SW18 9AB, *www.bedbreak.com.*

Fleurs de Soleil, *www.fleursdesoleil.fr.* Offers *maisons d'hôtes* and B&Bs throughout southern France.

Youth Hostels

Most cities and resort areas have youth hostels (*auberges de jeunesse*) that offer simple dormitory accommodation and breakfast to people of any age for around €10–€25 a night. Most offer kitchen facilities as well, or inexpensive meals. They are the best deal going for people travelling on their own; for people travelling together, a 1-star hotel can work out just as cheaply. Another downside is that many are in the most ungodly locations – in the suburbs where the last bus goes by at 7pm, or miles from any transport at all in the country.

For further information on youth hostels in France, contact the **Fédération Unie des Auberges de Jeunesse**, 27 Rue Pajol, 75018 Paris, **t** 01 44 89 87 27, *www.fuaj.org.*

In summer the only way to be sure of getting a room is to arrive early in the day. Most require a **Hostelling International** (HI; *www.hihostels.com*) membership card, which you can usually purchase on the spot, although regulations say you should buy them in your home country.

UK: HI International Youth Hostel Federation, 2nd Floor, Gate House, Fretherne Road, Welwyn Garden City, Herts AL8 6RD, **t** (01707) 324 170, *www.hihostels.com*. Also contact **YHA**, Trevelyan House, Dimple Rd, Matlock, Derbyshire DE4 3YH, **t** 0870 770 8868, *www.yha.org.uk.*

USA: Hostelling International USA, 8401 Colesville Rd, Suite 600, Silver Spring, MD 20910, **t** (301) 495 1240, *www.hiayh.org.*

Canada: Hostelling International Canada, 205 Catherine Street, Suite 400, Ottawa, ON K2P 1C3, **t** (613) 237 7884, *www.hihostels.ca.*

Australia: AYHA, 11 Rawson Place, opposite Central Station, Sydney, 2000 NSW, **t** (02) 9218 9090, *www.yha.com.au.*

Another option in cities is single-sex hostels for young workers (*foyers de jeunes travailleurs et de jeunes travailleuses*), which rent out individual rooms if available, for slightly more than a youth hostel.

Gîtes d'Etape, Refuges and Fermes Auberges

A *gîte d'étape* (*www.gite-etape.com*) is a simple shelter with bunk beds and a rudimentary kitchen set up by a village along GR walking paths (*see* p.75) or scenic bike routes. Again, lists are available for each *département*; the detailed maps listed under 'Getting Around' (*see* p.75) mark them as well. In the mountains, similar rough shelters along the GR paths are called *refuges*, most of them open in summer only. Both charge around €15 a night.

Fermes auberges, which combine rural living with B&B comforts, are becoming a popular option. Check with the regional tourist offices for lists.

Gîtes de France and Other Self-catering Accommodation

Provence offers a vast range of self-catering: inexpensive farm cottages, history-laden châteaux with gourmet frills, sprawling villas on the Riviera, flats in modern beach resorts, even canal boats.

The **Fédération Nationale des Gîtes de France** is a French government service offering inexpensive accommodation by the week in rural areas. Lists with photos arranged by *département* are available from the **Maison des Gîtes de France et du Tourisme Vert**, 56 Rue St-Lazare, 75009 Paris, **t** 01 49 70 75 75, *www.gites-de-france.fr.* If you want to stay in a château, request the *Chambres d'hôtes et gîtes de prestige* list. Prices range from €250–1,000 a week, depending very much on the time of year as well as facilities; nearly always you'll be expected to begin your stay on a Saturday. Many *départements* also have a second (and usually less expensive) listing of *gîtes* in the guide *Clévacances* (*www.clevacances.com*).

Other options are advertised in the Sunday papers, or contact one of the firms listed below. The accommodation they offer will nearly always be more comfortable and costly than a *gîte*, but the discounts that holiday firms can offer on the ferries, aeroplane tickets or car rental can make up for the price difference.

For private *gîte* rentals booked directly with the owners, try *www.frenchconnections.co.uk*, which also offers ferry discounts, and *www.abritel.fr*.

Camping

Camping is very popular, especially among the French, and there's at least one campsite in every town, often an inexpensive, no-frills place run by the town itself (*camping municipal*). Other campsites are graded with stars like hotels from four to one: at the top of the line you can expect lots of trees and grass, hot showers, a pool or beach, sports facilities, and a grocer's, bar and/or restaurant; on the coast, prices are rather similar to one-star hotels (although these, of course, never have all the extras).

Beware that July and August are terrible months to camp. If you want to camp outside official sites, ask permission from the landowner first, or risk a furious farmer, his dog and perhaps even the police.

Tourist offices have complete lists of campsites in their regions. If you plan to move around a lot, the *Guide Officiel Camping/Caravanning* is available in most French bookshops. Also see *www.camping france.com*. The Michelin Green Guide: *Camping/Caravanning France* is very informative and also lists sites with facilities suitable for disabled visitors. A number of UK holiday firms book camping holidays and offer discounts on ferries:

Canvas Holidays, t 0870 192 1154, *www.canvasholidays.co.uk*.

Eurocamp Travel, t 0844 406 0402, *www.eurocamp.co.uk*.

Keycamp Holidays, t 0870 7000 740, *www.keycamp.com*.

Special-interest Tour Operators

There are a number of ways to combine a holiday with study or a special interest. Contact the **Centre France Péguy**, 164–8 Westminster Bridge Rd, London SE1 7RW, t (020) 7960 2614, *www.cei-frenchcentre.com*; or the **Cultural Services of the French Embassy**, 58 Knightsbridge, London SW1X 7JT, t (020) 7073 1000, *www.ambafrance-uk.org*, or 972 Fifth Avenue, New York, NY 10075, t (212) 439 1400, *www.info-france-us.org*.

For language courses, see the Worldwide Classroom site at *www.worldwide.edu*.

In France

Alliance Française, 2 Rue de Paris, 06000 Nice, t 04 93 62 67 66, *www.alliance-francaise-nice. com*. French classes on all levels. Courses last a month, but they can tailor to your needs.

Association Neige et Merveilles, Hameau de la Minière de Vallauria, 06430 St-Dalmas-de-Tende, t 04 93 04 64 58 (weekends), t 04 93 87 64 33 (weekdays), *www.neige-merveilles.com*. Chalets from May-Oct, plus occasional courses in archaeology and restoration; also pony-trekking and walks for schools. In winter the village is practically cut off but you can stay in a *refuge*.

Cercle d'Echanges Interculturels et Linguistiques, Avignon (CEILA), 16 Impasse Jean-Pierre Gras, 84000 Avignon, t 04 32 76 39 94, *www.ceila.com*. Specializes in linguistics, conversational French and French as a foreign language.

Echanges Culturels Internationaux (ECI), 62 Av Maréchal de Lattre de Tassigny, 13097 Aix-en-Provence, t 04 42 21 07 68, *www.eci.asso.fr*. As the Cercle d'Echanges.

Routes de la Lavande, 2 Av de Venterol, 26110 Nyons, t 04 75 26 65 91, *www.routes-lavande. com*. All things lavender: stays in Provence, discovery circuits, well-being, garden visits.

Vedel – Cuisine et Tradition School of Provençal Cuisine, 11 Rue Portagnel, 13200 Arles, t 04 90 49 69 20, *www.cuisineprovencale.com*. Courses in traditional Provençal cuisine with chef supreme Erick Vedel: cookery workshops, B&B, meet the artisans.

In the UK

ACE Study Tours, Babraham, Cambs CB2 3AP, t (01223) 835 055, *www.acestudytours.co.uk*. Tours include a Provence river cruise taking in Avignon, Nîmes and the Camargue.

Alternative Travel Group (ATG), 69–71 Banbury Rd, Oxford OX2 6PE, t (01865) 315 678, *www. atg-oxford.co.uk*. Escorted walking tours tracking down the painters and gardens of

Provence, or independent walking and cycling along continuous routes.

Andante Travels, The Old Barn, Old Road, Alderbury, Salisbury SP5 3AR, **t** (01722) 713 800, *www.andantetravels.co.uk*. Archaeological and historical study tours led by experts in the field. They don't go every year to the south of France, so check.

Arblaster and Clarke Wine Tours, Cedar Court, 5 College St, Petersfield, Hampshire, **t** (01730) 263 111, *www.arblasterandclarke.com*. Expert-led luxury wine-tasting tours covering all the major wine-producing regions.

Destination Provence, 49 Stonegate, York YO1 8AW, **t** (01904) 622 220, *www.destination provence.co.uk*. Self-catering villas and hotels: special interest, golf, walking, wine, cycling, cooking and self-drive discovery tours.

Fleur Holidays, 4 All Hallows Road, Bispham, Blackpool, FY2 OAS, **t** 0870 750 21213, *www.fleur-holidays.co.uk*. Camping and walking holidays in Provence.

Headwater Holidays, Old School House, Chester Rd, Castle, Northwich, Cheshire, CW8 1LE, **t** 0870 066 2650 or (01606) 720 033, *www.headwater.com*. Off-the-beaten-track weekly/fortnightly cycling, walking holidays, staying in hotels with pools.

InnTravel, nr Castle Howard, York YO60 7JU, **t** (01653) 617 788, *www.inntravel.co.uk*. Walking and riding in hilltop villages of the Luberon and Lure, plus walks, hotels and short breaks in Roman and Haute Provence.

Martin Randall, Voysey House, Barley Mow Passage, London W4 4GF, **t** (020) 8742 3355, *www.martinrandall.com*. Lecturer-accompanied cultural and art tours; often staying in characterful 4-star hotels.

Page & Moy, Compass House, Rockingham Rd, Market Harborough, Leicestershire LE16 7QD, **t** 08708 334 012, *www.pageandmoy.com*. Escorted, expert-led tours.

Plantagenet Tours, 85 The Grove, Moordown, Bournemouth BH9 2TY, **t** (01202) 521 895, *www.plantagenettours.com*. Cultural tours with subjects including the Crusades, Roman remains and the troubadours. Not always in the south of France.

Sherpa Expeditions, 131a Heston Rd, Hounslow, Middlesex TW5 0RF, **t** (020) 8577 2717, *www.sherpa-walking-holidays.co.uk*. Walks, cycling and treks.

Susi Madron's Cycling for Softies, 2–4 Birch Polygon, Rusholme, Manchester M14 5HX, **t** (0161) 248 8282, *www.cycling-for-softies. co.uk*. Luxurious gourmet cycling holidays in Provence and the Camargue.

Travel for the Arts, 12–15 Hanger Green, London S5 3EL, **t** (020) 8799 8350, *www.travelforthearts. co.uk*. Visits to Aix-en-Provence music festival.

Waymark Holidays, 44 Windsor Rd, Slough SL1 2EJ, **t** 0870 950 9800, *www.waymarkholidays. com*. Walking tours, centre-based in Provence.

Winetrails, Vann Lake, Ockley, Dorking, Surrey, RH5 5NT, **t** (01306) 712 111, *www.winetrails. co.uk*. Six-night walking or cycling holidays through the olive groves of Avignon to Mont Ventoux, staying in 1- or 2-star hotels.

Your Golf Holidays, The Green, Blackmore, Essex CM4 0RT, **t** (01277) 824 100, *www. yourgolfholidays.com*. Fly-drive golf holidays staying in 4-star hotels based around Marseille.

In the USA and Canada

Abercrombie & Kent, 11411 Opus Place, Executive Towers, West II, Suite 300, Downers Grove, IL 60515-1182, **t** 800 554 7016, *www. abercrombiekent.com*. Quality city and country breaks, including Bordeaux, Provence, the Riviera, and escorted tours for individuals from Paris to Marseille.

Adventure Center, 1311 63rd St, Suite 200, Emeryville, CA 94608, **t** 800 228 8747, *www.adventurecenter.com*. Eight-day hiking trips for moderate walkers across the mountains of Haute Provence, taking in some rocky terrain (luggage transported).

Backroads, 801 Cedar St, Berkeley, CA 94701-1800, **t** 800 462 2848, *www.backroads.com*. Bicycling, hiking and multi-sport holidays in Provence and elsewhere.

Country Walkers, PO Box 180, Waterbury, VT 05676, **t** 800 464 9255, *www.countrywalkers. com*. Walking holidays in summer, in Provence and elsewhere, led by expert local guides.

Cross Country International, PO Box 1170, Millbrook, NY 12545, **t** 800 828 8768, *www.equestrianvacations.com*. Horse-riding in Provence, including the Camargue.

Dailey-Thorp Travel, PO Box 670, Big Horn, Wyoming, WY 82833, **t** 800 998 4677/**t** (307) 673 1555, *www.daileythorp.com*. Luxury escorted music tours, including the music festival at Aix-en-Provence and the opera at Nice.

DuVine Adventures, 124 Holland St, Suite 2, Somerville, MA 02144, **t** 888 396 5383, *www.duvine.com*. Six-night deluxe cycling tours through vineyards, with gourmet cuisine.

Horizons New England Crafts Program, PO Box 634, Leverett, MA 61054, **t** (413) 367 9200, *http://horizons-art.com*. Week-long photography, painting and drawing, fabric printing and design courses in Venasque, with time out for gourmet dining and sightseeing.

International Curtain Call, 3313 Patricia Ave, Los Angeles, CA 90064, **t** 800 669 9070, *www.iccoperatours.com*. Opera and music tours, including Paris–Avignon–Aix-en-Provence.

Self-catering Tour Operators

In the UK

A.I.P.L.V., *www.pour-les-vacances.com*. French site to match you with villa owners.

Allez France, **t** 0845 330 2059, *www.allezfrance.com*. Cottages, *gîtes*, châteaux.

The Apartment Service, 5–6 Francis Grove, London SW19 4DT, **t** (020) 8944 1444, *www.apartmentservice.com*. Apartment accommodation in cities.

Bowhills, **t** 0844 847 1333, *www.bowhills.co.uk*. Luxury villas, cottage holidays and farmhouses, mostly with pools.

Chez Nous, Spring Mill, Earby, Barnoldswick, Lancashire BB94 0AA, **t** 0870 197 1000, *www.cheznous.com*. Over 3,000 privately owned holiday cottages and B&Bs.

Destination Provence, 49 Stonegate, York YO1 8AW, **t** (01904) 622 220, *www.destinationprovence.co.uk*. Self-catering villas and hotels.

Dominique's Villas, The Plough Brewery, 516 Wandsworth Rd, London SW8 3JX, **t** (020) 7738 8772, *www.dominiquesvillas.co.uk*. Large villas and châteaux with pools.

Erna Low Consultants, 9 Reece Mews, London SW7 3HE, **t** 0870 750 6820, *www.ernalow.co.uk*. Self-catering villas/flats in villages.

Individual Traveller Co., Spring Mill, Earby, Barnoldswick, Lancs BB94 0AA, **t** 08700 780 189, *www.indiv-travellers.com*. Self-catering villas, cottages, farm and manor houses.

VFB Holidays, PO Box 2130, Anson Business Park, Gloucester GL2 9QN, **t** (01452) 716 830, *www.vfbholidays.co.uk*. Rustic *gîtes* and luxurious farmhouses and hotels.

In the USA and Canada

At Home in France, PO Box 643, Ashland, OR 97520, **t** (541) 488 9467, *www.athomeinfrance.com*. Apartments, cottages, farmhouses, manor houses and villas; moderate to deluxe.

Doorways Ltd., 900 County Line Rd, Bryn Mawr, PA 19010, **t** 800 261 4460, *www.villavacations.com*. Villas and apartments.

Families Abroad, **t** (212) 787 2434 or **t** (718) 768 6185, *www.familiesabroad.com*. Apartments, villas and châteaux in Provence and elsewhere.

France by Heart, 83 Sunrise Avenue, Mill Valley, CA 94942, **t** (415) 287 3256, *www.francebyheart.com*. Hundreds of properties.

Hideaways Aficionado, **t** 800 843 4433, *www.hideaways.com*. Villas, farmhouses and châteaux throughout South of France.

Vacances Provençales, 247 Davenport Rd, Suite 200, Toronto, Ontario M5R 1JT, **t** 800 263 7152 or **t** (416) 322 5565, *www.europeanhomerentals.com*. Moderate to luxury villas, country homes, chalets and apartments: can arrange train tickets, car hire, special interest trips, etc.

Villas of Distinction, PO Box 55, Armonk, NY 10504, **t** 800 289 0900 or **t** (914) 273 3331, *www.villasofdistinction.com*. Private villas, cottages and châteaux.

Villas of the World, **t** (631) 324 8455, *www.villasoftheworld.com*. Villas and apartments all over France.

VRBO, 3801 S Capital of Texas Highway, Suite 150, Austin, TX 78704, *www.vrbo.com*. Stands for 'vacation rentals by owner', a website where owners list their properties.

Practical A–Z

Conversion Tables 82
Children 83
Crime and the Police 83
Eating Out 83
Electricity 83
The Environment 83
Health and Emergencies 84
The Internet 84
National Holidays 84
Opening Hours 85
Post Offices 85
Racism 85
Shopping 85
Sports and Activities 86
Telephones 87
Time 88
Tipping 88
Toilets 88

07

Conversions: Imperial–Metric

Length (multiply by)
Inches to centimetres: 2.54
Centimetres to inches: 0.39
Feet to metres: 0.3
Metres to feet: 3.28
Yards to metres: 0.91
Metres to yards: 1.1
Miles to kilometres: 1.61
Kilometres to miles: 0.62

Area (multiply by)
Inches square to centimetres square: 6.45
Centimetres square to inches square: 0.15
Feet square to metres square: 0.09
Metres square to feet square: 10.76
Miles square to kilometres square: 2.59
Kilometres square to miles square: 0.39
Acres to hectares: 0.40
Hectares to acres: 2.47

Weight (multiply by)
Ounces to grams: 28.35
Grammes to ounces: 0.035
Pounds to kilograms: 0.45
Kilograms to pounds: 2.2
Stones to kilograms: 6.35
Kilograms to stones: 0.16
Tons (UK) to kilograms: 1,016
Kilograms to tons (UK): 0.0009
1 UK ton (2,240lbs) = 1.12 US tonnes (2,000lbs)

°C	°F
40	104
35	95
30	86
25	77
20	68
15	59
10	50
5	41
-0	32
-5	23
-10	14
-15	5

Volume (multiply by)
Pints (UK) to litres: 0.57
Litres to pints (UK): 1.76
Quarts (UK) to litres: 1.13
Litres to quarts (UK): 0.88
Gallons (UK) to litres: 4.55
Litres to gallons (UK): 0.22
1 UK pint/quart/gallon =
    1.2 US pints/quarts/
    gallons

Temperature
Celsius to Fahrenheit:
multiply by 1.8 then
add 32

Fahrenheit to Celsius:
subtract 32 then multiply
by 0.55

France Information

Time Differences
Country: + 1hr GMT; + 6hrs EST
Daylight saving from last weekend in March to end of October

Dialling Codes
Note: omit first zero of area code
France country code 33
To France from: UK, Ireland, New Zealand 00 / USA, Canada 011 / Australia 0011 then dial 33 and then the number without the initial zero
From France to: UK 00 44; Ireland 00 353; USA, Canada 001; Australia 00 61; New Zealand 00 64 then the number without the initial zero
Directory enquiries: 118 000
International directory enquiries: 00 33 12

Emergency Numbers
Police: 17
Ambulance: 15
Fire: 18

Embassy Numbers in France
UK: 04 91 15 72 10; **Ireland** 01 44 17 67 00;
USA: 04 91 54 92 00; **Canada** 04 93 92 93 22;
Australia 01 40 59 33 00; **NZ** 01 45 01 43 43

Shoe Sizes

Europe	UK	USA
35	2½ / 3	4
36	3 / 3½	4½ / 5
37	4	5½ / 6
38	5	6½
39	5½ / 6	7 / 7½
40	6 / 6½	8 / 8½
41	7	9 / 9½
42	8	9½ / 10
43	9	10½
44	9½ / 10	11
45	10½	12
46	11	12½ / 13

Women's Clothing

Europe	UK	USA
34	6	2
36	8	4
38	10	6
40	12	8
42	14	10
44	16	12

Children

France is very child friendly and there are few places – mostly hoity-toity bars and restaurants – where children aren't welcome. Under-4s travel free on trains and most buses, and 4- to 11-year-olds go for half-price; long-distance trains often have a play area.

Hotels will put a cot (child's bed) in a room for a small fee, and family-orientated ones often provide activities, watersports and baby-sitting services. Most restaurants offer a low-cost *menu enfant*.

Although all baby supplies are available in supermarkets and pharmacies, you may want to bring powdered formulas and prepared foods along if exact matches are important.

See Cadogan's *Take the Kids South of France* (Rosie Whitehouse, 2003).

Crime and the Police

Police t 17

Everyone in Marseille seemed most dishonest. They all tried to swindle me, mostly with complete success.

Evelyn Waugh

There is a fair chance that you will be had in the south of France, though probably not in Marseille; thieves and pickpockets go for the flashier fish on the Côte d'Azur. Road pirates prey on motorists blocked in traffic; train pirates prowl the overnight compartments looking for handbags and cameras; car bandits just love the ripe pickings in cars parked in isolated scenic areas or tourist car parks.

In cities, beware bands of children who push cardboard notes in the faces of their victims to distract them as they go through their pockets. Although violence is rare, the moral of the story is to leave anything you'd really miss at home, carry traveller's cheques and insure your property.

Report **thefts** to the nearest *gendarmerie*, not a pleasant task but the reward is the bit of paper you need for an insurance claim. If your **passport** is stolen, contact the police and your nearest consulate for emergency travel documents. Carry photocopies of your passport, driver's licence, etc.; it makes it easier when reporting a loss. By law, the police in France can stop anyone anywhere

Restaurant Price Categories

For full meal, per person, but not including wine, based on set menus; *à la carte* is normally more expensive.

very expensive	€€€€	over €60
expensive	€€€	€30–60
moderate	€€	€15–30
inexpensive	€	below €15

and demand to see ID; in practice, they only tend to do it to harass minorities, the homeless and scruffy hippy types. If they really don't like the look of you they can salt you away for a long time without any reason.

The **drug** situation is the same in France as anywhere in the West: soft and hard drugs are widely available and the police only make an issue of victimless crime when it suits them. Smuggling any amount of marijuana into the country can mean a prison term.

Eating Out

In this guide, price ranges have been used based on the set menu for one person that almost every restaurant offers in addition to its *à la carte* menu, or for an average two-course meal for one without wine (*see* box). For more information about food and local specialities, *see* **Food and Drink**, pp.51–62.

Electricity

French electricity is all 220V. British and Irish appliances need an adapter with two round prongs; North American 110V appliances usually need a transformer as well.

The Environment

As elsewhere in the Mediterranean, a sad litany of forest fires heads the television news every summer. Most forests are pine – Aleppo pines in limestone, maritime pines in the Maures and Esterel. Here they often close roads in the summer to decrease the chance of fires. Most fires are caused by twits with matches (*you'll* be more careful, won't you?), though many fires are deliberately started by speculators who burn off protected forests to build more holiday villas and suchlike. Fires often lead to erosion and flooding, though the local governments now do a good job of reforestation. The weird wasteland of Blausasc in a valley north of Nice, caused by greedy logging in the 1800s, shows what Provence would soon look like if they didn't.

The most spectacular environmental non-issue continues to be the overbuilding of the coast. The damage is done; one of the most exceptional parts of the Mediterranean coast has been thoroughly, thoughtlessly, irreparably ruined. Since the war there has simply been too much money involved for governments to act responsibly; most of the buildings you'll see were put up illegally. Local government continues to promote industrial and tourist growth in areas where there is absolutely no room for it. And Paris bureaucrats are as responsible as local politicians; they have insisted, for example, on pushing a new TGV route around the coast, bringing even more people to the area, instead of improving local transport and cutting down on the ferocious traffic.

Other enemies of the Midi include: the army, which has commandeered enormous sections of wilderness and regularly blows them to smithereens in manoeuvres and target practice; the nuclear industry, with France's nuclear research centre at Cadarache and most of its nuclear missiles hidden away on the Plateau de Vaucluse; the *chancre coloré*, a fungus that, like phylloxera, came from the USA (on wooden crates during the Second World War) and now threatens the lovely plane trees of Provence; and, finally, the villainous national electric company, EDF, which once tried to flood the Grand Canyon du Verdon. The one genuine contemporary ecological disaster is the Etang de Berre, now entirely surrounded by the industrial and suburban sprawl of Marseille, a ghastly horror of power pylons, pollution and speculative development. Here, too, the EDF is involved: heated water, pumped from their giant power plant into the lagoon, is killing off the few remaining fish. Local groups are fighting hard to make them stop.

Health and Emergencies

Ambulance (SAMU) **t** 15
Fire t 18

Local **hospitals** are the place to go in an emergency (*urgence*). **Doctors** take turns on duty at night and on holidays, even in rural areas: ring one to listen to the recorded message to find out what to do. To be on the safe side, always carry a phonecard (*see* 'Telephones', p.87).

If it's not an emergency, **pharmacists** are trained to administer first aid and dispense free advice for minor problems. In rural areas there is always someone on duty if you ring the bell; in cities pharmacies are open on a rotating basis on Sundays and holidays, and addresses are posted in their windows and in the local newspaper.

For information on **EHIC cards** and health and travel **insurance**, *see* p.68.

The Internet

Most cities and towns now have **cybercafés**, and you can often e-mail from the tourist office or your hotel, and from some post offices (using a France Telecom phonecard; *see* p.87).

Most French hotels and institutions happily give out their e-mail addresses (we've included them in the text if you can't e-mail via the website), but don't rely on this as your only means of communication with them.

National Holidays

On national holidays, banks, shops and businesses close; some museums do too, but most restaurants stay open. The French have a healthy approach to holidays: if there is a holiday near a weekend, they often 'make a bridge' (*faire le pont*) to the weekend, and take the extra day in between off too.

1 January New Year's Day
Easter Sunday (Mar or April)
Easter Monday
1 May *Fête du Travail* (Labour Day)
8 May VE Day, Victory 1945
Ascension Day (usually end of May)
Pentecost (Whitsun) and following Monday (late May or early June)
14 July Bastille Day
15 August Assumption of the Virgin Mary
1 November All Saints' Day
11 November Remembrance Day (First World War Armistice)
25 December Christmas Day

Opening Hours

Shops: While many shops and supermarkets in Marseille and other large cities now open continuously Tues–Sat from 9 or 10am to 7 or 7.30pm, businesses in smaller towns still close for lunch from 12 or 12.30pm to 2 or 3pm (4pm in summer). There are local exceptions, but nearly everything shuts on Mon, except grocers and *supermarchés*, which open in the afternoon. In many towns, Sunday morning is a big shopping time. **Markets** (daily in cities, weekly in villages) usually run mornings only, except clothes, flea and antiques markets.

Banks: Banks generally open 8.30am–12.30pm and 1.30–4pm. They close on Sun, and most either on Sat or Mon as well.

Post offices: Open in cities Mon–Fri 8am–7pm and Sat 8am–noon. In villages, offices may not open until 9am, then break for lunch and close at 4.30 or 5pm.

Museums: Most museums close for lunch, and often all day Mon or Tues, and sometimes for all of Nov or the entire winter. Hours change with the season: longer summer hours begin in May or June and last until the end of Sept – usually. Most museums close on national holidays. We've done our best to include opening hours in the text, but some change their hours every month, so call in advance if you're making a special trip. Most museums give **discounts** on admission (which ranges from €2–10) if you have a student ID card, or are an EU citizen under 18 or over 65. National museums are free if you're under 18. The third weekend of Sept is usually the *Journées du Patrimoine*, when state-owned museums throw open their doors to the public for free entry to give everyone a taste of France's national heritage. Though queues can spiral around the museums and the hordes have to shuffle past the national treasures, everyone is very cheerful at the thought of a freebie, and nobody seems to mind not seeing very much.

Churches: Churches are either open all day, or closed all day and only open for Mass. Sometimes notes on the door direct you to the *mairie* or priest's house (*presbytère*) to pick up the key. There are often admission fees for cloisters, crypts and special chapels.

Post Offices

Known as **La Poste**, post offices (for opening times, *see* left) are discernible by their sign of a blue bird on a yellow background. Larger offices are equipped with special machines for you to weigh and stamp your package, letter or postcard without having to even see a real person. They are surprisingly easy to use, with an English-language option. You can receive letters *poste restante* at any post office; the postal codes in this book should help your mail get there in a timely fashion. To collect it, take some ID; you may have to pay a small fee.

You can purchase **stamps** in tobacconists (*tabacs*) as well as post offices.

Racism

Unfortunately, in the south of France the forces of bigotry and reaction are strong enough to make racism a serious concern. We've heard some horror stories, especially about Marseille, where campsites and restaurants suddenly have no places if the colour of your skin doesn't suit the proprietor; the bouncers at clubs will inevitably say it's really the cut of your hair or trousers they find offensive. If any place recommended in this book is guilty of such behaviour, please write and let us know; we will not only remove it in the next edition, but forward your letter to the regional tourist office and relevant authorities in Paris.

Shopping

Some villages have more boutiques than year-round residents, but their wares are rarely compelling. Traditional handicrafts have all but died out, and attempts to revive them have resulted in little model houses and *santons*, terracotta Christmas crib figures dressed in 18th-century Provençal costumes, usually as artful as the concrete studies of the Seven Dwarfs sold at your local garden centre. Every town east of the Rhône has at least one boutique specializing in Provençal skirts, bags, pillows and scarves, printed in intense colours with floral, paisley or geometric designs. Block-print fabrics were first made in Provence after Louis XIV, wanting to protect the French silk industry, banned the import of popular Indian prints. Clever entrepreneurs in the papal-owned Comtat Venaissin responded by producing cheap imitations still known today as *indiennes*. The same shops usually sell the other essential bric-a-brac of the south – dried lavender pot-pourri, sachets of *herbes de Provence* (nothing but thyme and bay leaves) and perfumed soaps.

Moustiers has hand-made ceramics, and in Provence scores of artists wait to sell you their works. Fontaine-de-Vaucluse has a traditional paper and stationery industry. The sweet of tooth will find western Provence heaven. Nearly every town has its own speciality: candied fruits in Apt; the choco-lates and *calissons* (marzipan candies shaped like little boats) of Aix; *berlingots* (mint-flavoured caramels) in Carpentras; orange-flavoured chocolates called *papalines* in Avignon.

Sports and Activities

Bullfights

The Roman amphitheatres at Nîmes and Arles had hardly been restored in the early 1800s when they once again became venues for *tauromachie*. Attempts to abolish the sport in the 1900s fell flat when the poet Frédéric Mistral, the self-appointed watchdog of all things Provençal, intervened; if anything, bullfights are now more popular than they ever were.

However, the most traditional bullfights in Provence are not bloody. The *courses provençales* (or *courses libres*) can be traced back to the bull games described by Heliodorus in ancient Thessaly. Played by daring young men dressed in white called *razeteurs*, the sport demands grace, daring and dexterity, especially in leaping over the barriers before a charging bull. The object is to remove a round cockade from between the horns of the bull (or cow) by cutting its ribbons with a blunt razor comb – a sport far more dangerous to the human players than the animals. The animals used for the *courses provençales* are the small, lithe, high-horned breed from the Camargue; good sporty ones retire with fat pensions.

You will see three other types of bullfight advertised. *Corrida* is the traditional Spanish bullfight, where the bull is put to death. The bullfighters are usually Spanish as well, and the major festivals, or *ferias*, bring some of the top *toreros* to France, although beware that the already expensive tickets tend to be snapped up by touts. A *novillada*, pitting younger bulls against apprentice *toreros* (*novilleros*), is less expensive, but much more likely to be a butchery void of *arte*. In a *corrida portugaise* the bullfighter (*rejoneador*) fights from horseback, but doesn't kill the bull.

Canoeing and Kayaking

The **Fédération Française de Canoë-Kayak**, t 01 45 11 08 50, *www.ffck.org*, is the national centre for information. Some of the most dramatic rafting and canoeing is down the **Grand Canyon du Verdon** (*see* pp.279–81), but the journey requires considerable experience and considerable portage. Another disadvan-tage is that the electric company may be playing with the water.

Cycling

See pp.74–5, 'Getting Around'.

Fishing

You can fish in the sea without a permit as long as your catch is for local consumption. Freshwater fishing requires an easily obtained permit from a local club; tourist offices can tell you where to find them.

Horse-riding

Every tourist office has a list of *centres hippiques* or *centres équestres* that offer group excursions, though if you prove your-self an experienced rider you can usually head down the trails on your own.

The **Camargue**, with its many ranches, cowboy traditions and open spaces, is the most popular place to ride in the region, and there are increasing numbers of stables in the **Alps** for those who want to follow lone-some mountain trails. Most of the posher country inns can also find you a horse.

See also 'Tour Operators', pp78–80.

Pétanque

Like *pastis* and olive oil, *pétanque* is one of the essential ingredients of the Midi; even the smallest village has a rough, hard court under the plane trees for its practitioners – nearly all male, although women are welcome to join in. Similar to *boules*, the rules of *pétanque* were, according to tradition, developed in La Ciotat, near Marseille (*see* p.173). The object is to get your metal ball closest to the marker (*bouchon* or *cochonnet*). Tournaments are frequent and well attended.

Skiing

Ideally, if the weather ever decides to settle down, you can do as in California: ski in the morning and bake on the beach in the afternoon. The biggest **resorts** in the Alpes-Maritimes are Isola 2000, Auron and Valberg and, closest to Nice, Gréolières-les-Neiges.

Comité Régional de Tourisme Provence-Alpes-Côte d'Azur, t 04 91 56 47 00, *www.crt-paca.fr*.

Fédération Française de Ski, 50 Rue des Marquisats, B.P. 2451, 74011 Annecy Cedex, t 04 50 51 40 34, *www.ffs.fr*.

Association Nationale des Maires des Stations de Montagne, 9 Rue de Madrid, 75008 Paris, t 01 47 42 23 32, *www.skifrance.fr*.

Sailing

Most of the resorts along the southern coast have sailing schools and boats to hire. You can get a complete list from the **Fédération Française de Voile**, 17 Rue Henri Bocquillon, 75015 Paris, t 01 40 60 37 00, *www.ffvoile.org*.

Walking

See p.75, 'Getting Around'.

Watersports and Beaches

In 1763 the consumptive English writer and doctor Tobias 'Smelfungus' Smollett tried something for his health that shocked the doctors in Nice: he went bathing in the sea. Most extraordinary of all, it made him feel better, and he recommended that people follow his example, although it would be difficult for women 'unless they laid aside all regards to decorum'. There are scores of fine, sandy beaches along the coast. Anyone who arrives with the idea that access to the sea is a natural God-given right will be appalled to learn that paying concessions occupy most of the Provençal shore; free, quiet beaches require more effort (the *calanques* west of Cassis, the coves below the Esterel and the Maures, the Hyères islands).

The best diving is off Ile Port-Cros National Park. For a list of diving clubs, contact the **Fédération Française d'Etudes et de Sports Sous-Marins**, 24 Quai de Rive Neuve, 13284 Marseille, t 04 91 33 99 31, *www.ffessm.fr*.

If you're genuinely jaded and have a weakness for medical psychobabble, you can even indulge in *thalassothérapie* to help make you thin, fit, stress-free, or even turn you into a laid-back non-smoker.

Telephones

Nearly all public telephones have switched from coins to *télécartes* (phonecards) which you can buy at any post office or news-stand for €7.50 for 50 *unités* or €15 for 120 *unités*. You can also purchase the US-style phonecards which use a PIN-number system, and many boxes will accept credit cards. However, the prevalence of mobile phones is making phone boxes less useful.

The French have eliminated area codes, giving everyone a 10-digit number. If ringing France from abroad, the international dialling code is 33, and you drop the first '0' of the number. For international calls from France dial 00, wait for the change in the dial tone, then dial the country code (UK 44; US and Canada 1; Ireland 353; Australia 61; New Zealand 64), and then the local code (minus the 0 for UK numbers) and number.

The easiest way to reverse charges is to spend a couple of euros ringing the number and giving your number in France, which is always posted by public phones; alternatively, ring your national operator (for the UK dial 00 33 44; for the USA 00 33 11).

For **directory enquiries**, dial t 118 000, or see *www.pagesjaunes.fr* (the Yellow Pages website). For international directory enquiries call t 33 12.

British and Irish **mobile phones** work in France if they have a roaming facility; check with your service provider. If you're going to be in France a while and using your mobile a lot, and as long as your mobile is not locked to a UK network, avoid high charges (both outgoing and incoming) by temporarily replacing your UK SIM card with an international one (sold, for example, at *www.0044. co.uk*). or buying a pay-as-you-go phone from a large supermarket or phone shop.

Time

France is one hour ahead of UK time and six hours ahead of North American Eastern Standard Time, nine hours ahead of Pacific Coast Time.

French summertime (daylight-saving), as in the UK, runs from the last Sunday in March to the last Sunday in October.

Tipping

Many people leave a tip if they're happy with their meal and the service; if you eat *à la carte*, you might add a gratuity of around 10% (service is included in the price of set menus; *see* p.57).

Toilets

The hole-in-the-ground lavatory is still surprisingly common in rural France. Bars and cafés normally don't mind you using their facilities, but it's polite to make a small purchase at the same time. There are some public toilets for which you have to pay, either to get into – those funky, modern oval-shaped street facilities – or to get out of, when there's a caretaker (you should leave them a small tip).

Down the Rhône 1: Orange to Beaucaire

Despite Frédéric Mistral's best efforts in the epic 1896 Poème du Rhône, this is not a lyrical river, neither fair of face nor full of grace. Its nickname, 'malabar', the strongman, describes it well: deep and swift-flowing with muscular currents, banks like bulging biceps, and secret depths hosting legendary man-eating monsters such as the Tarasque and Drac.

For the Rhône is a Saturday's child and has to work for a living: after serving the industries and nuclear plants to the north, it does it all again in Provence, at France's biggest centre for the processing of nuclear waste, at the hydroelectric plant and satanic mills of Avignon's industrial quarter, and at the paper mills near Tarascon.

FRANCE

ITALY

SPAIN

08

Don't miss

⭐ **The Roman theatre and arch**
Orange **pp.92–5**

⭐ **Immaculate vines and wines**
Châteauneuf-du-Pape
p.97

⭐ **A lively Babylon that captivated medieval popes**
Avignon **p.100**

⭐ **Enguerrand Quarton's masterpiece**
Musée Pierre-de-Luxembourg, Villeneuve lez Avignon **p.117**

See map overleaf

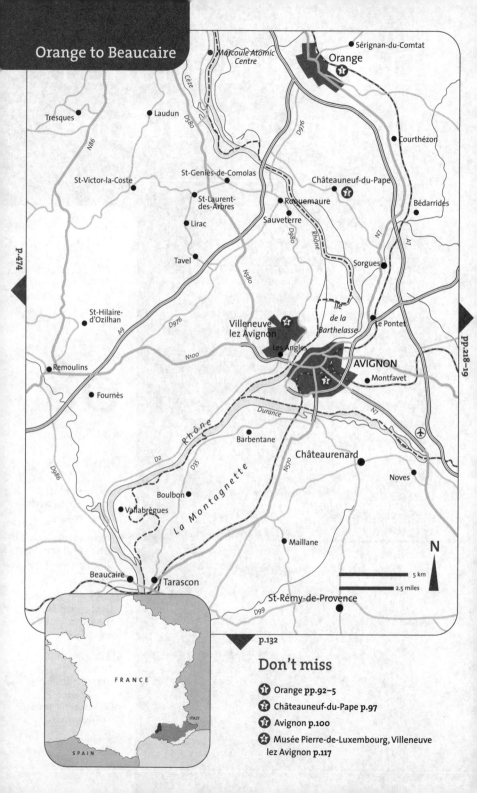

Historically, most of the Rhône's traffic has come south with the current, ferrying the blond barbarians, eaters of *frites* and drinkers of beer, down to the sultry Mediterranean. The river also divided the spoils: Provence, situated on the east bank, owed allegiance to the emperor and pope; Languedoc, on the west, belonged to the kingdom of France after the Albigensian Crusade. Rhône boatmen called the banks, not port and starboard, but Empire and Kingdom. On the empire's side are Orange, with its famous Roman theatre; Châteauneuf-du-Pape and Avignon, where 14th-century popes spent what Petrarch called their 'Babylonian exile'; and Tarascon, favoured home of Provence's Bon Roi ('Good King') René.

From Orange to Avignon

Orange

 Orange

There seems to have been a settlement of some kind around the hill of St-Eutrope in prehistoric times, and the city's chronicles date from 35 BC, giving it enough time for all imaginable Oranges to have come and gone. The present incarnation must be one of the sadder ones – this is a miasmic provincial town with a few cosy corners among the prevailing drabness. Fate, or the lack of a bypass road, has made its streets a kind of Le Mans for heavy lorries, fouling the air, menacing pedestrians and coating the old houses with a sooty film. Nevertheless, there are two ancient monuments unmatched in France, and some surprises besides. You'll probably like it best on a Sunday, when the law bans trucks from the road.

History

Rome took good care of its soldiers; keeping its word by them was one secret of the Empire's success. Nine years after Julius Caesar's death, many veterans of the Second Gallic Legion were ready for their promised retirement. The pattern was already set. Rome would establish a colony for them in the lands that they had conquered, often replacing a native village they had destroyed; the veterans farmed their allocated lands, and could look forward to real wealth in their declining years as the colony grew into a town. The colony that became Orange was called Colonia Julia Secundanorum Arausio. Exceedingly prosperous throughout Roman times, it survived the Visigothic conquest in 412; it was the site of two Church councils in the following decades.

The chronicles are largely blank from then until the mid-12th century, when the city's feudal lord was Raimbaut d'Orange, troubadour and patron of troubadours. Even then, history was on the back burner; the city and its hinterlands were often put in hock

Getting to and around Orange

The **train station, t** 04 90 11 88 03, on Avenue Frédéric Mistral has direct links with Paris, Avignon, Arles, Marseille, Nice and Cannes.

Buses depart from Cours Pourtoules, **t** 04 90 34 15 59, several times a day for Carpentras, Vaison-la-Romaine, Avignon and Séguret.

Bike Hire

Cycles Dupont, 745 Av Charles de Gaulle, **t** 04 90 34 15 60.
Cycles Picca, 795 Av de Verdun, **t** 04 90 51 69 53.

to pay Raimbaut's debts, while he presided over the most brilliant of Provençal courts. He died in 1173, at the age of only 29, and Orange passed to the counts of Baux.

In the 14th century it was a thriving place, with a municipal charter and even a university. In 1530 the city became the property of the German house of Nassau, just in time for the Reformation and the most unusual page of the city's history, an odd chance that would let Orange lend its colour to the Dutch, the Northern Irish, the Orange Free State and Orange, New Jersey. The Nassaus declared for Protestantism, and Orange rapidly became the dissenters' chief stronghold in Provence, a home for thousands of refugees and a thorn in the side of arch-Catholic Avignon, just to the south. Soon after, William of Nassau – William of Orange – became the first *stadhouder* of the United Provinces and led the fight for Dutch independence. Orange held fast through all the troubles of the Wars of Religion, and came out of it a Dutch possession, giving its name to the Netherlands' royal family.

Maurice of Nassau, in the early 17th century, did Orange a bad turn by destroying most of its ancient ruins, using their stone for the new wall he was building against the French. It didn't keep them out for long. In 1672, during one of his wars against the Dutch, Louis XIV seized the city and demolished its wall and castle.

French rule, particularly after the revocation of the Edict of Nantes in 1685 (*see* p.27), was a disaster; Orange, like many other towns in the south, lost many of its best citizens. The city has never really recovered, but it earns a fair living today from industry, and from the army and airforce bases that make it one of the most important military centres in France. Having twice elected a National Front mayor didn't help it either. Although the ultra-right Mayor Bompard claims to have spruced up the town, he also cut off all funds to cultural associations for ethnic minorities and banned a selection of left-wing literature from the public library.

Théâtre Antique
www.theatre-antique.com; open June–Aug daily 9–7; April, May and Sept daily 9–6; Mar and Oct 9.30–5.30; Jan, Feb, Nov and Dec daily 9.30–4.30; free audioguides; tours t 04 90 11 02 31; adm; ticket also valid for Musée Municipal, see opposite

Théâtre Antique

The architects might be distressed to hear it, but these days the most impressive part of this huge structure is its back wall. 'The best wall in my kingdom,' Louis XIV is said to have called it. If the old prints in the municipal museum are accurate, this rugged, elegant sandstone cliff facing Place des Frères Mounet was originally adorned with low, temple-like façades. In its present state, it resembles a typical Florentine Renaissance palace, minus the windows. The classically minded architects of the 15th century all travelled in Provence, and perhaps this stately relic of Rome at its best had a hidden influence that would have made its architects proud.

Built in the early 1st century AD, the theatre is a testimony to the culture and wealth of Arausio. Like the Colosseum in Rome, it even had a massive awning (*velum*), a contraption of canvas and beams that could be raised to cover most of the 9,000 spectators. All over the Mediterranean, theatres fell into disuse as part of the cultural degradation of the late Empire. This one was probably already abandoned when it burned down in the 4th or 5th century. In the Middle Ages, other buildings grew up over the ruins; old prints show the semicircular tiers of seats (*cavea*) half-filled in and covered with ramshackle houses.

The site is typical for a Roman theatre, backed into the hill of St-Eutrope, where the banks of seats could be built on the slope. These have been almost completely restored. Since 1869, Orange has used the theatre for a summer festival called *Les Chorégies*. Mistral and the Félibres (*see* pp.41–2) were active in its early years, when Greek and Roman plays were often on the bill; today contemporary drama and opera are more common.

Unlike Greek theatres, which always opened to a grand view behind the stage, those of the Romans featured large stage buildings, serious architectural compositions of columns, arches and sculptured friezes. This is what the great exterior wall is supporting; Orange's stage building (which is 115ft high) is one of two complete specimens that remain to us (the other is at Aspendos in southwestern Turkey), although the fragments of its decoration are mostly in the municipal museum across the street. A statue of Augustus remains, in the centre, over an inscription honouring the people of Arausio and welcoming them to the show. Outside the theatre, the foundations of a temple have been excavated, along with a semicircular ruin that may have been a *nymphaeum* or a gymnasium.

Musée Municipal

Musée Municipal
t 04 90 51 17 60; open April–Sept Mon–Sat 9–7, Sun 9–12 and 2–7; Oct–Mar Mon–Sat 9–12 and 1.30–5.30

Make sure you save some time for this bulging curiosity shop, directly opposite the theatre on Place des Frères Mounet; it is one of the most fascinating town museums in Provence. As expected, the main rooms focus on Roman art, including an exceptional frieze of satyrs and Amazons from the theatre. The *plan cadastral* (land survey) is unique: a stone tablet engraved with property records for the broad Roman grid of farmland between Orange and Montélimar. The first pieces of it were discovered in 1856, though no one guessed what they were until the rest turned up, between 1927 and 1954; since then they have been a great aid to scholars in filling in some of the everyday details of Roman life and law.

Climbing the stairs into the upper levels of the museum, you'll pass rooms of Dutch portraits and relics of Nassau rule, and a collection of works by the Welsh Impressionist Frank Brangwyn (born in Bruges): heroic compositions among wharves and factories, and country scenes. The most unexpected exhibit is the **Salle des Wetter**, a remarkable relic of the Industrial Revolution in France. The Wetters were a family of mid-18th-century industrialists who produced *indiennes*, printed cotton cloth much in demand at the time. They commissioned an artist named G. M. Rossett to paint a record of their business; this he did (1764) in incredible detail, on five huge naïve canvases showing every aspect of the making of *indiennes*, from the stevedores unloading the cotton on the docks to the shy, serious factory girls in the great hall – the Wetters were among the first in France to stumble on the factory system, and employed more than 500 people.

Old Orange and the Triumphal Arch

Touring old Orange does not handsomely reward the visitor. You can walk up the hill of **St-Eutrope** for a view over the town and a look at the foundations of the castle destroyed by the French; in the city centre, there is only an utterly pathetic **cathedral**, begun in 529 over a temple of Diana and rebuilt to death between 1561 and 1809. One thing Orange does have is original street names – sometimes unintentionally hilarious ones, such as Impasse du Parlement. **Rue Victor Hugo**, roughly following the route of the ancient Roman main street, leads out towards Orange's other Roman attraction. The **Arc de Triomphe**, which was built around AD 20, celebrates the conquests of the Second Gallic Legion with outlandish, almost abstract scenes of battling Romans and Celts. This is the epitome of the Provençal-Roman style: excellent, careful reliefs, especially in the upper frieze, portraying a naval battle, though with a touch of Celto-Ligurian strangeness in the details. Odd oval shields are a prominent feature, decorated with heraldic devices and thunderbolts. Seemingly random symbols at the upper left – a whip, a pitcher, something that looks like a bishop's crozier, and others – are in fact symbols of animal sacrifice and marine attributes (the 'crozier' is the prow of a ship). On the sides of the arch are heaps of arms – 'triumphs' – that were to influence the militaristic art fostered by rulers such as Emperor Charles V in the Renaissance. Little more than half a century before this arch was built, Orange was still Rome's wild frontier, and art such as this evokes it vividly. Note the standards the legionaries are carrying: not the Roman eagle, but a boar.

When frontier days returned to Orange, in the Middle Ages, the arch was expanded into a castle by Raymond of Baux. It is said that Raymond arranged it so that the battle reliefs would be a wall of his dining hall; we have his arrogance to thank for their relatively good state of preservation. To sample some of the area's more recently created marvels, try the **Palais du Vin**, on the RN7, which offers a *vinothèque* (wine library), tastings and a restaurant.

Palais du Vin
t 04 90 11 50 00, www. lepalaisduvin.com; open daily 10–7

Around Orange: Sérignan-du-Comtat and the 'Virgil of Insects'

Eight kilometres northeast of Orange on the D976, you can pay your respects to the great entomologist, botanist, scientist and poet **Jean-Henri Fabre** (1823–1915). Born into poverty, the largely self-taught Fabre qualified as a *lycée* teacher of sciences in Avignon, only to be fired in 1870 for explicitly describing the sex life of flowers to a night class of spinsters. Left without means, he borrowed money from his friend John Stuart Mill and settled in Orange for nine years, cranking out books on popular science on the average of one every four months – he was to produce more than 100 in total. He made enough in royalties to pay back his debts and in 1879 to buy an abandoned property in Sérignan that he called **L'Harmas**, the 'fallow land'. Fabre walled in the garden and planted 1,000 species of flowers and herbs, letting them run wild to create the perfect environment for his true passion: observing insects. Over the years he wrote 10 volumes of *Souvenirs entomologiques*, works of such beauty that he was twice nominated for the Nobel Prize for Literature. The Japanese, in particular, are huge fans; reissues of Fabre's books in Japan in 1991 sold more than a million copies. L'Harmas was bought by the state in 1922 (it's part of the Muséum National d'Histoire Naturelle, based in Paris), and has been left as it was during Fabre's life: you can see his curious apparatus for observing insects, his collections of fossils, shells, rocks, insects, plants, eggs, coins and bones (including some human bones, chewed on by cannibals – not found locally, mind), letters from Darwin, and his harmonium, which he would play to accompany the lullabies and songs he wrote in Provençal. Most extraordinary of all is the display of a selection of his 700 watercolours of the fungi of the Vaucluse, so real that you can hardly believe they are only two-dimensional.

L'Harmas
t 04 90 70 15 61, www. museum-paca.org/ harmas-collections.htm; open July and Aug Mon, Tues, Thurs and Fri 10–12.30 and 3.30–7, Sun 3.30–7; April–June and Sept–Oct Mon, Tues, Thurs and Fri 10–12.30 and 2.30–6, Sun 2.30–6; closed Wed, Sat, and Nov–Mar

Sérignan-du-Comtat village has erected a **statue** to Fabre, magnifying glass in hand, in front of the convex Baroque façade of the parish **church**, and you can visit his grave in the village **cemetery**, with its Latin inscriptions, one from Seneca: 'Those who we believe lost have been sent in advance.'

Market Days in Orange

Thurs am: Cours Aristide Briand.

In summer, Sat am: Place de la République.

Where to Stay and Eat in Orange

Orange ✉ 84100

***Arène**, Place de Langes, t 04 90 11 40 40, *www.hotel-arene.fr* (€€€). A pleasant option on a quiet square, part of the Best Western group.

**St-Jean, 7 Cours Pourtoules, t 04 90 51 15 16, *www.avignon-et-provence. com/hotel-orange-france/hotel-saint-jean* (€€). A charmingly restored

17th-century *hostellerie* with private parking, just steps from the Roman amphitheatre.

**Le Glacier, 46 Cours Aristide Briand, t 04 90 34 02 01, *www.le-glacier.com* (€€–€). A typical Logis establishment, with friendly hosts and private parking. Some rooms have air-conditioning. *Closed end Dec.*

**St-Florent, 4 Rue du Mazeau, t 04 90 34 18 53, *www.hotelsaint florent.com* (€). A decent budget choice; all rooms have bath and TV. *Closed Jan and Feb.*

Le Yaca, 24 Place Sylvain, t 04 90 34 70 03 (€€). A friendly, pretty little restaurant with a range of appetizing Mediterranean menus. *Closed Tues eve, Wed and Nov.*

ⓘ **Orange >**
*5 Cours Aristide Briand,
t 04 90 34 70 88,
www.otorange.fr;
open April–Sept daily;
Oct–Mar Mon–Sat;
there's another office
opposite the Théâtre
Antique; open July
and Aug daily*

⭐ **Le Yaca >>**

South of Orange: Châteauneuf-du-Pape

🏛 **Châteauneuf-du-Pape**

*Je veux vous chanter, mes amis/Ce vieux Châteauneuf que j'ai mis
Pour vous seuls en bouteille/ Il va faire merveille!*

*Quand de ce vin nous serons gris /Vénus applaudira nos ris:
Je prends à témoin Lise/La chose est bien permise!*

(My friends, I want to sing to you/Of this old Châteauneuf that
I've bottled just for you/It will work miracles!

For when this wine makes us tipsy/Venus will crown our mirth:
I take Lise as my witness/No one will mind if I do!)

Pope John XXII's drinking song

You'll begin to understand why Châteauneuf's wines are so expensive when you pass through the vineyards between Orange and Avignon. Blink, and you'll miss them. This pocket-sized wine region, tucked between the outskirts of Avignon and Orange, has become one of the most prosperous corners of France; every available square inch is covered with vines of a rare beauty, so immaculately precise and luxuriant that they resemble bonsai trees. Such good fortune is not without its disadvantages, however.

Châteauneuf-du-Pape, the very attractive village that gives the wine its name, has not resisted the temptation to become the Midi's foremost oenological tourist trap; along the main street there are few grocers or boutiques but plenty of wine shops, and in places it is hard to see the buildings for the signs advertising other shops or the winemakers' estates in the hinterlands.

Wine: Châteauneuf-du-Pape

An inspiration to both popes and lovers, Châteauneuf-du-Pape's reputation has remained strong through the ages; to safeguard it, in 1923 its growers agreed to the guarantees and controls that formed the basis for France's modern *Appellation d'Origine Contrôlée* (AOC) laws.

Several factors combine to give the wine its unique character: the alluvial red clay and the pebbly soil, brought down by a Rhône glacier in the last ice age; the *mistral*, which chases away the clouds and haze, allowing the sun to hit the grapes like an X-ray gun; and the wide palette of 13 varieties of grape that each winemaker can choose from: grenache, syrah, cinsault, mourvèdre, terret noir, vaccarese, counoise and muscardin for the reds (grenache can also be white); and clairette, bourboulenc, roussane, picpoul and picardan for the whites (clairette and picpoul can be red and white), 30 years ago dismissed as mere novelties and today celebrated as some of Provence's top wines – pale blond, with greenish highlights and a fresh, floral bouquet.

Because of the complex blends that give Châteauneuf its voluptuous qualities, the grapes are sorted by hand – uniquely among southern wines. The end result must have the highest alcoholic minimum of any great French wine (12.5%), a level achieved by spacing the vines a good 6–7ft apart to soak up the maximum amount of sun, and from the heat-absorbing pebbles underneath the vines that keep the grapes toasty after dark. Light, soft and fast to mature, a Châteauneuf-du-Pape red can be enjoyed much earlier than its Rhône rivals (often in three years) but only gets better the longer you can bear to wait.

In its home town, the wine is not exactly hard to find; even in the cellars it's not cheap, though, because a good deal of the *cuvées* dating from the late 1980s and early 1990s are superb, if somewhat difficult to get hold of. Contact the tourist office for a copy of a map of the vineyards: perhaps the best-known among the array of excellent wineries that welcome visitors are the **Château La Nerthe, t** 04 90 83 70 11, *www.chateaulanerthe.fr*, with its fascinating ancient cellars, and the vaulted cellars of **Château de la Gardine, t** 04 90 83 73 20, *www.gardine.com*.

In Bédarrides, the vineyards of **Domaine du Vieux Télégraphe**, 3 Route de Châteauneuf, **t** 04 90 33 00 31, *www.vignoblesbrunier.fr*, occupy a rugged promontory topped by a tower once used for optic telegraphic experiments; the 1993 and '95 reds and whites are excellent buys.

The three finest estates are in a class of their own and have such highly individual styles as to be unmistakable even when they're tasted blind. **Le Clos des Papes, t** 04 90 83 70 13, *www.clos-des-papes.fr*, is run by the highly intelligent and innovative Paul Vincent Avril. Avril is alone in employing humidifiers in his cellar to alleviate the drying effects of the *mistral* wind in particular and the heat in general. As a consequence, his wines have the best-defined fruit of the region and are the most elegant. With age, Avril's Châteauneuf-du-Pape can taste like expensive claret.

The wines of **Château de Beaucastel**, in Courthézon, **t** 04 90 70 41 00, *www.beaucastel.com*, have been consistently among the top wines of the *appellation*.

The most extraordinary source of Châteauneuf-du-Pape and possibly one of the country's most interesting wines is made by Emmanuel Raynaud at **Château Rayas, t** 04 90 83 73 09, *www.chateaurayas.com*. His wines are a must for all keen wine-lovers: they are the product of a bygone era – wines of incredible concentration and depth with the capacity to age for 20 years or more. Wines such as these are increasingly rare in an age when technology, which has helped to ensure that most wine is well made, also means that too many are sound but mediocre.

Among the vintages, 2003 was exceptional, after a long, hot, sunny summer; 2002 was a virtual write-off because of violent storms and huge rainfall, and 2001 was mixed, with some excellent wines available from respected sources (try before you buy) and others lacking acidity or being over-alcoholic. Going further back, 2000 is a top-class vintage with plenty of fruit, ripe tannins and and overall roundness that makes it easy to drink but also capable of ageing, and 1999 and 1998 were both outstanding. Most 1998 and 1999 wines make very good drinking now, but the top estates and *appellations* have produced wines that can be kept many years. The top Châteauneuf-du-Papes from these two vintages are simply wonderful wines.

Market Days in Châteauneuf-du-Pape

Fri am: Av des Bosquets.

Festivals in Châteauneuf-du-Pape

July: *Floraisons Musicales.*
Aug: *Fête Médiévale de la Véraison,* a local town festival.

Where to Stay and Eat in Châteauneuf-du-Pape

Châteauneuf-du-Pape
✉ 84230

****Château des Fines Roches, 2km south of town on D17, **t** 04 90 83 70 23, *www.chateaufinesroches.com* (€€€€). An imposing and elegant but entirely fake château (19th-century vintage) with gardens, set among the vineyards. The kitchen shines when it comes to seafood dishes and desserts.

Closed Nov; Oct–April restaurant closed Sun–Tues lunch.

***La Sommellerie, on D17 towards Roquemaure, **t** 04 90 83 50 00, *www. hotel-la-sommellerie.com* (€€€). A restored 18th-century sheepfold with 12 peaceful rooms and 2 suites over-looking the pool or the vines. The restaurant, presided over by Pierre Paumel, *maître cuisinier de France*, serves delicately perfumed Provençal dishes. Don't miss his reproductions of Van Gogh's paintings in spun sugar. *Closed Jan; restaurant closed Sun eve and Mon in winter.*

La Mère Germaine, 3 Rue du Commandant Lemaître, **t** 04 90 83 54 37, *www.lameregermaine.com* (€€–€). A sweet old hotel-restaurant with a gourmet restaurant (€€€) serving tantalizing dishes such as *agneau aïoli* and *galet de Châteauneuf-du-Pape*. The adjacent brasserie offers a moderate *plat du jour* and dessert.

Le Verger des Papes, 2 Rue du Château, **t** 04 90 83 50 94, *www. vergerdespapes.com* (€€€–€€). Has a stupedous terrace with huge views, just below the castle ruins.

(★) La Mère Germaine >>

(i) Châteauneuf-du-Pape >
Place du Portail, t 04 90 83 71 08, www. ccpro.fr/tourisme; open Mon–Sat

Legend has it that one of the first things that Clement V did on leaving Rome was inspect his vineyards to the north of Avignon. In 1316 his successor John XXII, who was a celebrated imbiber, went one better by building a castle here, which the Avignon popes used as a summer residence – a 14th-century version of Lazio's Castel Gandolfo. Sacked by the Protestants in the Wars of Religion, it was finally blown up by the retreating Germans in 1944; two crenellated walls are all that remain of it. Even if you don't like ruins or crowds, brave the hordes to have a look at the huge plain below you, and the Rhône muscling away on its route south to Avignon; wait till dusk if you can, for a magnificent sunset.

Chocolaterie
Bernard Castelain
t 04 90 83 54 71

If you're bored with wine, down on the plain, on the Route d'Avignon, taste chocolate at the **Chocolaterie Bernard Castelain**.

The Left Bank of the Rhône

Once you cross the Rhône into the Gard region, the land takes on a more arid and austere profile, its knobby limestone hills and cliffs softened by crowns of silver olives and the green pinstripes of vines, especially in the river-bend north of Villeneuve lez Avignon along the D976. The landmark here is **Roquemaure**, where Pope

Clement V died his peculiar death (*see* p.43) in its now-ruined castle, although it's not his ghost who haunts it, but that of a lovely but leprous queen who was quarantined in the tower. After she died, Rhône boatmen would see her on summer nights, flitting along the bank, dressed in white and sparkling with jewels. Roquemaure's church of **St-Jean-Baptiste**, opened by Clement V in 1329, has sheltered since 1868 the relics of a certain St Valentine, whom it celebrates with a Festival of Lovers, involving locals in 19th-century costume (Terni, in Umbria, which enshrines the relics of its first bishop San Valentino in a basilica and celebrates his feast day on 14 February, would be surprised to learn this). The church also houses a superb organ of 1680, built for the *Cordeliers* in Avignon and transferred here in 1800, which still has all of its original pipes.

The D976 continues southwest past the charming little village of **Tavel**, a place that is just as haunted – in this instance by wine fiends come to slake their thirst on the pale ruby blood of the earth. **Lirac**, situated 2km to the north, is even smaller; a pretty kilometre's walk westwards from the village leads to the **Sainte-Baume**, a cave holy since time immemorial, and in which a statue of the Virgin was discovered in 1647; a hermitage was built on the outside of the cave-chapel.

To the north, little **St-Laurent-des-Arbres** used to be owned by the medieval bishops of Avignon, and has a fortified Romanesque church that was built in 1150, a tower and a castle keep.

Wine: Tavel and Lirac

The sun-soaked, pebbly limestone hills on the left bank of the Rhône are as celebrated for their rosés as Châteauneuf-du-Pape is for its reds and whites. Tavel, which has the longest pedigree, has been beloved of kings since the 13th century, when Philippe le Bel declared: 'It isn't good wine unless it's Tavel.' By the 1930s, the vine stocks – grenache, cinsault, bourboulenc, carignan and red clairette – were so old that Tavel nearly went the way of the dodo. Since revived to the tune of 825 healthy hectares, it has once again been crowned by the French as king of the rosé, the universal, harmonious summer wine that goes with everything from red meat to seafood. Be warned, however, that Tavel may be a little strong to less acclimatized, non-French constitutions.

Some growers add syrah and mourvèdre to give their Tavels extra body and colour, including the two best-known producers in the village, whom you can visit by ringing ahead: the de Bez family at the **Château d'Aquéria**, **t** 04 66 50 04 56, and the prize-winning **Domaine de la Mordorée**, **t** 04 66 50 00 75, *www.domaine-mordoree.com*, where the talented Christophe Delorme also bottles a potent red Côtes-du-Rhône, Lirac and Châteauneuf-du-Pape.

The Lirac district begins 3km to the north of Tavel and encompasses four *communes* – Roquemaure, Lirac, St-Laurent-des-Arbres and St-Geniès-de-Comolas. Its pebbly hills are similar to those of Tavel, and the *appellation* differs in the addition of two grape varieties – white ugni and maccabeo – and the fact that everything doesn't come up rosé: Lirac is making a name for its fruity whites, with a fragrance reminiscent of the wildflowers of the nearby *garrigue*, and for its well-structured reds. Wines can be sampled weekdays by appointment at **Domaine Duseigneur**, St-Laurent-des-Arbres, **t** 04 66 50 02 57, *www.domaineduseigneur.com*, and at **Château St-Roch**, Roquemaure, **t** 04 66 82 82 59, *www.chateau-saint-roch.com*.

Where to Stay and Eat on the Left Bank of the Rhône

(★) Château de Varenne >

Roquemaure ⊠ 30150

***Château de Varenne**, Sauveterre, 4km from town, t 04 66 82 59 45, www.chateaudevarenne.com (€€€€). An 18th-century building set in a beautiful park with a pool. Closed Jan–mid-Feb.

Le Clément V, Rue Pierre Sémard (Route de Nîmes), t 04 66 82 67 58, www.hotel-clementv.com (€€). An excellent, moderately priced hotel

complete with a swimming pool. Closed Jan; restaurant closed lunch.

Tavel ⊠ 30126

***Auberge de Tavel**, Voie Romaine, t 04 66 50 03 41, www.auberge-de-tavel.com (€€). Charming, quiet, well-equipped rooms and a good restaurant (€€€). Closed May–Oct; restaurant closed Wed and sometimes also Tues and Thurs.

La Louisia, north of town near St-Laurent-des-Arbres, at crossroads on N580, t 04 66 50 20 60 (€€). A good place to try gâteau de rascasse à l'américaine (scorpion fish). Closed Tues.

Avignon

(★) Avignon

Avignon has known more passions and art and power than any town in Provence, its mixture of excitement whipped to a frenzy by the mistral. But even the master of winds has never caused as much trouble as the papal court, a vortex of mischief that ruled Avignon for centuries, trailing violence, corruption and debauchery in its wake. 'In Paris one quarrels, in Avignon one kills,' wrote Hugo. In Avignon, Petrarch's platonic, courtly love for Laura was an aberration. 'Blood is hot there,' wrote an anonymous author in the 17th century, 'and the most serious occupation in the land is the search for pleasure... even most of the husbands are accommodating in love, and allow their wives the same freedoms they enjoy themselves.'

Avignon still has a twinkle in its eye; it is alive and ebullient, and has been one of France's most innovative cities ever since the Italian Renaissance filtered through here to the rest of Europe. As the cultural and publishing centre of the south, it rocked the cradle of the Félibrige, the Provençal literary movement (see pp.41–2), and since the Second World War it has been the stage for Europe's most exciting theatre festival. Charming it is not; yet, as an old Provençal proverb puts it: Quau se lèvo d'Avignoun,se lèvo de la resoun – 'He who takes leave of Avignon takes leave of his senses.'

History

Rome, AD 1303. Anarchy reigns, with popular riots, regular visits from foreign armies, and clans waging medieval gang warfare in the streets, transforming the tombs of the Caesars into urban fortresses. The papacy, although in the thick of it all, usually kept the papal person himself in places such as Viterbo and Anagni for safety's sake – just as it had the arrogant intriguer Boniface VIII,

Getting to and around Avignon

By Air

Avignon's **airport** (*www.avignon.aeroport.fr*), 8km southeast of town at Caumont, has Air France (**t** 04 90 81 51 51, **t** 0820 820 820) flights from many French and European destinations.
Avignon is also 20mins by taxi from Nîmes airport.

By Train

There are direct trains from London to Avignon on **Eurostar** in July–Sept, taking 6hrs, **t** 08705 186 186, *www.eurostar.com*. The **central train station** is on Bd St-Roch, central bookings **t** 08 36 35 35 35. The new **TGV station** is 3km to the south; there is a shuttle bus every 15mins to the centre. Avignon is on the Paris–Marseille TGV line, and has frequent links to Arles, Montpellier, Nîmes, Orange, Toulon and Carcassonne.

By Bus

The *gare routière* is next to the train station (Avenue Monclar, **t** 04 90 82 07 35). There are plenty of daily buses to Carpentras, Cavaillon, St-Rémy-de-Provence, Orange, Arles and Nîmes, one early-morning run to Nice changing at Aix-en-Provence and Cannes (plus 5 to Aix), several to Marseille and Salon-de-Provence, Fontaine-de-Vaucluse, and some services to the Pont du Gard, Uzès, Châteaurenard, Châteauneuf-du-Pape and Tarascon.
For Villeneuve lez Avignon, take city bus 11 from the post office, train station or Porte de l'Oulle (buy tickets on board).

By Boat

Travellers of yore approached Avignon by boat – a thrill still possible with a lunch or dinner cruise with the **Grands Bateaux de Provence**, based at Allées de l'Oulle, **t** 04 90 85 62 25, *www.mireio.net*; the food is delicious and an afternoon's exploration of Arles is included. From mid-June to mid-Sept, the same firm runs regular **Bateau-Bus** trips between Avignon and Villeneuve lez Avignon. The tourist office has information on other cruise boats. You can also spend a week on the Rhône and Saône on the *Princesse de Provence* (April–Nov); contact **Peter Deilmann Cruises**, *www.eurorivercruises.com*.
There is also a free **shuttle** from the foot of Pont St-Bénezet to the Ile de la Barthelasse (*July and Aug daily 11–9, April–June and Sept daily 10–12.30 and 2–6.30; Oct–Dec Wed 2–5.30, Sat and Sun 10-12 and 2–5.30*).

Car Hire

Veo, 151 Av Pierre Sémard, **t** 04 90 87 53 43, *www.veolocation.com*,
Rent a Car, 130 Av Pierre Sémard, **t** 04 90 88 08 02, *www.rentacar.fr*.
There are free **car parks** outside the city walls; **Parking de l'Ile Piot** has a free shuttle to the town centre.

Bike Hire

Holiday Bikes, 20 Bd St-Roch, **t** 04 32 76 25 88, *www.provence-bike.com*.
Provence Bike, 52 Bd St-Roch, **t** 04 90 27 92 61.
La Maison du Jardin, 80 Rue Guillaume Puy, **t** 04 90 86 32 49.

who was now fresh in his grave. Boniface's arch-enemy, Philip the Fair of France, had just bribed the conclave to elect a Frenchman, Clement V. Philip also suggested that the new pope flee the inferno of Rome for the safer havens of the Comtat Venaissin in Provence (*see* p.242) – and Clement didn't have to be asked twice.

The Church had picked up this piece of Provence real estate as its spoils after the Albigensian Crusade (*see* p.25). Isolated within it was the little city-republic of Avignon, belonging to the Angevin counts of Provence – old papal allies, who welcomed their illustrious visitor. Clement V always intended to return to Rome, but when he died the French cardinals elected a former archbishop

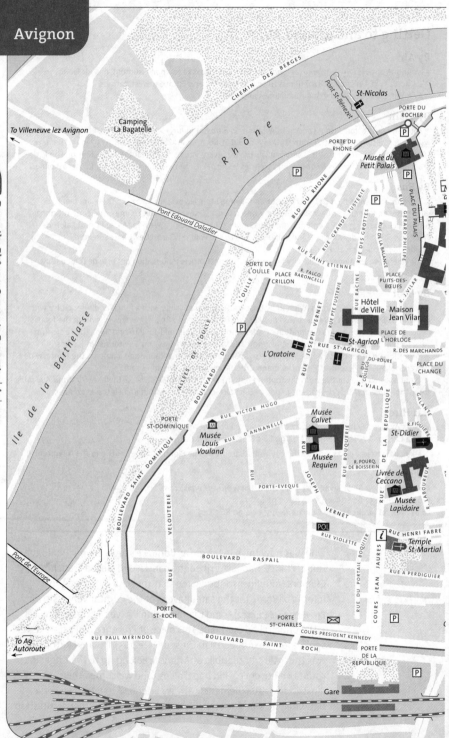

To Villeneuve lez Avignon

Camping
La Bagatelle

CHEMIN DES BERGES

Rhône

Pont St-Bénezet

St-Nicolas

PORTE DU
ROCHER

PORTE DU
RHONE

Musée du
Petit Palais

PLACE DU PALAIS

RUE GERARD PHILIPPE

Pont Edouard Daladier

BLD DU RHONE

RUE DE LA BALANCE

RUE GRANDE FUSTERIE

RUE DES GROTTES

Île de la Barthelasse

PORTE DE
L'OULLE

PLACE BARONCELLI
CRILLON

R. FALCO

RUE SAINT ETIENNE

RUE RACINE

RUE PTE FUSTERIE

PLACE
PUITS-DES-
BŒUFS

R. J. VILAR

Hôtel
de Ville

Maison
Jean Vilar

ALLÉES DE L'OULLE

BOULEVARD DE L'OULLE

RUE JOSEPH VERNET

RUE ST-AGRICOL

St-Agricol

PLACE DE
L'HORLOGE

R. DES MARCHANDS

L'Oratoire

R. DU COLLEGE DU-ROURE

R. VIALA

PLACE DU
CHANGE

RUE DE LA REPUBLIQUE

R. CALANTE

PORTE
ST-DOMINIQUE

RUE VICTOR HUGO

RUE D'ANNANELLE

Musée
Louis
Vouland

Musée
Calvet

RUE BOUQUERIE

R.FIGUIERE

St-Didier

BOULEVARD SAINT DOMINIQUE

RUE

Musée
Requien

RUE JOSEPH

R. POURQ.
DE BOISSERIN

Livrée de
Ceccano

R. LABOUREUR

PORTE-EVEQUE

VERNET

Musée
Lapidaire

Pont de l'Europe

RUE VELOUTERIE

POL

RUE VIOLETTE

RUE DU PORTAIL BOQUIER

RUE HENRI FABRE

Temple
St-Martial

BOULEVARD RASPAIL

COURS JEAN JAURES

RUE A PERDIGUIER

PORTE
ST-ROCH

RUE PAUL MERINDOL

PORTE
ST-CHARLES

BOULEVARD SAINT ROCH

COURS PRESIDENT KENNEDY

PORTE
DE LA
REPUBLIQUE

To A9
Autoroute

Gare

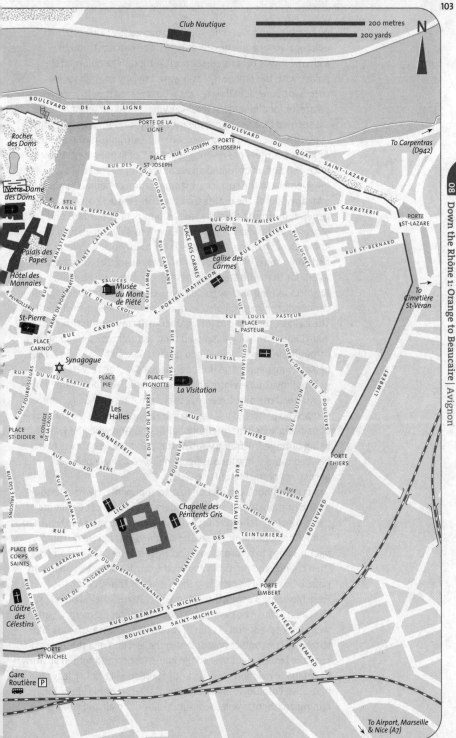

Club Nautique

200 metres
200 yards

N

BOULEVARD DE LA LIGNE

PORTE DE LA
LIGNE

BOULEVARD DU QUAI SAINT-LAZARE

To Carpentras
(D942)

Rocher
des Doms

PORTE
ST-JOSEPH

RUE ST-JOSEPH

PLACE
ST-JOSEPH

RUE DES TROIS COLOMBES

Notre-Dame
des Doms

STE-
ESCALIER ANNE R. BERTRAND

R.

RUE SAINTE CATHERINE

R. BANASTERIE

RUE DES INFIRMIERES

Cloître

PLACE DES CARMES

RUE CARRETERIE

RUE CARRETERIE

RUE LUCHET

RUE CARRETERIE

PORTE
ST-LAZARE

RUE ST-BERNARD

Palais des
Papes

Hôtel des
Monnaies

R. ARME DE PONTMARTIN

RUE CAMPANE

Eglise des
Carmes

R. SALUCES

Musée
du Mont
de Piété

R. OXIFLAMME

R. PORTAIL MATHERON

RUE DE LA CROIX

R. PEYROLLERIE

St-Pierre

RUE CARNOT

RUE PAUL SAIN

RUE LOUIS PASTEUR

PLACE
L. PASTEUR

RUE NOTRE-DAME DES 7 DOULEURS

To
Cimetière
St-Véran

PLACE
CARNOT

RUE TRIAL

RUE GUILLAUME

RUE BUFFON

Synagogue

R. DES FOURBISSEURS

RUE DU VIEUX SEXTIER

PLACE
PIE

PLACE
PIGNOTTE

La Visitation

R. DU FOUR DE LA TERRE

RUE

RUE

RUE PUY

LIMBERT

BOULEVARD

R. COLLEGE DE LA CROIX

Les
Halles

BONNETERIE

RUE

THIERS

PORTE
THIERS

PLACE
ST-DIDIER

RUE DU ROI RENE

R. BOURGNEUF

RUE PETRAMALE

RUE SAINT

RUE CHRISTOPHE

RUE SEVERINE

RUE DES 3 FAUCONS

Chapelle des
Pénitents Gris

LICES

RUE DES

RUE GUILLAUME

PUY

RUE DES

TEINTURIERS

PLACE DES
CORPS
SAINTS

RUE BARACANE

RUE DU PORTAIL MAGNANEN

RUE DE L'AIGARDEN

R. BON MARTINET

PORTE
LIMBERT

RUE ST MICHEL

Cloître
des
Célestins

RUE DU REMPART ST-MICHEL

BOULEVARD SAINT-MICHEL

AVE PIERRE

SEMARD

PORTE
ST-MICHEL

Gare
Routière P

To Airport, Marseille
& Nice (A7)

of Avignon, John XXII (1316–34), who moved the Curia into his old episcopal palace and greatly enriched the papacy (through alchemy, it was rumoured: *see* p.43). Although he enlarged the palace with the proceeds, it still wasn't roomy enough for his successor, Benedict XII (1334–42), who replaced it with another palace, or for Clement VI (1342–52), who added yet another.

It seemed that the popes meant to stay forever, especially after 1348, when Clement purchased Avignon outright from the young Angevin Countess of Provence, Jeanne Iere of Naples, for the sale price of 80,000 florins and an absolution for her possible involvement in the suspicious strangulation of her husband.

Meanwhile, all the profits that the 14th-century papal machine generated – from tithes, the sale of indulgences, pardons and offices, and the visits of pilgrims – went to Avignon instead of Rome. Overcrowding, debauchery, dirt, luxury, plague, blackmail and crime came with the deal – troubles exacerbated by papal tolerance that admitted outcasts from everywhere else into Avignon, as long as they could pay. Such refugees included not only common criminals but also Jews and, during the Schism, heretics. The Italians, mortified at losing their cash cow during this 'Babylonian captivity', expressed their self-righteous indignation through the long-time Avignon resident Petrarch: 'Avignon is the hell of living people, the thoroughfare of vice, the sewers of the earth... Prostitutes swarm on the papal beds.' Yet these same popes summoned the best *trecento* artists from Italy, especially from Siena, who perfected in Avignon the elegant, courtly, fairytale style of painting known as International Gothic. And when he wasn't being outraged, Petrarch wrote incomparable love sonnets to his beloved Laura, a mysterious figure believed to have been an ancestress of the Marquis de Sade.

In 1377 Avignon's population rose to approximately 30,000 souls, a third of them under religious orders. In that year, St Catherine of Siena convinced the seventh Avignon pope, Gregory XI, to return to Rome. The pope came, he saw, he sickened, but before he could pack his bags to return to Avignon, he died. The Roman mob seized their chance and physically forced the cardinals to elect an Italian pope who would re-establish the papacy in Rome. When the French cardinals escaped the Romans' clutches, they sparked off the Great Schism by electing a French antipope, Clement VII, and went back to Avignon. A Church council held in Pisa 30 years later to resolve the conflict only ended in the election of a third pope. In 1403 the French went over to the Rome faction and sent in an army to persuade Avignon's second antipope, Benedict XIII, to leave for his native Catalunya – where he spent the rest of his life bitterly raining anathemas and excommunications on all and sundry.

When the Church finally decided on one pope, Avignon and the Comtat Venaissin settled in for three and a half centuries of relaxed rule by cardinal legates, under whom the debauchery and violence continued, although on a more modest level. The party really came to an end when the Comtat Venaissin was incorporated into France during the Revolution in a blood rite of atrocities and the destruction of centuries of art and architecture.

But even as part of France, Avignon has maintained its lively international character. Publishers who first set up shop with the popes stayed on under the cardinal legates, beyond the bounds of French censorship (there were 20 in town before the Revolution); in the 1850s they took on a new life publishing the works of the Félibrige. In 1946 actor Jean Vilar founded the Avignon Festival of Theatre and Film, the liveliest and most popular event in the Provençal calendar. The city was also European City of Culture in 2000, and some of its monuments have been listed as UNESCO World Heritage sites. The TGV has made Paris less than 3 hours away, and a summer Eurostar route direct from London brings even more of Europe to its door.

The Famous Half-Bridge

From the north, Avignon is a brave two-tiered sight: in front rise the sheer cliffs of the **Rocher des Doms**, which has been inhabited since Neolithic times, and behind it the sheer artificial cliffs of the **Palais des Papes**, the same colour as the rock and almost as haphazard a pile. The ensemble includes the **walls** that the popes wrapped around Avignon: bijou, toothsome garden walls ever since Viollet-le-Duc recrenellated them and filled in the moat in 1860.

From the walls, four arches of a bridge leapfrog into the Rhône, sidle up to a waterbound, two-storey Romanesque **chapel** (the lower half of which is dedicated to St Nicolas, the patron of Rhône boatmen) and then stop abruptly mid-river, long before reaching Villeneuve lez Avignon on the distant bank. This is the famous

Pont St-Bénezet
t 04 32 74 32 74, www.palais-des-papes.com; open Aug 9–9; July and 1–15 Sept 9–8; 15 Mar–June and 16 Sept–Oct 9–7; 1–14 Mar 9–6.30; Nov–Feb 9.30–5.45

Pont St-Bénezet, otherwise known simply as the **Pont d'Avignon**, begun in 1185. It was built during a time when all bridges were the work of either devils or saints; in this case a shepherd boy named Bénezet, obeying the mandates of heaven, single-handedly laid the huge foundation stones. Originally 22 arches and three-quarters of a kilometre long, the bridge enriched Avignon with its tolls: its presence was a major factor in the popes' decision to live here. In 1660 the Avignonnais got tired of the constant repairs it demanded, however, and abandoned it to the monsters of the Rhône. Now only the four arches remain.

And did they ever '*danse, tout en rond*' on their bridge, as the nursery song would have it? No, they didn't, the historians say, although they may well have danced *under* it on the mid-river

Ile de la Barthelasse, formerly a hunting reserve and the head-quarters for Avignon's prostitutes and thieves. It was here that in later years the Avignonnais came for Sunday picnics. The Félibres (*see* pp.41–2) liked to bring pretty 'Félibresses' here to recite poetry. In summer people still come to cool off in its Olympic-size pool.

Palais des Papes

Palais des Papes
t 04 90 27 50 00, www. palais-des-papes.com; open Aug 9–9; July and 1–15 Sept 9–8; 15 Mar–June and 16 Sept–Oct 9–7; 1–14 Mar 9–6.30; Nov–Feb 9.30–5.45; adm; last ticket 1hr before closing; optional English audioguide

For a curious sensation, park directly under the popes' palace and take the lift up to the traffic-free **Place du Palais**. Once crowded with houses, it was cleared by antipope Benedict XIII to emphasize the message of the palace's vertical, impregnable walls: 'You would think it was an Asiatic tyrant's citadel rather than the abode of the vicar of the God of peace,' wrote Prosper Mérimée. But the life of a 14th-century pope justified paranoia. What is less obvious is that the life of a 14th-century pope and his cardinals, courtiers, mistresses and toadies was also extremely luxurious. The palace was spared in the Revolution only to end up serving as a prison and a barracks, and until 1920 its bored residents chipped off frescoes to sell to tourists, so that on most of the walls the only remaining decoration is an extraordinary variety of masons' marks. The entrance is up the steps, in the centre of Clement VI's façade.

Old Palace: Ground Floor

After crossing the **Cour d'Honneur**, the great courtyard dividing Benedict XII's stern Cistercian **Palais Vieux** (1334–42) from Clement VI's flamboyant **Palais Neuf** (1342–52), you start the tour in the **Jesus Hall**, so called for its decorative monograms of Christ. Once used to house the pope's treasure and account books, it now contains a hoard of maps, views of old Avignon and curios, such as a pair of 17th-century bell-ringing figures (*jacquemarts*). The most valuable loot was stored behind walls 10ft thick in the windowless bowels of the **Angels' Tower**, its ceiling supported by a single stone pillar resembling an enormous palm tree.

Next is the **Consistory**, where the cardinals met and received ambassadors; as its lavish frescoes and ceiling burned in 1413, it now displays 19th-century pictures of Avignon's popes and Simone Martini's *Virgin of Humility* fresco, detached from the cathedral porch in 1960. Under the fresco, the restorers found Martini's *sinopia*, or initial line sketch, etched in the stone. As an artist could only paint a small patch of fresh, wet plaster a day, such *sinopie* were essential to maintain the composition, and these, as is often the case in Italy, give a clearer idea of the painter's intent than the damaged fresco itself. There are traces of *sinopie in situ* in the **Chapelle St-Jean**, dedicated to both Johns, the Baptist and the Evangelist. Matteo Giovannetti of Viterbo, a *trecento* charmer who left the bulk of his work in Avignon, did the frescoes for Clement VI:

saints floating overhead in starry blue landscapes (recall that at the time ultramarine blue paint was even more expensive than gold). On one wall, John's head is served to Herod at table, as if in a restaurant.

Old Palace: First Floor

The tour continues to the first floor and the banqueting hall, or **Grand Tinel**, hung with 18th-century Gobelin tapestries. Although big enough for a football pitch, the Grand Tinel was too small to hold all the cardinal-electors who would gather in a conclave 10 days after a pope's death. Masons were brought in to accommodate them: the arches at the far end were knocked down to give the cardinals more room to manoeuvre (in both senses of the word), while the doors and windows were bricked up to keep them from bringing in more food and endlessly prolonging the conclave. The trick always worked, for the appetites of the 14th-century Curia were Pantagruelian – the adjacent **Upper Kitchen** boasts a pyramidal chimney that could easily handle a roast elephant, or the menu of Clement VI's coronation feast: a total of 1,023 sheep, 118 cows, 101 calves, 914 kids, 60 pigs, 10,471 hens, 1,446 geese and 300 pike, topped off by 46,856 cheeses and 50,000 tarts, all consumed by just 3,000 guests – some 16 tarts per person, with a few thousand left over for the pope's midnight snack. Off the Grand Tinel, more delightful frescoes by Matteo Giovannetti decorate the **Chapelle St-Martial**, celebrating the French saint who came from the same Limousin village as Benedict XII.

New Palace

The tour continues to the **Pope's Antechamber**, where he would hold private audiences, and then on to the **Pope's Bedroom** in the Angels' Tower, a room covered with murals of spiralling foliage, birds and birdcages. It leads directly into the New Palace and the most delightful room in the entire palace, the **Chambre du Cerf**, Clement VI's study, where he would come 'to seek the freedom of forgetting he was pope'. In 1343 he had Matteo Giovannetti (probably) lead a group of French painters in depicting outdoor scenes of hunting, fishing and peach-picking that not only quickened the papal gastric juices, but expressed what was then a revolutionary new interest in the natural world, where flowers and foliage were drawn from observation rather than copying a 'source'. The arrows direct you next to the **Sacristy**, crowded with statues of kings, queens and bishops escaped from Gargantua's chessboard, followed by Clement VI's **Great Chapel**, longer even than the Grand Tinel and just as empty, though the altar has been reconstructed. The **Robing Room** off the chapel contains casts of the Avignon popes' tombs. Revolutionaries bashed most of the

08 Down the Rhône 1: Orange to Beaucaire | Avignon

figures that once adorned the elaborate **Chapel Gate**; through the bay window in front of this, the pope would bless and give indulgences to pilgrims. A grand stair leads down to the flamboyant **Great Audience Hall**, where Matteo Giovannetti's *Prophets* remains intact, along with outline sketches of a *Crucifixion* that would certainly have been splendid if it had ever been completed.

Around the Palace: Notre-Dame-des-Doms

Before spray paint, the posterity-minded had to record their passing with family emblems. None did it better than the family of the Borghese pope, Paul V; his nephew, legate in Avignon, produced the striking 1619 **Hôtel des Monnaies**, or mint, just across from the Palais des Papes, where reliefs of the Borghese dragon and eagle prance in garlands of fruit salad. To the left of the palace is Avignon's cathedral, **Notre-Dame-des-Doms**, built in 1150, its landmark square bell-tower ridiculously dwarfed by a massive gilt statue of the Virgin added in 1859 – an unsuccessful attempt to make the church stand out next to the overwhelming papal pile. The interior has been fuzzily Baroqued like a soft-centre chocolate, but it's worth focusing on the good bits: the dome at the crossing, with an octagonal drum pierced by light, the masterpiece of this typically Provençal conceit; the 11th- or 12th-century marble bishop's chair in the choir; and, in a chapel next to the sacristy, now the **Trésor** (*adm*), the flamboyant Tomb of John XXII (d. 1334) by English sculptor Hugh Wilfred, mutilated in the Revolution and restored in the 19th century with a spare effigy of a bishop on top to replace the smashed pope.

Next to the cathedral, ramps lead up to the oasis of the **Rocher des Doms**, which is now a garden enjoying panoramic views from the Rhône below to Mont Ventoux rising to the northeast. Peacocks squawk and preen in trees so crippled by the *mistral* that they need crutches; you can tell the hour with your own shadow on a sundial called the *cadran solaire annalemmatique*, and admire a statue dedicated to an Armenian refugee named Jean Althen who 'introduced the cultivation of madder to the Midi' (don't laugh; used for producing dyes, madder was once the south's most important cash crop).

Musée du Petit Palais

Musée du Petit Palais
t 04 90 86 44 58,
www.petit-palais.com;
open June–Sept
Wed–Mon 10–6;
Oct–May Wed–Mon
10–1 and 2–6; adm

Overlooking the Rhône at the end of the Place des Papes stands the Petit Palais, built in 1318 and modified in 1474 to suit the tastes of Cardinal Legate Giuliano della Rovere – one day to become Michelangelo's patron and nemesis as Pope Julius II. In 1958 the Petit Palais became a museum to hold all the medieval works remaining in Avignon.

Although the scale of the Petit Palais can be daunting, it contains rare treats from the dawn of the Renaissance by artists hailing for the most part from Siena or Florence. But Avignon gets its say as well: the sculptures and pretty courtly frescoes from the 12th to the 14th centuries in the first two rooms demonstrate the city's role in creating and diffusing the late International Gothic style. The third room contains some fascinating fragments of the 35ft, eight-storey **tomb of Cardinal Jean de Lagrange** (1389), which stood in Avignon's temple of St-Martial before the Revolution. One bit that survived was the *transi*, or relief, of the decomposing corpse that occupied the lowest level of the tomb and was carved with morbid anatomical exactitude. Such *memento mori*, always used to contrast the handsome effigy of the deceased while alive, would soon become popular in northern France. The mouldering Cardinal Lagrange is one of the earliest examples, and may even be the prototype of the genre.

The next six rooms glow with the gold backgrounds (the better to show up in dim churches) of 14th- and early 15th-century Italian painting. Nearly all depict the Virgin and Child, a reflection of the cult of Mariolatry and chivalric ideals of womanhood that began where the troubadours left off. Although the subject matter is repetitive, it makes it easy to trace the medieval revolution in art and seeing, back in the good old days when art was content merely to imitate nature and not try to outdo her. The iconic, Byzantine flatness of the earliest paintings (especially Paolo Veneziano's *Virgin* of 1340, which has, remarkably, never been restored in its 660 years) begins to give way to a more natural depiction of space, composition and human form after the innovations of Giotto in Italy (especially Taddeo Gaddi, Pseudo Jacopino di Francesco, Lorenzo Monaco and Gherardo Starnina). Meanwhile, Sienese artists, following the lead of the great Duccio di Buoninsegna, took up a more elegant, stylized line and richer colours (Simone Martini and many works by Taddeo di Bartolo).

The taste of Avignon's popes for Sienese art made the latter the strongest influence in the International Gothic style forged at the papal court (Room 8), a style that the Sienese kept at long after the Florentines had moved on to new things – see Giovanni di Paolo's *Nativity* (1470), or Pietro di Domenico da Montepulciano's kinky *Vierge de Miséricorde* (1420), a delicate portrayal of a congregation sheltered under the Virgin's mantle while a band of flagellants whip themselves. Bridal chests (*cassoni*) were often used to illustrate cautionary tales for women: in Room 9 see Domenico de Michelino's *cassone* panels of 1450 on the story of *Susanna and the Elders*.

Renaissance Gems, Sacred and Profane

Beyond the *salon de repos* hangs the museum's best-known work, Botticelli's *Virgin and Child*, a tender, lyrical painting from his youth, inspired by his (and Leonardo da Vinci's) master, Verrocchio. The next few rooms offer nothing as striking until Room 15 and its four delightful narrative panels from bridal chests (*c.* 1510) by the Maestro dei Cassoni Campana. This unknown master's meticulous miniaturist style is as rare as the subject of his cautionary tale, *The Minotaur*, beginning with Queen Pasiphae of Crete's love for a white bull, resulting in the birth of the Minotaur. The third panel shows Ariadne and her ball of twine and Theseus slaying the Minotaur in an exquisite circular labyrinth.

The sacred equivalent of the *cassoni* is in Room 16b: the *Sacra Conversazione* by Venetian Vittore Carpaccio, lyrical master of charm, colour and incidental detail. Such 'sacred conversations' portray the Virgin and saints meditating together on matters sublime, to the accompaniment of angelic music. To this, Carpaccio has added a landscape dominated by a natural rock bridge, where episodes from the lives of saints Jerome, Augustine and Paul the Hermit take place.

Lastly, Rooms 17–19 are devoted to works by French artists in Avignon, who after 1440 formed one of the most important schools of French Renaissance art. Influenced by the realism of Flemish oil painting (introduced to Avignon by Benedict XIII) and the almost abstract, decorative lines of the Italians, it concentrates on strong, simple images, as in the altarpiece *Virgin and Child between Two Saints* (1450), by the school's greatest master, Enguerrand Quarton, with a pair of luminous shutters with saints Michael and Catherine on the reverse by Josse Lieferinxe. Or take two works by an accomplished but unknown hand: the striking *Jacob's Dream* and the lyrical *Adoration of the Child* (*c.* 1500), where the well-dressed donor seems to have stumbled unexpectedly on to the divine mystery.

Place de l'Horloge and Quartier des Fusteries

Just below the Place du Palais, an antique carousel spins gaily in the lively centre of old Avignon, **Place de l'Horloge**, site of the old Roman forum, now full of buskers and holiday layabouts. The timepiece of its name is in the 1363 tower of the Hôtel de Ville; this originally belonged to a Benedictine monastery on the site, but was secularized with a clock and two *jacquemarts* who sound the hours. They aren't the only archaic figures here: many first-time visitors do a double-take when they notice the windows on the east side of the square, filled with *trompe-l'œil* paintings of historic personages who all are linked in some way to the city.

Behind the Hôtel de Ville lies the **Quartier des Fusteries**, named after the wood merchants and carpenters who had their workshops here in the Middle Ages. These were replaced in the 18th century with *hôtels particuliers*: in one, the **Maison aux Ballons** (with little iron balloons on the window sills) at 18 Rue St-Etienne, Joseph de Montgolfier discovered the principle of balloon flight in 1782, when he noticed how his shirt, drying by the fire, puffed up and floated in the hot air. From the Quartier des Fusteries, the steep picturesque lanes of the **Quartier de la Balance** wind back up to the Place du Palais.

Off Place de l'Horloge and Rue St-Agricol, Rue du Collège-du-Roure leads to the fine mid-15th-century **Palais du Roure**, marked by a flamboyant gate topped with intertwining mulberry branches in memory of the Taverne de Mûrier that it replaced. Equally flamboyant was the 19th-century descendant of the Florentine family who built it, the Félibre poet Marquis Baroncelli-Javon, who preferred to spend his time as a cowboy in the Camargue and lent this town house to Mistral as a headquarters for his Provençal-language journal *Aïoli*. It now houses a **study centre** and exhibits on the language.

Palais du Roure study centre
t 04 90 80 80 88; open to students only Mon–Fri 9–12 and 2–5.30; closed Aug; free guided tours Tues at 3pm, and by appt

Rue St-Agricol is named after the restored Gothic church of **St-Agricol** (1326); its treasure is the *Doni Retable*, a rare Provençal work from the Renaissance. At No.19 is the **Librairie Roumanille**, founded in 1855 by the Avignon poet Joseph Roumanille, father of the Félibrige (*see* pp.41–2). The bookshop published the movement's first masterpiece, Mistral's epic *Mireio* (1859), and continues to put out books in Provençal, while Avignon's literati chum around in the shop's atmospheric 19th-century *salon*.

Museums around Avignon

At the end of Rue St-Agricol curves Rue Joseph Vernet, lined with 18th-century *hôtels particuliers*, antiques shops, and pricey restaurants and cafés. The kind of overly ornate spindly furniture, porcelains and knick-knacks that originally embellished these mansions is on display nearby at No.17 Rue Victor Hugo, in the **Musée Louis Vouland**.

Musée Louis Vouland
t 04 90 86 03 79, www.vouland.com; open May–Oct Tues–Sat 10–12 and 2–6, Sun 2–6; Nov–April Tues–Sun 2–6; adm

More exciting are the contents of the handsome **Hôtel de Villeneuve-Martignan**, at 65 Rue Joseph Vernet, first opened to the public as a 'cabinet of curiosities' in the late 18th century by collector Esprit Calvet. Now the **Musée Calvet**, it offers something for every taste: 6,000 pieces of wrought iron, Greek sculpture, 18th-century seascapes by Avignon native Claude-Joseph Vernet and paintings of ruins by Hubert Robert and Panini, mummies, a portrait of Diane de Baroncelli (grandmother of the Marquis de Sade), a bust of a boy by Renaissance sculptor Desiderio da

Musée Calvet
t 04 90 86 33 84; open Wed–Mon 10–1 and 2–6; adm

Settignano, tapestries, prehistoric statue-steles, dizzy kitsch paintings of nude men (David's *Mort de Bara* and Horace Vernet's *Mazeppa and the Wolves*), as well as an excellent collection of 19th- and 20th-century paintings by Corot, Guigou, Soutine, Daumier, Dufy, Morisot, Utrillo, Seurat, Toulouse-Lautrec, Vlaminck and Rouault. For all that, the best part of this museum may be the building itself, a light and airy palace from the Age of Enlightenment that complements perfectly the soft, romanticized landscapes and portraits on the walls.

Musée Requien
t 04 90 82 43 51; open Tues–Sat 10–1 and 2–6

Adjacent to the Calvet museum, the **Musée Requien** is Avignon's fuddy-duddy natural history collection, where a massive beaver found in the Sorgue steals the show. Lastly, at 27 Rue de la République, in the chilly 17th-century chapel of a Jesuit college, are the stone sculptures of the **Musée Lapidaire**. It's worth popping in for the 2nd-century BC (or Merovingian) man-eating *Tarasque de Noves*, each hand gripping the head of a Gaul, while an arm dangles from its greedy jaws; for the statues of Gallic warriors, looking much nattier in their mail than Astérix; or for the unlabelled masks in petal-like hoods. There is good Renaissance sculpture as well, but the best is in the nearby church of **St-Didier** (1359), just to the north in Place St-Didier: Francesco Laurana's polychrome reredos of Christ bearing the Cross, called *Notre-Dame du Spasme* for the spasm of pain on Mary's face; it was one of the first Renaissance sculptures to reach France, executed for the Bon Roi René in 1478. Opposite, in the first chapel on the left, are some *c.*1360 Florentine frescoes, uncovered in 1952.

Musée Lapidaire
t 04 90 85 75 38; open Wed–Mon 10–1 and 2–6; adm

More 14th-century frescoes have been restored opposite the church in the **Livrée de Ceccano**, now the town library. Nearby, at 5 Rue Laboureur, the treasures of a serious art collector named Jean Angladon-Dubrujeaud have been opened to the public as the **Musée Angladon**. These include Renaissance and Art Deco furniture, bronzes and African art, but the main reason for coming is a fine assortment of modern painting never before seen: works by Modigliani, Picasso, Manet, Degas and Cézanne, as well as the only Van Gogh on display in Provence, called *Les Wagons de chemin de fer*.

Musée Angladon
t 04 90 82 29 03, www. angladon.com; open May–Nov Tues–Sun 1–6; Dec–April Wed–Sun 1–6; hols 3–6; other times for groups by appt; adm

Lambert Collection
t 04 90 16 56 20, www. collection lambert.com; open July–Aug daily 11–7; Sept–June Tues–Sun 11–6

Situated in the 18th-century Hôtel de Caumont at 5 Rue Violette off the southern end of Rue Joseph Vernet, the **Lambert Collection** features modern art by the likes of Basquiat, and has a café and bookshop attached.

Musée du Mont de Piété
t 04 90 86 53 12; open Mon–Fri 8.30–11.30 and 1.30–5

Back past the Hôtel des Monnaies towards the Place des Carmes, the **Musée du Mont de Piété** at 6 Rue Saluces, the oldest pawn-broker's in France, houses the town archives and some silk desiccators that were used to work out the dry weight of Avignon's former chief commodity.

The Eastern Quarters

From Place St-Didier, Rue du Roi René is lined with chiselled palaces, one built on the site of the church of **Ste-Claire** (No.22), where Petrarch first saw his Laura on Good Friday 1327. ('It was the day when the sun darkened, as God Himself vanished into death, when I was taken,' he wrote.) Laura died, probably of the plague, in 1348, and was buried nearby in the Franciscan **Couvent des Cordeliers**, by the corner of Rue des Lices and Rue des Teinturiers; only the Gothic bell-tower survived the fury of the Revolution. In 1533 a humanist from Lyon claimed to have found Laura's tomb in the church, and such was Petrarch's reputation that François Ier made a special trip to Avignon to see it.

Rue des Teinturiers, the most picturesque street in Avignon, was named after the dyers and textile-makers who powered their machines on waterwheels in the Sorgue, two of which survive. Shaded by ancient plane trees, crossed by little bridges, it is a pleasant place to dawdle over a beer or dinner; it's hard to believe this Sorgue is the same stream that comes bursting like a bomb out of that other Petrarchan shrine, the Fontaine-de-Vaucluse (*see* pp.240–41). Rue des Teinturiers turns into Rue Bonneterie on its way to Avignon's shopping district and **Place Pie**, home of the ugly-duckling new market (**Les Halles**), although the produce inside is fit for a swan.

Another evocative street, **Rue du Vieux-Sextier**, once the site of the Jewish ghetto, is the address of Avignon's 19th-century **synagogue**, while, just beyond Place Carnot, **St-Pierre**'s flamboyant façade boasts a set of beautifully carved walnut doors (1551). Facing St-Pierre, Avignon's cosiest museum, Musée Théodore Aubanel, is a private institution dedicated to printing in Avignon, and to the romantic poet and Félibre Théodore Aubanel, whose family still owns one of Avignon's oldest publishing houses. From Place St-Pierre, Rue Carnot continues towards the charming **Place des Carmes**, which is dominated by the 14th-century **Eglise des Carmes** (church of the White Friars), Avignon's biggest church, with a pretty cloister that has been refurbished as a Festival venue.

Visitors in the 19th century would continue from here along Rue Carreterie, out of the city gate and down the Lyon road to the **Cimetière St-Véran**, a romantic, shady park where John Stuart Mill and his wife Harriet are buried. Harriet died at the Hôtel d'Europe in 1858 – a loss so devastating for the philosopher of utilitarianism that he lived in a house by the cemetery until he himself died in 1873. Another celebrated tomb belongs to Maurille de Sombreuil, who became a heroine during the Revolution when, to save the life of her father, the governor of the Invalides, she drank a goblet of human blood. Contemporaries noted that she favoured white wine after that.

Musée Théodore Aubanel
t 04 90 86 35 02; open for weekday morning visits by appt only; closed Aug; adm

Services in Avignon

Post office: Cours Président Kennedy, just inside the Porte de la République, near the train station.

Market Days in Avignon

Tues–Sun am: covered market, Les Halles, Place Pie.

Sat am: flower market, Place des Carmes.

Sun: flea market, Place des Carmes.

Festivals in Avignon

In 1947 Jean Vilar with his Théâtre National Populaire founded the **Avignon Festival**, with the aim of bringing theatre to the masses. It is now rated among the top international theatre festivals in Europe, and in July and August Avignon overflows with performances by the Théâtre National and others, the cinemas host films from all over the world, and there are concerts in the churches.

The **Maison Jean Vilar**, 8 Rue de Mons, t 04 90 86 59 64, *www.maisonjeanvilar.org (open July daily 10.30– 6.30; Sept–June Tues–Fri 9–12 and 1.30–5.30, Sat 10–5; closed Aug)*, is the nerve centre and hosts exhibitions, films and lectures the rest of the year. For festival bookings, contact the **Bureau du Festival d'Avignon**, Espace Saint-Louis, 20 Rue Portail Boquier, 84000 Avignon, t 04 90 27 66 50, *www.festival-avignon.com*.

During the festival, Avignon's squares and streets overflow with fringe (or 'Off') performers, *www.avignonleoff.com* or *www. avignon-off.net*. You can relax and discuss the latest events during the festival in **Le Bar du Off**.

Otherwise, there seems to be some sort of festivity every month, whether it's the **New Wine Festival** (Nov), **Passion for Horses** (*Cheval Passion*, Jan), **contemporary dance** (Feb), a **Triathlon** (June) or **fireworks** on 14 July. The monthly broadsheet *Rendez-Vous*, from the tourist office, has exhaustive listings.

(i) **Avignon >>**
41 Cours Jean Jaurès, t 04 32 74 32 74, www.avignon-tourisme.com; open April–Oct daily; Nov–Mar Mon–Sat and Sun am; guided city tours April–Oct

Shopping in Avignon

Chic designer shops are found along Rue St-Agricol and Rue Joseph Vernet. *Pâtisseries* in this area sell Avignon's gourmand speciality, *papalines*, made of fine chocolate and a liqueur, *d'Origan du Comtat*, distilled from 60 herbs picked from the slopes of Mont Ventoux and said to be a sure cure for cholera. You will find all the regional specialities: *fruits confits d'Apt*, *berlingots de Carpentras*, *melon de Cavaillon*, *nougat de Sault*, *truffe de Carpentras et du Tricastin*, garlic, olives, honey, *pastis*, goat's cheese, *fougasse* (a kind of French *focaccia*) and *herbes de Provence*. There are also essential oils, *santons*, bold Provençal fabrics, local pottery and soaps.

Behind the Hôtel de Ville, in Place de l'Horloge, the **Maison des Pays de Vaucluse**, t 04 90 85 55 24, has a large display of regional products and crafts.

Where to Stay in Avignon

Avignon ✉ 84000

Avignon gets packed in July and August and many places raise their rates. There are other choices across the river in Villeneuve lez Avignon (*see* p.119), and a huge number of chain hotels around the suburbs.

The area also has a large number of *gîtes* and rooms in private homes, some on the idyllic Ile de la Barthelasse. For one of these, contact the **CDT Vaucluse**, 21 Rue Collège de la Croix, t 04 90 80 47 00, *www. vaucluse.fr*.

*****Hôtel-Restaurant La Mirande, 4 Place de la Mirande, t 04 90 14 20 20, *www.la-mirande.fr* (€€€€€). With views of the Popes' Palace through its antique glass windows, *toile de jouy* wallpaper or ancient woodcuts, marble bathrooms and oak floors, this is a luxurious place to stay by any standard. Also offers cooking courses.

****Hôtel d'Europe, 14 Place Crillon, t 04 90 14 76 76, *www.heurope.com* (€€€€€–€€€). The oldest hotel in town, built in the 16th century and converted to an inn in the late 18th century. Classically formal, it has Louis XV furnishings. Napoleon stayed here, as did the eloping Robert Browning and Elizabeth Barrett. *Restaurant closed Sun and Mon.*

****Clarion Cloître Saint-Louis**, 20 Rue Portail Boquier, **t** 04 90 27 55 55, *www.cloitre-saint-louis.com* (€€€€€–€€€). A beautiful cloister built in 1589 as part of a Jesuit school of theology, now an island of tranquillity. Rooms have been modernized for its chain hotel status; meals (€€€) are served under the portico or by the rooftop pool. *Restaurant closed Sat lunch.*

 La Ferme >

****Hôtel-Restaurant La Ferme**, Ile de la Barthelasse, **t** 04 90 82 57 53 (€€). A 16th-century farmhouse with rooms ranging in style from traditional Provençal to a Gypsy caravan, set around a tennis court and a swimming pool. *Closed Nov–mid-Mar; restaurant closed lunch.*

****Hôtel du Palais des Papes**, 3 Place du Palais, **t** 04 90 86 04 13, *www. hotel-avignon.com* (€€). The hotel with the best views of the palace. There is a restaurant, **Le Lutrin** (€€).

Hiély-Lucullus >>

****Hôtel d'Angleterre**, 29 Bd Raspail, **t** 04 90 86 34 31, *www.hoteldangle terre.fr* (€€). Friendly, simple place. *Closed mid-Dec–mid-Jan.*

***Le Splendid**, 17 Rue Agricol Perdiguier, **t** 04 90 86 14 46, *www.avignon-splendid-hotel.com* (€€). Good-value option offering bright and comfortable rooms. *Closed mid-Nov–mid-Dec.*

***Mignon**, 12 Rue Joseph Vernet, **t** 04 90 82 17 30, *www.hotel-mignon.com* (€€). Bright hotel with small, air-conditioned rooms. *Closed Jan.*

****Saint-Roch**, 9 Rue Paul Mérindol, **t** 04 90 16 50 00, *www.hotelstroch-avignon.com* (€). Quiet hotel with a delightful garden, just outside the walls of Porte St-Roch.

Ile de la Barthelasse has four **campsites**, one of which, **Bagatelle**, **t** 04 90 86 30 39, *www.camping bagatelle.com* (€), offers dormitory rooms during the summer months.

Around Avignon

There are two exceptional hotel-restaurants within easy driving distance of Avignon.

****Hostellerie Les Frênes**, 645 Av des Vertes Rives, 84140 Montfavet (5km east of town on N107), **t** 04 90 31 17 93, *www.lesfrenes.com* (€€€€€–€€€€). Set around a beautiful garden and pool; antiques furnish the rooms. The food (€€€) is as marvellous as the setting. *Closed Feb.*

****Auberge de Cassagne**, 84130 Le Pontet (5km north of town on N7), **t** 04 90 31 04 18, *www.aubergede cassagne.com* (€€€€€–€€€). A plush option with a pool, tennis courts, a sauna and a gym, and access to a golf course. The food and the wine cellar are faultless (€€€€). *Closed Jan.*

Eating Out in Avignon

Christian Etienne, 10 Rue de Mons, **t** 04 90 86 16 50, *www.christian-etienne.fr* (€€€€). A very chi-chi but nonetheless popular choice for gourmet Provençal cuisine. *Closed Sun and Mon exc July.*

Hiély-Lucullus, 5 Rue de la République, **t** 04 90 86 17 07, *www.hiely-lucullus. com* (€€€). Avignon's gourmet bastion for the past 60 years, and resolutely old-fashioned with a first-floor dining room. The kitchen never disappoints, with dishes such as *tourte* of quail and the legendary *cassoulet de moules aux épinards* (mussel stew with spinach). *Closed Sat lunch.*

Le Petit Bedon, 70 Rue Joseph Vernet, **t** 04 90 82 33 98 (€€€). An Avignon institution offering well-prepared dishes seldom found elsewhere, such as *lotte au gigondas*, angler fish cooked in wine. *Closed Sun and Mon lunch.*

Le Bain Marie, 5 Rue Pétramale, **t** 04 90 85 21 37, *www.lebainmarie.com* (€€€). A popular place serving a range of traditional French fare. *Closed all day Sun, Mon lunch and Sat lunch.*

L'Entrée des Artistes, 1 Place des Carmes, **t** 04 90 82 46 90 (€€€–€€). A restaurant located in a quiet square, with a menu brimming with traditional Provençal cooking, including *pied de veau. Closed Sat lunch and Sun, plus Aug.*

La Fourchette, 17 Rue Racine, **t** 04 90 85 20 93 (€€€–€€). Hiély-Lucullus' less expensive sister restaurant, serving equally good cuisine at prices that won't bust your wallet. *Closed Sat, Sun, and 3 weeks Aug.*

Woolloomoolloo, 16 bis Rue des Teinturiers, t 04 90 85 28 44, *www. woolloo.com* (€€). A popular place with 'world cuisine' and live music.

Entertainment and Nightlife in Avignon

Outside the Festival

Théâtre du Chêne Noir, 8 bis Rue Ste-Catherine, t 04 90 86 58 11, *www.chenenoir.fr*. One of Provence's most talented theatre companies.

Théâtre des Carmes, 6 Place des Carmes, t 04 90 82 20 47, *www. theatredescarmes.com*. Avignon's oldest permanent company, performing in the restored Gothic cloister of the Eglise des Carmes.

AJMI, 4 Rue Escaliers Sainte-Anne, t 04 90 86 08 61, *www.jazzalajmi.com*. A jazz club with live music on Thurs.

Bars and Clubs

Pub Z, 58 Rue Bonneterie, t 04 90 85 42 84. A black and white bar with DJs.

Le Red Zone, 25 Rue Carnot, t 04 90 27 02 44, *www.redzonebar.com*. Bar with music.

Villeneuve lez Avignon

In 586, on Puy Andaon, the rock that dominates Villeneuve lez Avignon, a Visigoth princess-hermit named Casarie died in the odour of sanctity (holiness smells like crushed violets, apparently). In the 10th century, Benedictines built the abbey of St-André to shelter her bones and lodge pilgrims on the route to Compostela. St-André grew to become one of the mightiest monasteries in the south of France, and in 1226, when Louis VIII besieged pro-Albigensian Avignon, the abbot offered the king co-sovereignty of the abbey in exchange for royal privileges. And so what was once an abbey town became a frontier-fortress of the king of France, a new town (*ville neuve*), heavily fortified in case the pope over the river should start feeling frisky.

But Villeneuve was soon invaded in another way; wanton, squalid Avignon didn't suit all tastes, and the pope gave permission to his cardinals who preferred it not-so-hot to retreat across the Rhône into princely *livrées cardinalices* (palaces 'freed' from their original owners by the Curia). Though a dormitory suburb these days, Villeneuve still maintains a separate peace, with well-fed cats snoozing in the sun, leisurely afternoons at the *pétanque* court and some amazing works of art.

Around Town

Tour Philippe-le-Bel

t 04 32 70 08 57; open April–Sept 10–12.30 and 2–6.30; Oct–Nov and Mar Tues–Sun 10–12 and 2–5; closed Dec–Feb

In 1307, when Philip the Fair ratified the deal that made Villeneuve royal property, he ordered that a citadel be built on the approach to Pont St-Bénezet, named after guess who. As times grew more perilous, this bright white **Tour Philippe-le-Bel** was made higher to keep out the riff-raff, and from its terrace, reached by a superb winding stair, it offers splendid views of Avignon, Mont Ventoux and, on a clear day, the Alpilles.

Getting to Villeneuve lez Avignon

Bus 11 runs every 30mins from the train station, Porte de l'Oulle or the post office in Avignon to Villeneuve lez Avignon.

Collégiale Notre-Dame
t 06 70 01 22 74; open April–Sept 10–12.30 and 2–6.30; Oct–Nov and Mar Tues–Sun 10–12 and 2–5; closed Dec–Feb

From here, Montée de la Tour leads up to the 14th-century Collégiale Notre-Dame, once the chapel of a *livrée* and now Villeneuve's parish church. From Villeneuve's Chartreuse (charterhouse) it has inherited an elaborate marble altar of 1745, and it contains a copy of Enguerrand Quarton's famous *Pietà de Villeneuve lez Avignon* (the original is in the Louvre). The church's most famous work, a beaming, swivel-hipped, polychrome ivory statue of the Virgin, carved in Paris out of an elephant's tusk *c.* 1320, has been removed to safer quarters in the nearby Musée Pierre-de-Luxembourg, which is housed in yet another *livrée*.

✪ Musée Pierre-de-Luxembourg
t 04 90 27 49 66; open April–Sept 10–12.30 and 2–6.30; Oct–Nov and Mar Tues–Sun 10–12 and 2–5; closed Dec–Feb; adm

The museum's other prize is the masterpiece of the Avignon school: Enguerrand Quarton's 1454 *Couronnement de la Vierge*, one of the greatest works of 15th-century French painting, commissioned for the Chartreuse (*see* below). Unusually, it portrays God the Father and God the Son as twins, clothed in sumptuous crimson and gold, like the Virgin herself, whose fine sculptural features were perhaps inspired by the ivory Virgin. Around these central figures the painting evokes the spiritual route travelled by the Carthusians through vigilant prayer, to purify the world and reconcile it to God. St Bruno, founder of the Order, saints, kings and commoners are present, hierarchically arranged, while the landscape encompasses heaven, hell, Rome and Jerusalem, and local touches such as the Montagne Ste-Victoire (*see* pp.213–14) and the cliffs of L'Estaque (*see* p.197).

Other notable works in the museum include a curious 14th-century double-faced Virgin, the 'Eve' face evoking original sin and the 'Mary' face human redemption; Simon de Châlon's 1552 *Entombment*; and, amid the uninspired 17th-century fluff, Philippe de Champaigne's *Visitation*.

La Chartreuse and Fort St-André

From the museum, take Rue de la République up as far as No.53, the **Livrée de la Thurroye**, the best-preserved in Villeneuve; a cardinal would maintain a household of 100 or so people here.

Chartreuse du Val de Bénédiction
t 04 90 15 24 24; www.chartreuse.org; open April–Sept daily 9–6.30; Oct–Mar daily 9.30–5.30; adm

Further up the street and up the scale rises what used to be the largest and wealthiest charterhouse in France, the Chartreuse du Val de Bénédiction. This began life as the *livrée* of Etienne Aubert who, upon his election to the papacy in 1352 as Innocent VI, deeded his palace to the Carthusians for a monastery. For 450 years it was expanded and rebuilt, acquired immense estates on either side of the Rhône from kings and popes, accumulated a precious library, two more cloisters and various works of art, and in general lived high on the hog by the usual Carthusian standards. In 1792, the Revolution forced the monks out, and the Chartreuse was sold in 17 lots; squatters took over the cells and outsiders feared to enter the cloisters after dark. Now repurchased and beautifully restored, the buildings house the **CNES** (Centre National des Ecritures du Spectacle), where playwrights and others are given grants to work in peace and quiet in some of the former cells; it hosts seminars, exhibitions and performances, especially during the Avignon Festival.

Still, the sensation that lingers in the charterhouse is one of vast silences and austerity, the hallmark of an order where conversation was limited (at least at the outset) to one hour a week; monks who disobeyed the rule of prayer, work and silence ended up in one of the seven prison cells that are set around the laundry in the Great Cloister, each with a cleverly arranged window on the prison chapel altar. Explanations (in English) throughout offer an in-depth view of Carthusian life: one cell has been furnished as it originally was. Pierre Boulez discovered that the dining hall, or *tinel*, has some of the finest acoustics in the whole of France, designed so that everyone could hear the monk who read aloud during mealtimes. In the *tinel*'s **chapel** are some ruined 14th-century frescoes by Matteo Giovannetti and his school: originally their work covered the walls of the huge **church**, now bare except for their masons' marks and minus its apse, which collapsed. The star attraction here is **Innocent VI's tomb**, which boasts an alabaster effigy under a fine Gothic baldachin. Innocent was solemnly reburied here in 1960: a century ago the tomb was being used as a rabbit hutch. Popes who took the name Innocent have tended to suffer similar posthumous indignities: the great Innocent III was found stark naked in Perugia cathedral, a victim of poisoned slippers, while the corpse of Innocent X – the last of the series – was dumped in a toolshed in St Peter's.

Gazing down into the charterhouse from the summit of Puy Andaon are the formidable bleached walls of **Fort St-André**, built by the French kings around the old abbey in the 1360s, not only to stare down the pope over the river but to defend French turf during the heyday of the *Grandes Compagnies* (bands of unemployed mercenaries who pillaged the countryside and held towns to ransom). The two round towers afford a famous vantage point over Avignon; the southwestern tower is called the **Tour des Masques** (or Tour des Sorcières, or Tour des Fées); no one remembers why. Jumbly ruins are all that remain of the once splendid **Abbaye St-André** amid beautiful Italian gardens – sumptuous in springtime – restored and presided over by Roseline Bacou, a former curator at the Louvre.

Fort St-André
t 04 90 25 45 35; open mid-May–Sept daily 10–1 and 2–6; April–mid-May daily 10–1 and 2–5.30; Oct–Mar 10–1 and 2–5

Abbaye St-André
t 04 90 25 55 95; open April–Sept Tues–Sun 10–12.30 and 2–6, Oct–Mar Tues–Sun 10–12 and 2–5

Market Days in Villeneuve lez Avignon

Thurs: Place Charles David.

Sat am: Place Jean Jaurès, Provençal market.

Sat am: flea market.

Where to Stay in Villeneuve lez Avignon

Villeneuve lez Avignon
✉ 30400

Villeneuve makes an attractive alternative to Avignon, and has some fine places to stay.

****Le Prieuré, 7 Place du Chapitre, t 04 90 15 90 15, *www.leprieure.com* (€€€€€–€€€€). An exquisite, central hotel that gives you the option of sleeping in a 14th-century *livrée*, where the rooms are furnished with antiques, or in the more comfortable annexe by the large swimming pool. Further attractions are its gardens, tennis court and splendid restaurant (€€€€–€€€). *Closed Nov–Mar*.

****Hostellerie La Magnaneraie, 37 Rue Camp-de-Bataille, t 04 90 25 11 11, *www.hostellerie-la-magnaneraie.com* (€€€). A Best Western hotel with old-fashioned rooms in a former silkworm nursery, and a modern annexe, plus a swimming pool, gardens and Le Prieuré's rival for the best restaurant in town (€€€€). *Restaurant closed Wed,*

Sat lunch and Sun eve in Nov-April; Sat lunch in summer.

Aux Ecuries des Chartreux, 66 Rue de la République, t 04 90 25 79 93, *www.ecuries-des-chartreux.com* (€€€–€€). Nicely decorated 17th-century B&B with studios next to the Chartreuse.

**L'Atelier, 5 Rue de la Foire, t 04 90 25 01 84, *www.hoteldelatelier.com* (€€). A beautifully restored central 16th-century building with stylishly furnished rooms and a walled garden.

**Les Cèdres, 39 Av Pasteur Bellevue, t 04 90 25 43 92, *www.lescedres-hotel.fr* (€€). A 17th-century building with a swimming pool, restaurant (€€€–€€) and bungalows. *Closed Nov–Mar; restaurant closed Mon lunch except in July.*

Centre International de Séjour YMCA, 7 bis Chemin de la Justice, t 04 90 25 46 20, *www.ymca-avignon.com* (€). A hostel with superb views of the Rhône and a pool.

Eating Out in Villeneuve lez Avignon

Aubertin, 1 Rue de l'Hôpital, t 04 90 25 94 84 (€€€). An intimate, popular restaurant *gastronomique* under the porticoes. *Book ahead. Closed Sun, Mon eve, and last week Aug.*

La Maison, 1 Rue Montée-du-Fort, t 04 90 25 20 81 (€€). A friendly old favourite with traditional Provençal food. *Closed Tues, Wed and Aug.*

ⓘ **Villeneuve lez Avignon** >
1 Place Charles David, t 04 90 25 61 33, www.villeneuvelez avignon.fr/tourisme; open daily all year; in summer there is also a branch office in the main Avignon tourist office (see p.114).

 Le Prieuré >

South of Avignon

La Montagnette

Just south of Avignon and its confluence with the Durance, the Rhône curves to accommodate La Montagnette, a micro-region that is still something of a well-kept secret, near the tourist fleshpots of Provence and yet distant in spirit, self-contained and serene. La Montagnette itself is a striking, 10km-long outcrop of white stone, isolated from its sisters in the Alpilles and surrounded by orchards, a bijou landscape that **Barbentane** fits into like an old shoe. This friendly old town, which so loved its *farandole* that a man who could not dance it was not considered a fit husband, is still defended by the 14th-century **Tour Angelica**, its medieval gates and, near the church, the arcaded Renaissance **Maison des Chevaliers**. Outside the walls, the château was built in 1674, not for defence but for pleasure, by the Marquis de Barbentane, the king's ambassador to Tuscany. It would not look out of place in the Ile de France: the furnishings are Louis XV and Louis XVI, but the builder's Italian tastes permeate the other decoration. The enormous plane trees in the garden were brought over from Turkey by an earlier marquis in the 1670s.

Barbentane Château
t 04 90 95 51 07; open July–Sept daily 10–12 and 2–6; April– June and Oct Mon, Tues and Thurs–Sun 10–12 and 2–6; Nov and 16 Feb–Mar Sun 10–12 and 2–6; closed Dec– 15 Feb; adm

On the D35 south of Barbentane, **Boulbon** was known as Bourbon until 1792, when the guillotine cut into the name's popularity. Still defended by its fairytale 10th-century walls built dramatically into and onto the rocky escarpment overlooking the Rhône, Boulbon is known for its unique 1 June *Cérémonie du St-Vinage*, in honour of its patron saint Marcellin: the men of the village each bring a full bottle of wine to the saint's Romanesque chapel and hear the Gospel in Provençal, after which the wine is blessed and God is toasted with a mighty swig. The bottle is then corked and for the rest of the year the blessed wine is used as a remedy for illnesses.

Abbaye St-Michel-de-Frigolet
t 04 90 95 70 07, www.frigolet.com; open daily 7–12 and 1.30–6; guided tours available for groups by appt, and on Sun at 4pm for individuals; adm; you can also stay here, see p.125

Leaving Barbentane on the D35E will bring you to the **Abbaye St-Michel-de-Frigolet**, founded around 1000. The word *frigolet* comes from the Provençal *férigoulo*, or thyme; this invigorating herb scents the air of La Montagnette. The monks of Montmajour (*see* p.142), enervated by the swamps, would come up here for a *cure* – some of it in the form of a liqueur called *Elixir du Révérend Père Gaucher*, still distilled and on sale here. It may also have an effect on sterility: in 1632, Anne of Austria, barren after 20 years of marriage, prayed in the Romanesque **Chapelle de la Conception Immaculée** for a son, and soon after gave the world Louis XIV. In gratitude, she sent the gilt *boiseries* framing 14 turgid Mignards. Another celebrity to pass through was young Frédéric Mistral, for whom the stories and customs of these hills were to become a powerful source of inspiration.

The Petite Crau

East of Barbentane and La Montagnette, **Châteaurenard** is one of Provence's main wholesale fruit and vegetable markets, a big, bustling place under its plane trees. It lords over the rich, verdant plain of the **Petite Crau**, a large marshland drained by the Romans, planted with market gardens and orchards of cherries and apricots, and protected from the huffing and puffing of the *mistral* by hedgerows and poplars – nothing at all like the rocky waste of the 'big' Crau. Two proud **towers** on Châteaurenard's hill are all that remain of the castle that first belonged to Reinardus, a friend and ally of Charles Martel, who was killed below its walls fighting the

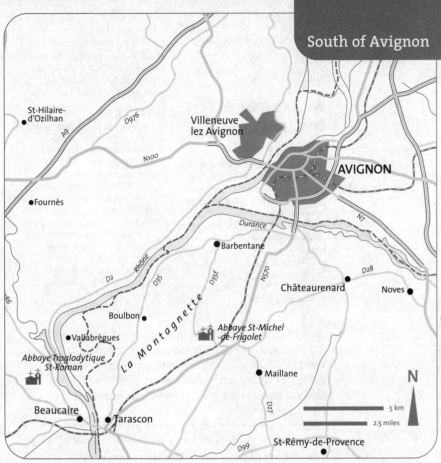

Tour du Griffon
*tours May–Sept Tues–Sat
10–12 and 2.30–6.30, Sun
2.30–6.30; Oct–April
Sat–Thurs 3–5; adm*

**Musée des
Outils Agraires**
*t 04 90 90 11 59; open
May–Sept Tues–Sat
10–12 and 2.30–6.30,
Sun 2.30–6.30; closed
Oct–April; adm*

**Musée Frédéric
Mistral**
*t 04 90 95 74 06; open
April–Sept Tues–Sun
9.30–11.30 and 2.30–
6.30, Oct–Mar Tues–Sun
10–11.30 and 2–4.30; adm*

Saracens; his wife Emma took over the command and fought bravely, keeping the enemy at bay, then died of a broken heart. Her ghost haunts the **Tour du Griffon**, which contains the **Musée des Outils Agraires**. Just east of Châteaurenard, **Noves** claims to have been the home, or summer residence, of Petrarch's Laura: you can see her supposed house.

In 1830, Mistral was born in **Maillane**, southwest of Châteaurenard, and spent as much time as possible there. It's been bypassed by the main routes, leaving a quaint, dusty nowhere with two old-fashioned bars, dogs sleeping in the middle of the streets, and a *tabac* selling keychains sporting Mistral's mug – the only noticeable effort by the locals to cash in on their Nobel Prize slinging hero (he does look like Buffalo Bill).

The house the master Félibre had built after 1876 is now the **Musée Frédéric Mistral** – don't mistake it for the rotting concrete Centre F. Mistral, which is something else. Preserved as it was the

Market Days South of Avignon

Barbentane: Fri am.

Where to Stay and Eat South of Avignon

ⓘ Barbentane ›
*4 Cours J-B Rey,
t 04 90 90 85 86,
www.barbentane.fr;
open summer Mon–Sat;
winter Mon–Fri
and Sat am*

Barbentane ✉ 13570

Hôtel Castel Mouisson, at foot of La Montagnette in Quartier Castel Mouisson, **t 04 90 95 51 17, *www.hotelcastelmouisson.com* (€€–€). A typical Provençal hotel, with a swimming pool and tennis court, and bike hire. *Closed mid-Oct–mid-Mar.*

Le Saint-Jean, 1 Le Cours, **t** 04 90 15 45 22 (€). Decent rooms in the centre and a restaurant (€€) with average fare. *Restaurant closed Wed, plus Xmas and New Year.*

Châteaurenard ✉ 13160

Les Glycines, 14 Av Victor Hugo, **t 04 90 94 10 66 (€). A simple base with an average restaurant (€€). *Restaurant closed Sun eve and Mon.*

Noves ✉ 13550

****Auberge de Noves, 2km northwest of town on D28, **t** 04 90 24 28 28, *www.aubergedenoves.com* (€€€€€–€€€€). A Relais & Châteaux *bastide* converted into one of the most prestigious Provençal hotels with heli-pad and lobster pools in a 15-hectare forest. The air-conditioned rooms have every comfort, and there are tennis courts and a swimming pool in the grounds, and riding and golf nearby. The restaurant (€€€€–€€€) is a gastro-temple. *Restaurant closed Sat lunch, plus Sun eve and Mon in winter.*

day he died in 1914, the house is 'as sympathetic and as cosy as a coffin,' as author James Pope-Hennessy described it. The guide won't let you in until the tour begins, and then his high-speed spiel won't be stopped. If you do interrupt, he'll forget where he is and have to start again. There are no concessions to non-French speakers.

Mistral's tomb, in the ghastly, gravelly graveyard over the road, is modelled after the Pavillon de la Reine Jeanne near Les Baux-de-Provence (*see* p.140), and decorated with a seven-pointed star and other Félibre symbols. If you can, leave Maillane southwards by the D27, and travel over beautiful fields and streams.

Tarascon

Few towns in Provence are as determinedly unglamorous as Tarascon. Most of the houses are not only unrestored but cry out for a lick of paint, and garages outnumber craft shops. Meanwhile, the rival fairytale castles of Tarascon and Beaucaire muse at each other across the Rhône like the embodiments of a bicommunal Walter Mitty daydream, reminders of heroism, romance, international markets, man-eating monsters and Alphonse Daudet's buffoonish anti-hero Tartarin, who never told a lie but, under the hot sun, was prone to imagine things. Provençal nationalists accuse Daudet (a native of Nîmes) of creating a stereotype that only heightened Paris' already smug attitude

Getting to and around Tarascon

By Train

Nearly every east–west train between towns in Provence and Languedoc stops in Tarascon.

By Bus

Société des Transports Départementaux du Gard buses run regularly between Tarascon, Nîmes and Avignon (**t** 04 66 29 27 29); **CTM**, from Tarascon station, go to Arles and Avignon (**t** 04 90 93 74 90).

---

towards the Midi, to which Daudet replied that 'All Frenchmen have in them a touch of Tarascon.'

Tarascon and St Martha

All centuries have quirks that seem quaint to later generations: tulip-bulb speculation in the 18th, ladies' bustles in the 19th, muzak in the 20th. In the 11th and 12th centuries it was a mania for the body parts of saints – a fad so passionate that a sure candidate for the inner circle, such as St Francis, had bodyguards in his dying days to stop rival towns kidnapping him. If it had no fresh relics, every town with a saintly legend linked to it began digging for bones; and in Tarascon, *voilà*, in 1187 they just happened to stumble across the relics of St Martha.

The 9th-century legend told how she found Tarascon bedevilled by the Tarasque, a man-eating amphibian whose ancestors are portrayed in Celtic sculpture chomping on human heads. Martha neatly tidied away the monster by showing it a cross, lassoing it with her girdle, then ordering it to the bottom of the Rhône, never to return. The new-found relics attracted so many pilgrims that the 12th-century **Collégiale Ste-Marthe** was enlarged in the 13th and 16th centuries into a curious Romanesque-Gothic hybrid.

The church was bombed in the Second World War, but worse mischief had been done earlier, in the Revolution, when the great south portal of 1197 was shorn of its sculptures. Nowadays, the chapels of the attractive five-aisled Gothic nave are filled with the lukewarm efforts of Mignard and Parrocel, masters of the Baroque fruitcake style, while in the crypt (part of the original church) there's a king-sized statue of Martha from 1400, and the slightly later *Effigy of Jean de Cossa*, seneschal of Provence, which is attributed to Francesco Laurana.

Château du Roi René

Château du
Roi René
t 04 90 91 01 93;
open April–Aug daily
10–6.30; Sept–Mar
Tues–Sun 10.30–5; adm

Rooted in a limestone rock over the Rhône, Tarascon's château gleams like white satin between the sun and the water. It's a storybook feudal castle with crenellations and a moat, named after the one character in Tarascon's history who was actually rounded out in flesh and blood. The Bon Roi René earned the 'Good' in his name for his good appetite and fondness for the good things of life, as well as for having the good sense not to let troubles or sorrows, of which he had many, get under his skin. He spent the last decade of his life (1471–80) surrounded by poets and artists in Tarascon, in this castle begun in 1401 by his father, Louis II of Anjou. After René's death and Provence's annexation to France, it underwent the usual conversion into a prison.

While the exterior is all business, the interior was designed with the good taste of René in mind – it's flamboyant and elegant, and now eloquently empty except for ten 17th-century tapestries on the *Life of Scipio* and a collection of 18th-century pharmaceutical pots. In the courtyard there are busts of the king and his second wife, Jeanne de Laval; here and there, sculptural titbits and faded ceiling panels offer clues to the original decoration. Graffiti by British sailors imprisoned here between 1754 and 1778 recalls the castle's later use.

Taking in the precipitous views from the top, you can see why no one ever tried to sneak up on it; and why, during the Revolution, Tarascon never needed to invest in a guillotine.

Elsewhere around Town

Perhaps because they haven't been prettified to death as in some Provençal towns, the streets of Tarascon, lined with rose, lemon and ochre houses with geraniums in the windows and laundry flapping in the breeze, make it a delightful place to wander around. The main **Rue des Halles** is still covered by medieval arcades. Halfway up it from the tourist office you'll find the Franciscan **Cloître des Cordeliers** (1450s), now open only for special exhibitions. At the top of Rue des Halles stands the handsome **Hôtel de Ville** (1648) – compare it with Beaucaire's, built 35 years later; the ceilings and original consuls' stalls are still intact.

Near here, at 39 Rue Proudhon, the **Musée Souleiado** is run by Souleiado (Provençal for 'sunray piercing through clouds'), France's leading manufacturer of block-printed textiles. Founded here in 1938 by Charles Deméry in the hopes of reviving a 200-year-old Tarascon industry, the museum holds 40,000 18th-century fruitwood blocks – still the basis for all the company's patterns. Brought back to fashion in the 1950s on such diverse backs as Bardot's and Picasso's, Souleiado's colour-drenched prints can be purchased in the nearby shop, or in the many boutiques in the south of France.

Lastly, there's the so-called **Maison de Tartarin** at 55 bis Boulevard Itam. The modern Tarasconnais say they have forgiven Alphonse Daudet for making them ridiculous, for in the age of Tourist Man he has also made them famous. Daudet claimed that the character

Cloître des Cordeliers
t 04 90 91 38 71

Musée Souleiado
t 04 90 91 50 11; open May–Sept daily 10–6; Oct–April Tues–Sat 10–1 and 2–6; adm

Maison de Tartarin
t 04 90 91 05 08; open July and Aug Mon, Tues and Thurs–Sat 9.30–12 and 2–7; April–June and Sept Mon, Tues, Thurs and Fri 9.30–12 and 2–7; Oct Tues, Thurs and Fri 9–12 and 1.30–7; closed Nov–Mar; adm

of Tartarin was derived from his cousin, a big-game hunter whom he accompanied on a lion hunt in Algeria, but there's another version: in the original story, published as a newspaper serial, Tartarin was named Barbarin after an old Tarasconnais family, the head of which had rejected the author's suit for the hand of his daughter. The family threatened to sue if Daudet used their name in his novel, so he changed it to the fictional Tartarin, then got his own back by making the whole town the butt of his jokes. In the house are mementoes from the three Tartarin novels, and photos from the plays and films. The garden has been planted to fit the book's exotic flora and baobab tree, where Tartarin held court with his tall tales.

Also on display is the famous **Tarasque**, a moustachioed armadillo covered with red spikes. Scholars argue whether the monster is named after the town or vice versa; when King René founded the *Jeux et courses de la Tarasque* in 1474, it was given a thick carapace to hide the men that made it walk, while fireworks blasted dramatically out of its nostrils and the people sang '*Lagadigadèu, la Tarasco, Lagadigadèu! Leisses la passa, La vieio Masco!*' or 'Let her pass, the Tarasque, let her dance.'

Market Days in Tarascon

Tues am: Provençal market, Place de Verdun.
Fri: Mediterranean market, Place du Marché.

Festivals in Tarascon

The *Fête de la Tarasque* lasts for 5 days around St John's Day (24 June), and includes a procession headed by a reconstruction of the Tarasque, bonfires, costumes, bullfights, an opera (the *Mireio*), dances, cavalcades and – yes – someone dressed up as Tartarin.

Where to Stay and Eat in Tarascon

Tarascon ✉ 13150
***Hôtel Les Mazets des Roches**, Route de Fontvieille (D33), t 04 90 91 34 89, *www.mazets-des-roches.com* (€€€–€€). A quiet, comfortable place with modern, air-conditioned rooms in a large park of tall pines, with a restaurant (€€), pool, tennis courts and bike rental. *Closed Nov–Mar; restaurant closed Thurs lunch and Sat lunch.*

***Hôtel de Provence**, 7 Bd Victor Hugo, t 04 90 91 06 43, *www.hotel-provence-tarascon.com* (€€€–€€). A *hôtel particulier* in the centre, with large rooms and a restaurant (€€).

**Le Terminus, Place du Colonel Berrurier, t 04 90 91 18 95 (€). A fairly basic sleeping option, with a buffet restaurant offering 16 starters and 10 main dishes. *Closed Mon lunch in winter.*

Hôtel-Restaurant Saint-Michel, Abbaye St-Michel-de-Frigolet (*see* p.120), t 04 90 90 52 70, *www.frigolet.com* (€). A hotel run by the Prémontré monks, with rooms and a restaurant (€€), offering guaranteed quiet. *Closed 2 weeks Dec, Jan–Feb; restaurant closed Mon and Tues.* There is also a separate retreat, but you will sleep in a cell and must attend services.

Auberge de Jeunesse, 31 Bd Gambetta, t 04 90 91 04 08, *www.fuaj.org/tarascon* (€). A hostel offering inexpensive food and bike hire. *Closed mid-Oct–mid-Mar.*

ⓘ Tarascon >
16 Bd Itam, t 04 90 91 03 52, www.tarascon. org; open June–Sept Mon–Sat and Sun am; Oct–May Mon–Sat

Bistrot des Anges, 20 Place du Marché, t 04 90 91 05 11 (€). A great place for lunch or snacks, with well-priced salads and tarts, in a nicely decorated building located in a lively part of town. Dinner is available at the weekends. *Closed Sun except during festivals.*

Beaucaire

Beaucaire can match Tarascon's stories tit for tat. It, too, was plagued by a river monster, called the **Drac** – a dragon in some versions, or a handsome young man – who liked to stroll invisibly through Beaucaire, before luring his victims into the Rhône by holding a bright jewel just below the surface. When the Drac became a father, he kidnapped a washerwoman to nurse his baby for seven years, during which time the woman learned how to see him when he was invisible. Years later, during one of his prowls through Beaucaire, she saw him and greeted him loudly. He was so mortified that he was never seen again, although like the Tarasque he makes an annual reappearance by proxy, on the first weekend in June.

Beaucaire was also the setting of one of the most charming medieval romances: of **Aucassin**, son of the count of Beaucaire, and his 'sweet sister friend' **Nicolette**, daughter of the king of Carthage, whom Aucassin loved so dizzily that he fell off his horse and dislocated his shoulder, among other adventures.

But in those days Beaucaire was on everyone's lips. It was here, in 1208, that a local squire assassinated Pope Innocent III's legate, who had come to demand stricter measures against the Cathars. It gave Innocent the excuse he needed to launch the **Albigensian Crusade** against Beaucaire's overlords in Toulouse, and all their lands in Languedoc. In 1216, when the war was in full swing, Raymond VII, the son of the count of Toulouse, recaptured the town from its French occupiers, who took refuge in the castle. As soon as word reached Simon de Montfort, he set off in person to succour his stranded men and to teach Beaucaire a lesson, besieging the town walls, while his troops took up the fight from inside the castle, so that Beaucaire was sandwiched in a double attack. The siege lasted 13 weeks before the troops in the castle ran out of food and surrendered and Simon de Montfort had to admit to one of his very few defeats. In gratitude, Raymond VI granted Beaucaire the right to hold a duty-free fair. But five years later the town was gobbled up by France along with the rest of Languedoc.

In 1464, Louis XI restored its freedoms and fair franchise; before long its *Foire de la Ste-Madeleine* became one of the biggest in western Europe. For 10 days in July, merchants from all over the

Mediterranean, Germany and England would wheel and deal in the *pré*, a vast meadow on the banks of the Rhône; by the 18th century, when the fair was at its height, Beaucaire (with a population of 8,000) attracted some 300,000 traders, as well as acrobats, thieves and sweethearts, who came to buy each other rings of spun glass as a symbol of love's fragile beauty. So much money changed hands that Beaucaire earned as much in a week as Marseille did in a year.

The loss of Beaucaire's duty-free privileges just after Napoleon lost at Waterloo put an end to the fair, and since then Beaucaire has had to make do with traffic on the Rhône and Rhône–Sète Canal, its quarries and its wine, ranging from good plonk to the more illustrious AOC Costière du Gard. But in the spring you can try one last legacy of the great fair in Beaucaire: the *pastissoun*, a patty filled with preserved fruits, introduced by merchants from the Levant. Nowadays Beaucaire is slightly down on its luck – roadworks occupy the main streets and driving and walking are not a pleasure.

The Château and Historic Centre

Les Aigles de
Beaucaire
t 04 66 59 26 72,
www.aigles-de-
beaucaire.com; open
mid–end Mar, Sept, Oct
Thurs–Tues 2.30–4.30;
April, May and June
Thurs–Tues 2–4.30; July
and Aug Thurs–Tues
3–5; closed Wed and
Nov–mid-Mar; adm

Louis XI's restoration of Beaucaire's rights paid off for a later Louis (XIII); in 1632, when the **château** was besieged by the troops of the king's rebellious brother, Gaston d'Orléans, the loyal citizens forced them out. To prevent further mishaps, Richelieu ordered Beaucaire's castle razed to the ground. But after the south wall had been demolished, the shell was left to fall into ruins romantic enough for an illustration to *Aucassin et Nicolette*. It's a fitting background to **Les Aigles de Beaucaire**, displays of the falconer's art in Roman costume. There are sweeping views of the Rhône and the old fairgrounds, the Champ de Foire, from the 80ft **Tour Polygonale**.

Musée Municipal
Auguste Jacquet
t 04 66 59 47 61; open
July–Aug Wed–Mon
10–12 and 2–7.15;
April–June Wed–Mon
10–12 and 2.15–6.15;
Sept–Oct Wed–Mon
10–12 and 2–6;
Nov–Mar Wed–Mon
10–12 and 2–5.15; closed
Tues; adm

In the castle gardens below, the **Musée Municipal Auguste Jacquet** has finds from Roman Beaucaire (then clumsily called Ugernum), including a fine statue of Jupiter on his throne, and another of the lusty Priapus found in a villa. There's a geological collection, popular arts, and advertising posters and mementos from the fair, when thousands of brightly coloured cloths swung over the streets, each bearing a merchant's name, his home address and his address in Beaucaire; it was the only way in the vast, polyglot throng to find anyone.

From the château, arrows point the way to the venerable **Place de la République**, shaded by giant plane trees, and the grand, elegant Baroque church of **Notre-Dame-des-Pommiers** (1744), which perhaps more than anything proves how many annual visitors this town once expected. It replaced a much smaller Romanesque

ⓘ **Beaucaire >>**
24 Cours Gambetta,
t 04 66 59 26 57,
www.ot-beaucaire.fr;
open July Mon–Sat and
Sun am; Easter–June
and Aug–Sept Mon–Sat;
Oct–Easter Mon–Fri;
guided tours in English

⭐ **Les**
Doctrinaires >>

Market Days in Beaucaire

Beaucaire: Thurs am and Sun am, Place de la Mairie and Cours Gambetta; Fri eves in July and Aug there's a market along the canal, with local produce, crafts and entertainment.

Where to Stay and Eat in Beaucaire

For a real escape from the hustle and bustle, why not hire a houseboat and make the leisurely loop down the Rhône–Sète canal to the Camargue, west to Aigues-Mortes and up the Languedoc canal past St-Gilles to Beaucaire? To book, you can contact **Connoisseur Cruisers**, 14 Quai de la Paix, **t** 04 66 59 46 08, UK **t** 0870 160 5648, *www.connoisseurafloat.com*.

The tourist office can also provide lists of *chambres d'hôtes*.

Beaucaire ✉ 30300
***Les Doctrinaires, 6 Quai du Général de Gaulle, **t** 04 66 59 23 70, *www.hoteldoctrinaires.com* (€€€). A rather old-fashioned hostelry set in the former home of the Doctrinaire fathers of Avignon before the Revolution. The restaurant (€€€–€€), which in summer is set in the hotel's pretty courtyard, is a very pleasant place in which to have a meal. *Closed Sat lunch, and mid-Dec–mid-Jan.*

***Robinson, 2km north of town on Route de Remoulins (D986), **t** 04 66 59 21 32, *www.hotel-robinson.fr* (€€). Thirty rooms set in acres of countryside, with a swimming pool, tennis court, playground and restaurant (€€). *Closed Feb.*

church but conserves, on its exterior transept wall (facing Rue Charlier), a superb 12th-century frieze depicting Passion scenes in the same strong, lively relief as at St-Gilles (*see* pp.166–8).

The stately French classical **Hôtel de Ville** (1683) situated in Place Georges Clemenceau, was designed by Jacques Cubizol and bestowed on Beaucaire by Louis XIV, who wanted to provide it with a monument worthy of its importance: note Louis' sun symbols on the façade, the town's coat of arms set in the Collar of St Michael (the French equivalent of the Order of the Garter – Beaucaire was the only town in France awarded the honour), and Beaucaire's motto: 'Renowned for its Fair, Illustrious for its Fidelity'.

If it's a holiday, there's likely to be some dramatic bull follies in the **Arènes**: 100 bulls are brought in for the *Estivales*, a week-long re-creation of the medieval market and other celebrations in late July. Beaucaire's *razeteurs* have a reputation as the most daring of them all; statues of Clairon and Goya, the bulls that gave them the best sport, greet visitors respectively by the Rhône bridge and in Place Jean Jaurès.

Le Vieux Mas
t 04 66 59 60 13; open
July–Aug daily 10–7;
April–June and Sept
daily 10–6; Oct–Mar
Wed, Sat, Sun and hols
1.30–6; adm

Around Beaucaire

The outskirts of Beaucaire are home to two attractions. **Le Vieux Mas**, 8km south on the road to Fourques, is a living evocation of a Provençal farmhouse at the turn of the 19th century, complete with a working blacksmith and other artisans to view at their labour, plus farm animals dotted around, and regional products to buy and take home.

Mas Gallo Romain des Tourelles
t 04 66 59 19 72;
www.tourelles.com;
open April–June and Sept–Oct daily 2–6; July and Aug Mon–Sat 10–12 and 2–7, Sun 2–7; Nov–Mar Sat 2–6, other days by appt

The **Mas Gallo Romain des Tourelles**, 4km southwest at 4294 Route de Bellegarde, is more original: since 1983 archaeologists have been working on the 210-acre vineyard of the Château des Tourelles (which has been owned by the Durands for 250 years), excavating a huge 1st-century AD agricultural estate that produced olives, wheat and wine, complete with a vast and efficient pottery factory capable of producing 4,000 amphorae a day.

The current Durand in charge, Hervé, became so fascinated with the digs that, together with the Centre National de la Recherche Scientifique, he has recreated a Gallo-Roman winery – during the harvest you can watch the grapes as they are gathered and pressed in the old Roman way and later see the wine bottled, or rather amphora-ed, in jars ranging in size from 5 to 1,000 litres, wrapped in straw to keep them from breaking in transit. You can taste and buy the result, although there's really no way of knowing how close it comes to the stuff quaffed by Nero and company – the Romans added lime, egg whites, plaster, clay, mushroom ashes and pig blood to 'improve' their wines, and Durand, thankfully, does not.

Beaucaire's Roman incarnation made its living transferring goods (including its wine) along the Roman 'superhighway', the **Via Domitia** that linked Rome to Spain. An 8km stretch of this ancient roadway has come through in remarkably good nick, especially in a place known as **Les Bornes Milliaires** (take the D999 1km northwest past the train tracks, turn left and continue for 800m, following the Enclos d'Argent lane). Nowhere else along the route have the milestones survived so well: these three, on the 13th mile between Nîmes and Ugernum, were erected by Augustus, Tiberius and Antoninus Pius.

Abbaye Troglodytique Saint-Roman de l'Aiguille
t 04 66 59 19 72,
www.abbaye-saint-roman.com; open daily April–June and Sept 10–6; July and Aug 10–6.30; Oct–Mar Sat and Sun 2–5; adm

In the same area, the unique and vaguely spooky **Abbaye Troglodytique Saint-Roman de l'Aiguille**, 4km up the D999, was founded in a cave during the perilous 5th century and was laboriously carved out of the living rock. It was mentioned in the chronicles in 1363, when Pope Urban V made it a *studium*, a school open even to the poorest children; but by 1537 it had lost its importance and was engulfed in the construction of a fortress. When the fortress in turn lost its importance in the 19th century and was destroyed, the abbey was rediscovered: you can see the chapel, with its remarkable abbot's chair; the subterranean cells; the water cisterns and wine press; and 150 rock-cut tombs in the necropolis on the upper terrace, from where the dead monks had better views than the live ones down below.

130

08 Down the Rhône 1: Orange to Beaucaire | South of Avignon: Around Beaucaire

Musée de la Vannerie et de l'Artisanat
t 04 66 59 48 14; open Easter–Oct daily 3–7; Nov–Easter by appt only; adm

Northeast of Beaucaire, **Vallabrègues**, 'the most Provençal town of Languedoc', was cut off from the rest of the Gard when the Rhône changed its bed. Surrounded by clumps of osier, it makes its living from wicker and basketry: learn all about the long-standing local craft in the interesting **Musée de la Vannerie et de l'Artisanat**.

Down the Rhône 2:
The Alpilles, Crau and Camargue

The Rhône that flows so majestically from the Swiss Alps down half of France comes to a rather messy end in the Camargue, dithering indecisively through a delta of swamps, salt pans and sand dunes. And yet if all the chapters of this book had to compete in a talent show, this would be the one to beat. It has wild bulls, horses and pink flamingos; it has the cowboys, Gypsies and fancy dress of the Arlésiennes; it has Roman ruins, the best Romanesque art and the most romantic stories; it has the sharpest mountains, a plain so uncanny that it took a myth to explain it and the mistral-whipped landscapes painted by Van Gogh; and it has the biggest bullring, France's only AOC hay (from Arles) and all the aluminium ore you could ask for.

09

Don't miss

⭐ **The 'Rome of France'**
Arles **p.144**

⭐ **A treasure house of waterfowl and other wildlife**
The Camargue **p.158**

⭐ **The great Gypsy pilgrimage church**
Saintes-Maries-de-la-Mer **p.161**

⭐ **Romanesque sculpture**
Abbey of St-Gilles **p.166**

⭐ **Saint Louis' walled city**
Aigues-Mortes **p.169**

See map overleaf

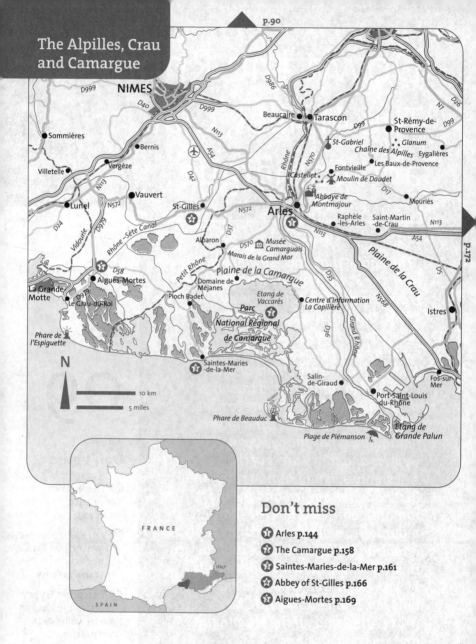

p.90

The Alpilles, Crau and Camargue

p.172

Don't miss

⭐ Arles **p.144**

⭐ The Camargue **p.158**

⭐ Saintes-Maries-de-la-Mer **p.161**

⭐ Abbey of St-Gilles **p.166**

⭐ Aigues-Mortes **p.169**

St-Rémy-de-Provence

Enclosed by a garland of boulevards lined with plane trees, St-Rémy's tranquillity has attracted its share of the famous. Nostradamus was born here, Gertrude Stein spent years here, Charles Gounod stayed here while writing his opera based on Mistral's *Mireille*, and Princess Caroline of Monaco drops in for

Getting to and around St-Rémy-de-Provence

By Bus

Although there are no trains, St-Rémy is surrounded by several big towns, so the bus service is a bit better than in other places. All buses leave from Place de la République. There's at least one a day to Tarascon, more to Avignon. You can walk to Les Antiques and Glanum, but buses from St-Rémy to Les Baux-de-Provence only run July–Aug. Les Baux is better connected to Arles, with 4–5 buses a day, stopping at Tarascon.

By Bicycle

The Alpilles are not too steep for cycling in most places; try **Holiday Bikes**, Av de Fauconnet, t 04 90 92 54 00, www.holiday-bikes.com. You might enjoy a tour around the southern slopes of the Alpilles, looking for the spots where Van Gogh painted many of his landscapes (*inaccessible July–Sept*).

Musée des Alpilles
t 04 90 92 68 24;
open July and Aug
Tues–Sat and 1st Sun of
month 10–12.30 and
2–7; Mar–June and
Sept–Oct Tues–Sat and
1st Sun of month 10–12
and 2–6; Nov–Feb
Tues–Sat and 1st Sun of
month 2–5; closed Sun
and Mon; adm

Musée Archéologique
t 04 90 92 64 04;
closed for renovation

Musée Estrine Centre Présence Van Gogh
t 04 90 92 34 72; open
Mar–Nov Tues–Sun
10–1 and 3–7; closed
Dec–Feb; adm

Florame
t 04 90 92 54 50; open
Easter–mid-Sept daily
10–12.30 and 2.30–7;
mid-Sept–Easter
Mon–Sat 10–12.30
and 2.30–7

Chapelle Notre-Dame-de-Pitié Donation Mario Prassinos
t 04 90 92 35 13; open
July–Aug Wed–Sun 11–1
and 3–7; Mar–June and
Sept–Dec Wed–Sun 2–6;
closed Jan and Feb

discreet visits (St-Rémy used to belong to the family). Vincent Van Gogh spent his tragic last year in St-Rémy's asylum, which was commandeered to hold interned Germans in the First World War – the one who got Van Gogh's room was Albert Schweitzer.

Nowadays, St-Rémy is home to a good many artists, and there are always exhibitions going on. The newest attraction is the bizarre-looking organ in the church of **St-Martin** on Boulevard Marceau. Built in 1983, it is said to be one of the finest in the world; the Organ Festival in August pulls out all the stops, as do the Saturday afternoon concerts in summer (*July–Sept 3pm*).

Older attractions are two fine Renaissance palaces, both around Place Flavier, behind the church one street to the north. The **Hôtel Mistral de Mondragon** (1550) contains the Musée des Alpilles, of local folk life and arts, with a special section on Nostradamus; the **Hôtel de Sade** has a small but interesting Musée Archéologique. St-Rémy is the medieval successor to the abandoned Roman town of Glanum (*see* p.135); finds on display here include architectural fragments, statues and reliefs of deities from Hermes to the Phrygian god Attis, and Roman glass and jewellery.

The Grimaldi representative in St-Rémy lived in the beautiful 18th-century **Hôtel Estrine**, in Rue Estrine, now the Musée Estrine Centre Présence Van Gogh, where you'll find a permanent exhibition of photos and documents, plus a film on Van Gogh's life, as well as changing exhibitions of classic and contemporary art.

Other places to visit in the centre include the perfume museum **Florame** at 34 Bd Mirabeau, with a display of scents, classic bottles and other items dating back 3,000 years; and the 12th-century **Chapelle Notre-Dame-de-Pitié Donation Mario Prassinos**, near the tourist office on Avenue Durand Maillane, containing 11 *Peintures du Supplice* painted for the chapel by Greek painter Mario Prassinos, long-time resident of nearby Eygalières, as well as a video on the artist and displays of some of the 105 works he donated to the government in 1985.

Les Antiques and Van Gogh's Asylum

The Romans had a habit of building monuments and impressive mausoleums on the outskirts of their towns, along the main roads. Just a 15-minute walk from the centre of St-Rémy-de-Provence, to the south on the D5, stand two of the most remarkable Roman relics in France. They were here long before the D5, of course; originally they decorated the end of the Roman road from Arles to Glanum, the ruins of which lie just across the D5. The **Triumphal Arch**, probably built in the reign of Augustus, was one of the first to be erected in Provence. Its elegant form and marble columns show the Greek sensibility of the artists – they are very far different from the strange Celtic-influenced arches of Orange and Carpentras. In the Middle Ages it inspired the creators of St-Trophime in Arles (*see* pp.149–50). Evidently, someone long ago carted off the top for building stone; the slanted tile roof is an 18th-century addition to protect what was actually left.

Next to it, the so-called **Mausoleum** was really a memorial to Caesar and Augustus, erected by their descendants in the early 1st century AD. There is nothing else quite like this anywhere, and it is one of the best-preserved Roman monuments. The form is certainly original: it is a narrow four-faced arch on a solid plinth, surmounted by a cylinder of columns and a pointed roof, 56ft above the ground; inside are statues of Caesar and Augustus. The **reliefs** on the base are excellent: mythological scenes including a battle with Amazons, a battle of Greeks and Trojans and a boar hunt. At the top of the arch, you can make out a pair of winged spirits holding a civic crown of laurel – Augustus' symbol for his new political order.

St-Paul-de-Mausole
t 04 90 92 77 00; open April–Oct daily 9.30–7; Nov–Mar daily 10.15–5.45; adm

Just across the road from Les Antiques, a shady path leads to the monastery of St-Paul-de-Mausole, in a beautiful setting with gardens all around. Founded in the 10th century, the complex includes a simple Romanesque church and a cloister. In 1810 the monastery buildings were purchased for use as a private hospital. This is the place Vincent Van Gogh chose as a refuge from the troubles of life in the outside world, in May 1890, not long after he chopped off the ear. He spent a year here, the most intense and original period of his career, painting as if possessed – 150 canvases and more than 100 drawings, including many of his most famous works, such as the *Nuit étoilée à Saint-Rémy* (*Starry Night*). The bluish mountains in the background of his work are the Alpilles. Appropriately enough, the patients and staff of the hospital have taken a keen interest in art therapy: you can see the results on the walls of the lovely cloister, as well as some interesting carved capitals.

Van Gogh painted the impressive Greco-Roman quarries just down the road, writing that they resembled a Japanese drawing.

Mas de la Pyramide
t 04 90 92 00 81;
open daily 9–12
and 2–5, until 7 in
summer; adm

In the midst of the quarries, excavated out of the rock, the **Mas de la Pyramide** is one of the oldest farmhouses in the region – it dates at least from the 8th century. It contains typical Provençal furnishings and a collection of 19th-century farm tools.

Glanum

Glanum
t 04 90 92 23 79;
open April–Aug daily
10–6.30; Sept–Mar
Tues–Sun 10.30–5; adm

Glanum began as a Celtic settlement – a proper town, really, under a heavy cultural influence from the Greeks at nearby Marseille. The Romans under Marius snatched it around 100 BC, but not until the great prosperity of the Augustan Empire did the city begin to bloom. Almost all of the ruins visible today (as well as Les Antiques) date from this period. In a prelude to the fall of the Empire, the Franks and Alemanni ranged throughout Gaul in the 250s and 260s. In one of their last hurrahs before the recovering Roman legions drove them out, they sacked Glanum in 270. After that, the townspeople relocated to a healthier and safer site, today's St-Rémy; silt washed down from the Alpilles gradually covered the city and it passed out of memory until the 19th century, when some accidental finds alerted archaeologists to its presence. Excavations began in 1921, and have since uncovered a fascinating cross-section of Glanum, including its **forum**. More than Vaison-la-Romaine (*see* pp.254–6) or anywhere else in France, this is the place to really feel at home in the Roman world. But you'll have to work for it; only the foundations remain, and recreating Glanum will require a bit of imagination (if it's reopened, see the museum in the Hôtel de Sade first, *see* p.133).

From the entrance, to the left are the **Maison des Antes** and the **Maison d'Atys**, two typical wealthy homes built around peristyle courtyards. The latter had apparently been transformed into a sanctuary of Cybele and Attis; this cult was one of the most popular of the mystery religions imported from the east in Imperial times. Across the street are remains of a fountain and the *thermae* (baths), with mosaics, a *palaestra* (exercise yard) and a *piscina* (pool). Next door is a building with an exedra that was probably a temple; altars to Silenus were found inside. In this part of the street the sewers have been uncovered. The forum wasn't very impressive, by the standards of most Roman towns, and it is hard to make anything out today from the confusion of buildings from various ages that have been excavated. Beyond it, to the right, are foundations of temples; to the left are the bases of another fountain and a monument. The street closes at a gate from Hellenistic times that was retained as the city expanded outside the original walls. Also retained was the *nymphaeum* beyond it, to the left; these decorated fountains were a common feature of Greek cities, built to allow travellers to refresh and clean up before entering the town.

(i) **St-Rémy-de-Provence >**
Place Jean Jaurès, on the way to Les Antiques, t 04 90 92 05 22, www.saintremy-de-provence.com; open June–Sept Mon–Sat and Sun am; Oct–May Mon–Sat; offers guided tours of Van Gogh's landscapes and the old town

(★) **Château des Alpilles >**

Market Days in St-Rémy-de-Provence

St-Rémy-de-Provence: Wed am.

Where to Stay in St-Rémy-de-Provence

St-Rémy-de-Provence ✉ 13210
St-Rémy gets heaps of tourists and has a wide choice of places to stay; it makes a convenient base for visiting the Alpilles and the Camargue.

****Hostellerie du Vallon de Valrugues, Chemin Canto Cigalo, t 04 90 92 04 40, www.hotelprestige provence.com or www.vallonde valrugues.com (€€€€€). A hotel waiting to spoil you with lovely Provençal-style rooms, a pool, a sauna and Jacuzzi, a putting green, and delicious meals in the palatial restaurant. *Closed Nov–Feb.*

****Hôtel Les Ateliers de l'Image, 36 Bd Victor Hugo, t 04 90 92 51 50, www.hotelphoto.com (€€€€€–€€€€). A photography gallery and workshop-cum-hotel, this place oozes contemporary style in its 24 rooms and 8 suites (one with a treehouse). There are two different kinds of accommodation, Espace Atelier and the more expensive Espace Provence, plus a swimming pool and two eateries, a French-Japanese restaurant, **Le Resto** (€€€), with a terrace with views on to the landscaped garden and beyond to the Alpilles, and **Le Provence** (€€€). *Closed Jan and Feb; restaurant closed lunch and Oct–May.*

****Château des Alpilles, D31, t 04 90 92 03 33, www.chateaudesalpilles.com (€€€€€–€€€€). A real haven outside the busy one-way rush of traffic around the centre, yet just a few steps outside town, in a park full of trees (some of them rare), with a tennis court and a swimming pool. It's all mirrors, period furniture (19th-century) and creature comforts. The restaurant (€€€) is reserved for hotel guests. *Closed Jan–mid-Mar; restaurant closed Wed.*

***Gounod, Place de la République, t 04 90 92 06 14, www.hotel-gounod. com (€€€€–€€€). Recently renovated old staging post full of 19th-century French charm (but modernized with king beds, flatscreen TVs, and other mod cons), where Charles Gounod composed his opera *Mireille* in 1863. Free private parking, tea room, broadband access, pool, and garden are other amenities. No smoking, children or pets. *Closed Xmas and New Year.*

**Villa Glanum, 46 Av Vincent Van Gogh, t 04 90 92 03 59, www villaglanum.com (€€€–€€). A place near the ruins, with surprising amenities for its price range: a pool and garden. *Closed Jan.*

***Le Castelet des Alpilles, 6 Place Mireille, t 04 90 92 07 21, www. castelet-alpilles.com (€€). An old country mansion with pretty rooms and a lovely terrace under a century-old cedar. *Closed Nov–early Mar.*

**Hôtel du Cheval Blanc, 6 Av Fauconnet, t 04 90 92 09 28, (€). A centrally located and therefore noisy hotel, but a good spot if you want to look out on to the *place* when you wake. The owners are cheerful and helpful, and there's a private garage. *Closed Nov–Feb.*

Eating Out in St-Rémy

La Maison Jaune, 15 Rue Carnot, t 04 90 92 56 14 (€€€). For dining in the centre of town, you won't do better than the panoramic terrace here, especially if you plump for the menu of Provençal specialities. *Closed winter Sun eve and Mon, summer Mon, and Tues lunch, plus Jan and Feb.*

Le Bistrot des Alpilles, 15 Boulevard Mirabeau, t 04 90 92 09 17 (€€). Fresh pasta, great desserts and a pleasant terrace. *Closed Xmas.*

Charmeroy, 26 Bd Mirabeau, t 04 32 60 01 23. A *salon de thé* serving genuine madeleines, Provençal-flavoured ice cream and a wide variety of teas. *Open Tues–Sun 10.30–12.30 and 3–7.*

The Chaîne des Alpilles

The ruins were nice, but there is an even greater treat ahead. The five twisting kilometres of the D5 that take you from Les Antiques into the heart of the Alpilles are, in fact, one of the greatest sensual experiences that Provence can offer. Vincent Van Gogh and cypresses, lushness and flowers are left behind; in a matter of minutes the road has brought you to another world. This world, incredibly, is at most 16km across, and a stone's throw away from the swamps of the Camargue and the sea. It is made up of thin, cool breezes and brilliant light; its colours are white and deep green, almost exclusively – in an astringent landscape of limestone crags and patches of scrubby *maquis*.

Les Baux-de-Provence

*A l'asard,
Bauthezar!*
('*Kill 'em at
random,
Balthazar!*')
Battle cry of the
Seigneurs des Baux

From as early as 3000 BC, this exotic *massif* attracted its fair share of residents. The Alpille mountains are full of caves, many of which were once inhabited. The Ligurians took advantage of its natural defences to found an important *oppidum* at Les Baux, a steep, barren plateau located in the centre of the *massif*, 11km from St-Rémy-de-Provence. In the Middle Ages, this made the perfect setting for the most feared and celebrated of Provence's noble clans. The Seigneurs des Baux are first heard of in the 10th century. 'A race of eaglets, vassals never', as their slogan went, they never acknowledged the authority of the French king, the emperors, or anyone else, and their impregnable crag in the Alpilles allowed them to get away with it. They claimed to be descended from Balthazar, one of the magi at Bethlehem, and put the Christmas star on their feudal escutcheon.

The symbol was never a harbinger of glad tidings to their neighbours, however, for over the course of the following two centuries the lords of Baux waged incessant warfare on all comers, and occasionally on each other, gradually becoming a real power in Provence. They did it with flair, however, and the chronicles are full of good stories about them: one *seigneur* once besieged the castle of his pregnant niece and sent sappers to undermine her bed-chamber. And they met memorable ends: one was stabbed to death by his wife, another flayed alive when he fell into the hands of his enemies.

All the while, the family headquarters at Les Baux maintained a polished court where troubadours were always welcome. It ended with a bang in 1372, when an even nastier fellow took over: Raymond de Turenne, a distant relation who was also a nephew of Pope Gregory IX. Taking advantage of confused times in the reign of Queen Jeanne, this ambitious and bloodthirsty intriguer found enough support, and enough foreign mercenaries, to bring full-scale civil war to Provence, bringing it the same kind of misery to which the rest of France had become accustomed in the Hundred Years' War.

When the last heir of Les Baux died in 1426, the possessions of the house were incorporated into the county of Provence. That isn't quite the end of the story; in the 16th century Les Baux began to thrive once more, first under Anne of Montmorency, who rebuilt the *seigneurs'* castle in the best Renaissance taste, and later under the Manvilles, who inherited it and made it a Protestant stronghold in the Wars of Religion. Cardinal Richelieu finally put this eternal trouble spot to rest in 1632, demolishing the castle and sending the owners the bill for the job. Until the Revolution, the remains of Les Baux were, like St-Rémy, in the hands of the Grimaldis of Monaco.

After the demolition, the village that surrounded the castle of Les Baux almost disappeared; Prosper Mérimée, in the 1830s, reported only a few beggars living among its ruins. But Provençal writers kept the place from being forgotten – men such as Mistral (born at Maillane, near St-Rémy; *see* p.121), and Alphonse Daudet, whose famous windmill is just over the Alpilles (*see* p.141). In the last 50 years, Les Baux has become the second-biggest tourist attraction in France after the Mont St-Michel. The village below the castle has been rebuilt and repopulated in the worst way, and whatever spark of glamour survives in this tremendous ruin, you'll have to run the gauntlet of shops peddling trinkets, scowling dolls, herbs, *santons* and soaps to reach it.

The first sight to greet you as you trudge up from the car park is an elegant carved Renaissance fireplace, open to the sky and standing right next to a souvenir shop. Walk a bit further, bearing right, and you will come to the **Musée des Santons** on Place Louis Jou, which you could easily give a miss to. Further up the street, past the ramparts, is the **Porte d'Eyguières**, which until the 18th century was the only entrance to the city.

Up Rue de la Calade you come to Place de l'Eglise, where the 16th-century **Hôtel des Porcelet** has become the **Musée Yves Brayer**. Brayer (1907–90), a respected figurative painter, left his major works here – pictures of Spain and Italy as well as Provence. You can get a preview of his work in the 17th-century **Chapelle des Pénitents Blancs** opposite the museum, where he frescoed scenes of a shepherds' Christmas.

St-Vincent, in the same square, dates from the 12th and 16th centuries. This is probably the coolest and least crowded place in Les Baux; there's a Cistercian nave, and some stained glass by Max

Musée Yves Brayer
t 04 90 54 36 99;
www.yvesbrayer.com;
open daily April–Sept
10–12.30 and 2–6.30,
Oct–Dec and mid-
Feb–Mar 10–12.30 and
2–5.30; closed Jan and
first half Feb; adm

**Chapelle des
Pénitents Blancs**
open same hours
as museum

Ingrand (1955), donated by Prince Rainier of Monaco. The domed turret with gargoyles on the south side is a *Lanterne des Morts*, a rare medieval survival: whenever anyone died in Les Baux, it would be announced by a flame.

Also in the village are the **Hôtel Jean de Brion** and the **Hôtel de Manville**, on the Grand-Rue. The first houses the **Fondation Louis Jou**, containing Jou's engravings, as well as pre-20th-century ones, engravings by Dürer, Rembrandt and Goya, and early books. The second is the Hôtel de Ville. Both these and the Hôtel des Porcelet date from the architectural development of the 16th century, before the castle was destroyed.

Fondation Louis Jou
t 04 90 54 34 17; open for groups of at least 30 by appointment; adm

Next comes the **Citadel**, with a museum to keep tramping tourists from the thing itself. The **Musée d'Histoire des Baux** is perfectly pleasant, with illustrations and archaeological finds as well as models in glass cases, to give you an overview, or to save you the walk over the site outside if the *mistral* is blowing. When you see Les Baux itself, the ambience changes abruptly – it is a rocky chaos surreally decorated with fragments of once-imposing buildings. The path leads through this '*Ville Morte*' (on the left are the remains of the **hospital** and the **Chapelle Saint-Blaise**, where you can watch a slide show on the olive tree) to the tip of the plateau, where there is a monument to Provençal poet Charlon Rieu, and a grand view over the Alpilles. Turning back, the path then climbs up to the château itself, which has bits of towers and walls everywhere, including the apse of a Gothic **chapel** that was carved out of the rock, and the long eastern wall that managed to survive Richelieu's explosives, dotted with a number of finely carved windows. What resembles a monolithic honeycomb is really a 13th-century pigeonry. Medieval siege engines have been

Citadel
t 04 90 54 55 56; open daily summer 9–7.30; spring and autumn 9–6; winter 9–5; adm

Wine: Coteaux des Baux-en-Provence

The AOC wine of the Alpilles is rosé, like most of Provence's vintages, but in recent years the reds of Les Baux have made a quantum leap in terms of quality and have attracted the most attention. This relatively new *appellation* comes under the heading of Coteaux d'Aix-en-Provence, and a majority of its growers are good environmentalists dedicated to growing grapes that are free from artificial fertilizers, pesticides and herbicides; the grapes that go into it include grenache, cabernet sauvignon, syrah, cinsault, carignan and counoise.

A good source is the charming **Domaine de la Vallongue**, in Eygalières, **t** 04 90 95 91 70, which uses traditional methods to create organic wines: fresh, fruity, fragrant rosés and intense reds, hinting at vanilla and spice. **Domaine Hauvette**, in St-Rémy, **t** 04 90 92 03 90, is a tiny estate but one of the very few vineyards in the region that is both owned and run by a woman, Dominique Hauvette, whose wines (which are also organic) have a warm, velvety quality.

In Les Baux itself, at the foot of the cliffs, visitors can take a didactic nature walk through the vines of **Mas Ste-Berthe**, **t** 04 90 54 39 01, and learn all about the grapes, some of which (ugni blanc, sauvignon and grenache blanc) go into the white wine.

reconstructed to add something of the spirit of the gangsters who built the place. The only intact part is the *donjon*. It's a rather treacherous climb to the top for a bird's-eye view over the site. Locals say the best time to see it is at night, with a blanket, under a starry sky.

An Infernal Valley and a Blonde Sorceress

South of Les Baux, on the western side, the **Pavillon de la Reine Jeanne** has nothing to do with the famous queen, but is a pretty Renaissance garden folly of 1581. The road that passes it will take you in another 3km to the **Val d'Enfer**, the wildest corner of the Alpilles, a weird landscape of eroded limestone, caves and quarries. One thing the Alpilles has a lot of is aluminium ore – bauxite – which was a useless mineral until the process for smelting it was discovered in the 19th century. Now there are bauxite mines all over southern Provence; those to be seen here are exhausted, but Jean Cocteau took advantage of the landscape to shoot part of his last film, *Le Testament d'Orphée*, here. Today the quarries host one of Les Baux's big attractions, the **Cathédrale d'Images**, a slick show where 30 projectors bounce giant pictures over the walls; the theme of the show changes annually.

Cathédrale d'Images
*t 04 90 54 38 65;
www.cathedrale-images.com; open Mar
and Oct–Dec 10–6;
April–Sept 10–7;
closed Jan–Feb; last
entry 5.15 or 6.15; adm*

Off the D27A, near the crossroads for Les Baux, the **Col de la Vayède** holds scanty remains of the pre-Roman *oppidum*; the lines of the walls can be traced in some places, and there are bits of wall and no fewer than three necropoli, with small niches carved into the rock to hold the ashes of the deceased. On the side of the hill facing the D27A, you can climb up a dirt path to see the mysterious relief called the **Trémaïe**. Neatly carved on a smoothed rockface are three figures and an effaced Latin inscription. It seems to be a Roman funeral monument, but local legend has it that the figures represent Marius, his wife and a blonde Celtic sorceress named Marthe who helped Marius in his campaigns against the Teutones. Another relief, less well preserved, can be seen a few hundred metres to the south.

Finally, for hikers, there is the **GR6** trail, which traverses the best parts of the Alpilles from east to west. It passes right through Les Baux.

St-Gabriel and Fontvieille

The eastern half of the Alpilles is the more scenic, and, if you're heading in that direction, lonely roads such as the D78 and D24 make worthwhile detours that won't take you more than a few kilometres out of the way; **Eygalières**, on the D24B, is a lovely village with a ruined castle.

Along the western fringes of the Alpilles, on the D33, you will pass the canal port of **Ernaginum**, later called St-Gabriel, which flourished from Roman times until the Middle Ages. You won't see anything; the drying-up of the old canal doomed the city to a slow death, and Ernaginum has disappeared more completely than any ancient city of Provence, leaving only the impressive 12th-century church of **St-Gabriel** standing alone in open fields. There is little to see inside and it's never open anyhow; the real interest is one of the finest Romanesque façades in the Midi. Very consciously imitating Roman architecture, it shows a stately portal with a triangular pediment, flanked by Corinthian columns. There are excellent sculpted reliefs on and above the tympanum: *Daniel in the Lions' Den*, an *Annunciation*, and *Adam and Eve*, apparently just realizing they have no clothes on. Above it, a small Italianate rose window is surrounded by figures of the four Evangelists.

From here, the only village on the way to Arles is **Fontvieille**, best known for the **Moulin de Daudet**, south on the D33, a rare survivor among the hundreds of windmills that once embellished every hilltop of southern Provence. Alphonse Daudet never really lived here, but his *Lettres de mon moulin*, a collection of sentimental tales of the dying life of rural Provence in the late 19th century, is still popular across France today. The windmill has become a museum to Daudet, with photographs and documents. It has a huge car park where coaches like fridges on wheels disgorge cooled tourists, and local driving instructors take their pupils to practise.

Two kilometres further south, there are sections of two Roman **aqueducts** that served Arles, along with vestiges of a **Roman mill**, unique in Europe. This huge installation was a serious precursor to the Industrial Revolution, using the flow of the water to power 16 separate mills along a stretch of canal over a kilometre long; nothing like it has been found anywhere else. There's no tourist tack, not even a railing. Give Daudet a miss and visit this instead.

The Hypogeum of Castellet

On the D17, at the crossroads with the D82, you will find a very ruined castle that once belonged to the counts of Provence. The surrounding area, a low, flat-topped hill called Castellet, contains one of the most unusual and least-known Neolithic monuments in France. The **Hypogeum** consists of four covered avenues, carefully carved out of the rock or earth, under tumuli that have long since disappeared. They were made as collective tombs about 3500 BC or later by the Ligurians or their predecessors, and probably also served as a kind of temple. Many have carvings, cup-marks and sun-symbols, inside or near their openings. The sites are not marked, and you may have to scramble and scout to find their narrow, trapezoïdal entrances in the undergrowth. All are within 400 metres of the D17, three south of the road and one north.

From Castellet you'll see another hill, the **Montagne de Cordes**, located about half a kilometre to the south. Like Castellet, this was an island in Neolithic times. (Nearby Montmajour (*see* below) was a third.) The Cordes is private property and you'll need permission from the owner (in the farmhouse on the slopes) to see another remarkable tomb-temple, the **Grotte des Fées**, also known as the *Epée de Roland*; the tapering 230ft tunnel has two small side chambers that give it the shape of a sword.

Abbaye de Montmajour

Abbaye de Montmajour
*t 04 90 54 64 17;
open May–Aug daily
10–6.30; April and Sept
daily 10–5; Oct–Mar
Tues–Sun 10–5*

Just before Arles, the D17 passes one of the most important monasteries of medieval Provence. Founded in the 10th century, on what was at that time almost an island amidst the swamps, this Benedictine abbey was devoted to reclaiming the land – a monumental labour that would take centuries to complete. By the 14th century the monastery had grown exceedingly wealthy – a real prize for the Avignon popes, who gained control of it and farmed it out, along with its revenues, to friends and relations. Under such absentee abbots, it languished thereafter, and its great church was never completed. An attempt to reform it in 1639 included importing new monks; the old crew refused to go and sacked the abbey before they were chased out by royal troops.

Montmajour became a national property not in the Revolution, but five years earlier. The 1786 'Affair of the Diamond Necklace' was a famous swindle that involved both Marie-Antoinette and the great charlatan Cagliostro. One of the principal players was Montmajour's abbot, the Cardinal de Rohan; he got caught, and all his property, including the abbey, was confiscated. The abbey did service as a farmhouse, and its church as a barn, before restorations began in 1907. Consequently, there isn't a great deal to see.

At the church entrance you'll notice the **piers**, built into the adjacent wall of the cloister, that would have supported the nave had it been completed. The **interior** is austere and empty, but gives a good idea of the state of Provençal architecture *c.* 1200, in transition from Romanesque to Gothic. The most interesting part is the **lower church**, a crypt with an unusual plan, including a long, narrow nave and a circular enclosure under the high altar, with radiating chapels behind it; its purpose remains obscure.

The **cloister** has some fanciful sculptural decoration; see if you can find the camel. Around the back of the church, you'll see a number of **tombs** cut out of the rock; these are a mystery, too, and may predate the abbey. The mighty 85ft *donjon* was built in the 1360s for defence, in that terrible age when the lords of Les Baux and a dozen other hoodlums were tearing up the neighbourhood; next to it, the tiny **chapel of St-Pierre** (usually closed) was the original abbey church, built on the spot where St Trophime (Trophimus) of Arles (*see* pp.149–51) had his hermitage.

Ste-Croix

A few hundred metres behind the apse of the church, in the middle of a farm, stands what was the abbey's funeral chapel, Ste-Croix. Don't miss it, though you have to walk through the farmyard muck (it's visible from the road, near a barn). There are few buildings that demonstrate so convincingly the architectural sophistication of the Romanesque as this small work of the late 11th century, a central-plan chapel with apses along three sides and an elegant lantern on top. Some complex geometry and a mastery of proportions went into this simple but perfect form, based on the Golden Section. Too much decoration would be superfluous; there is only a discreet carved floral frieze along the cornice, along with some Moorish-style interlocking arches.

Market Days in the Chaîne des Alpilles

Fontvieille: Mon and Fri.

Where to Stay and Eat in the Chaîne des Alpilles

Les Baux-de-Provence ✉ 13520

Les Baux, with its tourist hordes, isn't the most desirable place to stop over, and you'll have to pay a lot for the privilege.

****Oustau de Baumanière, Route d'Arles, t 04 90 54 33 07, *www. oustaudebaumaniere.com* (€€€€€). A restored Relais & Châteaux-affiliated farmhouse in magical setting in the Val d'Enfer, with all the amenities that you could hope for, including a highly rated restaurant (two Michelin stars; €€€€) affording spectacular views from its terrace, fabulous desserts and a formidable wine list boasting more than 100,000 bottles of Provençal treasures. *Closed Jan and mid–end Feb; restaurant closed Wed and Thurs lunch in winter.*

****La Cabro d'Or, on D27, t 04 90 54 33 21, *www.lacabrodor.com* (€€€€). A charming Relais & Châteaux hotel offering similar facilities to the Oustau de Baumanière, including a

gourmet restaurant (€€€€–€€€). *Closed Tues lunch, plus Sun eve and Mon in Nov–Mar.*

***Mas de L'Oulivié, on D78F towards Fontvieille, t 04 90 54 35 78, *www. masdeloulivie.com* (€€€). A modern hotel built in the traditional Provençal style among the olive groves and lavender fields. Lunch is served around a landscaped pool. An elegant, comfortable option with attentive service. *Closed Oct–Mar.*

***Le Mas d'Aigret, on D27 (south of Les Baux), t 04 90 54 20 00, *www. masdaigret.com* (€€€–€€€). Great views from some rooms, others opening on to the gardens, and still others (*chambres troglodytes*) hewn from the rock face. There is a swimming pool and a restaurant, and attention is paid to every detail. *Closed Nov and Jan.*

**Hostellerie de la Reine Jeanne, Grand' Rue, t 04 90 54 32 06, *www. la-reinejeanne.com* (€€–€). A basic, relatively cheap option in the village itself, with a bird's-eye view and a restaurant (€€). *Closed last 2 weeks Nov, and Jan.*

Fontvieille ✉ 13990

****Auberge La Régalido, Rue Frédéric Mistral, t 04 90 54 60 22, *www. laregalido.com* (€€€€€–€€€). Luxurious Relais & Châteaux hotel in a restored mill, with lovely gardens and a

---

ⓘ **Les Baux-de-Provence >**
Maison du Roy, t 04 90 54 34 39, www.les bauxdeprovence.com; open daily all year

⭐ **Oustau de Baumanière >**

ⓘ **Fontvieille >>**
5 Av des Moulins, t 04 90 54 67 49, www. fontvieille-provence. com; open mid-June– mid-Sept Mon–Sat and Sun am; mid-Sept–mid- June Mon–Sat

restaurant that is a little temple of *haute cuisine* (with prices to match), serving *agneau des Alpilles* and a special menu dedicated to olives. *Closed Nov–Feb; restaurant closed Mon, and Tues lunch.*

⭐ Le Homard >>

***La Peiriero, 36 Av des Baux (just north of town) **t** 04 90 54 76 10, *www.hotel-peiriero.com* (€€€€–€€). A family-friendly hotel with a large garden, a pool and table tennis. There are family rooms sleeping 4, and an inventive kid's menu. *Closed Nov–Mar.*

***Le Val Majour, Avenue d'Arles, **t** 04 90 54 62 33, *www.valmajour.com* (€€€–€€). A hotel with well-furnished, quiet rooms, plus a swimming pool, a tennis court and Internet access for guests.

Hostellerie de la Tour, 3 Rue des Plumelets, **t 04 90 54 72 21, *www. hotel-delatour.com* (€€–€). Budget Logis de France rooms in bungalows around a pool. *Closed mid-Oct–Mar.*

La Cuisine au Planet, 144 Grand-Rue, **t** 04 90 54 63 97 (€€€–€€). Tuck into excellent Provençal *haute cuisine. Closed 1st week Mar.*

Le Homard, Route du Nord, **t** 04 90 54 75 34 (€€). Appetizing home cooking; there's no lobster, despite the name, but *terrine de poisson, filet de rascasse* (scorpion fish) and *cassoulet* feature on the menus. You can accompany them with local Coteaux des Baux-en-Provence wines (*see* p.139). Make sure to reserve a table in advance. *Closed Nov–Feb.*

Arles

⭐ Arles

Like Nîmes, Arles has enough intact antiquities to call itself the 'Rome of France'; unlike Nîmes, it lingered in the post-Roman limelight for another thousand years, producing enough saints for every month on the calendar – Trophimus, Hilarius, Césaire and Genès are some of the more famous. Pilgrims flocked here for a whiff of their odour of sanctity, and asked on their deathbeds to be buried in the holy ground of the Alyscamps (*see* p.153). Nowadays, Arles is the largest *commune* in France; it's ten times larger than Paris, embracing 750 square km of the Camargue and Crau plains; it has given the world the rhythms of the Gypsy Kings and the pungent joys of *saucisson d'Arles*, France's finest donkey sausage.

Henry James wrote: 'As a city Arles quite misses its effect in every way: and if it is a charming place, as I think it is, I can hardly tell the reason why.' Modern Arles is charming, in spite of a scruffiness that seems more intentional than natural. For all the tourists, no town could seem less touristy; a paper mill across the Rhône wafts its stink over the down-at-heel old quarters, while grass grows between the pavement cracks around the Roman ruins and medieval palaces. Unhappily, Jeanne Calment, born here in 1876, who met Van Gogh as a young girl and was for a long while the oldest person in the world, died in 1997. The city's pride in her longevity continues, though, and the way to her grave is clearly marked in the cemetery at Trinquetaille.

History

In 1975 the remains of a Celto-Ligurian settlement were uncovered close to the Boulevard des Lices. It's hard to imagine

Getting to and around Arles

By Train

The **train station** on Av Paulin Talabot has connections to Paris, Marseille, Montpellier, Nîmes, Aix-en-Provence, and towns in Spain. There are also services to Avignon and Tarascon, and to Orange.

By Bus

The *gare routière* is just across the street from the train station, t 04 90 49 38 01. There are several daily buses to Albaron and Saintes-Maries-de-la-Mer in the Camargue, as well as daily buses to Salon-de-Provence, Aix, Marseille, Avignon, Nîmes, among other destinations; in July and Aug there are services to Aigues-Mortes; and there is a limited service to Tarascon and St-Gilles.

(Before you hurry into Arles from here, step over the road for a minute to the bank of the Rhône and admire the city on the bend of the river – an unlikely spot for an unparalleled view.)

By Taxi

For a taxi day or night, call t 04 90 96 90 03/07 94 (Jardin d'Eté, Bd des Lices), or t 04 90 96 09 00 (Av Paulin Talabot).

Car Hire

Europcar, t 04 90 93 23 24, and **Hertz**, t 04 90 96 75 23, can both be found on Av Victor Hugo.

Bike Hire

Hire a bike at the train station, or at **Dall'Oppio Hugues**, Rue Portagnel, t 04 90 96 46 83 (*Mar–Oct*).

what its builders thought in the 6th century BC, when Greek traders from Marseille arrived and began to haggle over prices. We know at least that the Greeks were pleased, and over the years they established the site as their principal 'counter' for dealings with the Ligurians, calling it Arelate (meaning 'near sleeping waters' or, less poetically, 'bog town').

Business picked up considerably after Marius' legionaries transformed Arelate into a seaport by digging a canal to Fos (104 BC). In 49 BC the populace, tired of getting bum deals from the wily Greeks, readily gave Caesar the boats he needed to punish and conquer Marseille for siding with Pompey. In return, Arles was rewarded with the spoils and received a population boost with a colony of veterans from the Sixth Legion. Most important of all, it got all the business that had previously gone through Greek Marseille. A bridge of boats was constructed over the Rhône, and the Colonia Julia Paterna Arelate Sextanorum became known far and wide for its powerful maritime corporations, called *utriculares* from their rafts that floated on inflated bladders.

Fortuitously situated at the crossroads of Rome's trading route between Italy and Spain and the Rhône, Arles increased rapidly in size, with each new century adding more splendid monuments – a theatre, several temples, a circus, an amphitheatre, at least two triumphal arches, and a basilica. Constantine had himself a grand palace built, together with baths that were as big as Caracalla's in Rome. In AD 395, Emperor Honorius made it the capital of the 'Three Gauls' – France, Britain and Spain – and as late as 418 it was

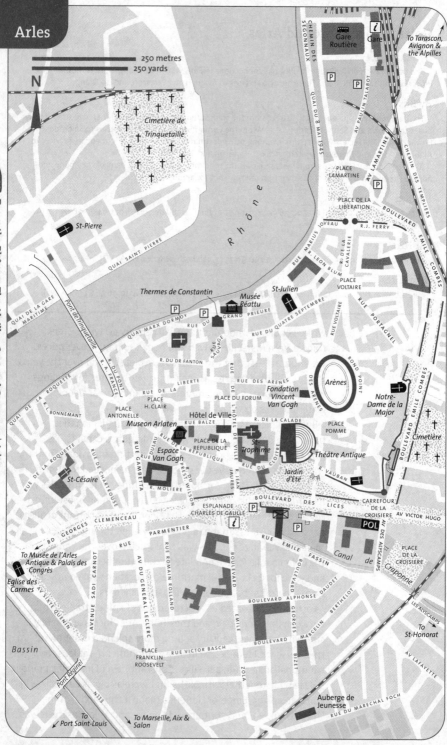

250 metres
250 yards

N

Cimetière de
Trinquetaille

Rhône

Gare
Routière

Gare

i

To Tarascon,
Avignon &
the Alpilles

CHEMIN DES SÉGONNAUX

QUAI DU 8 MAI 1945

AV PAULIN TALABOT

AV LAMARTINE

CHEMIN DES TEMPLIERS

P

P

P

PLACE
LAMARTINE

PLACE DE LA
LIBERATION

BOULEVARD

EMILE COMBES

R.J. FERRY

St-Pierre

QUAI SAINT PIERRE

RUE MARIUS JOUVEAU

RUE DE LA
CAVALERIE

PLACE
VOLTAIRE

RUE PORTAGNEL

Thermes de Constantin

Musée
Réattu

St-Julien

RUE R. LEON BLUM

RUE VOLTAIRE

Quai de la Gare
Maritime

Pont de Trinquetaille

R. DU PONT

QUAI MARX DORMOY

RUE DU
GRAND PRIEURE

RUE
SAUVAGE

RUE DU QUATRE SEPTEMBRE

ROND
POINT

Notre-
Dame de la
Major

R. DU DR FANTON

RUE DE LA
LIBERTE

RUE DES ARENES

RUE
DES
ARENES

Arènes

BOULEVARD EMILE COMBES

R. DU PONT

R. A. FRANCE

Quai de la Roquette

R. L. BONNEMANT

PLACE
ANTONELLE

RUE DE LA ROQUETTE

RUE DE CHARTROUSE

RUE GAMBETTA

PLACE
H. CLAIR

Museon Arlaten

Espace
Van Gogh

R. MOLIERE

RUE DE
LA REPUBLIQUE

RUE DE
L'HOTEL DE VILLE

PLACE DU FORUM

Fondation
Vincent Van Gogh

Hôtel de Ville

RUE BALZE

PLACE DE
LA REPUBLIQUE

St-
Trophime

R. DE LA CALADE

R. DU CLOITRE

R. JEAN
JAURES

Théâtre Antique

Jardin
d'Eté

PLACE
POMME

Cimetière

St-Césaire

R. DU PRESIDENT WILSON

BD GEORGES

CLEMENCEAU

AV SIXTE QUENIN

AV SADI CARNOT

RUE

PARMENTIER

AV DU GENERAL LECLERC

RUE ROMAIN ROLLAND

ESPLANADE
CHARLES DE GAULLE

i

BOULEVARD DES LICES

P

P

R. VAUBAN

CARREFOUR
DE LA
CROISIERE

AV VICTOR HUGO

POL

AV DES ALYSCAMPS

PLACE DE LA
CROISIERE

Craponne

LES ALYSCAMPS

To
St-Honorat

To Musée de l'Arles
Antique & Palais des
Congrès

Eglise des
Carmes

Bassin

Pont Réginel

N113

To
Port Saint-Louis

BOULEVARD

BOULEVARD

EMILE

RUE EMILE FASSIN

BOULEVARD ALPHONSE DAUDET

BOULEVARD

GEORGES

MARCELIN BERTHELOT

BIZET

Canal de

PLACE
FRANKLIN
ROOSEVELT

RUE VICTOR BASCH

ZOLA

Auberge de
Jeunesse

RUE DU MARECHAL FOCH

AV LAFAYETTE

To Marseille, Aix &
Salon

recorded that 'Arles is so fortunately placed, its commerce is so active and merchants come in such numbers that all the products of the universe are channelled there: the riches of the Orient, perfumes of Arabia, delicacies of Assyria...'

Arles was one of the last cities to fall to the Visigoths, only to become their capital in 476. The Franks inherited it in 536, and Saracen raids were frequent. But on the whole the Dark Ages were not so dark in Arles; from 879 to 1036 it served as the capital of Provence-Burgundy (the so-called 'Kingdom of Arles'), a vast territory that stretched all the way to Lorraine. Most importantly, Arles was a centre of power for Christianity. Several major Church councils convened here, including one back in 314 that condemned the heresy of Donatism (the quite reasonable belief that sacraments administered by bad priests had no value). Arles' cathedral of St-Trophime became the most important church in Provence; in 597 its bishop, St Virgil, consecrated St Augustine as first Bishop of Canterbury, and, as late as 1178, Emperor Frederick Barbarossa was crowned King of Arles at its altar.

After a busy career during the 11th and 12th centuries as a Crusader port and a pilgrimage destination, the city's special history ended in 1239 when Raymond Bérenger, count of Provence, evicted Arles' imperial viceroy. As the city declined, even the sea abandoned it, leaving the former port stranded between marshes and the rocky plain of the Crau, compressed in a time capsule of Roman monuments and ancient customs.

With the improved communications of the 19th century, Arles slowly resurfaced. The Roman amphitheatre was restored. The city's women, celebrated for their beautiful Attic features, inspired Daudet's story *L'Arlésienne* (1866) and Bizet's opera (1872). Its furniture-makers invented what has become the traditional south Provençal style, more elegantly rococo than the heavy pieces of northern Provence. The Félibres made much of the city for the striking costumes the women continued to wear, for its bullfights and for its *farandole*, a dance in 6/8 time dating back at least to the Middle Ages and perhaps to the ancient Greeks.

The Arles of Van Gogh

Vincent Van Gogh was a fervent admirer of Daudet, and it may well have been his stories that first brought him to Arles in February 1888. To his surprise, the city was blanketed with snow – a very rare occurrence and, in a way, an omen. When the snow melted it revealed an Arles made mean and ugly by new embankments along the Rhône, cutting the city off from its lifeblood (previously the flooding of the river had fertilized the countryside like the Nile in Egypt). At the same time, a new railway line was being installed by workers brought in from Belgium and housed in cheap buildings. Arles had never looked shabbier. But Van Gogh stayed, found a room to rent in a poor neighbourhood by the station, and painted the shabby Arles around him – the *Café de nuit* with its hallucinogenic lightbulb, *La Maison jaune* and *Le Pont de Langlois* (part of a ghastly irrigation project) – with colours so intense in their chromatic contrasts that they seem to come from somewhere over the rainbow.

Van Gogh's dream was to found an art colony in Arles, similar to the one in Pont Aven in Brittany. He begged his overbearing friend Gauguin to join him, but when Gauguin finally arrived in October he found little to like in Arles, dashing Van Gogh's hopes. The tension between the two reached such a pitch in December that the overwrought Van Gogh went over the edge and confronted Gauguin with a razor. Gauguin stared him down and Van Gogh, despising himself, went back to his room, cut off his own ear and gave it to a prostitute. Arles was scandalized, and breathed a sigh of relief when Van Gogh committed himself to the local hospital, the Hôtel Dieu.

In May 1889 he left for the hospital in St-Rémy (*see* p.134). Van Gogh's output in Arles was prodigious (from February 1888 to May 1889 he painted 300 canvases), but not a single painting remains in the city. His admirers, looking for the places he painted, have just as little to see: the famous bridge, yellow house and café were destroyed in the Second World War or after; only the clock in Café de l'Alcazar in Place Lamartine remains as Van Gogh painted it (in *Café de nuit*), along with some of the plane trees around the Alyscamps. To make up for its belated appreciation of the mad, lonely genius who sojourned here, Arles has converted the Hôtel Dieu into a multimedia gallery, the **Espace Van Gogh** on Rue Molière, which displays work by other artists and also contains the town's library; it's worth a look inside at the lovely, colourful courtyard, restored to look as it did when Van Gogh painted it. Here, as elsewhere around Arles, the town has put up reproductions of his works. The **Fondation Vincent Van Gogh** at 24 bis Rond-Point des Arènes exhibits work inspired by Van Gogh.

Espace Van Gogh
t 04 90 52 05 50; call for opening times

Fondation Vincent Van Gogh
t 04 90 49 94 04; www.fondationvan gogh-arles.org; open July–Sept daily 10–7; April–June daily 10–6; Oct–Mar Tues–Sun 11–5

The Arènes and Théâtre Antique

Despite the pictures in children's history books, Rome was ruined not so much by tribes of horrid Vandals, but by the latter-day Romans themselves, who regarded the baths, theatres and temples they inherited as their private stone quarries. The same holds true of Arles' great monuments, except for the amphitheatre, the **Arènes**, all of 10ft wider than its rival in Nîmes. As enormous as it is, the amphitheatre originally stood another arcade higher and was clad in marble; as with most public buildings in the Roman Empire, no expense was spared on its comforts. A huge awning

Arènes
t 04 90 96 03 70, www.arenes-arles.com; open May–Sept daily 9–6.30; Nov–Feb daily 10–7; Mar–April and Oct daily 9–6

operated by sailors protected the audience from the sun and rain, and fountains scented with lavender and burning saffron helped cover up the stink of blood spilled by the gladiators and wild animals below. This temple of death survived in good repair because it came in handy. Its walls were tricked out with towers by Saracen occupiers and used as a fortress (like the theatres of Rome), and from the Middle Ages on it sheltered a poor, crime-ridden neighbourhood with two churches and 200 houses, built from stones prised off the amphitheatre's third storey. These were cleared away in 1825, leaving the amphitheatre free for bullfights and still able to pack in 12,000 spectators. The first was held in 1830, to celebrate the capture of Algiers.

Théâtre Antique
http://pagesperso-orange.fr/artgp/theatre arles/index.html; open May–Sept daily 9–6.30; Nov–Feb daily 10–12 and 2–5; Mar–April and Oct daily 9–12 and 2–6

A different fate was in store for the **Théâtre Antique**, just south of the Arènes: in the 5th century, in a fury usually reserved for pagan temples, Christian fanatics pulled it apart stone by stone. A shame, because the fragments of fine sculpture they left in the rubble suggest that the theatre, once capable of seating 12,000, was much more lavish than the one in Orange. Of the stage, only two tall Corinthian columns survived; they were nicknamed 'the two widows', after being pressed into service as gibbets in the 17th and 18th centuries. The most famous statue of Roman Provence, the *Venus of Arles*, lay buried at their feet until she was dug up in 1651 and presented to Louis XIV to adorn the gardens of Versailles. Tiers of seats have been rebuilt for modern performances and costume pageants.

South of the theatre runs the **Boulevard des Lices** ('of the lists'), where large cafés under the plane trees provide ringside seats for the rollicking markets. Since the 17th century, the boulevard, where visitors such as Van Gogh would go on Sunday to see the women dressed in their best costumes, has been the favourite promenade of Arlésiens. On either side of the street are the **Jardin d'Eté** (with a bust of Van Gogh) and **Jardin d'Hiver** (where the 5th-century BC *oppidum* was uncovered).

Place de la République: St-Trophime

From Boulevard des Lices, Rue Jean Jaurès (the Roman *cardo*) leads to the harmonious **Place de la République**, an attractive square on the Roman model, with a fountain built around a granite obelisk that once stood in the *spina* (or barrier) of the circus. Overlooking this pagan sun needle is one of the glories of Provençal Romanesque, the cathedral of **St-Trophime**. The original church, constructed by St Hilaire in the 5th century and dedicated to St Stephen, was rebuilt at the end of the 11th century, with the great **portal** added in the next – it is one of the best-preserved ensembles of Romanesque sculpture in the Midi. Inspired by the triumphal arches of Glanum and Orange, its reliefs describe the

Last Judgement, mixing the versions of the *Apocalypse* and *Gospel of Matthew*. As angels blast away on their trumpets, the triumphant Christ sits in majesty in the tympanum, accompanied by the symbols of the four Evangelists, the 12 Apostles, and a gospel choir of 18 pairs of angels. On the left side, St Michael weighs each soul, separating the good from the evil for their just deserts in the afterlife – the fortunate in their long robes are delivered into the bosoms of Abraham, Isaac and Jacob, while the damned, naked and bound like a chain gang, are led off in a conga-line to hell: as in all great Romanesque art, the figures on this portal seem to dance to an inner, cosmic rhythm.

The large saints set back in the columned recesses below are, from left to right: Bartholomew, James the Minor, Trophime as bishop, John the Evangelist, Peter (over the man-eating lions), Paul, Andrew, Stephen (being stoned), James the Major and Philip. Van Gogh found it admirable but 'so cruel, so monstrous, like a Chinese nightmare, that even this beautiful example of so good a style seems to me to belong to another world and I am glad not to belong to it...'

After the sumptuous portal, the spartan nudity of the long, narrow nave is as striking as its unusual height. Aubusson tapestries dating from the 17th century hang across the top, and there are several palaeo-Christian sarcophagi along the sides. The best decoration here, however, is by a Dutchman by the name of Finsonius, who came down to Arles in 1610. Like Van Gogh, he stayed, mesmerized by the light and the colour, and he similarly met a bad end, drowning in the icy Rhône in 1642. St-Trophime contains three of his paintings: in the crossing, a beautiful *Annunciation* dating from 1610, the *Stoning of St Stephen* over the triumphal arch in the nave and, on the right, a singular *Adoration of the Magi*, with nightmare architecture and animals in attendance.

The Cloister

Cloister
t 04 90 49 33 53;
open May–Sept daily 9–6.30; Mar–April and Oct daily 9–6; Nov–Feb daily 10–5; come around midday to see the sculptures at their best

Around the corner in Rue du Cloître is the entrance to St-Trophime's cloister. No other cloister in Provence is as richly and harmoniously sculpted as this one, which was carved in the 12th and 14th centuries by the masters of St-Gilles. Because Arles was as anti-Revolutionary as a town could be, this masterpiece was spared the wanton vandalism that destroyed so much elsewhere.

The north gallery is the oldest, supported by two monumental pillars adorned with statues; *St Peter* and *St Trophime* on the northwest are masterpieces of the classically influenced Arles school – even the foliage in the borders has a certain Corinthian air. The capitals in the Romanesque north and east galleries are carved with scenes from the New Testament, their figures moving to the

same wonderful rhythms as those on the portal. The capitals of
the more severe Gothic gallery to the south are elaborately carved
with the life of St Trophime, while on the west the capitals closely
resemble the south gallery of Montmajour's cloister (*see* p.142):
note the Magdalene kissing Christ's feet and St Martha with
the Tarasque.

Hôtel de Ville and the Cryptoportiques

Sharing Place de la République with the cathedral of St-Trophime
is Arles' palatial **Hôtel de Ville**, built in 1675 after plans by Hardouin-
Mansart, architect of the Hall of Mirrors at Versailles; here, his
virtuoso signature is in the remarkable flat vaulting of the
vestibule. Facing the inner courtyard are remnants of older civic
buildings: sections of the 12th–15th-century palace of the *podestats*
(or prefects of the Holy Roman Emperor), and the town hall of 1500,
with a Roman tympanum and bell-tower modelled after the
mausoleum of Glanum.

Cryptoportiques
*open May–Sept daily
9–12 and 2–6.30; Oct
daily 9–12 and 2–6;
Nov–Feb daily 10–12
and 2–5; Mar–April
daily 9–12.30 and 2–6*

Just around the corner on Rue Balze is the *cryptoporticus* of the
forum, the **Cryptoportiques**, entered through the Hôtel de Ville.
With the ramparts, this *cryptoporticus* was the first large
construction of the Roman colony. Forming three sides of a
rectangle 289 by 192ft, these subterreanean barrel-vaulted double
galleries of the 1st century BC were built as foundations for the
monumental forum above. You can see a model of the forum's
original appearance in the Musée de l'Arles et de la Provence
Antiques; like the Imperial Fora in Rome, this one was built all at
once, as a unified architectural grouping, consisting of a rectangle
of colonnades for public business and a temple in the centre. No
one knows for sure what other purpose a *cryptoporticus* may have
served – for storage, or perhaps, as on Rome's Palatine Hill, for cool
promenades. During the last war the galleries came in handy as an
air-raid shelter.

Museon Arlaten

Museon Arlaten
*t 04 90 93 58 11; open
June–Aug daily
9.30–12.30 and 2–6;
April–May and Sept
daily 9.30–12 and
2–5.30; Oct–Mar
daily 9.30–12.30
and 2–5; adm*

The indefatigable Frédéric Mistral (*see* pp.41–2) began his
collection of ethnographic items from Provence in 1896; in 1904,
when he won the Nobel Prize, he used the money to purchase the
16th-century **Hôtel de Castellane-Laval** at 29 Rue de la République
to house his Museon Arlaten. Mistral's aim was to record the
details of Provençal life for future generations. The evolution of
the traditional Arlésienne costume is thoroughly documented,
including the adjustments made to match fashion changes in
Paris. The wearing of it declined along with the use of the
Provençal language, in spite of the poet's folklore parades (the
'Festivals of Virgins') and his pronouncements that the costume,
'in the shadowy transition of the centuries, lets us see a lightning

flash of beauty!' Nowadays, the female museum attendants here are the last people to wear the traditional costume, as they sit crocheting by the windows and gossiping (not in Provençal, but French). Most memorable and strange are the life-size dioramas: a Christmas dinner at a *mas*, with a table groaning with wax food; a reed-thatched *cabane des gardians*; and a visit to a new mother and her infant. The curious gifts of salt, a match, an egg and bread brought by the visitors symbolize the hope that the baby may grow to be wise, straight, full and good. The gallery of rituals has a prickly Tarasque retired from the procession at Tarascon, and a lock of golden hair discovered in a medieval tomb at Les Baux-de-Provence. One room is dedicated to the Félibrige, and another to Mistral himself, with the great man's cradle under glass. In the courtyard, a section of the forum was uncovered, complete with an exedra cut with 10 niches for statues.

To the north of Museon Arlaten, the café-filled **Place du Forum** is the centre of modern life in Arles, watched over helplessly by a statue of Mistral, moustachioed and goateed like his near-double, Buffalo Bill. Mistral himself attended its unveiling in 1909, thanking his admirers, but regretting that they made him look as if he were waiting for a train.

The Thermes de Constantin and Musée Réattu

Thermes de Constantin
t 04 90 49 36 36; open May–Sept daily 9–12 and 2–6.30; Mar–April daily 9–12.30 and 2–6; Oct daily 9–12 and 2–6; Nov–Feb daily 10–12 and 2–5; adm

Musée Réattu
t 04 90 49 37 58; open July–Aug Fri only, 3–10.30; 1–15 Sept Sat–Thurs 10–7, Fri 10–10.30; Mar–June and 16 Sept–Oct daily 10–12.30 and 2–6.30; Nov–Feb daily 1–5; adm

From Place de la République, Rue de l'Hôtel de Ville leads north to the ruins of Constantine's palace, of which only part of the baths, or **Thermes de Constantin**, remain. Across the street stood the priory of the Knights of Malta, built in the 14th century. The knights, who came from all over Europe, were divided into eight *langues* (tongues), and this was the local HQ of the *langue de Provence*; the façade with gargoyles facing the river gives the best idea of its original appearance. After the Revolution, an academic painter named Jacques Réattu purchased the priory and his daughter made it into the **Musée Réattu**. Besides Réattu's own contributions, there are works by Théodore Rousseau, followers of Lorrain and Salvator Rosa, and one painting so marvellously, indescribably awful that it deserves a museum to itself: Antoine Raspail's portrait of himself and his family.

In 1972 the museum was jolted awake with a donation of 57 drawings from Picasso, in gratitude for the many bullfights he enjoyed in Arles. Nearly all date from January 1971 and constitute a running dialogue the artist held with himself on some of his favourite subjects – harlequins, men, women, the artist and his model – and, more unusually, the Tarasque. Other Picassos in the museum include a beautiful portrait of his mother, Maria, from the 1920s, and a sculpture of a woman with a violin. There are more recent works by César (a compacted motorbike) and Pol Bury (the bizarre *Monument horizontal no.3*, with 12,000 steel balls demonically clicking away on a table).

The Alyscamps

Alyscamps
*open May–Sept daily
9–6.30; Mar–April
and Oct daily 9–12
and 2–6; Nov–Feb daily
10–12 and 2–5; adm*

This is a 10-minute walk from the centre; follow Rue Emile Fassin, the first street south of Bd des Lices, eastwards.

One of the most prestigious necropoli of the Middle Ages, the Alyscamps owed its fame to the legend of St Trophime, a cousin of the proto-martyr St Stephen who became a disciple of St Paul. Paul sent Trophime to convert Gaul, and medieval hagiographers later confused him with a 2nd- or 3rd-century bishop of Arles of the same name. The story has it that Trophime arrived in Arles in the year AD 46 and held secret meetings with his new converts in the lonesome Roman cemetery of Alyscamps (believed to be a corruption of *Elisii Campi*, or Elysian Fields), which according to Roman custom was built outside the city walls, along the Via Aurelia. Trophime eventually attracted quite a following, and before he died he gave a special blessing to the Alyscamps; Christ himself attended the ceremony and left behind a stone imprint of his knee.

Burial in such holy ground was so desirable that bodies sealed in barrels with their burial fee attached were floated down the Rhône to Arles. Some rascals in Beaucaire took to robbing the dead of their coins as they floated downstream, but they were found out when the barrels miraculously returned upstream to the scene of the crime. At its greatest extent, the necropolis stretched for more than 2km and contained 19 chapels and several thousand tombs, many of them packed five bodies deep. Dante mentions it in the *Divine Comedy* (IX, 112), and it makes an appearance in numerous *chansons de geste*. Ariosto wrote how Charlemagne's peers, cut down at Roncesvalles, were flown here and buried by angels.

The Alyscamps' mystique began to decline in 1152, when the relics of St Trophime were transferred to the cathedral. Grave-robbers pillaged the tombs and the most beautiful sarcophagi were given away as presents to Renaissance potentates. Under Louis-Napoléon, the Alyscamps itself was dismembered by a railroad, a canal, factories and a housing estate, leaving only one romantic, melancholy lane lined with empty, mostly plain sarcophagi. Little holes of mysterious purpose are carved into the stone of many of them, similar to holes in other tombs from the megalithic era; they may have held tiny oil lamps. Of the 19 chapels, all that remains is a 15th-century chapel that now serves as the ticket booth, along with the restored Romanesque **St-Honorat** at the far end. Its two-storey octagonal tower still stands, rebuilt in the 12th century by the monks of St-Victor in Marseille; in the apse you can see three Carolingian sarcophagi.

Musée de l'Arles et de la Provence Antiques

Musée de l'Arles
et de la Provence
Antiques
t 04 90 18 88 88;
open April–Oct daily
9–7; Nov–Mar daily
10–5; adm

Arles' newest museum is in an eerie wasteland slightly out of town, opposite the Palais des Congrès (follow Boulevard des Lices to its western end, and pass under the motorway; the official address is Presqu'Ile du Cirque Romain, Av de la 1re D. F.L.).

In front of the museum you'll see foundations of the curve of Arles' Roman circus. The shiny modern building houses the contents of several of Arles' old museums. Though the ancient works themselves are not especially noteworthy, the detailed explanations (in French) and especially the brilliant architectural models bring the Roman city back to life in a way that few museums anywhere can match. Here you'll see how the Roman sailors wired up the sailcloth awning to shade the amphitheatre; how the city centre – the forum and temples – looked to the man in the street; how the army engineers made the floating bridge over the Rhône, and much more.

Among the exhibits are the pagan statues and sarcophagi that graced the former Musée d'Art Païen. Nearly everything was made in the Arles region, with the exception of the lovely white marble Hippolytus and Phaedra sarcophagus (2nd- or 3rd-century AD), with its hunting scenes. Two exceptional mosaics brought in from nearby Roman villas show the rape of Europa and Orpheus enchanting the wild beasts; there's a graceful but damaged dancing girl, and a headless statue of Mithras, the god of the legionnaires, his torso decorated with signs of the zodiac entwined by a serpent. The large statue of Augustus was found in the theatre, as was the *Venus of Arles*, represented here by a copy made before Louis XIV had it 'restored'. Although a fairly chaste specimen as marble love goddesses go, she earned from Théodore Aubanel the most ham-fistedly erotic of all Félibre poems:

Laisso ti pèd toumba la raubo qu'à tis ancò
S'envertouio, mudant tout ço qu'as de plus bèu:
Abandouno toun ventre i pountoun dóu soulèu!
Coume l'èurre s'aganto à la rusco d'un aubre,
Laisso din mi brassado estregne en plen toun maubre:
Laisso ma bouco ardènto e mi det tremoulant
Courre amouros pertout sus toun cadabre blanc!

(Throw to your feet the robe that around your hips
hangs, hiding all that is most beautiful about you:
Abandon your stomach to the kisses of the sun!
As ivy entwines the bark of a tree,
Let me in my embraces clasp all of your marble;
Let my ardent mouth and trembling fingers
run lovingly over your body so white!)

Arles' mothers use this armless Venus for their own ends – they bring their children to see her and warn: 'The same thing will happen to you if you keep biting your nails!'

Also here are the contents of the former Musée d'Art Chrétien, the best collection of 4th-century Christian sarcophagi of any museum. Carved by Arlésien sculptors between the years 330 and 395, these remarkably preserved tombs make a fascinating documentary of the newly victorious faith; as their pagan ancestors carved scenes from mythology, so these early Christians spared no expense to decorate their last resting places on earth with scenes from the bible. Nearly every figure of importance wears a Roman toga; on the *Sarcophage de Trinquetaille*, discovered in 1974, the three Magi sport Phrygian bonnets.

Tourist Information and Services in Arles

(i) **Arles** >
Bd des Lices, next to Jules César hotel, t 04 90 18 41 20, www.arlestourisme.com; open April–Sept daily; Oct–Mar Mon–Sat and Sun am

Train station, open April–Sept Mon–Fri; closed Oct–Mar

The **main office** on Bd des Lices is very helpful, and there's another office in the **train station**. If you intend to see more than two of Arles' monuments and museums, buy the €13.50 global ticket to save money (you can also pick one up at any of the museums). The office also sells tickets for various city tours in English, and an MP3 city tour. In summer (April–Oct) you can book open horse-drawn coach tours directly also, with **Sentiers de Découverte de la Palissade**, t 04 42 86 81 28, and there is a little train (Easter–Oct), plus World Heritage-themed walking tours.

Post office: 5 Bd des Lices, t 04 90 18 41 05.

Market Days in Arles

Sat: Bd des Lices.
Wed: Bd Emile Combes.
First Wed of month: *Foire à la brocante*, Bd des Lices.

Festivals and Annual Events in Arles

Arles does its best to keep visitors entertained. The free broadsheet *Farandole*, *www.journal-farandole.com*, gives details of everything from theatre, concerts, fairs and exhibitions to local basketball results.

Easter is celebrated by a *Féria Pascale*, *www.feriaarles.com*, with four days of bullfights, most of them Spanish *corridas* (for ticket reservations for Arènes events, call t 08 91 70 03 70). On 24 June, the *Fête de la St Jean*, there are typical Arlésien dances in costume around bonfires, and the distribution of blessed bread.

July is the busiest month, with a festival of music, dance and drama, the *Cocarde d'Or* bullfights, and the *Rencontres Internationales de la Photographie*, *www.rencontres-arles.com*, with shows and workshops, held in the Théâtre Antique.

At the end of Aug there's the *Festival du Film Peplum*, *www.festivalpeplum-arles.com*.

The last bullfights of the year, held on the second Sun in Sept, coincide with the *Fêtes des Prémices du Riz*, or rice harvest.

Shopping in Arles

Les Etoffes de Romane, 10 Bd des Lices, t 04 90 93 53 70. Colourful 'Les Olivades' Provençal fabrics.

Arlys, 35 Place Voltaire, t 04 90 96 45 89. Provençal fabrics and *santons*.

Camille, 5 Bd Georges Clemenceau, t 04 90 96 04 94. Authentic *gardian* costumes.

Lettry Micheline Créations, Mas des Troënes, 17 Rue Jean Boutière, t 04 90 96 72 09. Local gifts and trinkets.

La Main Qui Pense, 15 Rue Tour du Fabre, t 04 90 18 24 58. Pottery.

La Nouvelle Arlésienne, 12 Rue du Président Wilson, t 04 90 93 28 05. Traditional clothes for women.

Puyricard, 54 Rue de la République, t 04 90 93 46 91. The place to buy *calissons d'Aix,* or to come just to see the crystallized fruits, marzipan models, chocolates and other bright goodies stacked like small sugared mountains.

Any good butcher you come across in town will sell you spicy donkey-filled *saucissons d'Arles.*

Where to Stay in Arles

Arles ✉ 13200

Arles charges less for better accommodation than you'll get in cities such as Avignon or Aix-en-Provence. There is a wide choice of accommodation in the inexpensive bracket on the streets leading towards the train station.

The tourist office provides a room-finding service for a small fee.

****Nord Pinus, Place du Forum, t 04 90 93 44 44, *www.nord-pinus. com* (€€€€€–€€€€). The former favourite of the Félibres, poets and literati such as Stendhal, Mérimée and Henry James, now the haunt of top matadors and wealthy aficionados. The public spaces are full of heavy, dark furniture and bullfighting posters, rooms are spacious and beautifully decorated. Look out for the columns from a Roman temple in the façade. No restaurant.

****Jules César ('Chez Jules'), Bd des Lices, t 04 90 52 52 52, *www.hotel-julescesar.fr* (€€€€€–€€). The luxurious grand-daddy of hotels in Arles, now part of the Relais & Châteaux chain, in a former Dominican monastery with a Caesar-ish temple porch tacked on. The rooms are vast, air-conditioned and furnished with Provençal pieces; the pool is heated and the gardens are beautiful. *See* opposite for its restaurant, **Lou Marquès.** *Closed Nov–23 Dec.*

***Hôtel d'Arlatan, 26 Rue du Sauvage, t 04 90 93 56 66, *www. hotel-arlatan.fr* (€€€–€€). Near lively Place du Forum, this 12th–18th-century home of the comtes d'Arlatan

⭐ Hôtel
d'Arlatan >

has been run by the same welcoming family for five generations. Wait for the lift standing on glass over Roman excavations; the house was built over part of the Constantine basilica, and in 1988 a Roman drain and a statue plinth from the 1st century BC were uncovered. The smaller rooms (24 and 38, with shared bathroom; €€) have a view of the courtyard with its fountain. *Closed Jan.*

***Hôtel du Forum, 10 Place du Forum, t 04 90 93 48 95, *www. hotelduforum.com* (€€€–€€). Pool.

***Auberge du Mas de la Fenière, Allée des Prairies, Raphèle-les-Arles ✉ 13280, 5km east of Arles on N453, t 04 90 98 47 44, *www.lafeniere.com* (€€€–€€). An attractive, ivy-covered inn on the edge of the Crau, with pleasant rooms, some with air-conditioning, and a restaurant (€€€) with an outdoor terrace, offering Camarguaise beef, duck with olives, salmon roulades and the like. *Restaurant closed lunch and Sun.*

Ecole de Cuisine Provençale, 11 Rue Portagnel, t 04 90 49 69 20, *www. cuisineprovencale.com*(€€€–€€). Cooking workshops run by Erick Vedel, the high priest of Provençal cuisine, plus three B&B rooms (€€).

**Hôtel de l'Amphithéâtre, 5–7 Rue Diderot, t 04 90 96 10 30, *www. hotelamphitheatre.fr* (€€). Stylish, good-value hotel behind the amphitheatre.

**Le Calendal, 5 Rue Porte-de-Laure (just in front of Arènes), t 04 90 96 11 89, *www.lecalendal.com* (€€). A good hotel for families, with a buffet restaurant. Rooms overlook a garden with palms. *Closed Jan; restaurant closed eves May–Oct.*

**Saint-Trophime, 16 Rue de la Calade, t 04 90 96 88 38, *www.hotel-saint-trophime.com* (€€–€). A reasonable option situated in an old house with a central courtyard. *Closed mid-Jan–mid-Feb.*

**Hôtel Le Cloître, 16 Rue du Cloître, t 04 90 96 29 50, *www.hotelcloitre. com* (€€–€). A friendly and well-priced if somewhat austerely decorated hotel in the centre, once part of a 12th-century cloister. *Closed Nov–mid-Mar.*

Hôtel du Musée, 11 Rue du Grand-Prieuré, **t 04 90 93 88 88, *www.hoteldumusee.com* (€€–€). Attractively converted 17th-century residence located opposite the Musée Réattu. Quiet, subtly chic and friendly. *Closed Dec and Jan.*

Auberge de Jeunesse, 20 Av Maréchal Foch, **t** 04 90 96 18 25, *www.fuaj.org/arles* (€). Youth hostel reached by bus from Place Lamartine. *Closed mid-Dec–Jan.*

Eating Out in Arles

Lou Marquès, Jules César hotel (*see left*), **t** 04 90 52 52 52 (€€€). Arles' elegant citadel of traditional *haute cuisine*, offering dishes such as *carré d'agneau* with artichokes, and boasting an excellent wine cellar. *Closed Sat, Sun and Nov.*

Le Jardin de Manon, 14 Av des Alyscamps, **t** 04 90 93 38 68 (€€€–€€). A good place for lunch after a walk through Les Alyscamps, serving *cuisine provençale* on a pretty back terrace. *Closed Tues eve and Wed in summer, Sun in winter.*

La Charcuterie Arlésienne, 51 Rue des Arènes, **t** 04 90 96 56 96 (€€). Popular restaurant serving traditional Lyonnais cuisine. *Closed Aug, Xmas–New Year, plus Sun and Mon.*

Entertainment and Nightlife in Arles

The most sociable bars in the city can be found in Place du Forum; for a spot of lazy watching-the-world-go-by, go for a chair in Place Voltaire or Bd des Lices.

Le Méjan/Actes Sud, 23 Place Nina Berberova, **t** 04 90 49 86 91/56 78. The liveliest place in Arles after dark, a complex that includes a book and record shop, an art gallery, a concert venue, three cinemas showing films in their original language (*v.o.*), a hammam, and a bar and restaurant where you can enjoy a delicious couscous or other meals.

Le Fémina, 14 Bd Emile Zola, **t** 08 92 68 47 07. A recommended bar and arthouse cinema.

The Plaine de la Crau

Hercules, after completing his Tenth Labour, the theft of the cattle of Geryon, passed through Provence with the booty on his way home to Greece. He had some trouble with the native Ligurians, who apparently tried to pinch the cows. One thing led to another, and before long the big fellow found himself involved in a single-handed battle with the entire nation. As they advanced across the marshy plain, Hercules, armed only with his club, got down on his knees in despair at having nothing to throw at them. Zeus took pity on him and sent down a shower of stones, with which the hero soon put the Ligurians to flight. This was an unaccountably important story in the mythology of the Greeks; they and the Romans put the Hercules of this battle in the sky; the northern constellation that we know as Hercules, they called *Engonasis*, the 'kneeler'.

The carpet of stones Zeus sent is still there for all to see, on the weird wasteland called the **Crau**, which stretches from Arles to the Etang de Berre, between the Camargue and the Alpilles. The ancients found it fascinating, and many Greek and Roman writers attempted to explain it; Aristotle, a hopeless bird-brain at anything involving natural science, said the stones were formed by volcanoes, and 'rolled down naturally' to the low plain. In fact, the rounded stones are alluvial deposits from the Durance, from long ago when the river followed this path into the Rhône delta. The empty, wind-blown Crau is a major element of the Provençal mystique; Mistral, for example, dragged his poor Mireille across it before she met her sad end. Today it does its best to keep up a romantic appearance. More than 100,000 sheep make their winter home here, nibbling the tufts of grass between the stones before migrating in the old-fashioned way up to the Provençal Alps in May or June; the stone shepherd huts are still one of the few features of the Crau. The French, unfortunately, have been trying to make it disappear. Most of the northern part has been reclaimed for farmland. The rest is crisscrossed with railways, canals and roads, and decorated with army firing ranges and the gigantic Istres military airport; there's even a dynamite plant.

There are no good roads over the unspoiled parts of the Crau, and the only village, **St-Martin-de-Crau**, is a dismal spot, but you can still see something of the original effect along the N568 (for Fos-sur-Mer and Marseille) and the N113 (for Salon-de-Provence), both east of Arles.

The Camargue

⚛ The Camargue

To its handful of inhabitants, the Camargue was the *isclo*, the 'island' between the two branches of the Rhône. The river's course has taken many different forms over the millennia; the present one, with its two arms, has created a vast marshland – this is France's salt cellar, its greatest treasure house of waterfowl and the home of some of its most exotic landscapes. The two branches, the Grand and Petit Rhônes, really build separate deltas, leaving the space in between a soupy battleground where land and sea slowly struggle for mastery. With its unique coastline and wild expanses, the Camargue provides a soothing antithesis to the more crowded areas of the region. It is also ideal for outdoor activities, including hiking, climbing, diving, surfing and horse-riding (*see* p.159 and p.162 for details).

History

Ancient writers recorded the people of the Camargue hunting boar in the swamp forests and actually raking fish out of the mud; besides remarking on its curiosities, however, the Greeks and Romans left the area entirely alone. During the early Middle Ages,

Getting to and around the Camargue

Arles is the main jumping-off point for the Camargue.

By Bus

The only public transport to the centre of the Camargue begins at the *gare routière* in Arles (t 04 90 49 38 01; *www.lepilote.com* for bus timetables): there are one or two buses a day each to Saintes-Maries-de-la-Mer (via Albaron) and Salin-de-Giraud. St-Gilles has regular bus connections to Nîmes, a few to Arles and one to Lunel.

On Foot and Horseback, and by Bicycle and Jeep

Remember that the Camargue is really quite small – it's never more than 40km from Arles to the coast. A serious hiker could see the whole thing in 3 days.

It is perfect country for **cycling**, and there are a few places in Saintes-Maries-de-la-Mer to rent some wheels (*see* p.162). **Horses** are even more popular; there are many places to hire one.

Camargue Découverte, t 04 90 96 69 20, *www.camargue-decouverte.camargue.fr*, organizes trips into the Camargue by jeep.

Camargue Safaris, t 04 90 93 60 31, *www.camargue-decouverte.camargue.fr*. Trips into the Camargue by SUV, from 1½hrs to a day, starting from Arles or from Saintes-Maries-de-la-Mer.

By Boat

Blue-Line (t 04 66 87 22 66) and several other firms in St-Gilles rent out boats for trips through the Petite Camargue. At Saintes-Maries-de-la-Mer and St-Gilles there are various **excursion boats** that cruise around the Camargue.

---

on the other hand, at least four monastic colonies were founded on the edges of the Camargue, not only to reclaim land but to collect that most precious of medieval commodities, salt. In this inhospitable country, these colonies disappeared long ago; the most important was the abbey of **Psalmody**, which became quite a power in Provence. Today only scant ruins of it can be seen, on a farm still called Psalmody, to the north of Aigues-Mortes in the region called the Petite Camargue, west of the Petit Rhône.

By the 17th century, the monks gave way to cowboys (*gardians*), who created large ranches to exploit the two totem animals of the Camargue: the native black longhorn cattle that thrive on salt grass and have always been the preferred stock for Provençal bullfights, and the beautiful white horse, believed to have been introduced by the Arabs back in the Dark Ages. A true cowboy culture grew up – a romantic image dear to the Provençaux, and especially to Provençal writers such as Mistral.

There are still a few score *gardians* in the Camargue today, keeping up the old traditions. Big changes have come to the swampland in the last century. For a while, the French threatened to dispose rationally of this land altogether, with dykes and drainage schemes turning large areas into saltpans and rice fields. Fortunately, however, a few nature societies secured the creation of a wildlife reserve around the heart of the Camargue in 1928, and the government made a regional park of the area in 1970.

Camargue Flora and Fauna

First and most spectacularly, there are the flamingos (*flamants roses*), a symbol of the Camargue, and understandably so: several thousand of them nest around the southern lagoons. Probably no place in the Mediterranean has a wider variety of aquatic birds: there are lots of ducks, grebes, cormorants, curlews and ibis. The little egret is a common sight, though they spend the winter in Africa, as does the avocet, which looks like an aquatic magpie. There are also many purple herons, conspicuously striped on the head and breast. Not all are water birds; you may see an eagle or a majestic red kite (*milan royal*).

Deforestation in favour of ranches destroyed most of the natural habitat for land animals, but there are still boars, beavers and blue frogs. Trees are rare, although there are some umbrella pines and some scrubby, pink-flowered tamarisks. Common plants include the purple-flowered *saladelle* and the *salicorne* (samphire), which grows in tough clumps.

Among the fauna, we nearly forgot the most important – the hard-drilling, inescapable Camargue mosquito; make it your prime consideration when you visit, and take appropriate precautions.

Musée Camarguais

Musée Camarguais
t 04 90 97 10 82;
open April–Sept daily
9.30–6; Oct–Mar
Wed–Mon 10–5; adm

It was an inspiration on the part of the regional park management, creating this museum in what not long ago was a working Camargue cattle and sheep ranch, the **Mas du Pont de Rousty**, 9km southwest of Arles on the D570. The buildings are well restored and documented, giving a feeling of what life was like on the *mas* a century ago. There are special exhibitions on the *gardians*, on the fickle Rhône (you learn that 400,000 years ago it flowed past Nîmes), on Mistral's *Mireio*, and other subjects. Outside, there are marked nature trails leading into the surrounding swampy plain, the **Marais de la Grande Mar**.

About 4km beyond the museum on the D570, little **Albaron** was one of the first inhabited centres of the Camargue; a stout medieval tower survives, built to guard Arles from any attack or pirate raid up the Petit Rhône.

The Etang de Vaccarès

Domaine de Méjanes
t 04 90 97 10 10

For lazy motor tourists, the way to see the best of the Camargue is to take the D37, a left turn 4km south of the museum. After another 4km, a side road leads to the **Domaine de Méjanes**, with horse-riding and canoes; on summer weekends the *gardians* put on shows of cowboy know-how, and occasional bullfights. Further on, the D37 skirts the edges of the **Etang de Vaccarès**, the biggest of the lagoons and centre of the Camargue wildlife reserve. In some places, you can see flocks of nesting flamingos all year round.

Centre d'Information La Capelière
t 04 90 97 00 97;
open April–Sept daily
9–1 and 2–6; Oct–Mar
Wed–Mon 9–1
and 2–5; adm

A side road, the D36B, leads down to Salin-de-Giraud, passing the **Centre d'Information La Capelière**, with exhibits on flora and fauna and guided nature walks around the lagoon.

The scenery changes abruptly at **Salin-de-Giraud**, a 19th-century industrial village that was devoted to the largest saltworks in Europe – a staggering 110 square km network of pans, annually producing 800,000 tonnes of salt. There's another nature centre

Where to Stay and Eat in the Eastern and Central Camargue

Almost all accommodation in the area is in Saintes-Maries-de-la-Mer (*see* p.165), but if you want to stay in the eastern or central parts of the Camargue, away from the tourists, there are some possibilities.

Albaron ✉ 13123

Le Flamant Rose, on D37, **t 04 90 97 10 18, *www.leflamantrose.camargue.fr* (€). A simple Logis de France with a

restaurant (€€). *Closed end Feb–mid-Mar; restaurant closed Wed lunch.*

Salin-de-Giraud ✉ 13129

Hidden amidst vast saltpans, Salin doesn't even dream of drawing tourists.

*La Camargue, Bd de la Camargue, **t** 04 42 86 88 52 (€€–€). Simple and basic. *Closed mid-Oct–mid-Mar.*

Les Saladelles, 4 Av des Arènes, **t** 04 42 86 83 87 (€). Small hotel with a good, popular restaurant (€€) for family dining, with a wide choice of dishes, including spicy *bœuf à la gardian*, chops and fish.

Domaine de la Palissade
*t 04 42 86 81 28;
open mid-June–mid-Sept daily 9–6; mid-Sept–mid-June daily 9–5; adm*

on the D36, **Domaine de la Palissade**, with white horses, bulls, audiovisual displays, a small aquarium, walks, and information on the flamingo-filled **Etang de Grande Palun**. The *salins* are barred from the Mediterranean by one of the longest, emptiest beaches in France, the **Plage de Piémanson** at the mouth of the Grand Rhône; the current is a bit treacherous for swimming. To get away from it all, head west of Salin for the **Plage de Beauduc** (signposted), where you'll find a couple of places that grill the day's catch.

With good local maps, in summer determined swamp fans can hike the 40km or so to Saintes-Maries-de-la-Mer, through the most unspoiled parts of the Camargue; a sea wall, the **Digue de la Mer**, provides a crossing around the lagoons, and the only hazards are secluded beaches that have been taken over by bands of *naturistes*. You might even make it over to the Camargue's forest, the **Bois des Rièges**, on a large island at the southern end of the Etang de Vaccarès. Though officially off limits, as part of the nature reserve it can sometimes be reached on foot in summer. Be careful, though: this is the home of the Camargue's Abominable Snowman, the *Bête de Vaccarès*, a mysterious part-human creature first sighted in the 15th century.

Saintes-Maries-de-la-Mer

✪ Saintes-Maries-de-la-Mer

Set among the low sand dunes, the lively town of Saintes-Maries-de-la-Mer has an open-armed approach to visitors that long predates any interest in the Camargue and its ecological balance. For this is one of Provence's holiest places, and if you come out of season you may still sense the dream-like, insular remoteness that made it the stuff of legend.

The pious story behind it all was promoted to the hilt by the medieval Church: after Christ was crucified, his Jewish detractors took a boat without sails or oars and loaded it with three Marys –

Getting to and around Saintes-Maries-de-la-Mer

By Bus

There are at least 2 buses daily from Arles (55mins). In July and Aug there are direct services to Aigues-Mortes and Montpellier and St-Gilles and Nîmes.

By Boat

The paddle steamer *Tiki III*, t 04 90 97 81 68, *www.tiki3.fr*, plies the Petit Rhône (April–Sept). The *Camargue*, t 04 90 97 84 72, *www.bateau-camargue.com*, also offers trips.

On Horseback

The tourist office has a list of stables, some offering tours for beginners; they include the **Promenade à Cheval Pont de Gau** on the Route d'Arles, t 04 90 97 89 45.

By Jeep and Bike

Safari Nature Camargue, t 04 90 97 89 33, *www.manade-safari.com*. Among firms offering jeep tours.

Le Vélociste, 8 Place Mireille, t 04 90 97 83 26. Bike hire.

Camargue Safaris, t 04 90 93 60 31. Trips into the Camargue by SUV, from 1½hrs to a day, starting from Arles or from Saintes-Maries-de-la-Mer.

Mary Salome (mother of the apostles James and John), Mary Jacobe, the Virgin's sister, and Mary Magdalene – plus Martha and her resurrected brother Lazarus, St Maximin and St Sidonius. As this so-called Boat of Bethany drifted offshore, Sarah, the black Egyptian servant of Mary Salome and Mary Jacobe, wept so grievously that Mary Salome tossed her cloak on the water, so that Sarah was able to walk across on it and join them. The boat took them to the Camargue, to this spot, where the elderly Mary Salome, Mary Jacobe and Sarah built an oratory, while their younger companions went to spread the Gospel, live in caves and tame the Tarasque. In 1448, during the reign of the Bon Roi René (who was always pinched for money), the supposed relics of the two Marys were discovered, greatly boosting the local pilgrim trade. Saintes-Maries became, as Mistral called it, the 'Mecca of Provence'. A few facts blazed the trail for the legend's ready acceptance. In the 4th century, a Roman writer described a settlement on this site called *Oppidum priscum Ra*. This lent its name to the first Christian church, Notre-Dame-de-Ratis, built over the site of a spring of fresh water – where a Gallo-Roman temple had been dedicated to three sea goddesses. *Ratis* was taken to mean raft (*radeau*), hence the connection not only with the Boat of Bethany but to ancient Egypt, where in the *Book of the Dead* the deceased sails in a boat without oar or sail, but with the image of Ra. Even the name 'Marie' had a familiar ring to Provence's early Christians; not only for its resemblance to the word for mother (*Matre*), but also to Marius, a local cult figure after his defeat of the Teutones, who was advised by the blonde sibyl Marthe (as pictured near Les Baux-de-Provence; *see* p.140).

Today, Saintes-Maries-de-la-Mer is best known for the pilgrimage of Mary Jacobe on 24 and 25 May. This attracts Gypsies from all over the world, who have canonized her servant Sarah as their patron saint. The reason seems to owe something to yet another coincidence – the discovery of the relics coincided with a great convergence of Gypsies in Provence in the 1440s, some of whom wandered up from North Africa and Spain, while others crossed into Europe by way of Greece and the Balkans. The Gypsies, however, claim that Sarah was not Egyptian but one of their own, Sarah-la-Kâli ('the black', but also recalling Hindu goddess Kali), who met the Boat of Bethany here and was the first of their tribe to be converted to Christianity. The Church obliged by 'discovering' the bones of Sarah in 1496.

The Church

In 869, during the construction of a new church to replace the 6th-century oratory 'built' by the two Marys, the Saracens swooped down in a surprise raid and carried off the archbishop of Arles, who just happened to be down to inspect the work. The pirates demanded a high ransom in silver, swords and slaves for their hostage, and were dismayed when the bishop died on them – but not so put out as to risk losing the ransom. They tied the bishop's corpse in all its vestments to a throne and made off with the loot before the Christians realized the hostage was dead.

In the face of the threat of similar shenanigans, stones were shipped down from Arles at great expense to rebuild the church in 1130. The result is, along with St-Victor in Marseille, the most impressive fortified church in Provence: a crenellated ship with loopholes for windows in a small pond of white villas with orange roofs. Inside, along the gloomy nave, are wells that supplied the church-fortress in times of siege; pilgrims still bottle the water to ensure their protection by St Sarah. In the second chapel on the left, near the model of the Boat of Bethany that is carried in the procession to the sea, is the polished rock 'pillow' of the saints, discovered with their bones in 1448.

The capitals supporting the blind arches of the raised choir are finely sculpted in the style of St-Trophime in Arles (*see* pp.149–51). Under the choir is the crypt, where the relics and statue of St Sarah in her seven robes are kept; the statue has been kissed so often that the black paint has come off in patches. Here, too, is a *taurobolium*, or relief of a bull-slaying from an ancient *mithraeum*, the bits scratched away long ago by women who used the dust to concoct fertility potions, along with photos and *ex votos* left by the Gypsies.

You can take a stroll below the **bell-tower**, offering views stretching across the Camargue, which takes on a magical glow at

Bell-tower
t 04 90 97 87 60; open July and Aug daily 10–8; Mar–June and Sept–Oct Mon–Fri 10–12.30 and 2–6.30, Sat and Sun 10–7; Nov–Feb Wed, Sat and Sun 10–12 and 2–5; open daily in school hols

Upper chapel
usually closed

sunset. This roof walk circles the lavish **upper chapel**, dedicated to St Michael, which in times of need served as a *donjon*. The coffer holding the relics of the Marys is kept here, except during the arcane *deus ex machina* rites unique to this church: during feast days the coffer is slowly lowered through a door over the altar after the singing of a special hymn, 'Les Saintes de Provence'; the pilgrimage ends to the tune of 'Adieu aux Saintes', as the relics are slowly raised back into the chapel. In the 18th century this hocus-pocus had a reputation for curing madness, combined with the shock therapy of stripping the afflicted naked and throwing them in the sea. When Mistral attended the pilgrimage as a young man, a beautiful girl from Beaucaire abandoned by her fiancé dramatically flung herself across the altar just as the relics were being lowered, praying for the return of her lover. The girl made a considerable impression on Mistral and became the basis for his heroine Mireille, who arrives in Saintes-Maries-de-la-Mer to make a similar prayer and dies of too much sun and love in the upper chapel of this church, while the congregation in the lower church, like the chorus in a Greek tragedy, accuses the holy Marys: *Reino de Paradis, mestresso/De la Planuro d'amaresso* ('Queens of Paradise, mistresses/of the plain of bitterness').

The Rest of Saintes-Maries-de-la-Mer, and Around

Musée Baroncelli
*t 04 90 97 87 60;
open Wed–Mon 10–12
and 2–5*

Mireille, in statue form at least, lives on in the main square north of the church, while to the south in Rue Victor Hugo the **Musée Baroncelli** is devoted to zoology, archaeology and folklore. It is named after the Camargue's secular saint, the Félibre Marquis Folco de Baroncelli-Javon (1869–1943), a descendant of a Florentine merchant family in Avignon, who at the age of 21 abandoned everything to go and live the life of a *gardian*. Baroncelli spent the next 60 years herding bulls, writing poetry and doing all that he could to maintain the Camargue and its customs intact. Although he was by trade a cowboy, his heart was actually with the Native Americans and other oppressed minorities; Chief Sitting Bull, visiting France with Buffalo Bill and his Wild West Show, smoked the peace pipe with the marquis and named him 'Faithful Bird'.

Parc Ornithologique
*t 04 90 97 82 62, www.
parcornithologique.
com; open April–Sept
9–sunset; Oct–Mar
10–sunset; adm*

At **Pont de Gau**, 4km north, there's a **Parc Ornithologique**, with walks through the marshlands and aviaries, frequented by some 200 species of birds, including rare ones.

Market Days in Saintes-Maries-de-la-Mer

Saintes-Maries-de-la-Mer: Mon and Fri am, Place du Gitan.

Festivals in Saintes-Maries-de-la-Mer

The *Pèlerinage des Gitans* (Gypsy Pilgrimage) is held on 24–25 May. The Gypsies began making the pilgrimage in numbers in the mid-19th century.

In 1935, thanks to the Marquis de Baroncelli, 24 May was set aside as St Sarah's day. Although the famous all-night candle vigil by her statue has been abolished by bureaucratic killjoys, her statue is still carried to the sea by a procession of Gypsies, *gardians* and costumed Arlésiennes, where in imitation of ancient rain-making ceremonies it is sprinkled with sea water while all are blessed by the bishop. Afterwards, the beaches and streets are alive with music and flamenco, *farandoles*, horse races and bullfights, attended by as many tourists as Gypsies.

The whole ceremony happens again, with considerably fewer Gypsies and tourists, on the Sunday nearest 22 Oct for Mary Salome.

★ Mangio Fango >>

Activities in Saintes-Maries-de-la-Mer

There are miles of white sand beaches, including a *plage naturiste* 6km to the east.

Where to Stay in Stes-Maries-de-la-Mer

ⓘ Saintes-Maries-de-la-Mer >
5 Av Van Gogh,
t 04 90 97 82 55,
www.saintesmaries.
com; open daily all year

ⓘ Maison du Parc Naturel Régional de Camargue
Pont de Gau, t 04 90
97 86 32, www.parc-
camargue.fr; open
summer daily
10–6; winter
Sat–Thurs 9.30–5

Saintes-Maries-de-la-Mer
✉ 13460

****Mas de la Fouque, Route du Petit-Rhône, 4km from town, t 04 90 97 81 02, *www.masdelafouque.com* (€€€€€–€€€€). A stunningly decorated 12-room hotel by a lagoon, with private terraces, a heated pool, a lake, its own boat for coastal trips, and a restaurant (€€€) using local organic produce. *Closed mid-Nov–mid-Mar.*

****Le Pont des Bannes, 3km north on the D570, t 04 90 97 81 09, *wwwpontdesbannes.com* (€€€€–€€€). Rooms in *cabanes de gardian*, plus a pool, a garden and stables for riding.

***Mas Sainte-Hélène, Chemin Bas-des-Launes, t 04 90 97 83 29, *www.pontdesbannes.com* (€€€€–€€€). The Pont des Bannes' annexe, spread out along an islet in the Etang des Launes, allowing you to get eye to eye with the pink flamingos that parade on its waterside terraces.

***Hôtel de Cacharel, Route des Cacharels, 5km from town, t 04 90 97 95 44, *www.hotel-cacharel.com* (€€€). Ranch-style hotel with a laid-back approach (no TVs) and excellent-value family rooms. There's no restaurant, but delicious snacks and wine are available midday–8pm. Horse-riding costs from €23 per hour.

****Mangio Fango, Route d'Arles (D570), t 04 90 97 80 56, *www.hotel mangiofango.com* (€€€–€€). A hotel offering a marriage of old materials and modern comfort, filled with crafts and paintings. There's a heated pool and a good restaurant (€€€) with a patio where you can enjoy wonderful seafood and excellent Camargue bull stew. *Restaurant closed to non-guests mid-Nov–Mar.*

*Le Delta, Place Mireille, t 04 90 97 81 12 (€). Five rooms and food. *Closed Jan–mid-Feb; restaurant closed Mon.*

Auberge de Jeunesse, Pioch Badet. t 04 90 97 51 72, *www.auberge-de-jeunesse.camargue.fr* (€). Accessible by bus from Arles and Stes-Maries.

Eating Out in Saintes-Maries-de-la-Mer

This is the place to try *bœuf gardian*, bull stewed in red wine with lots of garlic; *bouriroun*, an omelette with elvers from the Vaccarès; *salade de téllines*, made of tiny shellfish with garlic mayonnaise; and *poutargue*, Camargue caviar made from red mullet eggs.

Le Brûleur de Loups, Av Léon Gambetta, t 04 90 97 83 31 (€€€–€€). An elegant choice with a terrace overlooking the beach, serving delights from the sea. *Closed mid-Nov–Dec, Tues eve and Wed.*

Hostellerie du Pont de Gau, Rte d'Arles (D570), 4km north of town, t 04 90 97 81 53, *www.hotelpontdegau.com* (€€€–€€). Jolly Provençal décor and great *bouillabaisse*. Also has rooms (€). *Closed Wed in winter, and Jan–mid-Feb.*

Entertainment and Nightlife in Saintes-Maries-de-la-Mer

In summer, nightly *Courses Camargues* in the bullring; and guitars and buskers in the streets.

St-Gilles

West of Arles, the N572 takes you through the drier parts of the Camargue. After crossing the Petit Rhône, you're in the **Petite Camargue**, in the *département* of the Gard, approaching St-Gilles, the only town for miles in any direction.

History

In medieval times and earlier, St-Gilles was a flourishing port, much nearer the sea than it is now. Remains have been found of a Phoenician merchant colony, and the Greek-Celtic *oppidum* that replaced it, but the place did not really blossom until the 11th century. The popes and the monks of Cluny, who owned it, conspired to make the resting place of Gilles, an obscure 8th-century Greek hermit, a major stop along the great pilgrim road to Compostela. The powerful counts of Toulouse helped too – the family originally came from St-Gilles. Soon pilgrims were pouring in from as far away as Germany and Poland, the port boomed with the onset of the Crusades, and both the Templars and Knights Hospitallers (who owned large tracts in the Camargue) built important *commanderies*. In 1116 the abbey church of St-Gilles was begun, one of the most ambitious projects ever undertaken in medieval Provence.

Destiny, however, soon began making it clear that this was not the place. As the delta gradually expanded, the canals silted up and St-Gilles could no longer function as a port (a major reason for the building of Aigues-Mortes; *see* p.169).

The real disaster came with the Wars of Religion, when the town became a Protestant stronghold; the leaders of the Protestant army thought the church, that obsolete relic from the Age of Faith that took 200 years to build, would look much better as a fortress, and they demolished nearly all of it to that end. It was rebuilt, in a much smaller version, after 1650. What was left suffered more indignities during the Revolution – the loss of many of the figures' faces is nothing short of tragic – but it is a miracle that otherwise one of the greatest ensembles of medieval sculpture has survived more or less intact.

Abbey of St-Gilles

⭐ **Abbey of St-Gilles**
open Mon, Tues and Thurs–Sat; guided visits by arrangement; call the tourist office on t 04 66 87 33 75

This is the masterpiece of the Provençal school of 12th-century sculptors, the famous work that was copied, life-size, in the Cloisters Museum in New York.

Created roughly at the same time as the façade of St-Trophime in Arles, it is likewise inspired by the ancient Roman triumphal arches. Instead of Roman worthies and battle scenes, the 12 Apostles hold place of honour between the Corinthian columns. This is a bold, confident sculpture, taking delight in naturalistic detail and elaborately folded draperies, with little of the conscious stylization that characterizes contemporary work in other parts of France. In this, too, the Romans were their masters. The scheme is complex, and worth describing in detail.

The Church Façade

Left portal: tympanum of the Adoration of the Magi (1); beneath it, Jesus' entry into Jerusalem (2); flanking the door, a beautiful St Michael slaying the dragon (3); and on the right the first four Apostles, SS Matthew and Bartholomew, Thomas and James the Less (4–7).

Central portal: tympanum of Christ in Majesty (8), with symbols of the Evangelists; underneath, a long frieze that runs from one side portal across to the other: from left to right, Judas with his silver (9); Jesus expelling the money-changers from the temple (10); the resurrection of Lazarus (11); Jesus prophesying the denial of Peter, and the washing of the Apostles' feet (12); the Last Supper (13); the Kiss of Judas, a superb, intact work (14); the Arrest of Christ (15); Christ before Pilate (16); the Flagellation (17); Christ carrying the Cross (18). Left of the door, saints John and Peter (19); right of the door, saints James the Great and Paul, with the soul-devouring Tarasque under his feet (20). Beneath these, at ground level, are small panels representing the sacrifices of Cain and Abel and the murder of Abel (21); a deer hunt and Balaam and his ass, and Samson and the Lion (22).

Right portal: tympanum of the Crucifixion (23); beneath it, two unusual scenes: the three Marys purchasing spices to anoint the body of Jesus, and the three Marys at the tomb. To the left of this, the Magdalene and Jesus (24); to the right, Jesus

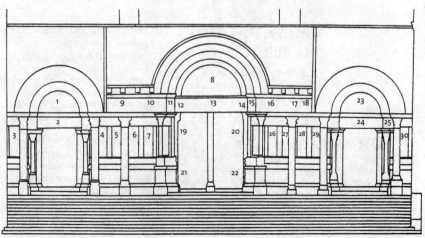

appearing to his disciples (25). Left of the door, four more unidentifiable Apostles (26–29; note how the 12 represented here are not the canonical list – better-known figures such as John the Evangelist and Paul were commonly substituted for the more obscure of the original Apostles). To the right of the door, Archangels combat Satan (30).

The Vis de St-Gilles

The 17th-century interior of the rebuilt church holds little of interest, but beneath it the original, wide-vaulted **crypt** or lower church (*adm*) survives (so many pilgrims came to St-Gilles that upper and lower churches were built to hold them). Behind the church, you can see the ruins of the **choir** and **apse** of the original, which was much longer than the present structure.

Here is the *vis* or 'screw' of St-Gilles, a spiral staircase of 50 steps that once led up one of the bell-towers. Built about 1142, it is a *tour de force*. The stones are cut with amazing precision to make a self-supporting spiral vault; medieval masons always tried to make the St-Gilles pilgrimage just to see it. Its author, Master Mateo of Cluny, also worked on the church of Santiago de Compostela, where he is buried.

The Maison Romane

Musée Lapidaire
t 04 66 87 40 42; open July and Aug Mon–Sat 9–12 and 3–7; June and Sept Mon-Sat 9–12 and 2–6; Feb–May and Oct–Dec 9–12 and 2–5; closed Jan; adm

The rest of the town shows few traces of its former greatness. The medieval centre is unusually large, if a bit forlorn. Near the façade of the church, on Place de la République, is a fine 13th-century mansion, claimed to be the birthplace of Guy Folques, who became Pope Clement IV. Today this 'Maison Romane' houses St-Gilles' **Musée Lapidaire**, with a number of sculptures and architectural fragments from the church, and collections displaying the folk life and nature of the Camargue.

Market Days in St-Gilles

St-Gilles: Thurs and Sun am.

Where to Stay and Eat in St-Gilles

(i) **St-Gilles >**
Place Frédéric Mistral, t 04 66 87 33 75, www.ot-saint-gilles.fr; open Mon–Sat

St-Gilles ✉ 30800

During the Middle Ages scores of pilgrims (sometimes thousands of them), would stay over at St-Gilles every night; if you tried it today, even the innkeepers would wonder what you were thinking of.

**Le Cours, 10 Av François Griffeuille, t 04 66 87 31 93, *www. hotel-le-cours.com* (€€–€). A typically traditional Logis de France residence (you pay extra for air-conditioning), with a shady restaurant terrace (€€) where you can try the likes of Camargue *pilaf* and frogs' legs. *Closed mid-Dec–Feb.*

***L'Héraclée, 30 Quai du Canal, t 04 66 87 44 10, *www.hotel-heraclee.com* (€). An unexciting but well-run choice.

Aigues-Mortes: History, Salt and Walls

⭐ **Aigues-Mortes**

Every French history or geography textbook has a photo of Aigues-Mortes in it, and every French person, most likely, carries in their mind the haunting picture of the great walls of the port from which Saint Louis sailed off to the Crusades, now marooned in the muck of the advancing Rhône delta. It is as compelling a symbol of time and fate as any Roman ruin, and as evocative of medieval France as any Gothic cathedral.

In 1241 the Camargue was the only stretch of Mediterranean coast held by France. To solidify this precarious strip, Louis IX (Saint Louis) began construction of a new port and a town, laid out in an irregular grid to stop the wind from racing up the streets. In 1248 the port was complete enough to hold the 1,500 ships that carried Louis and his knights to the Holy Land on the Seventh Crusade, which was to bring Louis disasters both at home and abroad (the town was the last he saw of France – he died in Tunis of the plague in 1270). His successor, Philippe III, finished Aigues-Mortes and built its great walls. Being the only French Mediterranean port, by the late 13th century it was booming, with perhaps four times as many inhabitants as its present 6,798, its harbour filled with ships from as far away as Constantinople and Antioch.

Aigues-Mortes means 'dead waters', and it proved to be a prophetic name. The sea deserted Aigues and, despite efforts to keep the harbour dredged, the port went into decline after 1350. Attempts to revive it in the 1830s failed, ensuring Aigues' demise, but allowing the works of Louis and Philippe to survive undisturbed. Forgotten and nearly empty a century ago, Aigues now makes its living from tourists, and from salt; half of France's supply is collected here, at the 10,000-hectare **Salins-du-Midi** pans south of town in the Petite Camargue. Now the sea wants to return, and attempts to keep the tides from draining the lucrative saltpans could be futile, or at least very expensive.

Salins-du-Midi
t 04 66 73 40 00,
www.salins.com; open
April–Sept, call for times

Tour de Constance
t 04 66 53 61 55; open
May–Aug daily 10–7;
Sept–April daily
10–5.30; adm

Aigues-Mortes' **walls** are more than 1.5km in length, streamlined and almost perfectly rectangular. The highly impressive **Tour de Constance** (entry inside the walls on Rue Zola) is an enormous cylindrical defence tower used to guard the northeastern land approach to the town. After the Crusades, the tower was turned into a prison, first for Templars and later for Protestants. One of them, Marie Durand, spent 38 years here in unspeakable conditions. On her release in 1768, she left her credo, *register* ('resist' in Provençal) chiselled into the wall, where it can still be seen.

The tower to the south was used as a temporary mortuary in 1431, during the Hundred Years' War, when the Bourguignons, who held the city, were suddenly attacked and decimated by their arch-enemies, the Armagnacs. There were so many gruesome bodies

Getting to and around Aigues-Mortes

For **trains** from Nîmes, contact **t** 08 92 35 35 35; the station is on the Route de Nîmes.
For **buses** to and from Montpellier and Nîmes, call **t** 08 25 34 01 34 and **t** 04 66 29 27 29 respectively.
There are signs around all the entrances to the town forbidding **cars**; ignore them (everyone else does).
There is no problem driving around Aigues-Mortes or finding parking, except in July and August.

lying around that the Armagnacs simply stacked them up in the tower, covering each of them with a layer of salt: hence the rather eloquent name – the **Tower of the Salted Bourguignons**.

Eight kilometres southwest of Aigues-Mortes, **Le Grau-du-Roi** with its 18th-century lighthouse doubles as France's most important fishing port (after Sète). No resort strip would be complete without a flashy new fish show, and **Seaquarium** here (Av du Palais de la Mer) is one of the Mediterranean's biggest: seals and orcas, the obligatory glass tunnel through the shark tanks, and a small museum dedicated to Le Grau-du-Roi and its seagoing traditions. Le Grau's **Port Camargue** is nothing less than Europe's largest marina, with 5,000 berths and a long waiting list, plus a Florida-style nest of holiday homes. To the south of this stretches the **Plage de l'Espiguette**, a remarkable stretch of natural sand dunes that go on and on and on, the only building in sight a lighthouse (the road ends there, by the *phare*, in an enormous car park).

Seaquarium
t 04 66 51 57 57,
www.seaquarium.fr;
open July and Aug daily
10am–midnight; May,
June and Sept daily
10–8; Oct–April daily
10–7; adm exp

Market Days in Aigues-Mortes

Aigues-Mortes: Av Frédéric Mistral: Wed and Sun am.

Activities in Aigues-Mortes

Like Saintes-Maries, Aigues-Mortes offers many guided tours of local flora and fauna.

Pescalune, t 04 66 53 79 47, *www.pescalune-aiguesmortes.com*, and **L'Isle de Stel, t** 06 09 47 52 59, offer barge tours of the Petite Camargue.

Four-wheel-drive safari tours are efficiently run out of Le Grau-du-Roi by **Manade des Chanoines, t** 06 08 60 97 56, *www.manade-safari.com*; and **Pierrot le Camarguais, t** 04 66 51 90 90, *www.pierrot-le-camarguais.fr*.

(i) **Aigues-**
Mortes »
Place Saint-Louis,
t 04 66 53 73 00, www.
ot-aiguesmortes.fr;
open daily all year;
offers historical tours of
the town, year-round

Where to Stay and Eat in Aigues-Mortes

Aigues-Mortes ✉ 30220
***Le Saint-Louis, 10 Rue de l'Amiral Courbet, **t** 04 66 53 72 68, *www. lesaintlouis.fr* (€€). A distinguished and beautifully furnished 18th-century building just off Place Saint-Louis, with gracious staff and a restaurant. *Closed mid-Nov–April.*

Hermitage de St-Antoine, 9 Bd Intérieur Nord, **t** 06 03 04 34 05, *www.hermitagesa.com* (€€). *Chambres d'hôtes* just inside the Porte St-Antoine in the medieval walls; all three rooms have *en suite* bathrooms. Added bonuses are a tranquil patio area and fantastic breakfasts.

La Camargue, 19 Rue de la République, **t** 04 66 53 86 88 (€€). The place where the Gypsy Kings got their musical start, and still the liveliest and most popular place in town, with flamenco guitars strumming in the background. Eat in the garden in summer.

Metropolitan Provence

Although this is the business end of Provence, the most densely populated, hurly-burly, industrial and everything-else-you've-come-to-get-away-from part of Provence, the region holds several trump cards: elegant and lively Aix-en-Provence, with its incredible markets and its landscape synonymous with the paintings of Cézanne; a tumultuous coastline ripped into the bones of the earth between La Ciotat and Marseille; and Marseille itself, every bit as good as its magnificent setting, as bad as any big port city, and as ugly as the fish in its heavenly bouillabaisse.

FRANCE

ITALY

SPAIN

10

Don't miss

⭐ **Towering white** *calanques*
Cassis **p.174**

⭐ **A** *bouillabaisse* **by the sea**
Marseille food **p.194**

⭐ **An aqueduct twice as high as the Pont du Gard**
Aqueduc de Roquefavour **p.215**

⭐ **Lovely streets and squares**
Aix-en-Provence **p.201**

⭐ **Cézanne's favourite view**
Montagne Ste-Victoire **p.213**

See map overleaf

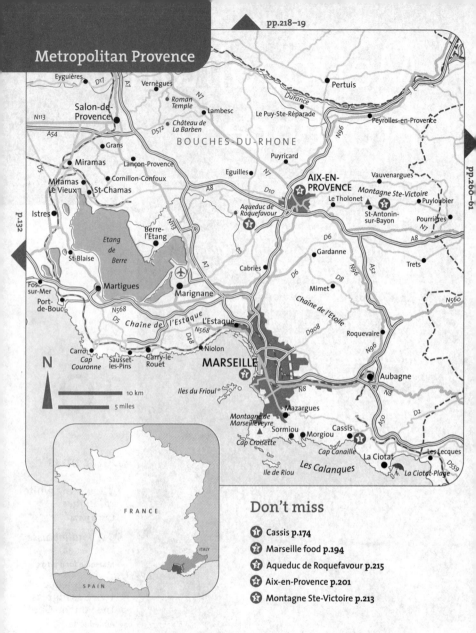

pp.260–61

p.132

Eyguières · N17 · Vernègues · Pertuis

Roman Temple · Lambesc · Le Puy-Ste-Réparade · Peyrolles-en-Provence

Salon-de-Provence · Château de La Barben · DS72

N113 · A54 · BOUCHES-DU-RHONE

Grans · Puyricard · AIX-EN-PROVENCE · Vauvenargues

Miramas · Lançon-Provence · Eguilles · D10 · Le Tholonet · Montagne Ste-Victoire · Puyloubier

Miramas-Le-Vieux · Cornillon-Confoux · St-Chamas · Aqueduc de Roquefavour · St-Antonin-sur-Bayon · Pourrières · N7

Istres · Berre-l'Etang · D6 · A8

St-Blaise · Etang de Berre · Cabriès · Gardanne · Trets

Fos-sur-Mer · Martigues · Marignane · Mimet · D6 · D8 · N96 · A52 · N560

Port-de-Bouc · N568 · Chaîne de l'Estaque · D5 · L'Estaque · Chaîne de l'Etoile · D908 · Roquevaire

Carro · Cap Couronne · Sausset-les-Pins · Carry-le-Rouet · Niolon · MARSEILLE · N8 · Aubagne · N96 · N8

Iles du Frioul · Mazargues · D2

Montagne de Marseilleveyre · Sormiou · Morgiou · Cassis · A50

Cap Croisette · Cap Canaille · La Ciotat · Les Lecques

Ile de Riou · Les Calanques · La Ciotat-Plage · DS59

10 km
5 miles

N

FRANCE

ITALY

SPAIN

Don't miss

1. Cassis **p.174**
2. Marseille food **p.194**
3. Aqueduc de Roquefavour **p.215**
4. Aix-en-Provence **p.201**
5. Montagne Ste-Victoire **p.213**

La Ciotat, Cassis and the *Calanques*

Before settling down and creating the broad, smooth bay that permits the existence of Marseille, the Provençal coast bucks and rears with the fury of wild horses. La Ciotat, halfway between Toulon and Marseille, is a hard-nosed and gritty shipbuilding town, while chic, well-heeled Cassis is endowed with a dramatic setting, a bijou harbour and delicate wine.

Beaches

The sandy beach at **Cassis** is pretty, with a dramatic backdrop of cliffs, but it gets crowded in summer. **Marseille** has an artificial town beach, the Plage de David, which is lively at all times of the year, with soccer, kite-flying, skateboarding and windsurfing.

For more adventurous sand you need head into the *calanques*, where you can walk the clifftop path and descend at will; boats run from Cassis and Marseille.

To the west of Marseille, the **Côte Bleue**, the playground of the Marseillais, gets crowded during weekends in summer. The beaches are mediocre; **Sausset-les-Pins** has sand and caravans; the best is at **Carro**, the furthest from Marseille, hence the quietest.

For real sand you need to continue west, to the **Camargue** (p.173).

La Ciotat: the World's First Film Set

A safe anchorage with fresh water and beaches, protected from the winds by an eroded rock formation known as the Bec de l'Aigle ('eagle's beak'), La Ciotat has seen ancient Greeks, pirates, fishermen and, since the time of François Ier, shipbuilders – though, instead of galleys to battle the Holy Roman Empire, the yards now produce vessels to transport liquefied gas. La Ciotat has also given the world two momentous pastimes. First came motion pictures, which were pioneered here in 1895 when Auguste and Louis Lumière filmed a train pulling into La Ciotat station (*L'Entrée d'un train en gare de La Ciotat*), a clip that made the first film spectators jump out of their seats as the locomotive seemed to bear down upon them; the **Eden Théâtre**, where it was shown on 28 December 1895, is presently closed, but the town is raising funds for its restoration. The second is *pétanque*, that most Provençal of sports, which came into being here in 1907, when one old-timer's legs became paralysed and he could no longer take the regulation steps before a throw, as laid down in the laws of *boules*. The rules were changed for him and, as everyone enjoyed working up less of a sweat, they stuck.

Most visitors to La Ciotat keep to the beaches and marina around **La Ciotat-Plage** (where you'll find a monument to the Lumière brothers), but it's really the business side of things, around the **Vieux Port**, that affords the best loafing opportunities; in the evening the shipyard cranes come to resemble luminous mutant insects. The Musée Ciotaden on Quai Ganteaume is dedicated to the history of La Ciotat and its shipyards.

Musée Ciotaden
*t 04 42 71 40 99,
www.museeciotaden.
org; open July–Aug
Wed–Mon 4–7;
Sept–June Wed–Mon
3–6; closed Tues; adm*

Beyond the latter, amid the wind-sculpted rocks and dishevelled Mediterranean flora of the Bec de l'Aigle, is the clifftop **Parc du Mugel** (*bus 3 from the Vieux Port*). Avenue de Figuerolles continues from here to the red pudding-stone walls and pebble beach of the **Calanque de Figuerolles**, with its hunchback monkish rock formation, once painted by Georges Braque.

Floating offshore, the tiny **Ile Verte** can be reached by boat from Quai Ganteaume; it has a restaurant and views back to the mainland that explain how the 'eagle's beak' got its name.

Getting to and around La Ciotat and Cassis

La Ciotat is a main stop for **trains** (**t** 08 36 35 35 35) between Marseille and Toulon; regular **buses** (**t** 04 42 08 90 90) cover the 3km from the station to the Vieux Port.

Cassis has less frequent services and its train station is just as far from the centre; if you're coming from Marseille, take one of the frequent coaches, which drop you off at Bd Anatole France, by the tourist office.

Boats leave from Cassis throughout the day for the *calanques* (**t** 04 42 01 90 83).

Bike Hire
Lleba Cycles,3 bis Av Frédéric Mistral, La Ciotat, **t** 04 42 83 60 30.
Carnoux Bikes, Av Foche, Cassis, **t** 06 03 78 57 85.

Route des Crêtes

If you sneer at vertigo and laugh in the face of hairpin turns, ignore the main road between La Ciotat and Cassis, and instead twist and turn along the 17km **Corniche des Crêtes**. Alternatively, a footpath cuts through the road loops, taking about four hours. You will be rewarded with plunging views from France's highest cliffs: the **Falaises du Soubeyran**, or Grande Tête (1,309ft), and craggy **Cap Canaille**. From Pas de la Colle, the road and path descend to the ancient Gallo-Roman Portus Carcisis, now known as Cassis.

Cassis and the *Calanques*

⭐ Cassis

The old coral-fishing village of Cassis, with its fish-hook port, white cliffs, beaches and quaint houses spilling down steep alleyways, was a natural favourite of the Fauve painters. Since their day, the village has made the inevitable progression from fishing to artsy to chic, and is now beyond the purse of most fishermen and artists. The swanky, modern **Casino Municipal** does a roaring trade thanks to its proximity to the gambling-mad Marseillais, and in summer so many tourists descend on the little port that it's often elbow-room only here and on the pebbly **Plage de Bestouan**. When they're not counting wads of banknotes, the Cassidans bestir themselves to make one of the most delicious, fragrant white wines of Provence (*see* opposite).

Until 1990, Cassis had yet another profitable trade: exporting crystal-white stone, hewn from the sheer limestone cliffs that stand like a great jagged sea wall between Cassis and Marseille. Here and there the cliffs are pierced by startling tongues of lapis-lazuli hue – mini-fjords known as *calanques*. The nearest, **Port-Miou**, is accessible by car or foot (a 30min walk): its hard white stone was cut for the Suez Canal. Another 1.5km hike will take you to **Port-Pin**, with a pretty beach, and from there it's another hour to **En-Vau**, the most beautiful of them all, with a small skinny-dippers' beach tucked under the sheer cliffs, where daring human flies dangle from threads (you can also reach En-Vau with less toil from a car park on the Col de la Gardiole). Serious walkers can continue along the GR98 all the way to Marseille. Note that since being

Wine: Cassis AOC

In Cassis, they say their white wine obtained its divine quality when God came down the road from heaven and shed a tear at the plight of a family trying to scratch a living from the rocky amphitheatre overlooking the village. The divine tear fell on a vine and *voilà*, it gave birth to a dry wine of a pale green tint, with a bouquet of heather and rosemary.

The Cassis district is minute but was one of the first to be granted AOC status (1936). Ugni blanc, marsanne, clairette and bourboulenc are the dominant grapes of this pale cocktail, popularized abroad by the late James Beard and considered by the Marseillais to be the only liquid worthy of washing down *bouillabaisse*, grilled red mullet and lobster. Try some in the vast, ancient cellars of **Clos Sainte-Magdeleine**, t 04 42 01 70 28, and **Château de Fontcreuse**, Route de La Ciotat, t 04 42 01 71 09, the district's only real château, which between the wars was the property of a retired English colonel who improved the stock and carved out new vineyards in the steep limestone hills.

ravaged by forest fires in 1990 the paths to the *calanques* have been off limits from mid-June to the second Saturday in September, when the only way to visit is by motorboat from Cassis port; excursions depart frequently through the day. If they let you disembark in the *calanques*, you must stick to the shore.

Market Days around La Ciotat and Cassis

La Ciotat: Tues and Sun am, plus July and Aug 8–12 on the Vieux Port.
Cassis: Wed and Fri am.

Festivals around La Ciotat and Cassis

La Ciotat: Carnival: April.
Cassis: Fishermen's Festival: last weekend in June; Harvest Fair: first Sun in Sept.

Where to Stay and Eat around La Ciotat and Cassis

La Ciotat ✉ 13600
Quai Stalingrad, near the shipyards, has the best choice of restaurants.
***Miramar, 3 Bd Beaurivage, t 04 42 83 33 79, *www.miramarlaciotat.com* (€€). A classy hotel amid pine groves by the beach. **L'Orchidée**, its restaurant, is the best in town. *Restaurant closed Sat lunch and Sun eve.*

**La Rotonde, 44 Bd de la République, t 04 42 08 67 50, *www.hotel-larotonde-ciotat.fr* (€€–€). The best bet near the Vieux Port.

(i) **Cassis** >>
Oustau Calendal, Quai des Moulins, t 08 92 25 98 92, www.ot-cassis.com; open July and Aug daily; Sept–June Mon–Sat and Sun am

(i) **La Ciotat** >
Bd Anatole France, t 04 42 08 61 32, www.tourisme-laciotat.com; open June–Sept Mon–Sat and Sun am; Oct–May Mon–Sat

*Beaurivage, 1 Bd Beaurivage, t 04 42 83 26 61 (€€). A good budget choice, at the lower end of the price range.
République Indépendante de Figuerolles, Calanque de Figuerolles, t 04 42 08 41 71, *www.figuerolles.com* (€). Grandly named *chambres d'hôtes* place on the beach, with a very good restaurant (€€) that becomes Russian between December and May. *Hotel closed Nov–mid-Mar.*

Cassis ✉ 13260
****Les Roches Blanches, 9 Av des Calanques, t 04 42 01 09 30, *www.roches-blanches-cassis.com* (€€€€€–€€€). The most spectacular hotel in the area, perched on the promontory overlooking Cassis bay. Rooms are a tad small but very comfortable; there's a private beach and sun terraces. *Closed Nov–Feb.*
***Les Jardins de Cassis, Rue Auguste Favier, t 04 42 01 84 85, *www.lesjardinsdecassis.com* (€€€–€€). A Provençal-style oasis set amidst lemon groves and bougainvillaea, with a pool and restaurant. *Closed Nov–mid-Mar; restaurant open lunch June–Sept only.*
***Le Royal Cottage, 6 Av du 11 Novembre, t 04 42 01 33 34, *www.royal-cottage.com* (€€€€–€€€). Just above the port, in a quiet park, with a pool, air-conditioning and well-

equipped rooms. No restaurant. *Closed Christmas–New Year.*

**Le Grand Jardin, 2 Rue Pierre Eydin, t 04 42 01 70 10, *www.hotel-grand-jardin-cassis.com* (€€). A hotel offering modern rooms, with a terrace, in the centre of town.

**Le Laurence, 8 Rue de l'Arène, t 04 42 01 88 78, *www.cassis-hotel-laurence.com* (€€–€). Reasonably priced option with views up to the château. *Closed Nov–Jan.*

Chez César, 21 Quai des Baux, t 04 42 01 75 47 (€€). Fresh seafood served up amidst Marcel Pagnol décor. The rosy-pink local sea urchins (*oursins*) feature prominently when in season. *Closed Sun eve and Mon.*

Nino, 1 Quai Barthélemy, t 04 42 01 74 32 (€€). A restaurant offering tasty fish soup, grilled prawns and more on a summery seaside terrace. *Closed Sun eve and Mon in winter; Mon in summer.*

Marseille

Marseille isn't a city; it's a shock.

Amid Provence's carefully nurtured image of lavender fields, rosé wine and *pétanque*, Marseille, France's second city and the world's eighth largest port, is the great anomaly. Like New York, it's been the gateway to a new world for hundreds of thousands of immigrants. Many have gone no further, creating in Marseille perhaps the most varied mix of cultures and religions in Europe, 'the meeting place of the entire world', as Alexandre Dumas called it. It is traditionally the great anti-Paris, ever defiant of central authority and bigwigs in any form, be they Julius Caesar, Louis XIV, Napoleon, Hitler or De Gaulle.

Unfortunately, Marseille has also shared some of New York's less savoury traits: racism, smuggling of all sorts, its lingering *French Connection* reputation earned by the petty crooks and hardened gangsters of the French mafia or *milieu* (one of whom, according to one theory, was the man on the famous grassy knoll who shot JFK). Unemployment is disproportionately high (up to 30 per cent in some *arrondissements*), and xenophobia thrives. 2002's presidential elections saw Marseille vote 25 per cent for National Front leader Jean-Marie Le Pen, yet the city was also the scene of the most seething anti-Le Pen demonstrations.

'These Marseillais make Marseilles hymns, and Marseilles vests, and Marseilles soap for all the world; but they never sing their hymns, or wear their vests, or wash with their soap themselves,' wrote Mark Twain. So what *do* they do? Marseille, in spite of character to spare, is a great unknown, a metropolis of 111 villages that in its 2,600 years has contributed precious little to civilization; it is the eternal capital of great expectations, 'a city that's been waiting for Godot', according to an editor in one of Marseille's young publishing houses. But one senses that its long bottled-up juices are about to be uncorked. Today's Marseille has a jaunty new look, through a renewed sense of local pride as well as through the state funds for restoration that came with its recently declared status as a *ville d'art*. But it's not all about looks; people are also

Getting to and around Marseille

By Air

Marseille's **airport**, *www.marseille.aeroport.fr*, is northwest of the city at Marignane; call **t** 04 42 14 14 14 for flight information. There are regular flights to Marseille from London; *see* **Planning Your Trip**, p.69. A **bus** every 20mins (**t** 04 91 50 59 34), between 4.30am and 12.50am, connects the airport with Gare St-Charles, taking 25mins.

By Train

Gare St-Charles (1er), the main **train station** with its great ironwork vault designed by Gustave Eiffel, has rail links with nearly every town in the south, **t** 0892 35 35 35, *www.voyages-sncf.com*. The TGV from Paris takes 3hrs.

By Boat

For **ferries** to Algeria (politics permitting), Corsica, Sardinia and Tunisia, contact **SNCM**, 61 Bd des Dames (2e), *www.sncm.fr*. On a smaller scale, there's a pedestrian-only '**ferryboat**' across the Vieux Port, immortalized by Marcel Pagnol.

By Métro, Bus and Tram

Marseille has an efficient **bus** network, two **métro** lines and two **tram** lines (*www.le-tram.fr*); the métro is safe, quick and highly efficient, but the buses can be pretty hard work. Pick up the useful *plan du réseau* at the tourist office or at the RTM (Régie des Transports Marseillais) information desk close to the Bourse, 6–8 Rue des Fabres (1er), **t** 04 91 91 92 10, *www.rtm.fr*. **Tickets** are valid for an hour, or you can buy a day pass; both are transferable between bus and métro. Night buses (Fluobus) run from La Canebière across town.

The *gare routière*, **t** 0891 024 025, *www.lepilote.com*, 3 Place Victor Hugo, has connections to Aix-en-Provence, Cassis, Nice, Arles, Avignon, Toulon and Cannes.

RTM also runs a daily multilingual hop-on, hop-off open-top **tour bus**, *Le Grand Tour*, with 1½hr guided tours of historic Marseille. It leaves at 10am from the Vieux Port directly in front of the boats for the islands. Or you could take a mini **tourist train**, touring Vieux Marseille or visiting Notre-Dame-de-la-Garde, **t** 04 91 25 24 69, *www.petit-train-marseille.com*.

By Taxi

Marseille's taxi drivers seem to be maniacs to a man. If you need one, call **t** 04 91 02 20 20, and make sure the meter is switched on at the start of your journey.

Car Hire

Car hire firms in Gare St-Charles include **Avis**, **t** 0820 61 16 36, *www.avis.fr*. **Hertz** is at 15 Rue Maurice Bourdet (1er), **t** 04 91 14 04 24, *www.hertz.fr*, and **EuropCar**, 121 Av du Prado (8e), **t** 0825 825 421. Driving in central Marseille is not for the faint-hearted, and, if you park in the street, only leave things inside the car that you don't want any more.

waking up to the fact that this very old city is the last place on the French Med with any real edge or swagger – you can feel it in the vibrant spontaneity in the streets and cafés, in the rhythms of the drum pounding at an OM game, and during Carnival, when a home-made explosion of energy and fun flow like hot lava down La Canebière. Luc Besson's film *Taxi* was an unexpected international hit that led to a sequel, and local group IAM continue to control the French hip-hop scene with their distinctive sound.

Yet as Marseille becomes hip and savvy, it also very much wants to remain distinctly *Marseille*, and residents are taking an increasingly jaundiced view of the new TGV trains that link the city to its old rival Paris in three short hours. The *envahisseurs* have already purchased their first holiday flats...

Central Marseille

250-metres
250 yards

N

Gare Maritime Internationale

Cathédrale de la Nouvelle Major

Ancienne Major

Le Panier

Vieille Charité

Hôpital de l'Hôtel-Dieu

Hôtel de Ville

Musée des Docks Romains

Vieux Port

Fort St-Jean

Fort St-Nicolas

To Parc du Pharo and Corniche J.F. Kennedy

Théâtre National de la Criée

Abbaye St-Victor

To Notre-Dame de la Garde

Centre Bourse

Musée d'Histoire de Marseille

Musée de la Mode

Musée de la Marine

VIEUX PORT-HÔTEL DE VILLE

Opéra Municipal

Musée Cantini

ESTRANGIN-PRÉFECTURE

Préfecture

Gare Routière

Gare St-Charles

Porte d'Aix

NOAILLES

Marché des Capucins

CANEBIÈRE-RÉFORMES

NOTRE-DAME DU MONT-COURS JULIEN

Musée Grobet-Labadié

To Palais Longchamp and Jardin Public

To L'Hôpital de la Timone

To Vélodrome Unité d'Habitation and Mazargues

Orientation

Marseille, with 11 neighbourhoods and 16 *arrondissements*, is one of Europe's largest cities, sprawling over twice as many acres as Paris. The northernmost neighbourhoods are the poorest, the first addresses of many new immigrants; the Panier (*see* p.183) and neighbourhoods around the station constitute the North African quarters, lively during the day although uncomfortable to wander in after dark on a poorly lit road. The southern neighbourhoods, with their parks and access to the beaches, are distinctly more monied and sanitized. A circle of hills divides the city from the mainland, physically and psychologically.

The Vieux Port, the heart of the city since its founding, is now used only for pleasure craft and boats out to the islets of Frioul and the Château d'If, while commercial port activities are concentrated to the north in the Rade de Marseille. To the south of the Vieux Port, the golden Virgin of Notre-Dame-de-la-Garde towers high over her beloved city, while to the west the Parc du Pharo marks the beginning of a corniche road along the coast to Cap Croisette, lined with coves, beaches and restaurants, with a mountain, Marseilleveyre, that you can climb at the end for a view of all of the above.

History

The story goes that in 600 BC Greek colonists from the Ionian city of Phocaea, having obtained the approval of the gods, loaded their ship with olive saplings and sailed towards Gaul. They found a perfect bay, and their handsome leader, Protis, went to the local king to obtain permission to found a city. It just so happened that that very day the king was hosting a banquet for the young men of his land, after which, according to tradition, his daughter Gyptis would select her husband. Protis was invited to join and, thanks to his great beauty, was chosen by the princess. For his new wife's dowry, Protis asked for the land the Greeks coveted near the mouth of the Rhône, including the Lacydon (the Vieux Port). He named the new city Massalia.

Massalia boomed from the start. By 530 BC it had its own treasury at Delphi, and its own colonies, from Málaga to Nice; it traded for tin with Cornwall; and its great astronomer, Pytheas, explored the Baltic and in 350 BC became the first scientist to calculate latitudes accurately. As a commercial rival of Carthage, the city allied itself with Rome in the Punic Wars, and profited from the latter's conquests in Spain and Gaul. By the 2nd century BC, Massalia had a population of 50,000 and was ruled by a merchant oligarchy whose political astuteness was admired by Aristotle and Cicero. This astuteness failed them when they sided with Pompey, calling down the vengeance of Caesar, who conquered their city after a long siege and seized all of Massalia's colonies with the exception of Nice and Hyères. Yet even after the 2nd century AD, when Massalia adopted Roman law, it remained a city apart, the westernmost enclave of Hellenism, with famous schools of Greek rhetoric and medicine.

As the Pax Romana crumbled, Marseille nearly went out of business, taking hard knocks from Goths, Franks, Saracens and then the Franks again in the 8th century under Charles Martel. It was plagued by pirates, and business stayed bad until the 11th century, when the Crusaders showed up looking for transport to the Holy Land. This was the get-rich-quick opportunity of the Middle Ages, and, though Genoa and Venice grabbed the biggest trading concessions in the Levant, Marseille too grew fat on the proceeds. Briefly a republic, the city soon saw its real power passed to a merchant oligarchy; from 1178 to 1192 the big boss was the cultivated En Barral, patron of two of Provence's greatest trouba-dours, the mad Peire Vidal (*see* p.45) and Folquet of Marseille.

Trumped by Kings: Charles d'Anjou to Louis XIV

When Charles d'Anjou acquired Provence in 1252, he confiscated Marseille's entire fleet to make good his claim on Sicily. Thanks to the monumental arrogance of the Angevins, the ships were annihilated in the revolt of the Sicilian Vespers (1282). With its legitimate commerce undermined by its own rulers, Marseille became a den for pirates and went into such a decline that it became an easy target for the Angevins' rival, Alfonso V of Aragon, who destroyed as much of it as he could in 1423.

Coming under French rule in 1481 meant, for Marseille, tumbling headlong into the power-grasping scrum known as the Wars of Italy (1494–1559). The city's galleys went to war again, this time for François Ier, earning the fury of Emperor Charles V, who sent his henchman, the rebel Constable of Bourbon, to besiege the city. Marseille resisted heroically and François Ier showed his gratitude by giving the city the freedom to trade at will in the eastern Mediterranean. Once again the money rolled in, to be pumped into new industries, especially soap and sugar.

Marseille's longing to be left alone to mind its own affairs put it squarely at odds with Louis XIV; for 40 years the city thumbed its nose at His Solar Majesty while scrambling to retain its autonomy. By 1660, the king had had enough: he opened up a great breach in Marseille's walls and humiliated the city by turning its own cannons back on itself. The central authority that Louis forced on Marseille was dangerously lax when it came to issues crucial to the running of a good port – such as quarantine. The result, in 1720, was a devastating plague that spread throughout Provence.

Tunes, Booms and Busts

Marseille buried its dead and went right back to business. New markets in the Middle East, North Africa and America made it Europe's greatest port in the 18th century. Its industries (soap, woollens, porcelain, tarot cards) blossomed – then withered away in the Revolution, which for 10 years bitterly divided workers and the oligarchy. The former did their share in upholding the Revolution; as 500 volunteers set off for Paris in July 1792, someone suggested singing the new battle song of the Army of the Rhine, composed by Claude-Joseph Rouget de l'Isle. It caught on, and as the Marseillais marched along they improved the rhythm and harmonies. By the time they reached Paris, the 'song of the Marseillais' was perfected and became the hit tune of the Revolution, and subsequently the most rousing and bloodcurdling of national anthems.

However, as the Revolution devolved into the Terror, Marseille was found so wanting in proper politics that it was known in Paris as the 'ville sans nom'. Any building that had sheltered an anti-Revolutionary was demolished, including the famous monastery of St Victor. The misery continued under Napoleon, who was added to the list of Marseille's bogeymen when he provoked the continental blockade by the British and ruined trade. Recovery came with the Second Empire, the conquest of Algeria in 1830 and the construction of the Suez Canal. Soon Marseille was more prosperous than ever, with some 60,000 new immigrants every decade between 1850 and 1930 – Greeks and Armenians fleeing the Turks, Italians fleeing Fascism and, later, Spaniards fleeing Franco.

After becoming one of the first French cities to vote socialist (in 1890), Marseille's reputation took a nosedive. Corruption, rigged elections and an open link between the Hôtel de Ville and the bosses of the milieu were so rampant that in 1938 Paris dissolved the municipal government and ran the city at a distance. Yet the 1930s also saw the film release of Marcel Pagnol's classic Marseillais trilogy Marius, Fanny and César, which helped create throughout France an insatiable appetite for opérette marseillaise; even Joséphine Baker sang the tunes of Marseille's great songwriter Vincent Scotto.

In 1953 Marseille elected a socialist mayor – Gaston Deferre, the antagonist of De Gaulle, who reigned until his death in 1986. Deferre oversaw rapid and difficult changes: a sharp decline in trade when France lost its colonies, and a population that exploded from 660,000 in 1955 to 960,000 in 1975. To accommodate the new arrivals (mostly North Africans and French refugees from Algeria), the city infested itself with the shoddy high-rise housing that scars it to this day. Unemployment rose as the traditional soap and fat industries plummeted, while new projects, such as the steel mills and port at Fos-sur-Mer, failed to provide as many jobs as expected, fuelling the racial tensions and organized crime that give the city its rough reputation. This image has softened, but there are still muzzled rottweilers at every métro station.

Even when the city, or at least its revered soccer team, L'Olympique de Marseille (OM), won the European championship in 1993, the team got itself banned from the 1994 European competition for match fixing and bribery. The team's flamboyant then-owner, maverick politician, businessman and Euro-deputy Bernard Tapie, served eight months in Marseille's most notorious jail for the offences. The scandal continued, with an audit revealing more than 85 per cent of the club's revenue going to players' salaries alone. Less well known than all the scandals is Marseille's reorientation, for the first time in its history, away from the Mediterranean and towards Europe. There's a new TGV rail link with Paris, and a canal will link the Rhône with the Rhine by 2010. Marseille is now the most important research centre in France after Paris, home of a major science university, inventor of a new, fifth-generation computer language, and site of COMEX, the world's leading developer of underwater technologies.

The Vieux Port

Marseille the urban mangrove entwines its aquatic roots around the neat, rectangular Vieux Port, inhabited for the past 2,600 years. It's now a huge marina with more than 10,000 berths; its cafés have fine sunset views, though in the morning the action and smells centre around the Quai des Belges and its boatside **fish market**, where the key ingredients of *bouillabaisse* are touted in a racy *patois* as thick as the soup itself. From the Quai des Belges, *vedettes* sail to the Château d'If and Iles de Frioul (*see* p.192), past the two bristling fortresses that still defend the harbour: to the north **St-Jean**, first built in the 12th century by the Knights of St John, and to the south **St-Nicolas**, built by Louis XIV to keep a close eye on Marseille rather than the sea.

A bronze marker in the Quai des Belges pinpoints the spot where the Greeks first set foot in Gaul. Yet Marseille concealed its age until the 20th century, when excavations for the glitzy new shopping mall, the **Centre Bourse**, revealed the eastern ramparts and gate of Massalia, dating back to the 3rd century BC, now enclosed in the **Jardin des Vestiges**. On the ground floor of the Centre Bourse, the **Musée d'Histoire de Marseille** displays models, everyday items, mosaics and a 3rd-century BC wreck of a Roman ship, discovered in 1974. Built from 15 different kinds of pine, it had become so fragile that it had to be freeze-dried, like instant coffee, to prevent further deterioration and aid preservation.

Elaborate antique models of later ships that sailed into the Vieux Port and items related to Marseille's trading history are the main focus of the **Musée de la Marine et de l'Economie de Marseille**. It's housed in the 1860 **Palais de la Bourse**, France's oldest stock exchange, built during the reign of Napoléon III to obliterate an unrepentant democratic quarter that spilled much blood in the Revolution of 1848. But this corner, stock exchange or not, remained a vortex for violence: a plaque on the Canebière side of the Bourse recalls that King Alexander of Yugoslavia was

Musée d'Histoire de Marseille
t 04 91 90 42 22; open Mon–Sat 12–7; adm

Musée de la Marine et de l'Economie de Marseille
t 04 91 39 33 33; open daily 10–6; adm

Musée de la Mode
*t 04 91 17 06 00; open
summer Tues–Sun 11–6;
winter Tues–Sun 10–5;
closed Mon; adm*

assassinated here in 1934. Just up La Canebière from here, at No.11, the **Musée de la Mode** has a wardrobe full of Chanel clothes and other pieces from the 1930s to the present, but they're not always on display. The emphasis is on changing exhibitions.

Le Panier

On sunny afternoons the Marseillais laze like contented cats in the cafés lining the north end of the Vieux Port – a custom probably as old as the city itself. Behind them is the oldest part of the city, known rather oddly as Le Panier ('the basket') after a popular 17th-century cabaret, although its weave of winding narrow streets and stairs dates from the time of the ancient Greeks. When the well-to-do moved out in the 18th century, Le Panier was given over to fishermen and a romanticized underworld; guides were published to its 'private' hotels and the hourly rates of their residents.

Before the war Le Panier was a lively Corsican and Italian neighbourhood, and later its warren of secret ways absorbed hundreds of Jews and other refugees from the Nazis, hoping to escape to America (*see* box, below). In January 1943, Hitler cottoned on to the leaks in Marseille and, in collusion with local property speculators, gave the order to dynamite everything between the Vieux Port and halfway up the hill, to the Grand'Rue/Rue Caisserie. Given just one day to evacuate, the 20,000 departing residents were screened by French police and the Gestapo, who selected 3,500 for the concentration camps and sent them out of the city in

One Good Man

In the early 1940s, in spite of open visa quotas, the US Department of State with its prejudiced, bury-its-head-in-the-sand bureaucracy maintained a policy of turning back ships of refugees from Hitler. Consulates in Europe were advised, as one memo put it, 'to resort to various administrative devices which would postpone and postpone and postpone the granting of the visas'. In one particularly shameful episode, the US Vice Consul in Lyon denied visas to Jewish children because their parents might be arrested, leaving their children to become public charges in the USA.

The one hero in the story was Varian Fry. Two months after the Nazis occupied Marseille, 32-year-old Fry, editor of a New York foreign policy review, arrived in the city as the representative of a privately funded group called the Emergency Rescue Committee. Although he had no previous experience in the field, and in spite of the considerable risks from the Gestapo and Vichy and the opposition of his own government, Fry quickly made himself an expert in obtaining false papers, forging documents and organizing safe transport out of Marseille: among the 1,500 people he saved were Marcel Duchamp, Marc Chagall, Hannah Arendt, André Breton and Max Ernst. Fry worked for 13 months before he was expelled from Marseille. On his return to the United States, he published an article on the systematic persecution of the Jews and the concentration camps, which made later pleas of official ignorance ring less than true. Just before Varian Fry died in 1967, the French government awarded him the Legion of Honour. And in October 2000 a square next to the American consulate (on Boulevard Paul Peytral) was named in his honour, Place Varian Fry. Presiding over the dedication ceremony was the US ambassador to France, Felix Rohatyn, who as a child was spirited out of occupied Marseille, in all likelihood by the good offices of Fry.

a long line of tram cars. A monument in the quarter commemorates the destruction and the deportees who never returned.

Two buildings were protected from the dynamite: the 17th-century **Hôtel de Ville** on the quay and, behind it, in Rue de la Prison, the **Maison Diamantée**, Marseille's 16th-century Mannerist masterpiece, named after the pyramidal points of its façade. It holds the **Musée du Vieux Marseille**, a delightful attic where the city stashes its odds and ends, including Provençal furniture; 18th-century Neapolitan Christmas crib figures and *santons* (*see* box, below); playing cards and tarot cards, long an important local industry; and poignant photos of Le Panier before it was blown to smithereens. Some of the cheap housing thrown up after the war in **Place du Mazeau** has been demolished in turn to make way for a museum dedicated to the flamboyant sculptor and native Marseillais César.

Hôtel de Ville
open for conferences and guided tours only; enquire at tourist office

Musée du Vieux Marseille
t 04 91 55 28 68; open summer Tues–Sun 11–6; winter Tues–Sun 10–5; closed Mon; adm

The dynamite that blew up lower Le Panier was responsible for revealing the contents of the **Musée des Docks Romains** at 2 Place Vivaux, built over a stretch of the vast 1st-century AD Roman quay, where wine and grains were stored in *dolia*, or massive jars. Exhibits describe seafaring in the ancient Mediterranean. One last survivor of the pre-war Le Panier is the oldest house in Marseille, the **Hôtel de Cabre** (1535), a Gothic–Renaissance confection on Grand'Rue. The city's oldest café, the 1903 **Café Parisien**, with colourful mosaics intact, is just up from here on Place Sadi Carnot.

Musée des Docks Romains
t 04 91 91 24 62; open summer Tues–Sun 11–6; winter Tues–Sun 10–5; adm

The Panier retains its original crusty character atop the well-worn steps of **Montée des Accoules** and around **Place de Lenche**, which was once the marketplace or *agora* of the Greeks: lanky cats prowl around, laundry flaps, cement mixers grind away, people sit on the pavement in kitchen chairs – it still feels more Greek than French, although that may soon change.

Signs point the way through the maze to the top of Rue du Petit Puits and the elegant **Vieille-Charité**, designed by Pierre Puget, a student of Bernini, court architect to Louis XIV and native of Le Panier. Built by the city fathers between 1671 and 1745 to take in homeless migrants from the countryside, this is one of the world's most palatial workhouses, with three storeys of arcaded ambulatories in pale pink stone, overlooking a court with a sumptuous

Santons

Christmas crèches with figures of the Nativity go back a long way in Provence. According to tradition, St Francis set up the first crèche in the 13th century, but some say it may have been his mother (from Tarascon or Beaucaire) who showed him how. At any rate, every church in Provence had a crèche at Christmas, and when the Revolution closed the churches in 1789 the people sorely missed their nativity scenes. It was then that Jean-Louis Lagnel (1764–1822) of Marseille invented *santons* (little saints) – hand-painted clay figures in traditional Provençal dress doing traditional Provençal things, that people could afford to buy and take home. They were an instant success, and in 1806 the first *santon* fair was set up along the Canebière. It's still going strong, from the end of November to Epiphany.

elliptical chapel crowned by an oval dome – a curvaceous Baroque work forced into a strait-laced neo-Corinthian façade in 1863. Although the complex became a barracks after the Revolution, it returned to its original purpose in 1860, housing families displaced first by the construction of the Bourse and later by the Nazis' destruction of Le Panier. By 1962, the Charité was in so precarious a state that everyone was evacuated, and Le Corbusier, happening through, warned the city it was in danger of losing a masterpiece. A long restoration ensued and in 1985 it reopened – a shelter no longer for the homeless but for culture.

Musée d'Archéologie Méditerranéenne
t 04 91 14 58 59; open summer Tues–Sun 10–6; winter Tues–Sun 10–5; adm

The middle gallery of the Charité houses the excellent **Musée d'Archéologie Méditerranéenne**, featuring a collection of ancient Mediterranean artefacts. The remarkable collection of Egyptian art (the second-best in France after the Louvre) has a range of fine art and sculpture plus bric-a-brac and cat, ibis and crocodile mummies; there are also beautiful works from ancient Cyprus, Mesopotamia, Susa, Greece (including a good section of vases), and pre-Roman and Roman Italy. Another section is devoted to the reconstructed **sanctuary of Roquepertuse** from Velaux, near Aix. Built by a head-hunting Celto-Ligurian tribe called the Salians, the sanctuary has pillars pierced with holes to hold skulls, a lintel incised with the outline of four horse heads (these symbolically transported the dead soul), and Buddha-like figures sitting in the lotus position. Similar temples found in Entremont (*see* p.215) and Mouriès suggest a common religion, perhaps a chthonic cult in which warriors went to commune with the spirits of their dead heroes.

Musée d'Arts Africain, Océanien et Amérindien
t 04 91 14 58 38; open summer Tues–Sun 11–6; winter Tues–Sun 10–5; adm

The Charité also houses the **Musée d'Arts Africain, Océanien et Amérindien**, with a fascinating collection of ritual artefacts, especially those dealing with more recent cultures obsessed with human heads and skulls, as in the Amazon and Vanuatu (don't miss the Aztec skull with the tiniest turquoise tiles imaginable). On the ground floor is a café, a cinema, and a bookshop with a good selection of world music and French-language art books.

Cathédrale de la Nouvelle Major
t 04 91 90 01 82; open Tues–Sat 10–12 and 2–5.30, Sun 9–12.30 and 2–6; closed Mon

Just to the west, looming over the tankers and cargo ships drowsing in Marseille's outer harbour basin, are the two 'majors'. The striped neo-Byzantine, empty and unloved **Cathédrale de la Nouvelle Major** was built in 1853 with the new money coming in from the conquest of Algeria – enough to make it the largest church built in France since the Middle Ages. Now utterly isolated by lanes of frantic traffic, the pile is held up by 444 marble columns; predictably, somehow, the monster is not only ugly but dangerous, and has to be encased in nets in order to keep the rare visitor from being brained by bits of falling stone. An EU-financed project is trying to remedy traffic problems by building a tunnel underneath the area, which may go some way to restoring the area's former tranquillity.

The cathedral's Romanesque predecessor, the **Ancienne-Major**, is in no better nick, having already had its transept brutally amputated for the new cathedral (note the poor angel, gesturing sadly without a hand); it's now fenced off and propped up with wooden planks. If you get a chance to go inside, don't miss the Ancienne-Major's crossing, a fantasy in brick that sets an octagonal dome on four stepped conical squinches, a typically Provençal conceit. One chapel has a *Descent from the Cross* (early 16th-century) by Nicolas della Robbia; the altar of saints Lazarus, Martha and Mary Magdalene in Carrara marble (1475–81) is by Francesco Laurana and was considered by Anthony Blunt 'the earliest purely Italian work on French soil'. What you never get to see is the Ancienne-Major's old curiosity shop of relics: part of Jesus' cradle and one of his tears, St Peter's tooth and, best of all, the fishbones left over from the feast at the Sermon on the Mount.

South of the Vieux Port: Quai de Rive Neuve and Abbaye St-Victor

Toweards the end of the 20th century, this part of the Old Port made a comeback: during lunchtimes and on summer evenings half of Marseille seems to descend on its bars, restaurants, theatres and clubs on the quay, Rue Saint-Saëns and Place Thiars. The oldest cultural institution here is the **Opéra**, two blocks south of the port in Place Reyer, built in 1924 and graced with Art Deco Greek gods and a pure Art Deco interior.

Opéra
contact the tourist office about tours

Two streets back, at 19 Rue Grignan, is a *hôtel particulier* housing the **Musée Cantini** with its modern art and frequent special exhibitions, which have included Francis Picabia, Max Ernst, André Masson, Francis Bacon, Balthus, César, Arman and Ben. Permanent displays at the museum include Paul Signac's shimmering *Port de Marseille*, and the first Cubist views of L'Estaque that Raoul Dufy painted with Georges Braque in 1908; the greater part of its post-1960 works have been moved into the Musée d'Art Contemporain (*see* p.191).

Musée Cantini
t 04 91 54 77 75; open summer Tues–Sun 11–6; winter Tues–Sun 10–5; adm

On **Quai de Rive Neuve** you'll find ship's chandlers' shops, restaurants and the national theatre, **La Criée**, installed in a former fish auction house (*see* p.196). For better or worse, its presence has tamed the once salty Rive Neuve bars, including the **Bar de la Marine**, which is no longer recognizable as the set for the famous card-playing scene in Marcel Pagnol's *Marius* (*see* p.181). Further along the *quai*, steps lead up to battlemented walls and towers good enough for a Hollywood castle, defending one of the oldest Christian shrines in Provence, the **Abbaye St-Victor**. St-Victor was founded in AD 416 by St Jean Cassien, formerly an anchorite in the Egyptian Thebaid. One account has it that he brought with him from Egypt the mummy of St Victor, though the more popular

Abbaye St-Victor
t 04 96 11 22 60, www.saintvictor.net; open daily 9–7

version says Victor was a Roman legionnaire who converted to Christianity and slew at least one sea serpent (see the relief over the door) before being ground to a pulp between a pair of millstones. In art he sometimes looks like Don Quixote, with windmill.

St-Victor may be Marseille's oldest church, but it's no fuddy-duddy: like Broadway, it has an electronic sign at the entrance reeling off news, and the side aisles are equipped with TV screens so all the parishioners can view mass at the high altar – doings Jean Cassien never imagined 1,600 years ago when he excavated the first chapels in the flank of an ancient stone quarry near a Hellenistic necropolis, which he expanded for Christian use as a *martyrium* (a rock-cut burial niche surrounding the tomb of a martyr). In the 11th century, when the monks of St-Victor adopted the Rule of St Benedict, they added the church on top, turning the old chapels into a labyrinthine **crypt**. Although now well lit, this curious *termitarium*, with ceilings 6–60ft in height, is suffused with ancient mystery – some of the beautifully sculpted sarcophagi date from the 3rd century AD and were found to contain seven or eight dead monks crowded like sardines, providing proof of the popularity of an abbey that founded 300 monastic houses in Provence and Sardinia. Then there's the 5th-century sarcophagus of St Jean Cassien, showing the saint preaching among the columns, and the cave-like 5th-century chapel, carved with a pair of weird old faces and stained green with moss, traditionally enshrining one of Marseille's three Black Virgins (supposedly Christian adaptations of Artemis, the patroness of Massalia). A primordial Candlemas rite begins here every 2 February: the archbishop comes to bless green candles before the Virgin, who gets to go out in a procession that ends at the abbey's bakery, where small loaves (*navettes*) are baked in the shape of boats – a similar custom, in the temples of Isis, once heralded the start of the navigation season. The faithful then take the green candles home to light at wakes as a symbol of rebirth.

Notre-Dame-de-la-Garde

Palais du Pharo
bus 83 from the Vieux Port, Quai des Belges

Notre-Dame-de-la-Garde
t 04 91 13 40 80, www. notredamedelagarde. com; open daily summer 7am–7.15pm; winter 7.30–5.30

Just northwest of St-Victor is Louis XIV's **Fort St-Nicolas**, and beyond that is the **Palais du Pharo**, built by Napoléon III as a gift for his wife, the Empress Eugénie, who never got around to seeing it. The gardens, with striking views over the port, were until recently used for concerts and summer theatre, though now host only conventions and weddings. You can still walk around the grounds, and beyond are the *calanques* (see pp.191–2). The prize 360° view, though, is from Marseille's watchtower hill, an isolated limestone outcrop towering 530ft above the city, crowned by **Notre-Dame-de-la-Garde**, a neo-Byzantine/Romanesque pile with an unfortunate resemblance to a locomotive. It's a killer walk, and even fairly hair-raising to drive – let bus 60 do the work from Place aux Huiles on Quai de Rive-Neuve. The landmark supports France's largest golden mega-Madonna, 33ft high and shining like a beacon out to sea. In 1214 a monk of St-Victor built the first chapel here and over the decades it gained a reputation for the miracles performed by a statue of the Virgin, Marseille's *Bonne Mère*. The chapel's florid Second Empire architecture attracted some real bombs when the Nazis made it their headquarters and last stand, and you can still see some of the dents. But besides the view, the main attraction is the basilica's great collection of *ex votos*, painted by fishermen and sailors.

La Canebière

Before La Canebière itself was laid out in Louis XIV's expansion scheme of 1666, this area was the ropemakers' quarter. The hemp they used has given its name to Marseille's most famous boulevard – *chanvre* in French, but in Provençal more like the Latin *cannabis*. It's a not entirely inappropriate allusion, for this was the high street of French *dolce far niente*, an essential ingredient of music-hall Marseille, which could swagger and boast that 'the Champs-Elysées is the Canebière of Paris'. In its day, the thoroughfare sported grand cafés, fancy shops and hotels where travellers of yore had their first thrills before sailing off to exotic lands, but these days La Canebière – or 'Can o' beer' as English sailors know it – has suffered the same fate as the Champs-Elysées: banks, airline offices and heavy traffic. Trees would do it some good.

Some of La Canebière's old pizzazz lingers in the lively streets to the south around 'Marseille's stomach', the **Marché des Capucins**, a grazer's heaven, where the air is filled with tempting, exotic smells and most of the shops are North African. Here, too, is **Noailles station**, the last resting place for the city's retired omnibuses and trams, the **Galerie des Transports**; Marseille's last working tram still has its terminus here. Behind this hurly-burly stretches the **Cours Julien**, a favourite promenade and *pétanque* court, lined with antiques shops, galleries and trendy restaurants, which gets distinctly more rough and ready towards **Place Notre-Dame-du-Mont**, with its spectacular displays of graffiti. Funky cafés and galleries are also to be found on the nearby **Rue des Trois Rois**.

North, and perpendicular to La Canebière, extends another tarnished *grand boulevard*, **Cours Belsunce**. Until 1964, No.54 was the site of the famous neo-Moorish/Art Nouveau **music hall** where Maurice Chevalier and Fernandel once starred, and where Tino Rossi and Yves Montand had their stage débuts. Now the *cours* leads only to the **Porte d'Aix**, a fuzzy-minded Roman triumphal arch, vintage 1823, erected to Louis XVI or Liberty or both, and adorned with statues of virtues such as Resignation and Prudence,

Galerie des Transports
t 04 91 54 15 15; closed for renovation

whose heads (much like Louis XVI's) suddenly fell off in 1937 and rolled down the street. This quarter, like Le Panier, is now mostly North African: Marseille's mosque is just the other side of the arch.

Palais Longchamp and Environs

In 1834 Marseille suffered a drought so severe that the city dug a canal to bring in water from the Durance. This 80km feat of aquatic engineering ends with a heroic splash at the **Palais Longchamp**, a delightfully overblown *nymphaeum* and cascade, populated with stone felines, bulls and a buxom allegory of the Durance, and having had a €6 million restoration programme (**Ⓜ** Cinq-Avenues-Longchamp; bus 80 from La Canebière). Behind the palace stretch the **public gardens**, an **observatory** (one of four in this city, which has been the home of many famous astronomers) and a little **zoo**; in the right wing of the palace itself, some of the creatures from it are embalmed in the **Muséum d'Histoire Naturelle**, sharing space with their fossilized ancestors.

Muséum d'Histoire Naturelle
t 04 91 14 59 50,
www.museum-marseille.org; open Tues–Sun 10–5; adm, free Sun am

The left wing of the Palais Longchamp houses the **Musée des Beaux-Arts**. Formed around art that was 'conquered' by Napoleon's army, it is home to some second-rate canvases by Italian masters such as Perugino, and some stagey burlesques such as Rubens' violent *Boar Hunt* (in which ladies daintily watch the spurting blood) or Louis Finson's *Samson and Delilah* (1600), with a nasty Delilah tugging the ear of a very dirty-footed Samson. The mood changes with Michel Serre's scrupulously dire *Scenes of the Marseille Plague of 1720*, where a large percentage of the plague's 40,000 victims are shown dropping like flies while healthy rich men in suits prance by on horseback, looking politely sympathetic. These same gentlemen never dismounted to assist Marseille's native artists, either – not even an establishment figure such as Baroque sculptor, architect and painter Pierre Puget (1620–94), who has a room devoted to him. Then there's Françoise Duparc (1726–76), a follower of Chardin, who worked in England for most of her life; and the satirist Honoré Daumier (1808–97), who went to prison for his biting caricatures of Louis-Philippe's toadies, here represented by *Spitting Image*-style satirical busts modelled after his drawings. Here, too, is Van Gogh's roving, bohemian precursor Adolphe Monticelli (1824–86), who sold his paint-encrusted canvases of fragmented colour for food and drink in the cafés along La Canebière. Also of note are paintings by Provençal pre-Impressionists, especially 18th-century scenes of Marseille's port by Joseph Vernet and sun-drenched landscapes by Paul Guigou.

Musée des Beaux-Arts
t 04 91 14 59 30;
closed for restoration until at least 2010

Just across Boulevard Longchamp at No.140, the **Musée Grobet-Labadié** contains a private collection as interesting for its eclecticism as for any individual painting, table, plate, instrument, tapestry or iron lock.

Musée Grobet-Labadié
t 04 91 62 21 82;
open summer Tues–Sun 11–6; winter Tues–Sun 10–5; adm

Heading South: Le Corbusier and Mazargues

The building that achieves speed will achieve success.

Le Corbusier

To pay your respects to Modular Man, you need to take bus 21 from the Bourse down Rue de Rome wide Avenue du Prado and Boulevard Michelet (a perfect spot for rollerblading, if you happen to have brought your skates) and past the swish Vélodrome football stadium to the *Corbusier* stop.

In 1945, during the height of Marseille's housing crisis, the French government commissioned Le Corbusier to build an experimental **unité d'habitation**, derived from his 1935 theory of '*La Cité Radieuse*'. Le Corbusier thought the solution to urban anomie and transport and housing problems was to put living space, schools, shops and recreational facilities all under one roof, in a building designed according to the human proportions of Leonardo da Vinci's Renaissance man-in-a-circle, reborn as Le Corbusier's wiggly Modular Man symbol. You can see the Man in relief on the concrete *pilotis*, or stilts – the most revolutionary aspect of the building. Le Corbusier, who anticipated the future importance of cars, intended that the ground level should be for parking.

For a city like Marseille, where people enjoy getting out and about at ground level, the building was a ghastly aberration, and was nicknamed the *casa de fada*, or 'house of the mentally deranged'. Plans for other *unités* were stifled and in 1952 the state sold the flats off as co-ops. But architects were entranced, and for the next 30 years thousands of buildings in every city in the world went up on *pilotis*, before everyone realized that the Marseillais were right all along: it is madness to deprive a building of its most important asset, a ground floor. The *unité*'s genuinely good points, unfortunately, had few imitators – each of its 337 flats is built on two levels and designed for maximum privacy; each has fine views over the mountains or sea. Of the original extras, only the school, the top-floor gym and the communal hotel for residents' guests (now open to all; *see* p.194) have survived. The hotel also offers tours by appointment.

From here you can take bus 23 or 45 towards **Mazargues**, a once-fashionable *banlieue* under the **Montagne de Marseilleveyre**, famous in the 19th century for its climate. When its residents died, at a ripe old age, they often chose to be remembered in the local cemetery by a mini-monument to their life's work – there are stone hedge-clippers, fishing boats, hoes and, on the tomb of an omnibus driver, a tram.

Marseille's Corniche and Parc Borély

Why go to the Riviera when Marseille has one of its very own? From the Vieux Port, you can catch bus 83 past the Parc du Pharo to **Corniche J.F. Kennedy**, a dramatic road overlooking a dramatic coast that must have reminded the ancient Greek colonists of home – now improved with artificial beaches, bars, restaurants, villas and nightclubs.

Amazingly, until the road was built in the 1850s, the first cove, the picture-postcard **Anse des Catalans**, was so isolated that the Catalan fisherfolk who lived there as squatters in the ruins of the old *lazaretto* (quarantine station) could hardly speak French. This now has the most popular (and the only real) sandy beach. From the bus stop *Vallon des Auffes* you can walk down to the fishing village of **Anse des Auffes** ('of the ropemakers'), isolated from the *corniche* until after the Second World War and still intact.

Other typical quarters with still more piquant names lie further on: **Anse de Maldormé** and **Anse de la Fausse Monnaie**. As soon as the corniche was built, the wealthy families of Marseille planted grand villas along it: the **Château Talabot** is one of the most spectacular. The corniche then descends to the artificial **Plage Gaston Deferre**, where a copy of Michelangelo's *David* holds court at the corner of Avenue du Prado, looking even more smugly ridiculous than he does in Florence. Beyond the big fellow opens the cool green expanse of **Parc Borély**, which is great for cycling or rollerblading and has a café/restaurant, golf course and running track, as well as a **botanical garden**, duck ponds and the **Château Borély**, an 18th-century palace built according to the strictest classical proportions for a wealthy merchant and unique for its surviving interior decoration. Behind it, Avenue de Hambourg leads into **Sainte-Anne**, another former village, where César's *Giant Thumb* emerges at the Boulevard de Haïfa, signalling the vast **Musée d'Art Contemporain** at No.69, with a large collection of post Second World War art (New Realists, Arte Povera, and more).

Parc Borély botanical garden
t 04 91 55 24 96; open daily 6am–9pm

Musée d'Art Contemporain
t 04 91 25 01 07; open summer Tues–Sun 11–6; winter Tues–Sun 10–5; adm

The *Calanques* and Grotte Cosquer

To continue east along the coast from Parc Borély, you'll need to change to bus 19, which passes by another beach and the **Musée de la Faïence**, in the 19th-century Château Pastré (157 Avenue de Montredon), with an exceptional collection of faïence from Neolithic times to the present, particularly the famous ware made in Marseille and Moustiers from the 17th century on.

Musée de la Faïence
t 04 91 72 43 47; open summer Tues–Sun 11–6; winter Tues–Sun 10–5; adm

Bus 19 stops just after **Calanque du Mont Rose**, Marseille's nudist beach. Bus 20 from here continues to **Cap Croisette**, a miniature end-of-the-world at the base of the Montagne de Marseilleveyre – which forms a backdrop to the fishing hamlet in the **Calanque des Goudes** – and the pebble beach at **Calanque de Samena**, facing the islets of Maire and Tiboulen. The road gives out at the narrow **Calanque de Callelongue**, where the GR98 coastal path to Cassis begins (*see* p.174). Another path from here leads in two hours to the summit of **Marseilleveyre** (1,417ft), with grand views over Marseille, its industrial *rade* and the islands.

In 1991 the next *calanque*, the beautiful, chalky, jagged **Calanque de Sormiou**, made national headlines when a local diver called Henri Cosquer discovered a hollow 130ft under the sea that hid the entrance to a tunnel. Cosquer swam up the tunnel and after 220 yards found himself in a subterranean cave above sea level, to his astonishment covered with paintings of running bison, horses, deer and the ancestors of the modern penguin. Along with the art, Cosquer found a number of 'negative' handprints, which were made by blowing colour around a hand in order to create its outline on the wall. Similar 'artists' signatures' mark the famous painted caves in the Dordogne. Although first dismissed as a forgery, mainly because no similar works have ever been found in Provence, the **Grotte Cosquer** is now recognized by prehistorians as a contemporary of Lascaux (*c.* 27,000 BC). At the time, when much of the northern hemisphere's water was concentrated in Ice Age glaciers, the level of the Med was much lower, so that the entrance to the cave was on dry land. The climate here was also considerably colder – hence the bison and penguins. To protect the art, the cave has been walled up, but reproductions are on display via the Internet at *www.culture.gouv.fr/culture/archeosm/fr/cosq.htm*.

Sormiou and the more distant *calanques* are most painlessly reached from Marseille by **boats** from the Quai des Belges. Or take bus 21 from La Canebière to the end of the line (*Luminy*) and walk 40 minutes to **Calanque de Morgiou**, dotted with seaside *cabanons*, or to the wilder **Calanque de Sugiton**.

Boats to Sormiou
t 04 91 55 50 09; mid-June–Sept

The Château d'If and Iles du Frioul

'*If*' in French means yew, a tree associated with death; it's an appropriately sinister name for this gloomy precursor of Alcatraz, the Château d'If, built by François Ier in 1524, to defend Marseille from Emperor Charles V. Even while Alexandre Dumas was still alive, visitors came to see the cell of the Count of Monte-Cristo, and a cell, complete with escape hole, was obligingly made to show to visitors. Real-life inmates included Mirabeau, imprisoned by his father-in-law for running up debts in Aix-en-Provence (*see* p.205); a Monsieur de Niozelles, condemned to six years in solitary for not taking his hat off in front of Louis XIV; and, after the revocation of the Edict of Nantes, thousands of Protestants, who either died here or went on to die as galley slaves elsewhere.

Château d'If
t 04 91 59 02 30; open except in rough seas Sept–Mar Tues–Sun 9.30–5.30; April daily 9.30–5.30; May–Aug daily 9.30–6.30; boats from Quai des Belges, t 04 91 55 50 09, departures summer hourly 9–5; winter every 90mins 9.30–4.30

The two other islands in the archipelago, **Pomègues** and **Ratonneau**, are white as bones and nearly as dry, tortured into crags and lumps by the mistral. They were originally hunting and fishing reserves and witnessed, in 1516, one of the first rhinos in Europe, who rambled here en route to Pope Leo X's menagerie in Rome. Later used as quarantine islands, they are now linked by a causeway at **Port du Frioul**, a marina designed by Le Corbusier's

Boats to Pomègues and Ratonneau
boats run as for the Ile d'If, with an early boat at 6.45 for Pomègues and Ratonneau only

pupil, José Luis Sert. Scores of swimming coves can be easily reached by foot, along paths lined with aromatic herbs and plants especially adapted to the extremely dry climate. A 20-minute path leads to the **Hôpital Caroline**, built in the 1820s on Ratonneau, where the winds blow the strongest – on the theory that they would help 'purify' infectious diseases. Now used as the venue for a summer festival, the hospital has excellent views of Marseille – as Marseille was meant to be seen, from the sea – that must have been heartbreaking to the imprisoned patients.

Tourist Information in Marseille

ⓘ **Marseille >**
4 La Canebière (1er), by the Vieux Port, t 04 91 13 89 00, www.marseille-tourisme.com; open daily all year; train station, t 04 91 50 59 18

ⓘ **CRIJPA >**
96 La Canebière (1er), www.crijpa.com, t 04 91 24 33 50

ⓘ **Service Municipal des Handicapés et Inadaptés >**
Mairie, 128 Av du Prado (8e), t 04 91 81 58 80

ⓘ **AVAD >**
7 Rue de la République (2e), t 04 96 11 68 80

Check at the main **La Canebière office** for **tours** of the Opéra Municipal and the Vieux Port forts, and for 'Taxis Tourism' – 4 set-price **taxi tours** of the city, with an English cassette guide. Ask also about the one-day (€20) or two-day (€27) **City-Pass**, with unlimited bus and *métro* travel, entrance to 14 museums, a boat trip to Château d'If, a trip on the Petit Train (*see* p.177), and discounts in shops. There's also an office in the **train station**.

Special information centres exist for young people at the very helpful **CRIJPA**; for disabled visitors, at the **Service Municipal des Handicapés et Inadaptés**, at the *mairie*; and for crime victims, at **AVAD**.

Services in Marseille

Post office: 1 Place de l'Hôtel-des-Postes (1er), t 04 91 15 47 00.
Emergencies: The **hospital** is at 264 Rue St-Pierre (5e), t 04 91 49 91 91.
SOS Médecin, t 04 91 52 91 52.
SOS Dentiste, t 04 91 85 39 39.

Internet Access

Cyberyann Café, 39 Bd Jeanne-d'Arc (5e), t 04 91 42 29 65.
Info-Café, 1 Quai de Rive Neuve (1er), t 04 91 33 74 98.

Market Days in Marseille

Every other Sun: Cours Julien (6e; Ⓜ Notre-Dame-du-Mont), flea market.

Mon–Sat: Place A. et F. Carli (1er, Ⓜ Noailles), old book, postcard and record market.

Festivals in Marseille

There are a number of festivals and street parties in Marseille at any given time in the summer, from the lively, eclectic neighbourhood parties of the *Fête du Panier* in late June to the *Foire à l'Ail* in early July.

If you're around in July it's hard to miss the celebrations for the city's largest party, the *Festival de Marseille* (for tickets call **t** 04 91 99 02 50 or see *www.festivaldemarseille.com*).

Shopping in Marseille

Rue St-Ferréol, home of the Galeries Lafayette and Virgin Megastore, is the centre of the city's shopping district; parallel **Rue Paradis** has the upmarket boutiques, and **Rue de Rome** is a good place to look for fake leopardskin.

Marseille holds its market of clay Christmas crib figures, the *Foire aux Santons*, from end Nov to Jan; at other times, you can see generations of and even buy *santons* at **Marcel Carbonel** (**t** 04 91 54 26 58, *www.santonsmarcel carbonel.com*) in the old port at 47 Rue Neuve Ste-Catherine (7e), and even see them being made.

Sports and Activities in Marseille

The **Olympique de Marseille** (OM; Stade Vélodrome Municipal, Bd Michelet, 8e, **t** 04 91 55 93 56) is France's most enthusiastically supported football squad and tickets for matches often sell out.

Windsurf boards can be hired at **Pacific Palissades**, Port de la Pointe Rouge (8ᵉ), t 04 91 73 44 11, *www. pacifique-palissades.com*, or the neighbouring **Sideral Times Club**, t 04 91 25 00 90.

Skatepark, Plage Vieille-Chapelle (8ᵉ; no.19 bus), *http://marseilleskatepark. free.fr*, is known as one of the best in the world, and has a strong family atmosphere.

Where to Stay in Marseille

Marseille ✉ 13000

Marseille's top-notch hotels are the bastion of expense-account business-men and women, while its down-market numbers attract working girls of a different kind. Be sure to book ahead if you're coming in mid-Sept, when Marseille holds its fair and there are no hotel rooms for love or money.

****Le Petit Nice Passédat, Anse de Maldormé (7ᵉ), off Corniche J.F. Kennedy, t 04 91 59 25 92, *www. passedat.fr* (€€€€€). Marseille's most refined, exclusive hotel, a former villa overlooking the Anse de Maldormé, with a fine restaurant, **Le Passédat** (*see* opposite). *Restaurant closed Sun lunch and Mon lunch in season.*

****Mercure Marseille Beauvau Vieux Port, 4 Rue Beauvau (1ᵉʳ), t 04 91 54 91 00, *www.mercure.com* (€€€€€–€€€€). A wood-panelled and comfortable hotel overlooking the Vieux Port, with quiet, air-conditioned rooms but no restaurant. Chopin and George Sand canoodled here.

****Le Pharo, 71 Bd Charles Livon (7ᵉ), t 04 91 315 315, *www.new-hotel.com* (€€€€€–€€€€). Brand new, very modern glass and steel hotel near the Vieux Port, with a pool and its own kitchen garden.

***New Hôtel Bompard, 2 Rue des Flots-Bleus (7ᵉ), t 04 91 99 22 22, *www.new-hotel.com* (€€€). A modern hotel that seems remote from the city, situated above the Corniche J.F. Kennedy (take bus 61 from ⓜ Joliette or St-Victor) in its own peaceful grounds, with rooms overlooking a

garden. There are also '*mas*' suites with kitchenettes.

***Le Corbusier, 280 Bd Michelet (8ᵉ), t 04 91 16 78 00, *www.hotellecorbusier. com* (€€€). A hotel-restaurant incorporated into the *unité d'habitation* designed by Le Corbusier (*see* p.190), providing a treat for students of architecture as well as lots of facilities such as a sauna and jogging track. The 22 rooms get booked up way in advance.

***Hôtel du Palais, 26 Rue Breteuil (6ᵉ), t 04 91 37 78 86, *www. hotel-palais-marseille-federal-hotel.com* (€€€–€€). Friendly, spotless small hotel decorated in white and cherry-red, a few minutes from the Vieux Port, recommended for its lovely breakfast.

**Azur, 24 Cours Franklin Roosevelt (1ᵉʳ), ⓜ Canebière-Réformés, t 04 91 42 74 38, *www.azur-hotel.fr* (€€). Average rooms with frills such as colour TV, air-conditioning and garden views.

**Hôtel Lutétia, 38 Allée Léon Gambetta (1ᵉʳ), t 04 91 50 81 78 (€€). Clean, bright little blue and white hotel, central, near La Canebière. The rooms are on the small side.

**Péron, 119 Corniche J.F. Kennedy (7ᵉ), t 04 91 31 01 41, *www.hotel-peron.com* (€€). An old-fashioned, family-run hotel with bright and colourful rooms.

**Le Richelieu, 52 Corniche J.F. Kennedy (7ᵉ), t 04 91 31 01 92, *www. lerichelieu-marseille.com* (€€). Good-value, nicely decorated rooms. The breakfast terrace overlooks the sea.

**Moderne, 11 Bd de la Libération (1ᵉʳ), t 04 91 62 28 66 (€). Nice enough rooms with *en suite* showers and TV.

**Montgrand, 50 Rue Montgrand (6ᵉ), t 04 91 00 35 20, *www.hotel-montgrand-marseille.com* (€). A palatable budget choice.

Auberge de Jeunesse de Bois Luzy, Allée des Primevères (12ᵉ), t 04 91 49 06 18, *www.fuaj.org* (€). The better of Marseille's two hostels, in a 19th-century château overlooking the city (take bus 6 or 8 from La Canebière, or bus K after dark; direction La Rose).

Eating Out in Marseille

The Marseillais claim an ancient Greek – even divine – origin for their ballyhooed *bouillabaisse*: Aphrodite invented it to beguile her husband Hephaestos to sleep so that she could dally with her lover Ares (seafood and saffron being a legendary soporific). Good chefs prepare it just as seriously, and display like a doctor's diploma their *Charte de la Bouillabaisse* guaranteeing that their formula more or less subscribes to tradition: the saffron and garlic-flavoured soup cooked on a low boil (hence its name) is based on *rascasse* (scorpion fish, the ugliest fish in the Med and always cooked with its leering head attached), which lives under the cliffs and has a bland taste that enhances the flavour of the other fish, especially *fielas* (conger eel), *grondin* (gurnard) and *saint-pierre* (John Dory).

On menus you'll usually find three degrees of *bouillabaisse*: simple or *du pêcheur*, made from the day's catch with a few shellfish thrown in; *royale*, with half a lobster included; and, most expensive of all, *royale marseillaise*, the real McCoy, with all the right fish. When it's served, the fish is traditionally cut up before you and presented on a side dish of *aïoli* or *rouille*, a paste of Spanish peppers.

General Restaurants

Une Table au Sud, 2 Quai du Port (2ᵉ), t 04 91 90 63 53 (€€€€). Acclaimed cuisine from a young chef who was taught by the legendary Alain Ducasse. *Closed Sun, Mon, 1st week Jan and 3 weeks Aug.*

Le Miramar, 12 Quai du Port (2ᵉ), t 04 91 91 10 40, *www.bouillabaisse.com* (€€€€–€€€). A restaurant where you can count on eating some reliable traditional fare. *Closed Sun and Mon.*

Restaurant Michel, 6 Rue des Catalans (7ᵉ), t 04 91 52 30 63 (€€€€–€€€). A posh joint with the best, swankiest *bouillabaisse*, the haunt of politicians and showbiz people.

⭐ **Les Mets de Provence Chez Maurice Brun** >

Les Mets de Provence Chez Maurice Brun, 2nd floor, 18 Quai de Rive-Neuve (7ᵉ), t 04 91 33 35 38, *www.maurice brun.fr* (€€€). A 50-year-old restaurant proving that there's more than *bouillabaisse* on the Marseille culinary scene. The genuine Provençal spreads include a grand three-course lunch

menu that starts with eight *hors-d'œuvre* and includes wine. *Closed Sat lunch, Sun, and Mon lunch.*

Les Arcenaulx, 25 Cours d'Estienne d'Orves (1ᵉʳ), t 04 91 59 80 30, *www.les-arcenaulx.com* (€€€). A restaurant situated in a busy square next to a bookshop, offering fresh market fare. *Closed Sun.*

Le Marseillois, Quai du Port (2ᵉ), t 04 91 90 72 52 (€€). A restaurant set on a sailing boat moored stern-on, with local fare and plenty of atmosphere. *Closed Feb.*

Country Life, 14 Rue Venture (1ᵉʳ), t 04 96 11 28 00 (€). A handy vegetarian option. *Open lunchtimes, Mon–Fri only.*

International and Late-night Eating

Marseille's unique ethnic mix, which includes Corsicans, Armenians, Jews, Greeks, Turks, Italians, Spaniards and Algerians, means it has an unrivalled selection of inexpensive cuisines from around the world.

Le Mas de Lulli, 4 Rue Lulli (1ᵉʳ), by the Opéra, t 04 91 33 25 90 (€€€–€€). A place where night owls can assuage their hunger pangs with good pasta dishes and grills. *Closed Sun, last 2 weeks Aug, 1st week Sept.*

Shabu Shabu, 30 Rue de la Paix (1ᵉʳ), t 04 91 54 15 00 (€€). Good Japanese cuisine. *Closed Sun, Mon lunch.*

La Gentiane, 9 Rue des Trois-Rois (6ᵉ), t 04 91 42 88 80 (€€). A good place for vegetarians. *Closed Sun, Mon and last week Sept.*

Au Roi du Couscous, 55 Rue de Forbin (2ᵉ), t 04 91 91 45 46 (€). The best couscous in town. *Closed eves.*

Along the Beaches and the *Calanques*

Le Passédat, Le Petit Nice Passédat hotel (*see left*), t 04 91 59 25 92 (€€€€). Ravishing food served in an exotic garden. *Closed Sun lunch and Mon lunch in season.*

L'Epuisette, Vallon des Auffes (7ᵉ), t 04 91 52 17 82, *www.l-epuisette.com* (€€€€–€€€). A seafood institution. *Closed Sun, Mon and Aug.*

Chez Fonfon, Vallon des Auffes (7ᵉ), t 04 91 52 14 38 (€€€). Provençal specialities in a peaceful spot on the fishing port overlooking the Château d'If and Frioul islands. *Closed Sun, Mon lunch, and 1st 2 weeks Jan.*

Pizzeria Jeannot, Vallon des Auffes, t 04 91 52 11 28 (€€€–€€). Fancy pizza. *Closed Sun eve and Mon in winter, Mon only in summer.*

La Grotte, 1 Rue Pebrons, Calanque de Callelongue (8ᵉ), t 08 26 10 11 24 (€€€). A pizza favourite by the sea.

Entertainment and Nightlife in Marseille

Marseille may be going on 3,000 years old, but the old girl's still kicking – sometimes in the wrong places, especially after 10pm in the streets between the station and the Port. But you don't have to be a brawny sailor to have a good time: Marseille has lively after-dark pockets, especially round **Place Thiars**, **Cours Honoré d'Estienne d'Orves** and **Cours Julien**.

Find out what's on in *Taktik*, free at the tourist office, or in *La Marseillaise* or *La Provence*.

Theatre

Marseille has a vibrant theatre scene.

Théâtre National de la Criée, 32 Quai Rive-Neuve (7ᵉ), t 04 91 54 70 54, *www.theatre-lacriee.com*.

Théâtre Les Bernardines, 17 Bd Garibaldi (1ᵉʳ), t 04 91 24 30 40, *www. theatre-bernardines.org*. A theatre hosting a mix of experimental dance and theatre.

Théâtre du Merlan, Av Raimu (14ᵉ), t 04 91 11 19 20. Avant-garde theatre.

Cinemas

Le César, 4 Place Castellane (6ᵉ), t 08 92 68 05 97, *www.cine-metro-art.com*. Showing first-run films in their original language (*v.o.*).

Cinéma Alhambra, 2 Rue du Cinéma (16ᵉ), t 04 91 03 84 66, *www. alhambracine.com*. Old movies and art films shown in *v.o.*

Les Variétés, 37 Rue Vincent Scotto, off La Canebière (1ᵉʳ), t 08 92 68 05 97, *www.cine-metro-art.com*. A swish place with first-run films in *v.o.*

Classical Music

The city has always had a special affinity with music; Berlioz claimed it understood Beethoven five years before Paris did.

Opéra Municipal, Place Reyer (1ᵉʳ), t 04 91 55 14 99, *http://opera.mairie-marseille.fr*. Italian opera and occasional ballets by the Ballet National de Marseille.

Ballet National de Marseille, 20 Bd Gabès (8ᵉ), t 04 91 32 72 72, *www.ballet-de-marseille.com*.

Iles du Frioul. A music festival venue in July.

Bars and Clubs

Nightlife in Marseille is concentrated in several zones. **Place Jean Jaurès/Cours Julien** and around is perhaps the trendiest place. There are also bars and Latin clubs aplenty along the seafront at **Plage Borély** (8ᵉ), and a number of places at **Escale Borély**.

Espace Julien, 39 Cours Julien (6ᵉ), t 04 91 24 34 10, *www.espace-julien. com*. Jazz, rock and reggae, plus a café with live music.

West of Marseille: The Chaîne de l'Estaque and the Etang de Berre

Whatever personality of its own this region once had has been thoroughly chewed and swallowed by the metropolis next door. Once sheltering attractive, out-of-the-way retreats, the Estaque coast and the broad lagoon of Berre behind it have totally succumbed to creeping suburbia in the last few decades; isolated corners that once knew only hamlets of poor fishermen now suffer some of the biggest industrial complexes in France. Still, the 'Côte Bleue', as the tourist offices call the Estaque coast, is a very attractive piece of coastline. Especially in the east, the mountains plunge straight into the sea, with sheltered *calanques* between them; there is no road along the coast until Carry-le-Rouet.

L'Estaque to Sausset-les-Pins

Leaving Marseille on the N568, you will pass the industrial suburb, docks and marinas of **L'Estaque** (take a bus from the Vieux Port). This was a favourite subject of Paul Cézanne, who came to this spot off and on for 15 years to paint, and whose vision of a new, classical Provence transformed the town's smokestacks into Doric columns. He was followed by Georges Braque, Raoul Dufy, Albert Marquet and other artists; the Marseille tourist office has a brochure pinpointing the spots where they set up their easels, but you'll be disappointed if you come expecting to recognize too many of the scenes. The road then crosses over the **Souterrain du Rove**, which holds the distinction of being the longest ship tunnel in the world. A partial collapse closed it in the 1960s, and no one has found it worth repairing since. Tortuous side roads from the N568 will take you down to two pleasant enclaves harbouring old fishing villages, **Niolon** and **Méjean**.

The reputation of **Carry-le-Rouet**, which is the biggest town on this stretch of the coast, is based on horse-faced actor Fernandel and on sea urchins; it celebrates the latter with a festival each February. The beach is often oversubscribed; Carry is fast being surrounded by the weekend villas of the Marseillais.

Sausset-les-Pins, the next town along the coast, suffers much the same problem; however, if you press on further, there are a number of popular, if also often crowded, beaches around **Carro** and especially at **Cap Couronne**, a favourite among the Marseillais.

Marignane and Martigues

On the lagoon side of the Chaîne de l'Estaque, facing inland across the Etang de Berre, the distinguished old city of **Marignane** has been completely engulfed by Marseille's sprawl and airport. In the centre of the old town, you can pay a visit to its 14th-century château (now the *mairie*), an eccentric work decorated with mythological frescoes.

From here, making a clockwise tour around the Etang de Berre, the next stop is **Martigues**, a sweet little city full of salt air and sailboats, not a compelling place to visit but probably a wonderful place to live. If Carry-le-Rouet serves up sea urchins to visitors in February, Martigues can answer with its own speciality – fresh sardines – during its Sardine Festival in July and August.

Martigues sits astride the **Canal de Caronte**, which links the lagoon and the sea, lending it a slight but much-trumpeted resemblance to Venice. According to legend, the city was founded by and named after the Roman general Marius; the oldest part of town is the **Ile Brescon**, at the head of the channel, with the Baroque church of the **Madeleine** and a number of 17th- and 18th-century buildings. One of its prettiest corners is a quay called the **Miroir des Oiseaux**, the 'mirror of birds'. On the mainland, the

Musée Ziem
*t 04 42 41 39 60;
open July and Aug
Wed–Mon 10–12 and
2.30–6.30; Sept–June
Wed–Sun 2.30–6.30*

Musée Ziem on Bd du 14 Juillet has paintings left to Martigues by landscape artist Félix Ziem, and works by Provençal painters Guigou, Monticelli and Loubon, as well as archaeology exhibits.

Fos-sur-Mer

The French, many of whom are fascinated with technology, actually come to visit this gigantic industrial complex. Fos has an

**Fos-sur-Mer
complex**
*Point Accueil Info,
Av Jean Jaurès,
t 04 42 47 71 96*

information centre on Avenue Jean Jaurès, and there are guided tours. You too might consider a drive through – in its way, Fos is the most astounding, unsettling sight in Provence. Before 1965, when France's Mephistophelean economic planners commandeered it to replace the overcrowded port of Marseille, this corner of the Camargue was pristine marshland. Today it is the biggest oil port, and the biggest industrial complex, on the entire Mediterranean. In area it is considerably larger than Marseille.

To a degree, it makes sense to concentrate unpleasant industry all in one place. But when you're driving past the 19km of chemical plants, steel mills and power lines rising out of the void like a mirage, your senses rebel. Economically, the 'ZIP' (*zone industrielle-portuaire*) is a failure; as planning, it is stupidly primitive, ecologically disastrous and demeaning to the people who live and work in it: the perfect marriage of corporate gigantism and bureaucratic simple-mindedness.

West and North of the Etang de Berre

Along the western shore of the Etang de Berre there is more of the same, engulfing a number of ancient villages, such as **St-Blaise**, which contains a Romanesque church and a wealth of ruins that have been excavated, including a rare stretch of Greek wall. Of the two large towns here, **Istres** has a Provençal-Romanesque fortified church, **Notre-Dame-de-Beauvoir**, and a **Musée Archéologique**,

**Musée
Archéologique**
*t 04 42 55 50 08;
open daily 2–6; adm*

filled with mostly Roman-era finds that were discovered by divers in the Golfe de Fos. **Miramas** is more attractive, with the ruins of its medieval predecessor nearby at **Miramas-le-Vieux**, and a **railway museum** at the SNCF depot.

St-Chamas, southeast, has an impressive Baroque church. The Via Domitia passed this way, and over a small stream south of the village stands one of the finest and best-preserved Roman bridges anywhere, the **Pont Flavien**. Built in the 1st century AD, the single-arched span features a pair of very elegant triumphal arches at the approaches, decorated with Corinthian capitals, floral reliefs and stone lions. But life went on here even earlier than that, and there are troglodyte dwellings to prove it.

North of the Etang, towards Salon-de-Provence, lie three pretty villages: **Cornillon-Confoux**, on a steep hill with a wide view, **Grans**, and **Lançon-Provence**; the latter is home of some of the most exquisite AOC Coteaux d'Aix-en-Provence wines (see p.215).

Salon-de-Provence

The home of Nostradamus should be a more interesting place. Aix-en-Provence's disagreeable little sister, Salon is quite well off from processing olive oil, making soap and being home to the French airforce training school. The town seems aptly named: it's a little bourgeois parlour, smug and stuffy and neat as a pin. Its spirit is captured perfectly in the antiseptic, gentrified **Vieille Ville**, ruined by an insensitive restoration programme in the last few years. Even the antiseptic has its surprises, however: surely the snazziest tiled loos in France (underneath Place du Général de Gaulle), and the **Ecole des Bergers**, France's national school for shepherds.

The old quarter, surrounded by a ring of boulevards, is entered by the 18th-century **Porte de l'Horloge**, with its ironwork **clock tower**. In the centre, at the highest point of Salon, is the **Château de l'Empéri**, parts of which go back to the 10th century. Long a possession of the archbishops of Arles, it now houses the **Musée National de l'Empéri**, which contains a substantial hoard of weapons, bric-a-brac and epauletted mannequins on horseback, covering the history of France's army from Louis XIV to 1918, with an emphasis on Napoleon. The slightly kitsch **Musée Grévin de la Provence**, run by the Parisian waxwork family Grévin, illustrates the history of Provence by means of 54 waxwork figures, from Marius'

Musée National de l'Empéri
t 04 90 56 22 36; open Wed–Mon 10–12 and 2–6; closed Tues; adm

Musée Grévin de la Provence
t 04 90 56 36 30; open Mon–Fri 9–12 and 2–6, Sat and Sun 2–6; adm

Nostradamus

Salon's most famous citizen was born in St-Rémy-de-Provence in 1503, to a family of converted Jews. Trained as a doctor in Montpellier, young Michel de Nostredame made a name for himself by successfully treating plague victims in Lyon and Aix-en-Provence. In 1547 he married a girl from Salon-de-Provence and settled down there, practising medicine and pursuing a score of other interests besides – studying astrology, publishing almanacs and inventing new recipes for cosmetics and hair dyes. The first of his *Centuries*, ambiguous quatrains written in the future tense, were published in 1555, achieving celebrity for their author almost immediately.

Nostradamus himself said that his works came from 'natural instinct and poetic passion'; in form they are similar to some other poetry of the day, such as the *Visions* of Du Bellay. It may be that he had never intended to become an occult superstar – but when the peasants start bringing you two-headed sheep asking for an explanation, and when the Queen Regent of France sends an invitation to court, what's a man to do? Nostradamus went to Paris, and later Charles IX and Catherine de Médicis came to visit him in Salon. The Salonnais didn't appreciate such notoriety; if not for Nostradamus's royal favour, they might well have put him to the torch.

battle with the Barbarians, through a lifeless Napoleon, to Pagnol's 'Manon des Sources'.

If you're on the Nostradamus trail (*see* box, previous page), you can visit the **Maison de Nostradamus**, just inside the Porte de l'Horloge at 11 Rue de Nostradamus. On his death in 1566, Nostradamus was, oddly, buried inside the wall of the Cordeliers' church; tales spread that he was still alive in there, writing his final book of prophecies. After his tomb was desecrated in the Revolution, he was moved to the Dominican church of **St-Laurent**, on Rue du Maréchal Joffre, where he remains.

East of Salon along the D572, the **Château de la Barben** once belonged to Napoleon's favourite sister, Pauline Borghese, and now has a little zoo in the grounds for kids.

North of Salon on the D17, **Eyguières** is an archetypal Provençal village, with some Celtic-Greek tombs above the ruins of a medieval castle; their contents may be seen in the **Centre d'Etudes Archéologiques**. Also note the 10th-century **Chapelle St-Vérédème**.

Vernègues, in a forgotten corner of Provence (take the D16 northeast of Salon), has a ruined castle and, just southeast, the ruins of a 1st-century BC Roman temple.

Maison de Nostradamus
t 04 90 56 64 31; open Mon–Fri 9–12 and 2–6, Sat and Sun 2–6; adm

Centre d'Etudes Archéologiques
t 04 90 59 82 44; open Sat am or by appointment; donation appreciated

ⓘ **Martigues >>**
Rond-Point de l'Hôtel de Ville, t 04 42 42 31 10, www.martigues-tourisme.com; open Mon–Sat and Sun am; provides details of walking/driving tours

ⓘ **Carry-le-Rouet >**
Espace Fernandel, Av Aristide Briand, t 04 42 13 20 36, www.carry-lerouet.com; open summer Mon–Sat and Sun am; winter Mon–Sat

ⓘ **Salon-de-Provence >>**
56 Cours Gimon, t 04 90 56 27 60, www.visitsalondeprovence.com; open summer Mon–Sat and Sun am; winter Mon–Sat

Market Days West of Marseille

Carry-le-Rouet: Tues and Fri.

Martigues: Thurs and Sun am, Place de la Libération and Parking Leclerc; Wed and Sat Port de Carro and Place du Marché à la Couronne; daily, fish market, Port de Carro.

Salon-de-Provence: Wed am.

Where to Stay and Eat West of Marseille

Carry-le-Rouet ✉ 13620

Most people here have villas or are on day trips from the city, so accommodation is scarce and functional.

**La Tuilière, 34 Av Draïo-de-la-Mar, t 04 42 44 79 79, www.hotel-tuiliere.com (€€). Modern, comfortable rooms, some with sea views, with a pool and air-conditioning.

L'Escale, 3 Bd des Moulins, t 04 42 45 00 47 (€€€). A monthly changing gourmet menu served on attractive seaside terraces. *Closed Sun eve and Mon out of season.*

Le Calypso, Quai Vayssière, t 04 42 45 10 64 (€€). A seafood restaurant behind the port, with great sea views.

Martigues ✉ 13500

**L'Eden, Bd Emile Zola, t 04 42 07 36 37, www.hoteleden.fr (€€–€). On the outskirts, with great sea views.

**Le Cigalon, 35 Bd 14 Juillet, t 04 42 80 49 16 (€€–€). A central hotel with modern rooms, air-conditioning and a restaurant for guests only.

Miroir aux Oiseaux, 4 Rue Marcel Galdy, t 04 42 80 50 45 (€€). Traditional gourmet food on a terrace overlooking the attractive quay. *Closed Mon, Wed eve and Sat lunch.*

Salon-de-Provence ✉ 13300

****Le Mas du Soleil, 38 Chemin Saint-Côme, t 04 90 56 06 53, www.lemasdusoleil.com (€€€€€–€€€). Elegant, air-conditioned rooms, a pool and terrace, and a traditional restaurant serving beautifully presented food. *Restaurant closed Sun eve and Mon.*

****Abbaye de Ste-Croix, Val-de-Cuech (D16), t 04 90 56 24 55, www.hotels-provence.com (€€€€€– €€€). A Relais & Châteaux place 5km out of town, with lovely rooms overlooking a medieval cloister. There's a pool, horse-riding and a posh restaurant. *Closed weekdays Nov–mid-Mar.*

Domaine de Roquerousse, on Route Jean Moulin, direction Avignon, 4km from town, t 04 90 59 50 11, *www.roquerousse.com* (€€). Pretty rooms and a restaurant in the individual buildings of a 19th-century *mas*, in a park, with a pool and tennis courts.

Citotel Vendôme, 34 Rue Maréchal Joffre, t 04 90 56 01 96, *www. hotelvendome.com* (€). A bright, pretty and old-fashioned hotel with spacious rooms and a courtyard.

La Salle à Manger, 6 Rue Maréchal Joffre, t 04 90 56 28 01 (€€). A restaurant in an exuberantly floral 19th-century mansion, offering a choice of delicious if extravagant dishes (ostrich *carpaccio*, for instance, and 40 puddings) to match the décor. *Closed Sun and Mon.*

La Table des Cordeliers, 20 Rue Hozier, t 04 90 56 53 42 (€€). The 13th-century chapel that once hosted Nostradamus' mortal remains, offering local cuisine. *Closed Sun.*

Aix-en-Provence

⭐ Aix-en-Provence

Elegant and honey-hued, the old capital of Provence is splashed by a score of fountains – a charming reminder that its very name comes from its waters, Aquae Sextiae. It's sweet water, mind you, with none of the saltiness and excesses of Marseille. For if chaotic Marseille is the great anti-Paris, Aix-en-Provence is the stalwart anti-Marseille – bourgeois, cultured, aristocratic, urbane, slow-paced and convivial. Since 1948, it has hosted France's most élite festival of music and opera, while its 600-year-old university not only teaches the arts and humanities to the French but instructs foreign students in the fine arts of French civilization (the more 'practical' science departments are in Marseille). If a fifth of Aix's 150,000 souls are students, another large percentage are doctors, lawyers and professors, financial and underworld nabobs who commute to Marseille. But as cultured as it is, Aix can never quite live down having mocked and laughed at Paul Cézanne, the one real genius it ever produced.

History

The first version of Aix, the *oppidum* of Entremont, was the capital of the Salyens, a Celto-Ligurian tribe who liked to decapitate their enemies and tie their heads to the tails of their horses. By 123 BC they had pulled this trick once too often on the Greeks of Massalia, who called in their Roman allies to teach them a lesson. Under Sextius Calvinus, the Romans did just that, and founded a camp by a nearby thermal spring that they named Aquae Sextiae Salluviorum.

Just 20 years later, in 102 BC, these Latin frontiersmen woke up one day to find 200,000 ferocious Teutones with covered wagons at their door, en route to Italy – looking not for a place to camp but for *Lebensraum*. The strategies of the great Roman general Marius caught them unawares, and, in the battle that raged around Aix,

10 Metropolitan Provence | Aix-en-Provence

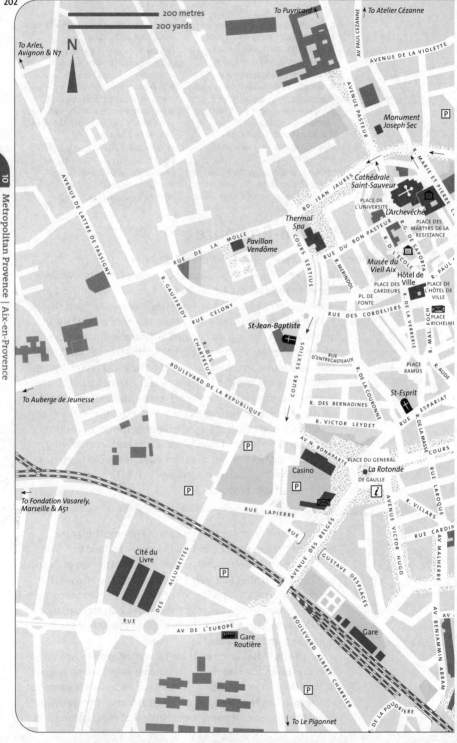

200 metres
200 yards

N

To Puyricard

To Atelier Cézanne

AV PAUL CÉZANNE

AVENUE DE LA VIOLETTE

To Arles,
Avignon & N7

AVENUE PASTEUR

Monument
Joseph Sec

P

R. MARIE ET PIERRE C

AVENUE DE LATTRE DE TASSIGNY

BD. JEAN JAURÈS

Cathédrale
Saint-Sauveur

PLACE DE
L'UNIVERSITÉ

L'Archevêché

PLACE DES
MARTYRS DE LA
RESISTANCE

Thermal
Spa

Pavillon
Vendôme

COURS SEXTIUS

RUE DE LA MOLLE

R. GAUFFREDY

RUE CELONY

RUE DU BON PASTEUR

R. MERINDOL

R.D. L'ÉCOLE

R.G. DE SAPORTA

Musée du
Vieil Aix

Hôtel de
Ville

PLACE DE
L'HÔTEL DE
VILLE

R. PAUL

R. DE LA VERRERIE

R. MAL

PLACE
RICHELME

R. DES
CHARTREUX

BOULEVARD DE LA RÉPUBLIQUE

St-Jean-Baptiste

COURS SEXTIUS

RUE
D'ENTRECASTEAUX

PLACE DES
CARDEURS

PL. DE
FONTE

RUE DES CORDELIERS

R. HOCHE

PLACE
RAMUS

R. AUDE

To Auberge de Jeunesse

R. DES BERNADINES

R. DE LA COURONNE

St-Esprit

R. DE LA MASSE

R. ESPARIAT

R. VICTOR LEYDET

COURS

AV N. BONAPARTE

PLACE DU GENERAL
DE GAULLE

La Rotonde

RUE LAROQUE

Casino

P

RUE
LAPIERRE

i

AVENUE VICTOR HUGO

R. VILLARS

RUE CARDIN

AV MALHERBE

To Fondation Vasarely,
Marseille & A51

P

P

RUE

AVENUE DES BELGES

GUSTAVE DESPLACES

Cité du
Livre

P

DES ALLUMETTES

RUE

AV DE L'EUROPE

Gare
Routière

BOULEVARD ALBERT CHARRIER

Gare

AV BENJAMIN ABRAM

AV A

DE LA POUDRIERE

To Le Pignonet

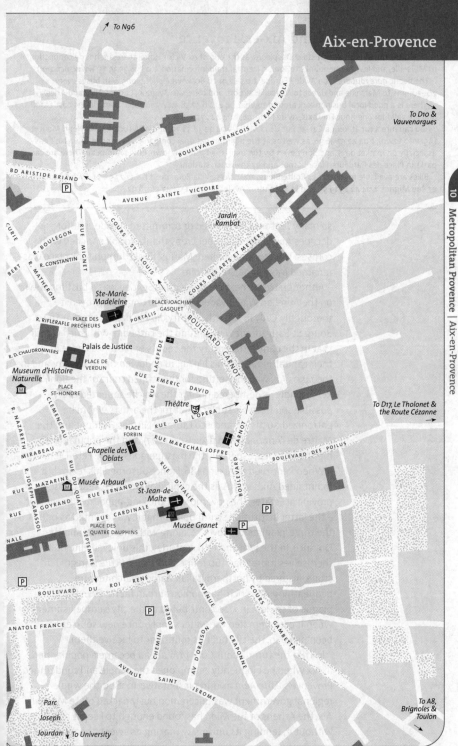

To N96

To D10 &
Vauvenargues

BOULEVARD FRANCOIS ET EMILE ZOLA

BD ARISTIDE BRIAND

AVENUE SAINTE VICTOIRE

Jardin
Rambat

CURIE

R. BOULEGON

RUE MIGNET

COURS ST LOUIS

R. CONSTANTIN

BERT

R. MATHERON

COURS DES ARTS ET METIERS

Ste-Marie-
Madeleine

PLACE JOACHIM
GASQUET

R. RIFLERAFLE

PLACE DES
PRECHEURS

RUE PORTALIS

BOULEVARD CARNOT

R. D. CHAUDRONNIERS

Palais de Justice

PLACE DE
VERDUN

RUE LACEPEDE

Museum d'Histoire
Naturelle

PLACE
ST-HONORE

RUE EMERIC DAVID

R. CLEMENCEAU

R. NAZARETH

Théâtre

RUE DE L'OPERA

To D17, Le Tholonet &
the Route Cézanne

MIRABEAU

Chapelle des
Oblats

RUE MARECHAL JOFFRE

CARNOT

BOULEVARD DES POILUS

R. JOSEPH CABASSOL

RUE MAZARINE

RUE DU QUATRE

Musée Arbaud

RUE FERNAND DOL

RUE D'ITALIE

BOULEVARD

GOYRAND

St-Jean-de-
Malte

RUE

RUE CARDINALE

PLACE DES
QUATRE DAUPHINS

Musée Granet

P

RUE DU QUATRE SEPTEMBRE

NALE

BOULEVARD   DU   ROI   RENE

P

ANATOLE FRANCE

P

CHEMIN   ROBERT

AVENUE   DE   CRAPONNE

AV. D'ORAISON

COURS   GAMBETTA

AVENUE   SAINT   JEROME

To A8,
Brignoles &
Toulon

Parc
Joseph
Jourdan   To University

Getting to and around Aix-en-Provence

The **train station** is on Rue Gustave Desplaces, at the end of Av Victor Hugo; there are hourly connections to Marseille, and less frequent links to Toulon (central train information, **t** 08 36 35 35 35, *www.sncf.com*).

The hectic **gare routière** is on Av de l'Europe, **t** 04 42 91 26 80, *www.lepilote.com*, with **buses** every 20–30mins to Marseille and direct to Marseille airport, and others to Avignon, Cannes, Nice and Arles.

There is a good **local bus** network around town, **t** 04 42 26 37 38, *www.aixenbus.com*. Tickets cost €1.10 and are valid for one hour. For **taxis**, Av de l'Europe, **t** 04 42 27 71 11.

You can **hire a car** at **Rent a Car**, 35 Rue de la Molle, **t** 04 42 38 58 29, and **ADA Location**, Av Henri Mouret (A51 into town), **t** 04 42 52 36 36, as well as at the big multinational companies. **Parking** in town isn't easy, especially on market days, and don't even try the main road through town, Cours Mirabeau. There are **car parks** in Place des Cardeurs, Place Carnot and by the coach station.

Bikes are available for hire at **La Route Bleue**, 20 Traverse Villa Romaine, **t** 04 42 27 92 34, **Cycles Zammit**, 27 Rue Mignet, **t** 04 42 23 19 53, and **La Rotonde**, 2 Av des Belges, **t** 04 42 26 78 92.

so many Teutones were killed or committed suicide that for decades Aix enjoyed bumper crops thanks to soil enriched with corpses. The mountain where Marius' final triumph took place was renamed Montagne Ste-Victoire.

Although by the next century Aquae Sextiae was a bustling town on the Aurelian Way, invaders in the Dark Ages destroyed it thoroughly. Only in the 11th century did Aix begin to revive: the Bourg St-Sauveur grew up around the cathedral with such vigour that in the early 13th century the counts of Provence chose it as their capital. In 1409, Louis II d'Anjou endowed the university, and in the 1450s Aix was the setting for the refined court of the Bon Roi René, fondly remembered not for the way he squeezed every possible *sou* from his subjects but for the artists whom he patronized, such as Francesco Laurana, Nicolas Froment and the Maître de l'Annonciation d'Aix (*see* p.207), and the popular festivities he founded, especially the masquerades of the Fête-Dieu.

When René died at Aix in 1486, France absorbed his realm but maintained Aix's status as the capital of Provence, seat of the provincial Estates, the governor and the king-appointed *Parlement* – the latter institution so unpopular that it was counted as one of the three 'plagues' of Provence, along with the *mistral* and the Durance. In the 17th and 18th centuries, this unloved élite built themselves more than 160 refined *hôtels particuliers* in golden stone, inspired by northern Italian Baroque architecture, bequeathing Aix a rich, harmonious urban fabric. Even the real plague of cholera in 1720 contributed to the city's embellishment when it contaminated the water supply; once new sources had been piped in, the city built its fountains to receive them.

In 1789 the tumultuous Count Mirabeau became a popular hero in Aix when he eloquently championed the people and condemned Provence's *Parlement* as unrepresentative; in 1800 the whole regional government was unceremoniously packed off to Marseille. Aix, the 'Athens of the Midi', has found enough to keep it busy without it, tending its university, making its sweets, hosting music festivals and, as of 1997, inaugurating a new thermal spa for the spring that gave the city its name.

Cours Mirabeau

Canopied by its soaring plane trees, decked with fountains and flanked by cafés, banks, *pâtisseries* and *hôtels particuliers* from the 17th and 18th centuries, **Cours Mirabeau** is the centre stage for Aixois society. Dubbed 'the most satisfying street in France' and laid out in 1649 to replace the south walls, it begins in Place du Général de Gaulle, which takes the old roads from Marseille and Avignon and spins them around the pompous Second Empire fountain, **La Rotonde**. Other fountains punctuate the *cours* itself: the lumpy, mossy **Fontaine d'Eau Chaude**, oozing up its much-esteemed 34°C water and, at the far end, the **Fontaine du Roi René**, with a fairytale statue of the good monarch holding up a bunch of the muscat grapes he introduced to Provence (along with the turkey and silkworm, discreetly omitted by the sculptor).

Of the fine *hôtels particuliers* on the *cours*, No.12 is where Count Mirabeau wed the aristocratic Emilie de Covet-Marignane in 1772, after playing a dastardly trick on her. When the young lady refused his marriage proposal, he sneaked into her house and appeared in the morning on her balcony, clad only in his nightshirt and socks, publicly compromising her virtue. In revenge, his new father-in-law refused the couple any money, and, when Mirabeau ran up huge debts, signed the order to have him locked up in the Château d'If. Mirabeau returned to Aix to plead in the subsequent divorce case, but despite his unparalleled eloquence he lost the appeal. Thus rebuked by his noble peers, he returned to Aix in 1789 as a member of the Third Estate and proceeded to attack their privileges – a trial run for his role in igniting the Revolution in Paris.

Artist Paul Cézanne grew up at 55 Cours Mirabeau, the son of a hatter who later turned banker (on the façade you can still make out the sign of the *chapelier*). Nearby, at No.53, the elegant café **Les Deux Garçons** ('Les Deux G') has been Aix's smartest place to see and be seen since the Second World War, with a reputation and prices similar to those of Paris' café-citadels of artsy existentialist mumbo-jumbo; until recently, North Africans were not admitted. It looks across towards the weighty façade of the 1647 **Hôtel Maurel de Pontevès** (No.38), the building that inspired Aix's secular Baroque, still supported after all these years by two muscle-bound stone giants, 'the only ones who do any work at all on the *cours*', as the saying went in the days of Aix's parliament.

South of Cours Mirabeau, the straight lanes of the **Quartier Mazarin**, lined with *hôtels particuliers* and antiques shops, were laid out according to the rules of Renaissance urban design by the archbishop brother of the famous cardinal.

Musée Paul Arbaud
t 04 42 38 38 95; open Mon–Sat 2–5; adm

At 2 Rue du Quatre-Septembre, the **Musée Paul Arbaud** is the city's overflow tank for odds and ends, especially Provençal ceramics and a few hundred portraits of Mirabeau's over-large pockmarked head.

Musée Granet

Musée Granet
Place St-Jean-de-Malte, t 04 42 52 88 32, www.museegranet-aixenprovence.fr; open June–Sept Tues–Sun 11–7; Oct–May Tues–Sun 12–6

Walk two streets south of the Musée Arbaud and then turn left at the Fontaine des Quatre Dauphins ('fountain of the Four Dolphins'), unusually equipped with teeth and scales, to reach the much more substantial archaeology and art collections of the Musée Granet, which is housed in the priory of the Knights of Malta (1675), next to the church of **St-Jean-de-Malte**, where the counts of Provence lie buried.

The museum's basement and ground floor are devoted to archaeology, especially everyday items and sculptures dating from the Celto-Ligurian *oppidum* of Entremont. Appropriately enough for residents of the land that would invent the guillotine, the overall theme is cult decapitation. The remains of 15 embalmed heads were discovered in the sanctuary, and the sculptures on display here, like death masks, may have been carved to replace real heads that mouldered away; according to Tertullian, the Celts would spend nights with their dead ancestors, seeking oracular advice. The heads, either singularly or in bunches, were once held as trophies by at least five statues of warriors: one has the same face as the famous gold mask of Agamemnon from Mycenae; another head resembles not so much that of a dead man as a resurrected youth. There are also finds from Roman Aquae Sextiae (note the fine sarcophagus depicting Leda and the swan, discovered in the cathedral), a superb statue of a Persian warrior (200 BC) of the Pergamon school, and Egyptian steles and cats.

Celtic head cults seem benign next to *Jupiter and Thetis* (1811), arguably Ingres' most objectionable canvas, holding court upstairs in a whole room of neoclassical mythologies inspired by Jacques-Louis David. The real culprit behind this smirking art is Napoleon, whose totalitarian approach to statecraft opened a Pandora's box of kitsch: art like this is born when cloying sentiment and a cynical manipulation of the classical past are used to serve political ends. The expression on Jupiter's sublimely stupid face not only sums up a whole era, but looks ahead to the even more cynical kitsch-mongers of the 20th century, who make Napoleon look like Little Red Riding Hood.

There are other, more palatable works by Ingres, including the *Portrait of François Granet* (1775–1849), the artist from Aix after whom the museum is named, painted while the two sojourned at Rome's Villa Medici. Granet himself was capable of neoclassical folderol and received more than his share of commissions from the clergy, but he also painted Provençal landscapes in the same vein as Guigou, Loubon and Monticelli, who are also present.

There are 17th-century portraits of Aixois nobility, made fluffy and likeable by Largillière and Rigaud; Dutch and Flemish masters (Teniers, Brit, Neefs, Rubens, Robert Campin, and a sumptuous anonymous 15th-century triptych of the *Adoration of the Magi*); and the Italians (Alvise Vivarini, Previtali, Guercino, Preti, the mysterious, grave 15th-century Maître de l'Annonciation d'Aix, and from Carlo Portelli a bizarre 16th-century Counter-Reformation blast, the *Allegory of the Church Suffering, Militant, and Triumphant*).

But what of Paul Cézanne, who took his earliest drawing classes in this very building? For many years he was represented by three measly watercolours (no one in Aix would buy his works), until 1984, when the French government finally rectified the omission by depositing eight small canvases here that touch on the major themes of his work.

Vieil Aix

North of Cours Mirabeau, the narrow lanes and squares of Vieil Aix concentrate not only some of Provence's finest architecture, but the region's most delightful shopping, especially on market days (*see* p.211). Enter the kasbah by way of Rue Espariat from Place du Général de Gaulle, and you'll come to a cast-iron Baroque campanile and the church of **St-Esprit**, where a 16th-century retable has portraits of 12 members of the first Provençal *Parlement* cast in the roles of the Apostles. Further up, just beyond Aix's most elegant little square, the cobbled, fountained **Place d'Albertas**, you can pop into the lavish, Puget-inspired **Hôtel Boyer d'Eguilles** of 1675 (6 Rue Espariat), now the **Muséum d'Histoire Naturelle** – well worth it for its impressive 17th-century interior, its grand staircase and its clutch of petrified dinosaur eggs.

Rue Espariat ends at **Place St-Honoré**, just south of the neoclassical **Palais de Justice**, a dull building of the 1760s that hardly merited the demolition of a well-preserved Roman mausoleum and the medieval palace of the counts of Provence.

Aix's flea and food markets take place in the adjacent Place de Verdun and **Place des Prêcheurs**, laid out in 1450 by King René for popular entertainments and executions of all sorts, including, in 1772, the burning in effigy of the Marquis de Sade and his valet after they were caught sodomizing prostitutes in Marseille. Here, the former Dominican church of **Ste-Marie-Madeleine** has a pleasant Second Empire façade, paintings by Rubens and Van Loo, and a gentle 13th-century polychrome statue of Notre-Dame-de-Grâce standing on a moon. However, the show-stopper is the central panel of the *Triptych of the Annunciation*, a luminous work of 1445 painted for a local draper – the two lateral panels are in

Muséum d'Histoire Naturelle
t 04 42 27 91 27,
www. museum-aix-en-provence.org;
open daily 10–12
and 1–5; adm

Rotterdam and Brussels. Commonly attributed to Barthélémy d'Eyck, illuminator of King René's courtly allegories in the *Livre du Cœur d'Amour Epris* (now in Vienna's National Library), the central panel has provoked endless controversy over its singular, possibly heretical iconography: the angel Gabriel, winged with owl feathers (a bird of evil omen), kneels in the porch of a Gothic church, decorated with a bat and a dragon. From on high, an unconventionally gesturing God the Father sends in a golden stream of breath a foetus bearing a cross, just missing a monkey's head; a vase of flowers holds poisonous belladonna.

The more orthodox blooms of Aix's flower market lend an intoxicating perfume to **Place de l'Hôtel de Ville** (or Place de la Mairie) in the very heart of Vieil Aix, a lovely square framed by the stately, perfectly proportioned **Hôtel de Ville** (1671), decorated with stone flowers and fruits and intricate iron grilles, and the flamboyant **Tour de l'Horloge** (1510), with clocks telling the hour and the phase of the moon, and wooden statues that change with the season. Note, too, the former grain market in the same square (now the post office), crowned by a handsome allegory of a river and city, the latter dangling a dainty foot over the cornice.

Musée du Vieil Aix
t 04 42 21 43 55; open April–Oct Tues–Sat 10–1 and 2–6; Nov–Mar Tues–Sat 10–12 and 2–5; adm

From here, 17 Rue Gaston de Saporta is home to the **Musée du Vieil Aix**, housed in another grand 17th-century *hôtel particulier* with another magnificent staircase. It stores some quaint paintings on velvet, a bevy of *santons* in a 'talking Christmas Crib' and marionettes made in the 19th century to represent the biblical, pagan and local personages who figured in King René's Fête-Dieu processions, beginning with a figure representing Moses and someone tossing a cat up and down, and ending with Death swinging his scythe.

Cathédrale Saint-Sauveur, Musée des Tapisseries and Monument Joseph Sec

Rue Gaston de Saporta continues north to Place de l'Université, which was once part of the **forum** of Roman Aix, and the **Cathédrale Saint-Sauveur**, a dignified patchwork of periods and styles crowned by an octagonal bell-tower. The flamboyant Gothic west portal of 1340, decorated with scenes of the Transfiguration and the Apostles said to be by King René, was mutilated in the Revolution and partially restored in the 1830s; only the lovely Virgin on the central pillar was spared, when someone popped a red cap of Liberty on her head and made Mary a Marianne. Fortunately, the Revolutionaries forgot to axe the doors; under their protective covers they have some beautiful high reliefs of prophets and sibyls by Jean Guiramand of Toulon, sculpted 1508–10.

The interior has naves for every taste: from right to left you'll fine Romanesque, Gothic and Baroque. Tucked away by the door inside the Romanesque nave, the octagonal baptistry dates from *c.* 375, when Aix was made a bishopric. The font is encircled by columns recycled from the temple of Apollo that once stood on this site in the forum.

The cathedral's most famous treasure, Nicolas Froment's *Triptyque du Buisson Ardent* (1476), is under restoration, and a copy is on view in the foyer. On the lateral panels are portraits of a well-fed King René, who commissioned the work, and his second wife, while the central scene depicts the vision of a monk of St-Victor of Marseille, who saw the Virgin and Child appear amidst the miraculous burning bush vouchsafed to Moses. The flaming green bush symbolizes her virginity (it burns without being consumed); the mirror held by the Child symbolizes his incarnation. The meticulously detailed castles in the background seem to have been inspired by those of Tarascon and Beaucaire.

On the same wall, from the same period, another triptych has scenes from the Passion with saints Maximin and Mitre. Mitre, a 4th-century Greek slave serving a cruel master in Aix, was accused of sorcery and had his head chopped off by Roman soldiers. His trunk then picked up the head (which was already adorned with a halo) and carried it into the cathedral. The sight scared the children but made the Romans, who had a modern sense of humour, laugh until they cried, at least according to the 15th-century *Martyrdom of St Mitre*, which may be on display in the chapel tucked behind the high altar, where the saint's 5th-century sarcophagus once emitted an ooze collected by the faithful to heal eye diseases. The high altar itself is decorated with tapestries on the lives of Christ and the Virgin made in Brussels in 1510. These originally hung in Canterbury Cathedral but were sold off by the Commonwealth and purchased by a cathedral canon in Paris for next to nothing in 1656.

In the Baroque aisle is the striking **Autel des Aygosi** (1470), formerly attributed to Francesco Laurana but now to Audinet Stephani, an itinerant sculptor from Cambrai. On top, the Crucifixion is surrounded by symbols: the sun and moon on either side represent universality; the skull of Adam set at the base of the cross is purified by the blood from Christ's wounds, while, above, the pelican feeds her nestlings with her own blood, according to a popular medieval misconception. Below stand saints Anne, Marcel and Marguerite, the latter emerging from the shoulders of an embarrassed-looking dragon who swallowed her whole. The guardian will on request also unlock the airy, twin-columned, 12th-century **cloister**, with capitals daintily carved, though in an awful state of repair.

To the right and back of the cathedral, the grand 17th–18th-century residence of Aix's archbishops, the **Archevêché**, is the setting for the festival's operas. The building also houses the

Musée des Tapisseries
t 04 42 23 09 91; open mid-April–mid-Oct Wed–Mon 10–6; mid-Oct–Dec and Feb–mid-April Wed–Mon 1.30–5; closed Tues and Jan; adm

Musée des Tapisseries, containing three sets of light-hearted Beauvais tapestries that were hidden under the roof during the Revolution and rediscovered only in the 1840s. The set known as the *Grotesques* (1689) features arabesques, animals, dancers and musicians; there are nine rococo scenes from the story of *Don Quixote* (1740s), and four on the subject of *Jeux Russiens* (1769–93), inspired by the rustic frolics that the court of Louis XVI got up to in the backwoods of Versailles.

Just north of the cathedral on Avenue Pasteur stands the 1792 **Monument Joseph Sec**, an eccentric discourse on the Revolution that spoiled those pampered bucolic daydreams. Sec, the builder, was a Jacobin who made his fortune floating timber down the Durance, and no one has ever satisfactorily explained the meaning behind the reliefs and statues of biblical characters, allegories and masonic symbols he chose for his monument 'dedicated to the municipality of a law-abiding town'. This obsession with law is continued in the inscriptions ('Risen from cruel slavery/I have no master but myself/But of my freedom I desire no other use/than to obey the law') and presence of Moses (with horns) on top. Behind the monument are seven more statues in exedrae, including one of a woman driving a stake into a man's head.

Cézanne, the Pavillon de Vendôme and Cité du Livre

Atelier Cézanne
t 04 42 21 06 53, www.atelier-cezanne. com; open July and Aug daily 10–6; April–June and Sept daily 10–12 and 2–6; Jan–Mar and Oct–Dec daily 10–12 and 2–5; adm

Paul Cézanne spent an idyllic childhood roaming Aix's country-side with his best friend, Emile Zola, and as an adult painted those same landscapes in a way that landscapes had never been painted before. The **Atelier Cézanne** at 9 Av Paul Cézanne, the studio that he built in 1897, located half a kilometre north of the cathedral, has been rather grudgingly maintained as it was when the master died in 1906, with a few drawings, unfinished canvases, his smock, palette, pipe and some of the bottles and skulls used in his still lifes. For a better understanding of Cézanne and his art, pick up the free *Circuit Cézanne* from the tourist office, which points out the places where Cézanne liked to plant his easel around Aix.

Fondation Vasarely
t 04 42 20 01 09, www. fondationvasarely.fr; open Tues–Sat 10–1 and 2–6; adm

Cézanne's family home at Jas-de-Bouffan is now dominated by the irritating black and white cubic forms of the **Fondation Vasarely**, inaugurated in 1976 by the late op/geometric/kinetic artist at the height of his fame. The foundation is unpersuasively dedicated to promoting 'more human' urban development.

Pavillon de Vendôme
t 04 42 91 88 75; mid-April–mid-Oct Wed–Mon 10–6; mid-Oct–Dec and Feb–mid-April Wed–Mon 1.30–5; closed Tues and Jan; adm

Along the boulevards to the west of Vieil Aix, in what was open country in 1665, a local cardinal built himself a lavish summer folly and park, the **Pavillon de Vendôme**, in Rue Célony. The building's delightful exterior includes a pair of atlantes who, judging by their pained expressions, have just been staring into one of Vasarely's optical illusions. Part of the interior décor is intact, complete with 17th- and 18th-century patrician furnishings and paintings.

Bibliothèque Méjanes
t 04 42 91 98 88, www. citedulivre-aix.com; open Tues, Thurs and Fri 12–6, Wed and Sat 10–6

Fondation St-John Perse
t 04 42 25 98 85, www. fondationsaintjohnperse. fr; open Tues–Sat 2–6

ⓘ **Aix-en-Provence >**
Place du Général de Gaulle, t 04 42 161 161, www.aixenprovence tourism.com; open daily all year

Near the bus station at 8 Rue des Allumettes, the modern **Cité du Livre** collects several cultural entities under one roof, including the **Bibliothèque Méjanes**, with a rich collection of incunabula and illuminated manuscripts, some of which are usually on display – you can also sit in a booth and take in a wide selection of celebrated operas and concerts filmed from 1950 to the present day – and the **Fondation St-John Perse**, a museum and study centre bequeathed to Aix by the French poet who won the Nobel Prize in 1960.

Tourist Information in Aix-en-Provence

Aix has one of the most pleasant tourist offices in the south of France, with details of a host of circuits to explore: by yourself with a map, or in guided groups; on foot, by bus or car; in town or around the countryside. The office also has a hotel booking service, and sells the €2 '**Carte Visa pour Aix et le Pays d'Aix**', with discounts on museums, concerts, dance programmes and buses.

Market Days in Aix-en-Provence

There's local produce every morning in **Place Richelme**, but **Tues**, **Thurs** and **Sat** are the days to come, when the centre of Aix overflows with good things: food in **Place des Prêcheurs** and **Place de la Madeleine**, flowers in **Place de l'Hôtel-de-Ville** (also known as Place de la Mairie), antiques and brocante in **Place de Verdun**, and clothes, fabrics and accessories on **Cours Mirabeau** and around the **Palais de Justice**; on Saturday nights in summer the stands stay open late, all bustling and brightly lit.

Festivals in Aix-en-Provence

The Aix authorities publish a free monthly guide to events, *Le Mois à Aix*, which comes in especially handy during the city's **summer festivals**. The headquarters and general booking office for these events is the **Boutique du Festival**, 11 Rue Gaston de Saporta, t 04 42 17 34 34. The most famous is the **International Opera Festival**, featuring celebrity opera and classical music in July. This highbrow (and very expensive) festival now features equally outstanding theatre.

It is preceded by a less formal **Music Festival** that includes jazz, big-band music and chamber music, during the 2nd and 3rd weeks of June.

Shopping in Aix-en-Provence

The traditional souvenirs of Aix are its marzipan and glazed melon sweets in the shape of boats, *calissons*, which have been made here since 1473. You can buy them at **Béchard**, 12 Cours Mirabeau, t 04 42 26 06 78, and **Confiserie Brémond**, 16 Rue d'Italie, t 04 42 38 01 70.

The better grocers sell the prize-winning *huile d'olive du pays d'Aix*: Aix calls itself 'the capital of the olive tree since the 18th century'. You can buy local, world-renowned **pottery** at **Terre è Provence**, 6 bis Rue Aude, t 04 42 93 04 54.

Where to Stay in Aix-en-Provence

Aix-en-Provence ✉ 13100
If you come in the summer during the festivals, you can't book early enough; Aix's less pricey hotels fill up especially fast (if you have a car, check around Aix as well, *see* p.216).

★★★★**Villa Gallici**, Av de la Violette, t 04 42 23 29 23, *www.villagallici.com* (€€€€€). A member of the Relais & Châteaux group, just north of the centre, with all the warm atmosphere of an old Provençal *bastide*, charming rooms, a garden, restaurant (€€€€), pool, and parking. *Closed Jan*.

⭐ Le Pigonnet >

****Le Pigonnet, 5 Av du Pigonnet, **t** 04 42 59 02 90, *www.hotelpigonnet. com* (€€€€€). A romantic old *bastide* on the southern outskirts of the city, with rose arbours, a swimming pool, lovely rooms furnished with antiques, an excellent restaurant (€€€€) and splendid views out over the Aix countryside. *Restaurant closed Sat plus Sun lunch in Oct–Mar.*

***Hôtel Cézanne, 40 Av Victor Hugo, **t** 04 42 911 111, *www.hotelaix.com* (€€€€). An exceptional little hotel located just two blocks from the train station, furnished with antiques and serving delicious breakfasts. There's air-conditioning and Internet access. No restaurant.

***Hôtel des Augustins, 3 Rue de la Masse, off Cours Mirabeau, **t** 04 42 27 28 59, *www.hotel-augustins.com* (€€€€–€€€). A 12th-century convent converted into a hotel, with elegant rooms. No restaurant.

***Grand Hôtel Nègre-Coste, 33 Cours Mirabeau, **t** 04 42 27 74 22, *www. hotelnegrecoste.com* (€€€–€€). A renovated, elegant 18th-century hotel that still hoists guests in its original elevator. No restaurant.

***Le Manoir, 8 Rue d'Entrecasteaux, **t** 04 42 26 27 20, *www.hotelmanoir. com* (€€). A quiet hotel built around a 14th-century cloister, with a garden and a private car park. *Closed 3 weeks in Jan.*

Artea, 4 Bd de la République, **t 04 42 27 36 00, *www.hotel-artea-aix-en-provence.com* (€€). The former home of composer Darius Milhaud (who grew up in the city), now a comfortable hotel with air-conditioned rooms with satellite TV and *en suite* baths (but no mementos of Milhaud). Discounts may be available out of season; check when booking.

Le Prieuré, 458 Route de Sisteron, 2km north of centre, **t 04 42 21 05 23, *http://hotel.leprieure.free.fr* (€€). A hotel situated in a charming 17th-century building overlooking a garden designed by Andre Le Nôtre of Versailles fame.

*Hôtel Paul, 10 Av Pasteur, **t** 04 42 23 23 89, *www.aix-en-provence.com/ hotelpaul* (€). An old-fashioned hotel near the cathedral, with a garden.

Hôtel des Arts, 69 Bd Carnot, **t** 04 42 38 11 77 (€). Basic, clean, good value.

Auberge de Jeunesse, 3 Av Marcel Pagnol, Jas-de-Bouffan (bus 4 or 6), **t** 04 42 20 15 99, *www.fuaj.org* (€). Far from the centre. *Closed mid-Dec–Jan.*

Eating Out in Aix-en-Provence

Le Clos de la Violette, 10 Av de la Violette, **t** 04 42 23 30 71, *www.closde laviolette.com* (€€€€–€€€). A lovely restaurant long considered the best in Aix, serving Provençal *haute cuisine*, including truffles in season. *Closed Sun, Mon and 2 weeks Aug.*

La Bastide du Cours, 43–47 Cours Mirabeau, **t** 04 42 26 10 06, *www. cafebastideducours.com* (€€). A constantly busy restaurant that's been in business since 1806, serving food and every imaginable kind of beverage throughout the day. There are also some plush *chambres d'hôtes* (€€€€).

Le Bistro Latin, 18 Rue de la Couronne, **t** 04 42 38 22 88 (€€). Imaginative variations on local themes, such as lentil and sausage terrine, at refreshingly reasonable prices. *Closed Sun, Mon lunch and 2 weeks Aug.*

Chez Maxime, 12 Place Ramus, **t** 04 42 26 28 51, *http://restaurant-chez maxime.com* (€€). Delicious meat or fish dishes, accompanied by a list of 500 wines, served on a shady terrace or by a cosy fireplace. *Closed Sun plus Mon lunch in winter, Sun lunch in summer.*

Café du Roi René, 61 Cours Mirabeau, **t** 04 42 38 21 30 (€€). Fresh pasta and other Italian and Provençal dishes served in a laid-back atmosphere.

Entertainment and Nightlife in Aix-en-Provence

Cinémazarin, 6 Rue Laroque, **t** 04 42 26 61 51, and **Renoir**, 7 Rue Villars, **t** 0892 687 270. Films in original language (*v.o.*).

Pasino, just off La Rotonde, **t** 04 42 59 69 00, *www.pasino-aixenprovence. com*. Aix's casino. *Open 10am–dawn.*

Bars and Clubs

Hot Brass, west of centre on Route d'Eguilles, **t** 04 42 21 05 57. One of the many jazz clubs kept in business by the student population.

Club 88, La Petite Calade, north of town near N7, **t** 04 42 23 26 88. A bustling club 8km from the centre.

Le Scat, Rue de la Verrerie, **t** 04 42 23 00 23. Live jazz at weekends.

Aix-urbia

East around the Montagne Ste-Victoire

The rolling countryside around Aix-en-Provence is the quintessence of Provence for those who love Cézanne: the ochre soil, the green cypresses – as still and classical as Van Gogh's are possessed and writhing – the simple geometry of the old *bastides* and villages and the pyramidal prow of the bluish-limestone **Montagne Ste-Victoire**. These landscapes are so inextricably a part of Cézanne's art that one can only wonder who created what. What if this grouchy genius had been born in Birmingham or New Jersey?

⭐ **Montagne Ste-Victoire**

Along the south flank of the Montagne Ste-Victoire runs the **Route Cézanne** (D17), beginning at the wooded park and Italianate château of **Le Tholonet** (3km from Aix). Here Cézanne often painted the view towards the mountain which haunts at least 60 of his canvases ('I am trying to get it right,' he explained). The château belongs to the local canal authority, while the park is used as a venue for Aix's music festival (take the bus from La Rotonde).

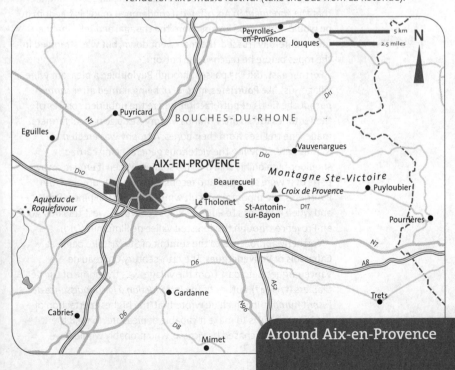

Around Aix-en-Provence

The entire 60km route around Montagne Ste-Victoire is striking and unspoiled; the mountain's wild shoulders are covered with maquis and holm oaks, growing back after a devastating fire in 1989, or tamed with vineyards. The short detour up to **Beaurecueil** is repaid with lovely views, while further east **St-Antonin-sur-Bayon** is home to the Maison de Sainte-Victoire, an information centre on the mountain; the GR9 (*see* p.75) begins nearby.

Maison de Sainte-Victoire
t 04 42 66 84 40

The ascent of Montagne Ste-Victoire takes about two hours (bring some sturdy shoes, a hat and a bottle of water); there's a 17th-century stone *refuge* with water and a fireplace if you want to spend the night. Crowning the precipitous west face, the 55ft **Croix de Provence** (which Cézanne never painted) has been here, in one form or another, since the 16th century. Legend has it that Marius stood on the spot, watching his troops annihilate the Teutones, then, at the urging of his sibyl Marthe, had 300 defeated chieftains brought up and tossed into the **Garagai**, Ste-Victoire's mighty chasm. One legend claims that the floor of the Garagai is occupied by an enchanted lake and meadows, the abode of the legendary Golden Goat of Provence; shepherds, they say, would lower their sick sheep and cows down on ropes so that they could graze on the therapeutic grass. Other stories claimed that the chasm was the entrance to hell, or linked to the Fontaine de Vaucluse (*see* p.240) – in fact, fluoride that was released here surfaced there three months later. In the 17th century, curiosity reached such a pitch that the *Parlement* in Aix offered a condemned man his freedom if he would agree to be lowered into the Garagai and tell what he found. Carefully trussed, the man went down, but was strangled in the ropes before he reached the bottom.

Further east, the D17 passes through **Puyloubier**, a pleasant wine village, just like **Pourrières**, in spite of being named after *campi putridi*, the fields of putrefaction, where the unburied corpses of the Teutones rotted after Marius' victory (*see* p.201); local farmers made vine trellises from their bones. A trophy was erected to Marius here, showing the victorious general being carried shoulder-high on his shield by his soldiers. When it eroded away, parts of it were salvaged and reconstructed as a fountain. From Pourrières, the mountain circuit winds through the pines (D23), and when it reaches Le Puits de Rians veers back west towards Aix-en-Provence through the forested Vallée de l'Infernet (D10).

Northerly approaches to the summit of Ste-Victoire begin at **Cabassols** or **Vauvenargues**. The 14th-century Château de Vauvenargues, set apart from the village, was the home of Luc de Clapiers (1715–47), author of the *Introduction à la connaissance de l'esprit humain*, in which he wrote that 'the highest perfection of the human soul is to make it capable of pleasure'. In 1958 the château was purchased by Picasso, who probably would have

Wine: Coteaux d'Aix-en-Provence and La Palette

This relatively recent AOC district has begun to make a name for its red, rosé and white wines. Coteaux d'Aix-en-Provence originates in 50 *communes* in the highlands stretching from the Durance to Marignane, west to Salon-de-Provence and east to the flanks of Montagne Ste-Victoire, and consists of the region's traditional syrah, grenache, cinsault, mourvèdre and carignan grapes, enhanced in the past 30 years with the addition of Cabernet Sauvignon, a stock that has improved the wine's ageing ability. Coteaux d'Aix's sunny whites are made from sauvignon, grenache blanc and ugni – but never from René's sweet muscat grapes, although these now grow merrily in Roussillon.

Many growers welcome visitors, such as Puyricard's **Château du Seuil**, **t** 04 42 92 15 99, a handsomely restored 13th-century *bastide*, where reds and whites from the late 1990s are an excellent buy.

Or head further north, 20km from Aix, to Le Puy Ste-Réparade and the lush estate of **Château de Fonscolombe**, on the banks of the Durance, **t** 04 42 61 70 00, where James de Roany produces classic, fragrant red, rosé and white wines.

Further afield, another estate that welcomes visitors also supplies some of France's best restaurants: Jean Bonnet's 120-hectare **Château Calissanne**, overlooking the Etang de Berre on the site of an ancient Celtic *oppidum* (on the D10, close to Lançon-Provence), **t** 04 90 42 63 03. On the south bank of the lagoon, one of the sunniest corners of France, **Château St-Jean**, at Port-de-Bouc near Fos-sur-Mer, **t** 04 42 44 70 14, produces prize-winning rosés (dominated by Counoise, an old-fashioned stock, mixed with grenache and carignan) and reds full of old-fashioned finesse.

La Palette is a venerable, microscopic AOC region on a north-facing limestone scree east of Aix, on the left bank of the Arc; although fairly sheltered from the mistral, it has cooler summer and winter temperatures than its environs. La Palette's red, white and rosé nectar has been served at the royal fêtes of such diverse monarchs as King René and Edward VII, but only two estates still produce this rare fine wine of the south, aged in small casks: the celebrated 150-year-old **Château Simone**, at Meyreuil, off the pretty D58H, **t** 04 42 66 92 58, where dark, violet-scented reds are kept for three years in caves carved out by 16th-century Carmelites; and **Château Crémade**, **t** 04 42 66 76 80, a 17th-century *bastide* in Le Tholonet, which bottles magnificent, well-structured red wines and a fruity blanc de blancs.

10

Metropolitan Provence | Aix-urbia

agreed with him; Picasso's grave is in the grounds but is off limits along with the rest of the château ('No admittance! Don't insist! The museum is in Paris!'). The idyllic D11 descends north of Vauvenargues for 13km to **Jouques**, sheltered in a cool, green valley.

Puyricard and the Arc Valley

Four kilometres to the north of Aix-en-Provence, overlooking the modern city, is the plateau where the city's story began, the Celto-Ligurian *oppidum* of **Entremont**. For a place that lasted less than a century – it was founded in the 2nd century BC and destroyed by the Romans in 122 BC – it was a highly impressive achievement, its clusters of stone houses once sheltering some 5,000 souls. You can trace the foundations of the large public building that produced the sculptures that now reside in the Musée Granet in Aix.

Entremont
www.entremont. culture.gouv.fr; bus 20 from Aix tourist office every half-hour; open Wed–Mon 9–12 and 2–6

The same bus continues north to **Puyricard**, and the **Chocolaterie Puyricard** at 420 Route du Puy-Ste-Réparade, where some of the most delectable (and expensive) fresh chocolates you'll ever taste are made in the traditional pre-Willy Wonka manner, 4km away in the factory; try the *clous de Cézanne*.

Chocolaterie Puyricard
t 04 42 96 11 21

To the west of Aix, the D64 continues for 10km from the Fondation Vasarely to the three-tiered **Aqueduc de Roquefavour**

 Aqueduc de Roquefavour

⭐ Relais Sainte-
Victoire >

Where to Stay and Eat around Aix

Le Tholonet ✉ 13100

Chez Thomé, La Plantation (in town centre next to *pétanque* courts), **t** 04 42 66 90 43, *www.chezthome.com* (€€). A restaurant offering good country fare, including some vegetarian dishes and a choice of divine desserts, served on a leafy terrace in summer. *Closed Mon all year and Sun eve in winter, and Jan.*

Beaurecueil ✉ 13100

***Relais Sainte-Victoire, **t** 04 42 66 94 98, *www.relais-sainte-victoire.com* (€€€–€€). A ravishing place to stay or eat, with a swimming pool, a gourmet restaurant (€€€) with a lovely veranda, and, above all, tranquillity. The guest rooms are air-conditioned and have terraces. *Book well in advance. Closed Sun eve, Mon, Fri lunch in summer, all day Fri in winter and school hols.*

Puyloubier ✉ 13114

Relais de Saint-Ser, on D17 between Puyloubier and St-Antonin-sur-Bayon, **t** 04 42 66 37 26, (€; restaurant €€). A small place for guests who want to get away from it all, though it's occasionally besieged by conference groups. *Closed Jan; restaurant closed Sun eve all year, closed Sun lunch only Oct–May.*

Les Sarments, 4 Rue-qui-Monte, **t** 04 42 66 31 58, *http://restosarments. free.fr* (€€). An old country inn, run by the family that owns the Relais Sainte-Victoire, providing well-prepared *cuisine du terroir*. *Closed Mon.*

Vauvenargues ✉ 13126

*Moulin de Provence, 33 Av des Maquisards, **t** 04 42 66 02 22 (€; restaurant €€). Twelve simple rooms and a breakfast terrace overlooking Picasso's château. An excellent place to begin or end a walk around the Montagne Ste-Victoire.

Roquefavour ✉ 13122

Arquier, Route du Petit-Moulin, **t 04 42 24 20 45, *www.logis-de-france.fr* (€€). Peaceful rooms immersed in trees in the Arc valley, next to the aqueduct, with a pleasant restaurant (€€) and a terrace along the river. *Closed Sun eve, Mon and mid-Feb–mid-Mar.*

Gardanne ✉ 13320

***L'Etape Lani, Route de Gardanne (D6), **t** 04 42 22 61 90, *www.lani.fr* (€€). A hotel with comfortable, well-equipped rooms and a nice restaurant (€€€–€€) where you can enjoy delicate seasonal dishes. *Closed Sat lunch and Sun eve out of season; Sat lunch, Sun and Mon lunch in July and Aug.*

(1847), twice as high as the Pont du Gard and built across the steep valley of the river Arc to bring the waters of the Durance to Marseille. The wooded setting is delightful – the Arc is the river where Cézanne painted his famous proto-Cubist scenes of bathers.

The edge of the Arc valley is dotted with old farms and *villages perchés*: **Eguilles**, north on the D543, with fine views from its William Morris-style medieval château (now the *mairie*); and south, off the busy Aix–Marseille routes, lofty **Cabriès** and **Mimet**. **Gardanne**, an old village often painted by Cézanne, has remained unchanged, though it is now defended by an ugly ring of industry.

Northern Provence: The Vaucluse

Two troublesome natural features serve to define the boundaries of this region: the long curve of the wicked, boat-sinking, valley-flooding Durance river to the south; and a long line of ridge-like mountains, Mont Ventoux and the Montagne de Lure, to the north, which folk wisdom has always credited as the source of Provence's terrible mistral wind.

But the lands between these natural prodigies are the eye of the hurricane, with some of the most civilized countryside and loveliest villages in the Midi. They have not passed without notice, of course, and the rural Vaucluse is now what the Côte d'Azur was 40 years ago: the in-place for both the French and foreigners to find a bit of sun-splashed holiday paradise amongst the vineyards.

FRANCE

ITALY

SPAIN

11

Don't miss

⭐ Touristy but magical
Fontaine-de-Vaucluse **p.240**

⭐ A village built on ochre
Roussillon **p.233**

⭐ An abbey set in lavender
Abbaye de Sénanque **p.240**

⭐ Vineyards under lacy peaks
Les Dentelles de Montmirail **p.252**

⭐ A quirky old town
Carpentras **p.245**

See map overleaf

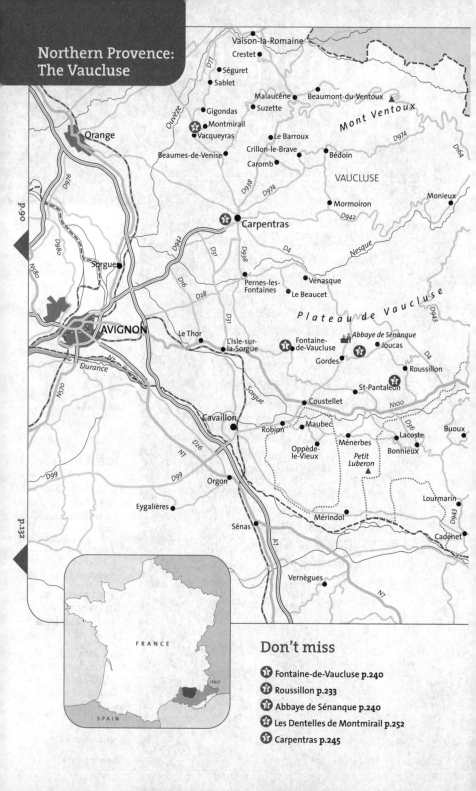

Vaison-la-Romaine
Crestet
Séguret
Sablet
Malaucène
Suzette
Beaumont-du-Ventoux
Gigondas
Montmirail
Vacqueyras
Beaumes-de-Venise
Le Barroux
Crillon-le-Brave
Bédoin
Caromb
Orange
Mont Ventoux
VAUCLUSE
Monieux
Mormoiron
Carpentras
Nesque
Sorgue
Pernes-les-Fontaines
Venasque
Le Beaucet
Plateau de Vaucluse
AVIGNON
Le Thor
L'Isle-sur-la-Sorgue
Fontaine-de-Vaucluse
Abbaye de Sénanque
Joucas
Gordes
Roussillon
St-Pantaleon
Durance
Coustellet
Cavaillon
Robion
Maubec
Ménerbes
Lacoste
Buoux
Oppède-le-Vieux
Petit Luberon
Bonnieux
Lourmarin
Orgon
Eygalières
Mérindol
Sénas
Cadenet
Vernègues

FRANCE
ITALY
SPAIN

Don't miss

⭐ Fontaine-de-Vaucluse **p.240**

⭐ Roussillon **p.233**

⭐ Abbaye de Sénanque **p.240**

⭐ Les Dentelles de Montmirail **p.252**

⭐ Carpentras **p.245**

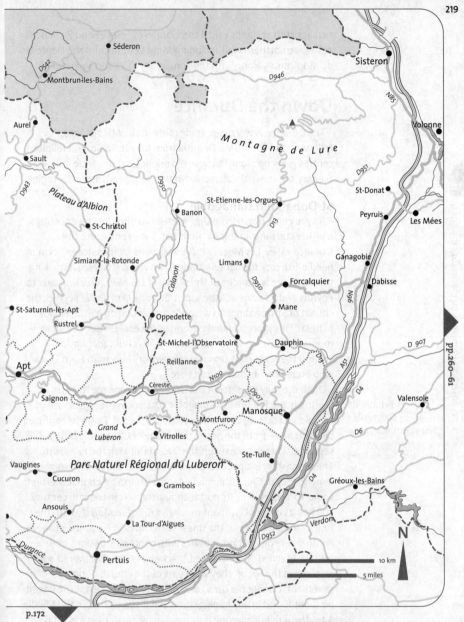

pp.260–61

p.172

Not everything included in this section is actually in the *département* of Vaucluse (Manosque and Forcalquier are in Alpes de Haute-Provence); and the Vaucluse's two cities, Orange and Avignon, will be found in the chapter **Down the Rhône 1: Orange to Beaucaire**. The remainder divides neatly into three areas: the mountainous Luberon, cradled in the Durance's arc, a *pays* of especially pretty villages; the old papal Comtat, nearer the Rhône, rich agricultural lands called the 'Garden of France'; and Provence's definitive northern wall, including Mont Ventoux and the Dentelles de Montmirail, along with the Roman city of Vaison-la-Romaine.

Down the Durance

The Durance was a major trade route in the Middle Ages, following the Roman Via Domitia from Italy to Spain, and religious centres grew up along it. These old priories, set in gentle rolling scenery, are the main attraction in this still fairly untouristy region.

St-Donat and Ganagobie

As you come down from Digne-les-Bains and the Provençal Alps, a rather startling landmark punctuates your entry into the Durance valley: **Les Mées** (a Provençal word for milestones), 2km of needle-like rock formations eroded into weird shapes, overlooking the D4. There is a bridge at the village of Les Mées, crossing over to **Peyruis** and its ruined castle. Up in the hills, 5km above Peyruis, the church of **St-Donat** enjoys a wonderful setting on a little wooded plateau. This graceful building, one of the earliest Romanesque monuments in Provence (11th century), was built for pilgrims visiting the relics of St Donat, a 5th-century holy man from Orléans who ended his life as a hermit here.

Of all the holy sites down the Durance, the one most worth visiting is the **Prieuré de Ganagobie**, just down the N96 south of Peyruis, in a setting as lovely as that of St-Donat. Don't be confused by the roads – from the north, the village of Ganagobie is up a separate side road; you want the D30, about 3km further south. The monastery is signposted. Founded in the 9th century as a dependency of Cluny, the monastery's remarkable **church** was built some 200 years later. Its portal, though rebuilt in the 17th century, still has its original tympanum relief: a *Christ in Majesty* with the four Evangelists, one of the finest such works in Provence. Inside is another rare decoration: **mosaics** with geometric designs and peculiarly styled animals in red, black and white. Discovered and restored in the 1960s, they were part of the church's original pavement. Ganagobie used to have the relics of a certain St Transit; he is not found in any hagiography, and it seems that in the Middle Ages the habit of carrying holy relics in procession on a holiday (a *transit*) led to the invention of a new saint. Such things happened all the time in the Midi. (And there must have been some Provençal colonists involved in a similar occurrence very much later, in New Orleans, where the faithful in one parish still beseech favours at the altar of Ste Expédite: a statue of a female saint had arrived during the building of the church; no one knew who she was – but then they found her name on the packing crate.)

Prieuré de Ganagobie
t *04 92 68 00 04, www. ndganagobie.com; open Tues–Sun 3–5*

Getting around the Durance Valley

The valley of the Durance is the main corridor for public transport. A **railway line** passes Manosque and continues along the bottom edge of the Luberon, serving Pertuis on its way to Aix-en-Provence and Marseille. Manosque is also the hub for **buses**, with several daily to Aix-en-Provence and Marseille, and also one or two a day to Forcalquier and Digne-les-Bains, stopping in Les Mées.

The lovely area around the priory is a great place for a picnic, or some unambitious hiking along the old trails, with a few *bories* (*see* p.239), medieval quarries and views over the valley.

Forcalquier, Mane and Around

Nowadays on the drowsy side, and a bit too large and musty to attract the holiday-home-restoring crowd, **Forcalquier** only bestirs itself for its market day. Yet in the 11th and 12th centuries, it was a miniature capital of a small-fry mountain state whose counts often made life difficult for the counts of Provence. Alphonse II managed to get it in 1209, by marriage, and later Provençal rulers such as Raymond Bérenger V made it a favoured residence during the 14th century. They left few traces: an **obelisk** in front of the stern Gothic cathedral commemorates Marguerite de Provence-Forcalquier, wife of Saint Louis; there's a Gothic **fountain** with the warrior angel and monkey faces in Place St-Michel; and also Europe's only listed

Cemetery
open daily 9–5

cemetery, its ancient yew hedges trimmed to form the arcades of a cloister. A **tower** and other scanty remains of Forcalquier's citadel overlook the town, next to an octagonal **chapel**, crowned with a statue of the Virgin, honouring Pope Urban II, who came here to raise men and money for the First Crusade. The well-restored 13th-century **Couvent des Cordeliers**, parts of which were originally the counts' palace, was given to the Franciscans by Raymond Bérenger V; it has medieval art, a Franciscan cloister garden and occasional summer exhibitions.

Prieuré de Salagon
t 04 92 75 70 50, www. musee-de-salagon.com; open June–Aug daily 10–7.30; May and Sept daily 10–12.30 and 2–6.30; Oct daily 2–5; Feb–April Mon-Fri 2–5; Nov and Dec Sun 2–5; closed Jan; adm

The lands around Forcalquier are some of the most beautiful in this part of Provence, full of oak forests and sheep meadows, rustic, peaceful and not yet as touristy as the Luberon to the south. Six kilometres southwest, in **Mane**, the 12th-century Benedictine **Prieuré (Musée) de Salagon** was built on the site of a Gallo-Roman farm and 5th-century Christian cemetery. Beautifully restored by the Conseil Général, the priory has medieval and medicinal gardens and houses the frequent exhibitions of the Alpes de Lumières, an organization dedicated to preserving and documenting local culture and customs. Mane's 18th-century **Château de Sauvan**, owned by a friend of Marie Antoinette, is a fine example of French classicism, with period furnishings.

Château de Sauvan
t 04 92 75 05 64; open July and Aug Sun–Fri 2.30–5.30; Sept–June Sun and hols 2.30–5.30; guided tours at 3.30 on days when open; adm

Observatoire de Haute-Provence
t 04 92 70 64 00, www.obs-hp.fr; open July and Aug Wed and Thurs 1.15–4.15; April–June and Sept Wed 2–4; Oct–Mar Wed 3pm; adm

Twelve kilometres south of Forcalquier lies the **Observatoire de Haute-Provence**, near St-Michel-l'Observatoire. Scientists were attracted to the area by a study in the 1930s that found that the *pays de Forcalquier* had the cleanest, clearest air and the least fog of anywhere in France. There are guided tours, sadly only by day.

This is also a region of *villages perchés*: **Dauphin**, just to the south, and **Oppedette**, to the northwest, overlooking the scenic canyon of the Calavon river. To the north, **Limans**, under the brooding, bald Montagne de Lure, is famous for its luxurious 16th-century *pigeonniers*, while **Banon** to the northwest is synonymous with Provence's most famous sheep's cheese, plus it holds a goat's cheese fair each May. Most impressive of all, perhaps, is **Simiane-la-Rotonde**, set high on a small plateau. The *rotonde* is a peculiarly shaped 12th-century *donjon* dominating the village, with Romanesque carvings around what may have been a chapel – all that's left of a feudal castle. Simiane is by far the most chic of the villages in this area, with plenty of restored second homes; it's a charming place nevertheless, with a late Gothic church and an old covered market supported on stone pillars.

Manosque

By far the biggest town in this part of the Durance valley (with a population of 20,000), Manosque is unavoidable. Nicknamed '*Manosque la Pudique*' (the modest or shamefaced) by François Ier after a beautiful girl from the village who disfigured herself rather than surrender to his unwanted advances, it was for centuries a drowsy place, with no other distinction than being the home town and lifetime abode of writer Jean Giono (1895–1970). Today, acres of concrete suburban sprawl press against the hilltop medieval centre, and the traffic can be as ferocious as Marseille's. The culprit is **Cadarache**, France's national nuclear research centre, a huge complex to the south across the Durance, which was set up in 1959; most of its workers live around Manosque.

Manosque's tidy, teardrop-shaped centre, an oasis amidst the sprawling disorder, is entered through two 14th-century gates, the **Porte Saunerie** and the **Porte Soubeyran**, designed more for decoration than defence. Inside are two unremarkable churches on quietly lovely squares: **St-Sauveur**, made in bits and pieces from the 13th to the 18th centuries but attractive nevertheless, and **Notre-Dame-de-Romigier**, with a Renaissance façade; the altar is an early Christian sarcophagus with reliefs of the Apostles.

Manosque also has a pair of newer attractions just outside the historic centre. A 19th-century *hôtel particulier* holds the **Centre Jean Giono**, just outside Porte Saunerie at 1 Bd Elémir Bourges, dedicated to Manosque's literary lion, with an exhibition, a library, and a *vidéothèque* with interviews and the films made from Giono's writings. A few doors down, the **Fondation Carzou**, in the neoclassical church at the **Couvent de la Présentation**, has frescoes by contemporary Armenian painter Jean Carzou.

Simiane *donjon*
t 04 92 75 91 40; open last 2 weeks June daily 10–12.30 and 3–7; July–mid-Sept Mon–Sat 10–7, Sun 3–7; April–mid-June and last 2 weeks Sept Wed–Mon 3–5; Oct–Mar by reservation for groups only; adm

Centre Jean Giono
www.centrejeangiono. com; open July–Aug Tues–Sun 9.30–12 and 2–6; April–June and Sept Tues–Sat 9.30–12 and 2–6; Oct–Mar Tues–Sat 2–6; adm

Fondation Carzou
open July and Aug Tues–Sun 10–12 and 2.30–6.30; June and Sept Tues–Sat 2.30–6.30; Oct–May Wed–Sat 2.30–6.30

Market Days in the Durance Valley

Forcalquier: Fri am.
Banon: Tues am.
Manosque: Sat am.

Where to Stay and Eat in the Durance Valley

Dabisse-Les Mées ✉ 04190

Le Vieux Colombier, on D4, t 04 92 34 32 32, http://levieuxcolombier.over-blog.fr (€€€–€€). A pleasant old farmhouse with a dovecote, specializing in succulent pigeon but also offering some superb cheeses and a wonderful selection of desserts. Closed Wed, Sun eve, and 1st 2 weeks Jan.

Forcalquier ✉ 04300

Auberge Charembeau, Route de Niozelles, 2.5km east of town, t 04 92 70 91 70, www.charembeau.com (€€). A hotel situated in a Revolutionary-era farmhouse outside of town, with a swimming pool. There's no restaurant, but some of the rooms have small kitchenettes; some are inexpensive,

some expensive. Closed mid-Nov–mid-Feb.

Le Colombier, Mas des Dragons, 3km south of town, t 04 92 75 03 71, www.lecolombier.fr (€€). A sensitively restored mas with a shady garden and a swimming pool, located out in the pretty countryside surrounding Forcalquier. Half-board obligatory in summer. Closed Feb.

Le Grand Hôtel, 10 Bd Latourette, t 04 92 75 00 35 (€). A perfectly acceptable option for its price range, with the attraction of a garden.

Manosque ✉ 04100

Le Provence, Route de la Durance, t 04 92 72 39 38, www.leprovence manosque.com (€€–€). A modern hotel on the outskirts; air-conditioning.

François Iᵉʳ, 18 Rue Guilhempierre, t 04 92 72 07 99, www.hotelfrancois1. com (€). A central, quiet, if a little old-fashioned small hotel.

Le Petit Pascal, 17 Promenade Aubert-Millot, near Porte Saunerie, t 04 92 87 62 01 (€). A one-woman operation in a hole-in-the-wall with no sign, offering delicious home cooking; worth looking out for. Open lunch only.

ⓘ **Manosque ››**
Place du Dr Joubert, t 04 92 72 16 00, www. manosque-tourisme. com; open mid-June–mid-Sept daily; mid-Sept–mid-June Mon–Sat and Sun am

ⓘ **Forcalquier ›**
13 Place du Bourguet, t 04 92 75 10 02, www.forcalquier.com; open daily all year

The Luberon

As is the case with many a fair maiden, the Luberon's charms are proving to be her undoing. This is Peter Mayle country, the stage-set for his surprise bestseller *A Year in Provence*. Yes, this is that magical place where the natives are endlessly warm and human, the vineyards ever-so-lovely in autumn, and the lunch in the little *bistrot* worth writing about for pages and pages. All true, in fact – but now everybody knows it, and the trickle of outsiders who began settling here in the 1950s, permanently or in holiday homes, has become a flood, to the extent that the French have even given up and dropped their accent – the Lubéron has become the Luberon, with a much-disputed change of pronunciation to go with it.

How you experience the Luberon also depends on what time of year you come. Most of the year it's quiet as a grave; in summer it can seem like St-Tropez-under-the-Poplars, with crowds of Brits, Americans and Parisians milling about. It's hard to imagine why anyone would want to come in August; if you insist, book a hotel months in advance.

Getting around the Luberon

Public transport is woefully inconvenient in the Luberon. It is possible to get around the villages, but just barely. Try to avoid the *villages perchés* in July and Aug, when tour buses cause traffic jams.

By Train and Bus

Apt is on an **SNCF** rail branch line, with a few trains daily to Cavaillon and Avignon.

Buses (**t** 04 90 74 03 18; timetables at Apt tourist office) from Apt leave from Place de la Bouquerie by the river; there are one or two daily to Avignon and Aix-en-Provence, stopping at Bonnieux, Lourmarin, Cadenet and Pertuis; and one to Digne-les-Bains, stopping at Céreste. From Cavaillon there are buses to L'Isle-sur-la-Sorgue, Pernes-les-Fontaines and Carpentras (several daily), to Apt and Avignon, and occasionally to Bonnieux.

By Horse

Finding a horse is no problem in most areas; in Lauris, try the **Mas de Rocaute**, **t** 04 90 08 29 58, and in Cairanne try **Les Ecuries de Muzet**, **t** 04 90 46 12 99, which offers 2-day tours of the Côtes-du-Rhône vineyards on horseback.

Like many parts of rural Provence, the Luberon presents a puzzling contrast. How did these villages become such civilized places, set amidst a landscape (and a population) that is more than a little rough around the edges? The real Luberon is a land of hunters stalking wild boar over Appalachian-like ridges, and

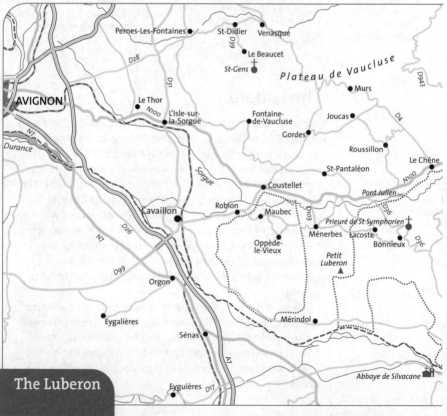

The Luberon

weatherbeaten farmers in ancient Renaults full of rabbit cages and power tools. There are equally scenic and rustic areas of Provence that merit being frozen into a nature preserve, but the Luberon was most in danger of being destroyed by a rash of outsiders and unplanned holiday villas.

The **Parc Naturel Régional du Luberon**, now ranked as a Biosphere Reserve by UNESCO, was founded in 1977, in a co-operative arrangement between the towns and villages that cover most of the territory between Manosque and Cavaillon, though quite a few places (often where the mayor is an estate agent or a notary) have decided not to participate at all. The Luberon is not an exceptional nature area like the Mercantour National Park (*see* pp.262–4). Still, the park protects rare species such as Bonelli's eagle, which is nearing extinction. It also keeps the Luberon from being over-whelmed by new buildings.

The Pays d'Aigues

The southern end of the Regional Park, the Pays d'Aigues, is the sleepier corner of the Luberon, a rolling stretch of good farmland sheltered by the Grand Luberon mountain to the north. **Pertuis**, a

ⓘ Natural Regional Park Information

Maison du Parc du Luberon, 60 Place Jean Jaurès, Apt, t 04 90 04 42 00, www. parcduluberon.com; open April–Sept Mon–Fri and Sat am; Oct–Mar Mon–Fri: an information centre with exhibitions, a shop, plus information on bike routes; see p.231

11 Northern Provence: The Vaucluse | The Luberon

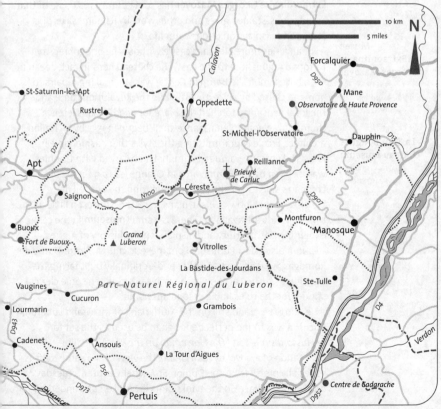

busy crossroads town along the D973, is the modest capital of the *pays*, with a bit of an aristocratic air; it earned the *fleur de lis* on its arms for its loyalty to the French crown during the Wars of Religion. Prosperity in the 17th century has left it a number of fine buildings in the historic town centre.

Of the smaller villages, a few stand out: **Grambois** to the north-east is a neatly rounded hilltop hamlet, a Saracen stronghold in the 8th–10th centuries and later one of the 12 citadels of Provence. Some walls remain, but the crenellated tower belongs to the church of **Notre-Dame-et-St-Christophe**. Both its patrons are represented in art inside: a good Renaissance altarpiece of the Virgin and an original 14th-century fresco of St Christopher, as well as, best of all, an anonymous 16th-century polyptych of John the Baptist, one of the masterpieces of the Provençal school.

Ansouis, to the north of Pertuis on the D56, is a *village perché* built around the sumptuously furnished **Château de Sabran**, first mentioned in print in 961 and still in the hands of the original family. A Henry IV monumental stair leads to Flemish tapestries, Italian Renaissance furniture, portraits and later Bourbon bric-a-brac. The atmosphere is wonderfully snooty. The **Musée Extraordinaire Georges Mazoyer** has some of this and some of that – sculptures, stained glass and other work by its namesake, plus fossils and displays on underwater life.

For an airier, more pleasant castle without the bric-a-brac, try **La Tour d'Aigues**, just to the east. The **château** here, in fact, doesn't even have a roof. The Baron of Cental was still making repairs to damage caused by a fire in 1782 when the Revolution came and the local peasantry torched the place for good. What's left is a thoroughly elegant Renaissance shell, begun in 1555 by an Italian architect, Ercole Nigra, imitating the styles then fashionable in Paris. The entrance, a huge triumphal arch carved with trophies, was inspired by the Roman arch at Orange (*see* p.94). One of the château's side towers has been rebuilt, and the Conseil de Vaucluse, which now owns it, plans to restore the rest a little at a time as funds are available. There is a small **museum** in the cellar, exhibiting both pottery and displays on the history of Aigues.

La Tour also has an unusual Romanesque church, **Notre-Dame de Romegas**, with an apse at either end – originally built facing the east, it was turned around in the 17th century when some clerical stickler for the rules had a second apse built.

Heading west, and still on the south flank of the Grand Luberon, **Cucuron** was found perfect enough to be used as the set for *Le Hussard sur le toit* (*The Horseman on the Roof*), the film adaptation of a novel by Jean Giono; the view of the same roofs is especially pretty from the **Donjon St-Michel**. Cucuron's Tuesday market takes place on the banks of its little lake, surrounded by

Château de Sabran
t 04 90 09 82 70, www. chateau-ansouis.com; open July–Sept daily 2.30–6; Easter–June and Oct Wed–Mon 2.30–6; Nov–Dec and Feb–Easter Sun 2.30–6; closed Jan; adm

Musée Extraordinaire Georges Mazoyer
t 04 90 09 82 64; open daily summer 2–7, winter 2–6; adm

La Tour d'Aigues château museum
t 04 90 07 50 33; www.chateau-latourdaigues.com; open July–mid-Aug daily 10–1 and 2.30–6; April–June and mid-Aug–Sept Wed–Sat 10–1 and 2.30–6, Sun 2.30–6, Tues 10–1; Oct Wed–Sat 10–1 and 2.30–6, Sun and Mon 2.30–6, Tues 10–1; Nov–Mar Wed–Sat 10–12 and 2–5, Sun and Mon 2–5, Tues 10–12; adm

ancient plane trees. The town also holds a renowned May tree celebration in late May, in which the highest poplar tree is cut down and paraded through the streets to the local church, where it remains until August. The D56 leads on to **Vaugines**, a lovely little place (the setting for many scenes in *Manon des Sources* and *Jean de Florette*) and Lourmarin.

Lourmarin and Cadenet

Further west, into the heart of the Luberon, **Lourmarin** was the last home of Albert Camus. This is an unusual village, densely packed almost to the point of claustrophobia; many of its houses have tiny courtyards facing the street. It's too cute for its own good – few villages, even in the Luberon, are so beset by tourists. Its landmark is a grand **bell-tower**, so everyone always knows what time it is, and its main attraction is another 16th-century château.

Lourmarin château

t 04 90 68 15 23; open July and Aug daily 10–12 and 2.30–6; May–June and Sept daily 10–11.30 and 2.30–5.30; Mar–April and Oct daily 10–11.30 and 2.30–4.30; Nov–Dec and Feb daily 10.30–11.30 and 2.30–4; Jan Sat and Sun 2.30–4; adm

This was the residence of the counts of Agoult for three centuries; its last countess was the mother of Franz Liszt's three children, one of whom, Cosima, married Richard Wagner. Well restored, the 'Villa Médicis de Provence', as it's called, is now the property of the Académie of Aix, who use it for cultural programmes, concerts and exhibitions. The rooms have rare furnishings (don't miss the Aztec fireplace) and art, including the lovely *Lute Player* by the school of Leonardo da Vinci and a collection of engravings by Piranesi. If you are looking for the existentialist, Albert Camus can be found buried on the left-hand side of the pretty **cemetery**.

Cadenet, a big village overlooking the rocky bed of the Durance, is only 5km away, but the difference is like that between day and night. An ancient place, Cadenet began as a pre-Celtic *oppidum*; even older are some of the cave dwellings that can be seen in the cliffs behind the village (others were refuges for persecuted Waldensian Protestants in the 16th century; *see* below). It's also a very attractive village. On the **Place du Tambour d'Arcole**, one of the focal points of the Monday market, is a bronze statue of Cadenet's favourite son, André Estienne, a 15-year-old drummer boy who once managed a difficult river crossing for Napoleon's troops – wading right in and beating the charge under direct Austrian fire. The embarrassed soldiers could only follow. Peek inside the parish church, **St-Etienne**, on the northern edge of town. The baptismal font has well-preserved reliefs of a Bacchic orgy; scholars call it 3rd-century but disagree over whether it was originally a sarcophagus or a bathtub. The **Musée de la Vannerie** is dedicated to Cadenet's age-old occupation, wickerwork and basketry.

Musée de la Vannerie

t 04 90 68 24 44; open April–Oct Mon, Thurs, Fri and Sat 10–12 and 2.30–6.30, Tues, Wed and Sun 2.30–6.30; closed Nov–Mar; adm

West of Cadenet, **Mérindol** isn't much to look at, but it's worth a mention as a symbol of a very dark page of the Luberon's history. When plagues and war depopulated the region in the 14th century, immigrants from the Alps and from Italy came to work the land.

Many were peaceful, hard-working Waldensian dissenters; when the Reformation began, the authorities would no longer tolerate them. In 1540, the *Parlement* of Aix oversaw the burning of 19 Waldensian villages in the Luberon, including Mérindol and Lourmarin. More than 3,000 innocents were butchered, and hundreds more were sent off to the king's galleys. There is a Waldensian museum, **La Muse**, in the village, which contains extensive archives. The ruins of Mérindol's **castle** house a Waldensian memorial; also note the curious onion-domed tower, called a 'Saracen bulb' in French.

La Muse
t 04 90 72 91 64; call for opening hours

The Abbaye de Silvacane

Abbaye de Silvacane
t 04 42 50 41 69; open June–Sept daily 10–6; Oct–May Wed–Mon 10–1 and 2–5; adm

Life as a medieval Cistercian was no picnic. Besides the strict discipline and a curious prejudice against heating, there was always the chance the Order might send you to somewhere in the middle of a swamp. They built this, the first of the 'Three Sisters of Provence', in just such a location – the 'forest of rushes' (*silva cana*), south of the Durance, 7km from Cadenet – because they meant to reclaim it. It took a century or two, but they did the job, as you can see today from the fertile farmlands around Silvacane.

A Benedictine community had already been established here when the Cistercians arrived in 1147. Work began on the present buildings soon after, partially financed by the barons of Les Baux, and Silvacane became quite prosperous. However, bad frosts in the 14th century killed off all the olives and vines, starting Silvacane on its long decline. When the government bought the complex to restore it in 1949, it was being used as a barn.

The **church** is as chastely fair as its younger sisters at Sénanque (*see* p.240) and Thoronet (*see* pp.288–9), and perhaps more austere and uncompromising still: even the apse is a plain rectangle. There is hardly any sculptural decoration (though there are scores of masons' marks on the columns and vaulting). The adjacent **cloister** now contains a herb garden and a lovely broken fountain. Note the capitals on the arcades, carved, oddly, with maple leaves.

Northern Luberon: Along the N100 to Apt

Starting at Forcalquier, this route follows the northern slopes of the mountains, which generally constitutes much more scenic country than the other side, with pretty villages such as **Reillanne**, which was nearly deserted 100 years ago but is now making a comeback, and **Céreste**, a village that grew up as a stopping point on the Via Domitia, with a Roman bridge as a landmark.

Prieuré de Carluc
t 04 92 79 00 03 to check for its occasional music performances in summer, which is the only time you can visit

Between the two is the **Prieuré de Carluc**, with a 12th-century Romanesque chapel and unique ruins of the original early Christian priory, partly carved out of a rocky outcrop. Like Notre-

Dame-du-Groseau on Mont Ventoux (*see* p.250), this was an ancient religious site built around a sacred spring; the ruins around the rock include a Gallo-Roman cemetery.

The narrow roads south of the N100 are some of the most beautiful in the Luberon, passing through **Vitrolles** or **Montfuron**, with its lofty ruined castle, on their way to the Pays d'Aigues. There are also several hiking trails, from Vitrolles or from Saignon, 5km southeast of Apt, leading up to the summit of the Grand Luberon, the **Mourre Nègre**, with views that take in all of the Vaucluse and beyond. **Saignon** itself is a beautiful *village perché* between two crags, boasting a well-preserved 12th-century church of **Ste-Marie**, with a curious lobed façade and a reliquary of the True Cross inside. You can also tour the **Potager d'un Curieux**, a beautiful collection of forgotten plants, flowers and herbs.

Potager d'un Curieux
t 04 90 74 44 68; open Mar–Oct by appt only

ⓘ **Lourmarin >>**
Av Philippe de Girard, t 04 90 68 10 77, www.lourmarin.com; open Mon–Sat and Sun am

★ **Moulin de Lourmarin >>**

ⓘ **Pertuis >**
Le Donjon, Place Mirabeau, t 04 90 79 15 56, www.vivreleluberon.com; open Mon–Sat

ⓘ **La Tour d'Aigues >**
Château, t 04 90 07 50 29, www.souriredu luberon.com; open summer Mon–Sat; winter Tues–Sat

Market Days in the Luberon Natural Park

Pertuis: Provençal market Fri; farmers' market Wed and Sat.
La Tour d'Aigues: farmers' market Thurs am.
Cucuron: Tues.
Lourmarin: Fri.
Cadenet: Mon.

Where to Stay and Eat in the Luberon Natural Park

Pertuis ✉ 84120

Le Boulevard, 50 Bd J.B. Pécout, t 04 90 09 69 31, *www.restaurant-le-boulevard.com* (€€). A good place to stop for tasty and kindly priced Provençal classics, if you're passing through at lunchtime. *Closed Sun eve, Tues eve and Wed.*

La Bastide-des-Jourdans ✉ 84240

*Auberge du Cheval Blanc, Cours de la République, t 04 90 77 81 08 (€€). Picture-postcard hotel with a restaurant specializing in game and trout, served on an outdoor terrace. *Closed Feb; restaurant closed Thurs and Fri lunch in winter.*

La Tour d'Aigues ✉ 84240

**Le Petit Mas de Marie, Le revol, t 04 90 07 48 22, *www.destinations-*

luberon.com (€€). Simple rooms and a swimming pool nearby, and a restaurant with outdoor tables that's the town's best bet for lunch. *Restaurant closed Mon, and Sat lunch.*

Lourmarin ✉ 84160

Lourmarin, small as it is, has become the chic destination in the southern Luberon and has some of the best restaurants in the region.

****Moulin de Lourmarin, Rue du Temple, t 04 90 68 06 69, *www.moulindelourmarin.com* (€€€€–€€). A classy one-time olive mill on the western perimeter of the village, with views over the château and nearby hills. Provençal meets Art Nouveau in the tasteful decoration, and the restaurant serves attractive and delicious Provençal dishes. Cookery courses are also available. *Book well in advance. Closed last 2 weeks Jan.*

***Mas de Guilles, Route de Vaugines, t 04 90 68 30 55, *www.guilles.com* (€€€€–€€). A restored farmhouse just east of the village, part of the Relais du Silence, with all the amenities, including a tennis court, a pool and gardens, and restaurant (€€€). *Closed Nov–Mar; restaurant open eves only.*

**Hostellerie Le Paradou, Route d'Apt (D943), t 04 90 68 04 05, *www.hostellerieleparadou.com* (€€). In a dreamy setting north of Lourmarin at the entrance to the Combe de Lourmarin (*see* p.234), with pleasant rooms and a restaurant (€€). *Half-board obligatory in season.*

11

Northern Provence: The Vaucluse | The Luberon

Villa St-Louis, 35 Rue Henri de Savournin, **t** 04 90 68 39 18, *www. villasaintlouis.com* (€€–€). Charming *chambres d'hôtes* in a 19th-century house on the edge of the village, with a very affable proprietress.

La Fenière, Route de Cadenet, **t** 04 90 68 11 79, *www.reinesammut.com* (€€€€). A restaurant offering old Provençal favourites cooked in an expert way, like batter-fried courgette flowers and *daube*. There is also a cheaper *bistrot* (€€), and 18 **rooms** (€€€). *Closed Mon, Tues lunch and Jan; bistrot closed Tues eve and Wed.*

Le Bistrot, Av Raoul Dautry, **t** 04 90 68 29 74 (€€). Overlooking the château, offering a wide choice of Provençal and Lyonnais cuisine, together with some vegetarian dishes. *Closed Fri lunch, Sun eve, and Jan.*

Michel-Ange, Place de la Fontaine, **t** 04 90 68 02 03 (€€). A restaurant offering a reasonably priced choice of vegetarian, fish and organic dishes. *Closed Tues and Wed in winter.*

La Récréation, 15 Rue Philippe de Girard, **t** 04 90 68 23 73 (€€). A good bet, with a terrace facing the château and a menu of fresh organic Provençal fare. *Closed Tues and Wed.*

Cadenet ✉ 84160

Cadenet is less expensive and less touristy than Lourmarin, and is a good alternative as a place to stay.

Le Mas du Colombier, Route de Pertuis, **t 04 90 68 29 00, *www. mas-du-colombier.com* (€€). A pleasant enough place with a swimming pool, set in an old vineyard. *Closed end Oct–early Nov and 1 week Feb.*

ⓘ **Cadenet >>**
*11 Place du Tambour-d'Arcole, **t** 04 90 68 38 21, www.ot-cadenet.com; open daily all year; includes a shop selling items by Cadenet's famous basket-weavers*

Apt

The capital of the Luberon (pop. 15,000 and growing) also claims to be the 'World Capital of Candied Fruits', with one big factory and plenty of smaller concerns that make these and every other sort of sweet. And there is a certain stickiness about Apt itself; everyone in the Luberon comes here for the huge, animated Saturday market, but no one has ever admitted to liking the place, at least not in print. Roman Colonia Apta Julia, a colony refounded over a Celtic village, was the capital of the area even then. Despite languishing for a few dark centuries before being rebuilt in the 12th century, the streets still bear traces of a rectangular Roman plan, bent into kinks and curves through the ages.

The Cathedral and More Dubious Provençal Saints

We can guess that the **Rue des Marchands**, the main shopping street of Apt, roughly follows the course of its Roman predecessor. It leads to the **Tour de l'Horloge** (1567), the bell-tower of Apt's old **Cathédrale Ste-Anne**. Begun in the late 12th century and tinkered with incessantly until the 18th, it has an ungainly exterior concealing a wealth of curiosities within. There is fine 14th-century stained glass in the apse, an early Christian sarcophagus and an odd golden painting of John the Baptist in two chapels on the north side, plus an interesting *trésor* with reliquaries, books of hours, and a number of Islamic ivories. Another trophy that made its way here from the east is a linen banner, which was brought back from the Crusades by a lord of Simiane; because its origin was forgotten, it came to be revered in Apt as the veil of St Anne.

Few regions of Europe had such a longing for relics as Provence in the Dark Ages. Other peoples, the Germans and Venetians, had a kleptomaniac urge to steal holy bones when no one was looking; the Provençaux, showing less initiative but greater imagination, simply invented them. We met St Transit at Ganagobie (*see* p.220), and the crypt here has two more. According to legend, the bones of St Anne, the mother of Mary, were miraculously discovered in this crypt in the 8th century, occasioning the building of the first cathedral. In those days, any early Christian burial dug up was likely to be elevated to saint status; beyond that, scholars guess that the Anne invented for the occasion was less the biblical figure than a dim memory of the primeval pan-European mother goddess, known as Ana, or Dana, to the Celts, the Romans (Anna Perenna), and nearly everyone else. Next to her are the bones of 'St Auspice', claimed to be Apt's first bishop but really the sacred auspices of pagan times (divination from bird flight or from the organs of sacrificed animals) – another verbal confusion like St Transit.

Fruits and Fossils

Musée d'Histoire et d'Archéologie
*t 04 90 74 05 30;
open for groups by
appt only*

Apt also has a good **Musée d'Histoire et d'Archéologie** at 27 Rue de l'Amphithéâtre, with archaeological finds going back to the Palaeolithic period, late Roman sarcophagi, recent Roman and medieval finds from the centre of Apt, painted *ex votos* and a display of Apt's once-flourishing craft of faïence, which had its heyday in the 18th century.

Maison du Parc du Luberon
*t 04 90 04 42 00;
open April–Sept
Mon–Sat;
Oct–Mar Mon–Fri*

The town's other attraction is the **Maison du Parc du Luberon** at 60 Place Jean Jaurès, the headquarters and information centre of the Natural Regional Park in a restored 17th-century building; it has exhibits on the region's natural life, including a push-button Palaeontology Museum for the children, an interesting gift shop, and all the information you need on the wild areas of the Luberon.

Aptunion Factory
*t 04 90 76 31 31,
www.kerryaptunion.
com and click on link to
Les Fleurons; shop open
Mon–Sat 9–12 and 2–6;
factory visits by appt*

Finally, you can take a tour of the **Aptunion Factory**, west on the N100, where they make most of those crystallized fruits, by sucking the water out of the fruit and replacing it with a sugar solution – a bit like embalming.

ⓘ **Apt** ›
*20 Av Philippe de
Girard, t 04 90 74 03 18,
www.luberon-apt.fr;
open May–Sept
Mon–Sat and Sun am;
Oct–April Mon–Sat*

Market Days in Apt

Apt: Sat general market; Tues farmers' market, Cours Lauze de Perret.

Where to Stay and Eat in Apt

Apt ✉ 84400

As rooms in the smaller villages are hard to come by, you'll probably end up staying in Apt. The tourist office has lists of *chambres d'hôtes*, *auberges* and campsites.

***Auberge du Luberon, 8 Place du Faubourg du Ballet, **t** 04 90 74 12 50, *www.auberge-luberon-peuzin.com* (€€€–€€). Pleasant rooms and a restaurant where the speciality is rabbit with figs, and dishes with *confit d'Apt. Closed Sun eve, Mon lunch and Tues lunch out of season, plus Nov.*

Le Palais, 24 Place Gabriel Péri, **t 04 90 04 89 32, *http://hotelrestaurant dupalais.com* (€). Simple, comfortable budget hotel. *Closed mid-Nov–Feb.*

Le Platane, 8 Rue Jules Ferry, **t** 04 90 04 74 36 (€€). Fresh dishes made using organic market produce. *Closed Sun.*

Around Apt ✉ 84400

Relais de Roquefure, Le Chêne, 4km west of town on N100, **t 04 90 04 88 88, *www.relaisderoquefure.com* (€€€–€€). An old stone-built inn with a pool and restaurant. *Closed Dec–Jan, and eves in winter.*

 Auberge du Presbytère >

Auberge du Presbytère, Place de la Fontaine, Saignon, **t** 04 90 74 11 50,
www.auberge-presbytere.com (€€€–€€). Two 10th- and 11th-century buildings in the town centre, with a magnificent view over the Luberon, charming, homey rooms and a fine intimate restaurant. Worth the detour. Make sure to book ahead. *Closed mid-Jan–mid-Feb; restaurant closed Wed.*

Bernard Mathys, Le Chêne, 4km west of town on N100, **t** 04 90 04 84 64 (€€€). A lovely restaurant set in an 18th-century house, offering delightful meals with all the trimmings (the vegetables are especially good). *Dinner only; closed Tues and Wed, and mid-Jan–mid-Feb.*

Red Villages North of Apt

Technically, this isn't part of the Luberon, though it is within the boundaries of the Regional Park. Above Apt, on the southern slopes of the Plateau de Vaucluse, the geology changes abruptly. The plateau is mostly limestone, which erodes away to make caves and water tricks such as the Fontaine-de-Vaucluse (*see* p.240). This part has sandy deposits full of iron oxides – ochre, the material used in prehistoric times as skin-paint, and later to colour everything from soap to rugs. Centuries of mining have left some bizarre land-scapes – cliffs and pits and peaks in what locals claim are '17 shades of red', as well as yellow and cream and a few other hues.

Rustrel to Roussillon

Roussillon

Rustrel, northeast of Apt on the D22, was one of the mining towns until 1890. The huge, ruddy mess they left is called the **Colorado**; there are hazily marked routes around it for tourists, although you may have to pay for a proper map. From here, the D179 west takes you to **St-Saturnin-lès-Apt** (St Saturnin is probably the Roman god Saturn). Inside a modern ring of bungalows, this old village had little to do with mining, but it has always grown nice red cherries; there are plenty of ruins, including a **castle** and bits of three different sets of walls (13th–16th centuries), a **windmill** for a landmark, and a simple Romanesque **chapel** from the 1050s. And you don't get the hordes of tour buses as in nearby Gordes or **Roussillon**. To the southwest, the latter occupies a spectacular hill-top site, and well it should – centuries of mining have removed nearly everything for miles around. The Association Terre d'Ocres, an organization that wants to get the business going again, has an information centre in the village and can direct you on a walk through the old quarries, known locally as the **Sables de Roussillon**.

Conservatoire des Ocres et Pigments Appliqués
t 04 90 05 66 69, www.okhra.com; open April–Sept daily; Oct–Mar Tues–Sun

Further information on the ochre is available at the **Conservatoire des Ocres et Pigments Appliqués**.

Samuel Beckett spent the war years exiled in Roussillon; the rural peace and quiet gave him a nervous breakdown. His house is being restored as the **Maison Samuel Beckett**, with an adjoining cultural centre. Roussillon was also 'Peyrane' in Laurence Wylie's *Village in the Vaucluse*; the one place readers will recognize from the 1950s is **Bar Castrum**, with its old poster of the film *Marius* on the wall.

South of Roussillon and the N100 is a well-preserved Roman bridge, the **Pont Julien**. The little stone village of **Joucas**, just north of Roussillon, is quiet and uncommercial, although its surrounding hotels have taken up catering for upper-class tourists. North of here, at **Murs**, you can pick up the scenic D4 across the Plateau de Vaucluse and its gorges to Venasque (*see* p.244).

Market Days North of Apt

Roussillon: Thurs, Place du Pasquier.

Where to Stay and Eat North of Apt

St-Saturnin-lès-Apt ✉ 84490

St-Saturnin-lès-Apt is a friendly village, and though it's bit out of the way it is a good, reasonably priced choice for a base.

Le Saint-Hubert, Place de la Fraternité, t 04 90 75 42 02 (€€–€). A hotel with eight rooms and a restaurant with a pretty terrace. *Closed Jan; restaurant closed Thurs.*

**Hôtel Les Voyageurs, Pl Gambetta, t 04 90 75 42 08 (€). Delightfully old-fashioned Logis de France with a restaurant (€€). *Closed Feb; restaurant closed Wed and Thurs lunch.*

ⓘ **Roussillon >**
Place de la Poste, t 04 90 05 60 25, www. roussillon-provence. com; open July and Aug daily; Sept–June Mon–Sat

Roussillon ✉ 84220

***Le Mas de Garrigon, Route de St-Saturnin-d'Apt, t 04 90 05 63 22, *www.masdegarrigon-provence.com* (€€€). A well-restored farmhouse with all the amenities that you could hope for, including lovely rooms named after writers and a gourmet restaurant (€€€€). It's a shame they are both rather overpriced. *Half-board is obligatory in summer. Restaurant closed Mon, and must be booked for other days.*

**Rêves d'Ocres, Route de Gordes, t 04 90 05 79 74 (€€). A pleasant, cheaper option, with convenient parking. *Closed mid-Nov–Jan.*

Le Val des Fées, Rue R. Casteau, t 04 90 05 64 99 (€€). Reasonably priced restaurant with lovely views over the ochre from its terrace. *Closed Wed exc July and Aug, and Nov–Feb.*

Joucas ✉ 84220

****Hostellerie Le Phébus, Route de Murs, t 04 90 05 78 83, *www.lephebus. com* (€€€€€–€€€€). Done in exquisite taste, with views over Roussillon's red hills, and a garden, pool, tennis court and excellent restaurant, with Provençal dishes made with the freshest herbs. *Closed mid-Oct–Feb.*

****Le Mas des Herbes Blanches, t 04 90 05 79 79, *www.herbesblanches. com* (€€€€€–€€€€). A sumptuous Relais & Châteaux spread in an old *mas*, with a beautiful setting and a restaurant (€€€€–€€€). *Closed Jan and Feb; restaurant closed Tues and Wed and mid-Oct–Dec.*

Le Mas du Loriot, Murs, t 04 90 72 62 62, *www.masduloriot.com* (€€€–€€). Intimate, friendly and refined option in a new Provençal *mas*, with 8 rooms and a pool, and a restaurant (€€). *Closed mid-Nov–mid-Mar; restaurant closed Tues, Thurs, Sat and Sun.*

**La Bergerie, Route de Murs, t 04 90 05 78 73 (€€). An average country hotel with 20 rooms, a pool and a restaurant (€€). *Half board obligatory in summer. Closed Nov–Mar.*

Villages of the Petit Luberon

West of Apt, and south of the N100, is a string of truly beautiful villages that have become the high-rent district of the Luberon, one of the poshest rural areas in France. Don't come here looking for that little place in the country to fix up; it's all been done, as long as 40 years ago. The first to arrive were the Parisians, including many artists, intellectuals and eccentrics, giving the place a reputation as 'St-Germain-in-the Luberon'. Since the 1960s, a wave of outsiders looking for Provençal paradise, including many Americans, have transformed the place. None of this is readily apparent, apart from the infestations of swanky villas on many hillsides outside the Regional Park boundaries. The villagers, a bit richer now, take it in their stride and carry on as they always have – separate worlds, existing side by side.

The biggest and busiest of the villages, **Bonnieux** is also one of the loveliest, a belvedere overlooking the whole of the Petit Luberon. The ungainly modern **church** at the bottom of the village contains four colourful 16th-century wood paintings of the *Passion of Christ*; the other attraction, so to speak, is the **Musée de la Boulangerie** in Rue de la République, which as the name suggests will tell you all you wanted to know about Provençal bread.

Musée de la Boulangerie
t 04 90 75 88 34; open April–Sept Wed–Mon 10–12 and 3–6.30; Oct Sat and Sun 10–12 and 3–6.30; closed Nov–Mar; adm

There are some wonderfully scenic excursions from here. The D36/D943 south to Lourmarin is the only good road across the spine of the Luberon; it passes through a long and beautiful gorge called the **Combe de Lourmarin**. East of Bonnieux off the D943, a side road, the D113, takes you up into the mountains, passing the slender, elegant Romanesque bell-tower of the **Prieuré de St-Symphorien**, and up to the hamlet and cliffs of **Buoux**, which has of late become something of a climber's mecca; above it, the ruined medieval **Fort de Buoux** offers tremendous views over the heart of the Luberon. Nearby is the beginning of a nature trail marked out by the Regional Park, with placards on the Luberon's flora and fauna all along the way.

Wine: Côtes-du-Luberon

Between the mountains of the lower Durance and the Calavon valley around Apt are the vineyards that produce AOC Côtes-du-Luberon – mostly young ruby wines made from grenache, syrah, cinsault, mourvèdre and carignan; the whites come from Bourboulenc and Clairette. One high-profile producer is the extraordinary hi-tech cellar at the **Château Val-Joanis**, in Pertuis, t 04 90 79 20 77, *www.val-joanis.com*, where the red, with a high percentage of syrah, is good quality and a good buy.

On the more traditional side, **Château de l'Isolette**, on the main road between Bonnieux and Apt, t 04 90 74 16 70, *www.chateau-isolette.com*, is run by the Pinatels, a family that has been making wine since the 16th century. Over the past decade the estate has won scores of medals, especially for its red wines aged in oak barrels, such as the Grande Sélection; they also do a fine blanc de blancs and rosé. In Bonnieux itself, look for **Château La Canorgue**, Route du Pont Julien, t 04 90 75 81 01, a beautiful 16th-century château whose wines, made from organically grown grapes, consistently win medals in international competitions.

Lacoste, located to the west of Bonnieux on the D109, is a trendy *village perché*, home to an American school run by the Cleveland Institute of Art. Overlooking the village is a gloomy ruined **castle**, the one-time home of no less a personage than the Marquis de Sade (d. 1814). The French are a bit embarrassed by the author of *Les 120 Journées de Sodome*, but he certainly wasn't insane, and he is a literary figure of some note, taking to extremes the urge for self-expression that came with the dawn of the Romantic movement. He did have his little weaknesses, which kept him in and out of the calaboose for decades, on charges such as pushing 'aphrodisiac bonbons' on servant girls, and worse. The scion of a respectable old Provençal family, he spent a lot of time here when Paris grew too hot for him. Oddly enough, the Marquis seems to have been a descendant of Petrarch's Laura – Laura de Sade (*see* 'Avignon', p.104). The thought of it obsessed him all his life, and he saw her in visions in the castle here. The castle, which was burned in the Revolution, is now fully restored. It has recently been bought by Pierre Cardin and is open to the public for concerts and theatre events.

Continuing along the D109, you come to **Ménerbes**, a honey-coloured, artsy and cuter-than-cute town. As the former home of professional expat Peter Mayle, it now attracts legions of fans, who come here by the busload to pay homage and buy a postcard; there's really not a good deal else to do here. Ménerbes is so narrow that from certain angles it resembles a ship, cruising out of the Luberon towards Avignon; at the top is a small square, measuring about 18ft across, with balconies on either side.

The D188 from here takes you amongst waves of vines, to, fittingly, the world's first and only corkscrew museum, the **Musée du Tire-Bouchon**, at **Domaine de la Citadelle** just to the west of Ménerbes. The museum houses a collection of bottle poppers, from 17th-century attempts to a bejewelled Cartier *de luxe* model and an extensive display of pornographic corkscrews.

From here the D188 continues through grand scenery almost to the top of the Petit Luberon, and **Oppède-le-Vieux**, with its even gloomier ruined castle, the home of the bloodthirsty Baron d'Oppède, leader of the genocide against the Waldensians in the 1540s (*see* pp.26–7). The road west of Oppède, by way of Maubec and Robion towards Cavaillon, is equally pretty; **Maubec**, with its Baroque church, may be the Luberon village of your dreams.

Musée du Tire-Bouchon
t 04 90 72 41 58, www. musee-tirebouchon. com; open April–Oct daily 10–12 and 2–7, Nov–Mar Mon–Sat 10–12 and 2–5; adm

ⓘ **Bonnieux >>**
7 Place Carnot, t 04 90 75 91 90, www.tourisme-en-luberon.com; open Mon–Sat

Market Days in the Petit Luberon

Bonnieux: Fri am.
Lacoste: Tues am.
Oppède-le-Vieux: Sat am.

Where to Stay and Eat in the Petit Luberon

Bonnieux ✉ 84480
***Le Prieuré**, Rue Jean Baptiste Aurard, t 04 90 75 80 78, *www.*

hotelprieure.com (€€€€). An 18th-century priory in the village centre; the rooms have a view and there's a garden and gourmet restaurant. *Closed Nov–mid-Mar.*

Hôtel Le César, Place de la Liberté, **t 04 90 75 96 35 (€€). 18th-century hotel in the centre. Ask for rooms at the back to avoid the street noise. There are some inexpensive rooms with shared bathrooms. *Restaurant closed Thurs, and mid-Nov–mid-Mar.*

Le Fournil, 5 Place Carnot, **t** 04 90 75 83 62 (€€). A restaurant carved out of the cliff, serving light fare. *Closed Mon, plus Jan and Feb.*

La Flambée, 2 Place du 4 Septembre, **t** 04 90 75 82 20 (€). A reasonable pizzeria. *Closed Mon–Fri in winter.*

Buoux ✉ 84480

Auberge des Seguins, Les Seguins (off D113), **t** 04 90 74 16 37 (€€). An isolated hotel above Buoux, near the fort, for those who really want to get away from it all and enjoy simple rooms and home cooking in a memorable setting with a pool. *Closed Jan; restaurant (€€€) open weekends only, plus by reservation Mon–Fri.*

Ménerbes ✉ 84560

***Le Roy Soleil, D103, **t** 04 90 72 25 61, *www.roy-soleil.com* (€€€€–€€€). A hotel in a 17th-century building in an olive grove overlooking Ménerbes, with a pool and an excellent restaurant. *Closed Jan.*

Oppède-le-Vieux ✉ 84580

Le Mas des Capelans, N100, **t 04 90 76 99 04, *www.masdescapelans-luberon.com* (€€€). A pleasant country hotel in a former stable, with a pool, a terrace and a playground; restaurant for guests only.

Cavaillon

Lacking anything more compelling, Cavaillon has become famous for its melons. As one of the biggest agricultural market towns in all of France, it ships a million tonnes or so of these and all the other rich produce of the surrounding plains to Paris every year. Back in the 19th century, Alexandre Dumas loved Cavaillon's melons so much that he agreed to supply the local libraries with his books in exchange for a dozen of them a year.

Cavaillon is built under a steep hill overlooking the Durance, the **Colline St-Jacques**, where a Neolithic settlement has been uncovered next to a medieval chapel; it is a short climb up from central **Place du Clos**, with views on top stretching from Mont Ventoux to the Alpilles. Roman-era Cavaillon has left behind only a 1st-century AD **arch**, at the foot of the hill. Unlike the arches of Carpentras and Orange, this one probably doesn't mark any particular triumph; it is four-sided, a *quadroporticus*, and, like the only similar construction, the Arch of Janus in Rome, it probably was a simple decoration for – appropriately enough – a market-place. Its decorative reliefs, mostly fruits and flowers, are now too eroded to be seen very clearly.

Musée de l'Hôtel-Dieu
t 04 90 76 00 34; open mid-April–mid-Sept Thurs–Mon 10–12 and 2–6.30, closed Tues and Wed; mid-Sept–mid-April Mon and Wed–Fri 10–12 and 2–6.30; adm

Cavaillon's other attractions include: a small **archaeological museum**, in the chapel of the Hôtel-Dieu off Cours Gambetta; the odd-shaped, rather forbidding Romanesque cathedral of **Notre-Dame-et-St-Véran**, with a tatterdemalion 17th-century interior and a pretty cloister; and an ornate 18th-century **synagogue**, similar to

Prévôt >>

Market Days in Cavaillon

Cavaillon: Mon; it competes with Apt's as the most important in the Vaucluse.

Festivals in Cavaillon

Cavaillon: Melon Festival, early July.

Where to Stay in Cavaillon

Cavaillon ✉ 84300

If you need a change from French food, there are Indian, Tex-Mex, Vietnamese and other restaurants along Bd Gambetta.

**Hôtel du Parc, 183 Place François Tourel, t 04 90 71 57 78, *www.hoteldu parccavaillon.com* (€€). An old hotel that makes a pleasant place to stay, with a homely feel and private parking.

**Toppin, 70 Cours Gambetta, t 04 90 71 30 42, *www.hotel-toppin.com* (€€–€). A venerable and well-kept option with private parking facilities. *Closed Christmas and New Year.*

(i) Cavaillon >

Place François Tourel, t 04 90 71 32 01, www.cavaillon-luberon.com; open July and Aug Mon–Sat and Sun am; mid-Mar–June and Sept–mid-Oct Mon–Sat; mid-Oct–mid-Mar Mon–Fri and Sat am

Eating Out in Cavaillon

Prévôt, 353 Av de Verdun, t 04 90 71 32 43 (€€€€–€€). Offering organic Provençal cuisine, and themed menus during the town's food festival. *Booking is required. Closed Sun eve and Mon, plus 2 weeks Aug.*

Le Pantagruel, 5 Place Philippe de Cabassole, t 04 90 76 11 98 (€€€–€€). A *restaurant gastronomique* under big stone arches opposite the market, using organic produce. *Closed Sun and Mon.*

Fin de Siècle, 46 Place du Clos, t 04 90 71 12 27 (€€). Famed for its old-fashioned décor; try stuffed chicken breast or salmon cakes. The café next door is a listed monument. *Closed Tues and Sun in winter, plus 2 weeks Aug.*

Côté Jardin, 49 Rue Lamartine, t 04 90 71 33 58 (€€). A popular local place with traditional dishes made from fresh market produce. *Book. Closed Sun, Mon eve and Tues eve.*

L'Oustau de Mathias, 21 Av Pierre Sémard, opposite station, t 04 90 76 04 58 (€€). Generous dishes, including a huge seafood salad. *Closed Mon.*

Synagogue museum
same hours and telephone number as Musée de l'Hôtel-Dieu

the one in Carpentras, with a small **museum**, on Rue Hébraïque. Before the Revolution, Cavaillon had the biggest Jewish population in the papal enclave; among them were the ancestors of the composer Darius Milhaud. Segregated in a tiny ghetto around the synagogue, the community prospered despite occasional gusts of papal persecution; after the Revolution most of Cavaillon's Jews moved to the larger cities of Provence, and there is none living in the town today. The museum offers guided tours of the synagogue and the old Jewish community, as well as of the old towns and countryside.

The Vaucluse

The Plateau de Vaucluse

The Plateau de Vaucluse is the high ground that runs between the Luberon and Mont Ventoux to the north. Beware that both Gordes and Fontaine-de-Vaucluse can get crowded out by the heaving coachloads in the summer.

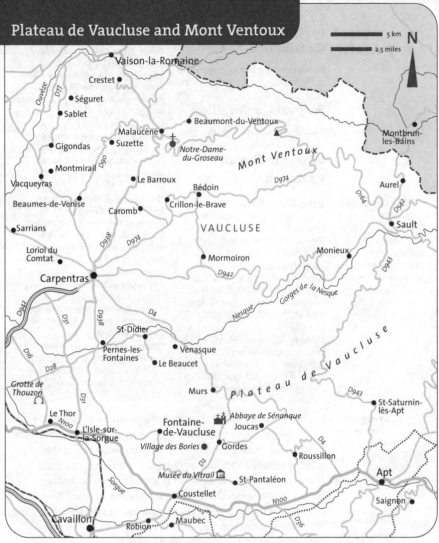

Gordes

The first thing you'll notice about this striking *village perché* is that it has a rock problem. They have it under control; the vast surplus has been put to use in houses and sheds, and also for the hundreds of thick stone walls that make Gordes seem more like a southern Italian village than one in Provence. The stones made agriculture a bad bet here, so the Gordiens planted olives instead, and became famous for them – at least until the terrible frost of 1976 killed off most of the trees. But without ever asking for it, Gordes has found something easier and more profitable: art tourism, with exhibitions and concerts in the summer.

Gordes was a Résistance stronghold in the war and suffered for it, with wholesale massacres of citizens and the destruction of much of the village; after the war it was awarded the *Croix de Guerre*. The damage the Nazis did has been repaired; the village centre, all steep, cobbled streets and arches, is extremely attractive. At the centre, you may see flocks of well-scrubbed art students lounging on the steps of the imposing château built by the lords of Simiane in the 1520s. They are making their pilgrimage to an avant-garde that no longer exists. Even the rearguard – a 'didactic museum' of the works of the late Hungarian op art/poster artist Vasarely – has ducked out of Gordes, apparently for good, victim of an unseemly quarrel over money between Vasarely's heirs and the management. If you're disappointed, the **Galerie Pascal Lainé** in Place du Château has an exhibition of his works.

To see what real art's all about, walk over to Gordes' parish church of **St-Fermin**, with its memorable 18th-century interior of purple, pink and gilded jiggumabobs, a lodge brother's fantasy seraglio. A statue of the Magdalene on the right looks down on it with a jaundiced eye. The **château** itself has a superb Renaissance fireplace, the second largest in France, and a hotchpotch of art in the **Musée Pol Mara** up on the second and third floors.

Around Gordes: *Les Bories* and Another Bore

Across the Midi they are called *bories*, or *garriotes*, or *capitelles*, or a dozen other local names. In Provence, there are some 3,000 of them, but the largest collection in one place is the **Village des Bories**, south of Gordes off the D2. A *borie* is a small dry-stone hut, usually with a well-made corbelled dome or vault for a ceiling. Because of their resemblance to Neolithic works (such as the *nuraghi* of Sardinia), they have always intrigued scholars. Recently it has been established, however, that, though the method of building goes way back, none of the *bories* you see today is older than the 1600s. Elsewhere they are usually shepherds' huts, but these are believed to have been a refuge for the villagers in times of plague. This group of 12 *bories* has been restored as a rural museum. You'll see other *bories* all around Gordes; some have been restored as holiday homes, and one has even become an expensive restaurant. Determined *borie*-hunters should also tour the large concentrations in the countryside around Bonnieux, Apt, Buoux, St-Saturnin-lès-Apt and Saumane-de-Vaucluse, north of Fontaine-de-Vaucluse.

South of Gordes, there is a beautiful, simple Romanesque church in the hamlet of **St-Pantaléon**. To the west of that, watch out for the well-publicized **Musée du Vitrail** (stained glass) and **Musée du Moulin des Bouillons**, where another little Vasarely has set up shop near the oldest intact olive oil press in France. There are indeed

Galerie Pascal Lainé
t 04 90 72 00 90

Gordes château
t 04 90 72 02 75; open daily 10–12 and 2–6; adm

Village des Bories
t 04 90 72 03 48, www.gordes-village-des-bories.com; open daily 9–sunset; adm

Musée du Vitrail/ Musée du Moulin des Bouillons
both t 04 90 72 22 11; open April–Oct Wed–Mon 10–12 and 2–6; adm

Musée de la Lavande
t 04 90 76 91 23; www. museedelalavande.com; open July and Aug daily 9–7; Sept–June daily 9–12 and 2–6; adm

exhibits on the history of stained glass here, and some others on Marseille soap, but their only purpose is to suck you into the adjacent gallery to look at the high-priced and gruesome work of Duran and others.

Further south still, at **Coustellet**, the **Musée de la Lavande** reveals all you have ever wanted to know about lavender.

Abbaye de Sénanque

🏆 **Abbaye de Sénanque**
t 04 90 72 05 72; www.senanque.fr; open for guided tours only, in a complicated timetable that changes; check website for details; adm

The loveliest of the Cistercian 'Three Sisters' lies 4km north of Gordes on the D177. The church may be almost a double of the one at Thoronet (*see* pp.288–9), but built in the warm golden stone of the Vaucluse and set among lavender fields and oak groves, it makes quite an impression. The Benedictine monks of the Ile St-Honorat, who hold the title, returned in 1988; they cultivate honey and lavender in the grounds.

The **church**, begun about 1160, shows the same early Cistercian seriousness as Thoronet and Silvacane (*see* p.228), and has been changed little over the centuries; even the original altar is present. Most of the **monastic buildings** have also survived, including a lovely cloister, the *chauffoir* (the only heated room, where the monks transcribed books), and a refectory with displays giving a fascinating introduction to Sénanque and the Cistercians.

Fontaine-de-Vaucluse

🏆 **Fontaine-de-Vaucluse**

More than a century ago, explorers found the source of the Nile. They're still looking for the source of the little Vaucluse river called the Sorgue. It's underground; the best spelunkers in France have been combing the region's caves for decades without success, and in 1983 a tiny, specially made submarine probe (the *Sorguonaute*) sent back data from some 820ft below the surface of the Fontaine-de-Vaucluse, where the Sorgue makes its daylight début through a dramatic hole in a cliff in the beautiful valley the Romans called Vallis Clausa – the origin of 'Vaucluse'. *Sorguonaute II*, a second probe, was sent down in 1984, and imploded soon after immersion; finally, in 1985, a device usually used in oil exploration – the *Modexa 350* – plunged to a bed 1,024ft below, though the passages that carry the stream into this remain unexplored.

Medieval legends record St Véran, patron of Cavaillon, dispatching a dragon near the source – a sure sign that this was an ancient holy place, given the close connection between underground water and mythological serpents everywhere in Europe. The more prosaic Romans channelled the water into an aqueduct, remains of which can still be seen along the D24 towards Cavaillon. In later times, among those attracted by Provence's greatest natural wonder was Petrarch, who from 1327 spent many seasons in a villa by the river bank writing his *De Vita Solitaria*, until 1353, when a band of brigands sacked the village and frightened him back to Italy.

Norbert Casteret's Musée de Spéléologie (Ecomusée du Gouffre)
t 04 90 20 34 13; open July and Aug daily 9.30–7.30; Feb–June and Sept–Nov daily 10–12 and 2–6; adm

Vallis Clausa
t 04 90 20 34 14; open daily 9–12.30 and 2–6.30

Musée d'Histoire 1939–1945
t 04 90 20 24 00; open June–Sept Mon 10–6; April–May and first 2 weeks Oct Wed–Mon 10–12 and 2–6; mid-Oct to All Saints' Day Wed–Mon 10–12 and 2–5; Nov–Dec Sat and Sun 10–12 and 2–5; Mar Sat and Sun 2–5; closed Tues and Jan–Feb; adm; combined ticket with Musée Pétrarque available

Musée Pétrarque
t 04 90 20 37 20; open June–Sept Wed–Mon 10–12.30 and 1.30–6; April, May and first 2 weeks Oct Wed–Mon 10–12 and 2–6; mid-Oct to All Saints' Day Wed–Mon 10–12 and 2–5; closed Tues and Nov–Mar; adm; combined ticket with Musée d'Histoire

The Fontaine is still an exquisite place, but the 540 or so residents of the town of Fontaine-de-Vaucluse have not been able to keep the place from being transformed into one of Provence's more garish tourist traps. To reach it, from the car park next to the church you'll have to walk a noisy 2km gauntlet of commerciality, with everything from *frites* stands to a museum of authentic Provençal *santons* and a museum of medieval torture instruments. Incredibly, many of the attractions are worthwhile. There is **Norbert Casteret's Musée de Spéléologie (Ecomusée du Gouffre)**, a 'subterranean world' of underground rarities and informative exhibits overseen by France's best-known cave explorer, and **Vallis Clausa**, an art gallery containing a paper mill powered by old wooden wheels in the river that continues to make paper the 15th-century way for art books and stationery. Most surprising of all, in a sharp modern building, is the **Musée d'Histoire 1939–1945**, a government-sponsored institution that opened in 1990 and recaptures the wartime years vividly with two floors of explanatory displays, vignettes of daily life under the Nazis, newsreels and magazines, weapons and other relics. As at Gordes, Résistance life around Fontaine-de-Vaucluse was no joke; among the exhibits is a tribute to Fontaine's mayor, Robert Garcin, whose aid to the *maquis* earned him a one-way ticket to Buchenwald in 1944.

Finally, there is the **spring** itself, which is well worth the trouble even if you come off-season. In spring, and occasionally in winter, it pours out at a rate of as much as 200 cubic metres per second, forming a small, intensely green lake under the cliff. From late spring until autumn it is greatly diminished, and often stops overflowing altogether (the water appears slightly further down the cliff); its unpredictability is as much a mystery as its source. It is a beautiful spot; if you're ambitious, it is also the beginning of two excellent hiking trails (the GR6 and GR97) leading up into some of the most scenic parts of the Plateau de Vaucluse. More easily, you can climb up to the ruined 13th-century **château**, once owned by Petrarch's friend Philippe de Cabassole.

Before you leave, have a look at the village church, **Ste-Marie-et-St-Véran**. Begun in 1134, this lovely Romanesque building incorporates Roman and Carolingian fragments, including some bits of floral arabesques and the columns and capitals around the altar. The cornice outside is decorated with winsome rows of human and animal faces. Inside, there is the 6th-century Merovingian tomb of St Véran, and a good painted altarpiece of the *Crucifixion*, donated in 1654 by the village's *confrérie* of paper-makers. Also on the way out, peek in at the **Musée Pétrarque**, a subdued look at the life and times of the poet during his stay in the town. Note the column, erected in 1804 by the Athenaeum Valclusianum to celebrate the 500th anniversary of his birth.

Market Days on the Plateau de Vaucluse

Gordes: Tues.
Coustellet: Sun am.

Festivals on the Plateau de Vaucluse

Roussillon: International String Quartet Festival, July–Sept, t 04 90 75 89 60.

Where to Stay and Eat on the Plateau de Vaucluse

Gordes ✉ 84220

Gordes is big business – several fancy villa-hotels have sprung up on the outskirts – but the whole scene is expensive, over the top and a bit exploitative of the credulous, who want it and deserve it. The tourist office has a list of the many *chambres d'hôtes* in the area.

**Auberge de Carcarille, southwest of town on D2, t 04 90 72 02 63, *www.auberge-carcarille.com* (€€). A carefully restored *mas* outside the village, with pretty rooms, some of them with balconies, a swimming pool, and a restaurant (€€€–€€) specializing in fish and game. *Closed Dec–Jan; restaurant closed Fri lunch in April–Sept and all day Fri in Oct–Mar.*

Fontaine-de-Vaucluse ✉ 84800

Fontaine-de-Vaucluse, in spite of its touristic vocation, is a pleasant place to stay or dine.

Hostellerie Le Château, in former *mairie*, Quartier Château Vieux, t 04 90 20 31 54 (€). A hotel with an outdoor terrace overlooking the Sorgue (behind glass, so you won't get splashed by the waterwheel in front). The excellent cooking includes *rouget à la tapenade* (red snapper), and there are 5 pleasant rooms. *Hotel closed Oct–Mar; restaurant open all year, but lunch only in Oct–Mar.*

Auberge de Jeunesse de Fontaine-de-Vaucluse, Chemin de la Vignasse, 1 km from village, t 04 90 20 31 65, *www.fuaj.org* (€). A tranquil hostel. *Closed mid-Nov–Jan.*

Philip, Chemin de la Fontaine, t 04 90 20 31 81 (€€€–€€). The closest restaurant to the spring, with a menu of mostly fish, and a pleasant outside terrace by the river. *Closed Oct–Mar.*

ⓘ **Fontaine-de-Vaucluse >>**
Chemin de la Fontaine,
t 04 90 20 32 22,
www.oti-delasorgue.fr;
open daily all year

★ **Hostellerie
Le Château >>**

ⓘ **Gordes >**
*Château, t 04 90 72
02 75, www.gordes-
village.com; open daily
all year*

From Cavaillon to Carpentras

Until the Revolution, the western Vaucluse plains stretching from Cavaillon north to Vaison-la-Romaine were known as the **Comtat Venaissin**, a county that was a part of the papal dominions in France, though legally separate from Avignon. Saint Louis had stolen the territory from the counts of Toulouse in 1229, as part of the French Crown's share of the booty after the Albigensian crusade, and Philip III passed it along to the popes in 1274 to settle an old dispute. It was a worthy prize – medieval irrigation schemes had already made the rich lands of the Comtat the 'Garden of France', an honorific it still holds today as the most productive agricultural region in the country. Besides Cavaillon's famous melons, this small area has five per cent of all France's vineyards, including its best table grapes, and still finds room to grow tonnes of cherries, asparagus, apples and more.

All this intensive agriculture doesn't do the scenery any harm, and passing through it you'll find some fat, contented villages that make the trip worthwhile.

L'Isle-sur-la-Sorgue and Le Thor

The Sorgue, that singular river that jumps out of the ground at Fontaine-de-Vaucluse and makes fly-fishermen happy all the way to the suburbs of Avignon (it's one of France's best trout streams), has one more trick to play before it reaches the Rhône. At **L'Isle-sur-la-Sorgue**, it briefly splits into two channels to make this Provençal Venice – a charming town of more than 17,000 souls – an island indeed. In the Middle Ages, as a scrappy semi-independent *commune*, L'Isle-sur-la-Sorgue dug two more channels and put the water to work running mills and textile factories; when trouble came, as during the Wars of Religion, the town knew how to keep out invaders by flooding the surrounding plains and making itself even more of an island. Today, L'Isle-sur-la-Sorgue still makes fabrics and carpets, but it is best known as the antiques centre of Provence, with a number of permanent shops on the southern edge of town, around **Avenue des Quatre-Otages**, and a big '**antiques village**' by the train station. Circumnavigating the town is a pleasant diversion; you pass a number of old canals and wooden mills, some still in use, and houses with little front terraces built over the rushing water. There are two **mills** along **Rue Jean Théophile**, a street that will also take you to the 18th-century **Hôtel-Dieu** (hospital), with a sumptuous chapel and a perfectly preserved **pharmacy** of that era that can be visited (*ask at tourist office*), an ensemble of Moustiers faïence and ornate carved wood.

There are frequent art exhibitions in an 18th-century palace at 20 Rue Dr Tallet, the **Maison René Char-Hôtel Donadeï de Campredon**, and right in the centre is the town's beached whale of a church, 17th-century **Notre-Dame-des-Anges**, sprawling across Place de l'Eglise. Even in a region full of marvellously awful churches, this one is a jewel – a mouldering imitation of Roman Baroque outside and gilt everything within. Opposite the façade, note the old firm of **Fauques-Beyret**, the prettiest drapery shop in Provence, with a fine Art Nouveau front; inside and out, nothing seems to have changed since about 1900.

To the west of L'Isle-sur-la-Sorgue, the N100 leads to **Le Thor**, which boasts one of the best Romanesque churches in the whole of Provence, carrying the intriguing name of **Notre-Dame-du-Lac**. Begun about 1200, it is a work of transition that bears witness to the giving way of the Provençal-Romanesque to Gothic influences, as can be seen in the pointed vaulting of the nave. The sculptural decoration is spare but elegant, emphasizing the perfect symmetry of one of the last great medieval buildings in this region.

Some 3km north of Le Thor on the D16 are the **Grotte de Thouzon**. Of all the caves in Provence, this may be the one most worth seeing – weird and colourful, with rare needle-slender stalactites hanging down as much as 10ft.

Antiques Village
open Sun (some booths also open Sat and Mon)

Maison René Char-Hôtel Donadeï de Campredon
t 04 90 38 17 41; adm

Notre-Dame-des-Anges
open Tues–Fri 10–12 and 3–5, Sat 10–12, Mon 3–5; closed Sun

Grotte de Thouzon
t 04 90 33 93 65; www.grottes-de-thouzon.com; open July and Aug daily 10–6.30; April–June and Sept–Oct daily 10–12 and 2–5.30; Mar Sun and bank hols 2.15–6.30; by guided tour only; adm

Pernes-les-Fontaines

L'Isle-sur-la-Sorgue's tiny neighbour to the north, Pernes-les-Fontaines, has only a single drowsy stream passing through it, the Nesque. In the 18th century, perhaps out of jealousy, the Pernois took it into their heads to build decorative **fountains** instead. They got a bit carried away and now there are 50 of them, or one for every 190 inhabitants. The fountains contribute a lot to making Pernes one of the most delightful towns in the Vaucluse. It is an introspective place, sheltering inside a circuit of walls that was demolished 100 years ago, to be replaced by a ring of boulevards.

The Pernois have used the centuries to make their town an integrated work of art, looking exactly the way they want it to look, and there's a surprise around every corner. Starting from the centre, the old **bridge** over the Nesque is embellished at both ends, with the 16th-century **Porte de Notre-Dame**, the **Cormorant fountain** and the small chapel of **Notre-Dame-des-Grâces**, from the same era. Behind it, the 12th-century church of **Notre-Dame-de-Nazareth** includes some Gothic chapels and reliefs of Old Testament scenes. The relative simplicity of its interior, in contrast with so many other Provençal churches, is a reminder of Pernes' earnest Catholicism through the centuries (one of its current economic mainstays, incidentally, is making the communion hosts for all the churches of France). Note the **Tour de l'Horloge**, once the keep of the castle of the counts of Toulouse, now crowned with a pussycat weather vane. Ask at the tourist office for a guide to take you around to the **Tour Ferrande**, on Rue Gambetta. This medieval tower, next to a fountain with carved grotesques, contains some of the oldest frescoes in France (c. 1275), with vigorous scriptural scenes, Charles of Anjou in Sicily, St Sebastian and St Christopher, and one Count William of Orange battling against a giant.

Tour de l'Horloge
t 04 90 61 31 04; you can climb up daily 9–5

East of Pernes-les-Fontaines is a very odd place, **Le Beaucet** (on the D39 south of St-Didier), where the people used to live in cave-houses, some of which can still be seen, along with a ruined castle. Above it, in the mountains, a **spring** similar to Fontaine-de-Vaucluse has given rise to one of the biggest pilgrimage sites in Provence, a well-decorated **chapel** dedicated to the 12th-century St-Gens, who was a rain-maker and a tamer of wolves.

Venasque, further east, was the old capital of the Comtat Venaissin, and gave the county its name. Though a pretty village, nothing is left of its former distinction but the usual ruined fortifications and a venerable baptistry (really a 6th-century Merovingian funeral chapel reworked in the 12th century).

The **D4**, connecting Carpentras and Apt, was the main road of the Vaucluse in medieval times; it is still a lovely route, passing southeast from Venasque through the **Forêt de Venasque** and some rocky gorges on the edge of the Plateau de Vaucluse.

Market Days between Cavaillon and Carpentras

L'Isle-sur-la-Sorgue: Thurs and Sun; antiques market Sun.

Le Thor: Sat and Wed am.

Pernes-les-Fontaines: Sat am; antiques Wed am.

Where to Stay and Eat between Cavaillon and Carpentras

L'Isle-sur-la-Sorgue ✉ 84800

L'Isle-sur-la-Sorgue can be a delightful place for a stay when not ravaged by tour buses.

***Mas de Cure Bourse, 120 Chemin de la Serre, Route de Caumont, Velorgues, 2km south of town on D938, **t** 04 90 38 16 58, *www.masde curebourse.com* (€€€–€€). A restored 18th-century inn, with a pool, big gardens, 13 rooms and a restaurant (€€€) where the marinated pheasant is a treat. *Restaurant closed first 3 weeks in Nov and 2 weeks in Jan, and Mon and Tues lunch.*

La Gueulardière, Route d'Apt, **t 04 90 38 10 52 (€). Cosy rooms and

a garden terrace for dining (€€); specialities include *gâteau d'aubergines aux foies de volaille* (aubergine cake with duck, chicken and goose liver). *Closed mid-Dec–mid-Jan; restaurant closed Wed, plus Tues lunch in winter.*

Le Vivier de la Sorgue, Cours Fernande Peyre, Rte de Carpentras, **t** 04 90 38 52 80, *www.levivier-restaurant.com* (€€). Tasty fish dishes served on a lovely terrace over the river. *Closed Sat lunch and Sun, and Mon eve out of season.*

Pernes-les-Fontaines ✉ 84210

***L'Hermitage, Route de Carpentras, **t** 04 90 66 51 41, *www.hotel-lhermitage.com* (€€). A quiet hotel with a pool. *Closed mid-Nov–Feb.*

Prato Plage, Route de Carpentras, **t 04 90 61 41 60, *www.pratoplage.com* (€€). A 20-room hotel with restaurant.

Le Clan 'Destin', Route de Carpentras, **t** 04 90 61 34 00 (€€). Health food restaurant serving only local produce. *Closed Wed.*

Venasque ✉ 84210

Auberge La Fontaine, Place de la Fontaine, **t** 04 90 66 02 96, *www.auberge-lafontaine.com* (€€€). Five luxurious suites and the best food in the village (€€€–€€). Cookery lessons are available. *Restaurant closed Wed.*

ⓘ Pernes-les-Fontaines >>
Place Gabriel Moutte, **t** *04 90 61 31 04, www.ville-pernes-les-fontaines.fr; open July and Aug Mon–Fri; April–June and Sept Mon–Sat; Oct–Mar Mon–Fri and Sat am*

ⓘ L'Isle-sur-la-Sorgue >
Place de la Liberté, **t** *04 90 38 04 78, www.oti-delasorgue.fr; open daily*

ⓘ Le Thor
Place du 8-Mai-et-11-Novembre, **t** *04 90 33 92 31, www.oti-delasorgue.fr; open Tues–Fri, Mon pm and Sat pm*

11 Northern Provence: The Vaucluse | Carpentras

Carpentras

The average French town of 30,000 or so, unless it has some great historical importance or major monument, is likely to be a rather anonymous place. Carpentras isn't. Perhaps because of its long isolation from the rest of France, under papal rule but really run by its own bishops, Carpentras has a subtle but distinct sense of place. Despite recent attempts at urban renewal in the old town, it is still a bit unkempt; there are some cockeyed monuments, and some surprises. The rest of Provence pays Carpentras little mind; ask, and they'll probably remember only that the town is famous for mint-flavoured caramels called *berlingots*.

As in many other French towns, you'll have to cross a sort of motorway to get to the centre: a ring road of boulevards was created when the town walls were knocked down in the 19th century (it's one-way and very fast). One part of the fortifications remains, the towering 14th-century **Porte d'Orange**, built in the 1360s under Pope Innocent IV. When you get in, you'll find an

Getting to and around Carpentras

Carpentras is the node for what little there is of **coach** transport in the northern Vaucluse, with good connections to Avignon (some by way of Pernes-les-Fontaines and L'Isle-sur-la-Sorgue) and Orange, one every day to Marseille, and one or two a day to Vaison-la-Romaine and some of the villages of the Dentelles de Montmirail, including Beaumes-de-Venise and Gigondas. Almost all buses stop at Place Aristide Briand on the ring boulevard. There are also several daily SNCF **trains** to Orange and Avignon.

amiable and lively town, especially when the produce of the Comtat farmers rolls in for the Friday **market**. The stands fill half the town, but the centre is Rue des Halles, with the **Passage Boyer**, an imposing glass-roofed arcade built by Carpentras' unemployed in the national public works programme after the 1848 revolution.

Cathédrale St-Siffrein

Cathédrale St-Siffrein
open Tues–Sat 10–12 and 3–5

Undoubtedly, this is one of the most absurd cathedrals in Christendom. It's had so many architects, in so many periods, and no one has ever been able to get it finished and get it right. Worst of all is the mongrel façade – Baroque on the bottom, a bit of Gothic and who knows what else above. Begun in the 15th century, it saw remodellings and restorations in fits and starts until 1902.

Some of the original intentions can be seen in the fine Flamboyant-Gothic portal on the southern side, called the **Porte Juive** because Jewish converts were taken through it, in suitably humiliating ceremonies, to be baptized. Just above the centre of the arch is Carpentras' famous curio, the small sculpted *Boule aux Rats* – a globe covered with rats. The usual explanation is that this has something to do with the Jews, or heretics. But bigotry was never really fashionable among 15th-century artists, and more likely this is a joke on an old fanciful etymology of the town's name: *carpet ras*, or 'the rat nibbles'.

The **interior**, richly decorated in dubious taste, includes some stained glass of the 16th century (much restored) and an early 15th-century golden triptych (left of the high altar) by the school of Enguerrand Quarton – an island of calm among so much busyness. The sacred treasures are in a chapel on the left: the relics of St Siffrein, one of the most obscure of all saints, not even mentioned in any early hagiographies; and the *Saint-Mors*, the 'holy bridle bit', said to have been made by St Helen out of two nails of the Cross as a present for her son, Emperor Constantine.

Palais de Justice
ask the concierge to show you around

Next to the cathedral, the **Palais de Justice** (1640) is the former archbishops' palace, occupying the site of an earlier palace, which, for the brief periods that popes such as Innocent IV chose to stay in Carpentras, was the centre of the Christian world. The present building, modelled after the Palazzo Farnese in Rome, contains interesting frescoes from the 17th and 18th centuries, including mythological scenes, and also views of Comtat villages and towns.

The Triumphal Arch and the Secret Cathedral

Everyone knows that if you walk around a church widdershins (against the sun or counterclockwise), you'll end up in fairyland, like Childe Harold. Try it in Carpentras, and you'll find some strange business. The 28ft Roman **triumphal arch**, tucked away in a corner between the cathedral and Palais de Justice, was built about the same time as that of Orange, in the early 1st century AD. Anyone who hasn't seen Orange's would hardly guess this one was Roman. Of all the ancient Provençal monuments, this shows the bizarre Celtic quality of Gallo-Roman art at its most stylized extreme, with its reliefs of enchained captives and trophies. In the 14th century, the arch was incorporated into the now-lost episcopal palace. By 1640, when it was cleared, it was serving an inglorious role separating the archbishop's kitchens from his prisons. Originally, it must have connected the palace with the earlier cathedral.

Now, look at the clumsily built exterior wall of the present cathedral, opposite. There are two large gaps, through which you can have a peek at something that few books mention, and that even the Carpentrassiens seem to have forgotten: the **crossing and cupola** of the 12th-century cathedral, used in the rebuilt church to support a bell-tower (later demolished) and neglected for centuries. In its time this must have been one of the greatest buildings of Provence, done in an ambitious, classicizing style – perhaps too ambitious, as its partial collapse in 1399 necessitated the rebuilding. The sculpted decoration, vine and acanthus-leaf patterns, along with winged creatures and scriptural scenes, is excellent work; some of it has moved to the town museum.

The Synagogue and Museums

Behind the cathedral and palace, two streets north up Rue Barret, is the broad **Place de l'Hôtel-de-Ville**, marking the site of Carpentras' Jewish ghetto. Before the Revolution, more than 2,000 Jews were forced to live here in unspeakable conditions, walled in and obliged to pay a fee any time they wanted to leave. A small population remains, one that is only just recovering from the trauma of some brutish desecration in the local Jewish cemetery by four neo-Nazis in 1990. The crime stirred up passions, rumours and bitterness on a national scale until March 1997, when some local skinheads finally confessed, and apologized in court. All that remains of the old ghetto is the **synagogue** at the end of the square. Constructed in 1741, it has a glorious decorated interior in the best 18th-century secular taste.

Synagogue
t 04 90 63 39 97;
open Mon–Thurs 10–12
and 3–5, Fri and hols
10–12 and 3–4

Hôtel-Dieu
t 04 90 63 00 78;
open twice weekly
on a changing
programme of visits

Other attractions in town include the **Hôtel-Dieu** on Place Aristide Briand, an 18th-century hospital with a well-preserved pharmacy and an attractive chapel containing the tomb of Carpentras' famous bishop and civic benefactor, Monseigneur

Market Days in Carpentras

Carpentras: Fri am (including truffles during the season, Nov–Mar); flea market Sun from 11am.

Where to Stay and Eat in Carpentras

Carpentras ✉ 84200

Accommodation here is limited.

***Le Comtadin**, 65 Bd A. Durand, t 04 90 67 75 00, *www.le-comtadin. com* (€€). Close to the town centre, and part of the reliable Best Western chain, with smart modern rooms and the usual three-star facilities.

****Hôtel du Fiacre**, 153 Rue Vigne, t 04 90 63 03 15, *www.hotel-du-fiacre. com* (€€). An elegant old hotel in an 18th-century building. The room on the top floor offers a view of Mont Ventoux. There is also a suite (€€€).

****Forum**, 24 Rue du Forum, t 04 90 60 57 00, *www.hotel-forum.fr* (€€–€). Pretty little hotel on the edge of the centre of town, charmingly decorated in Provençal style.

Franck, 30 Place de l'Horloge, t 04 90 60 75 00, *www.franckrestaurant.com* (€€€–€€). Elegant dining – scallops, monkfish, braised turbot, duck cannelloni and gingerbread ice cream – with a gastronomic tasting menu and a truffle menu in season. *Closed Tues and Wed.*

Chez Serge, 90 Rue Cottier, t 04 90 63 21 24, *www.chez-serge.com* (€€). A stylish restaurant in the centre, with a rooftop terrace. Wood-fired pizzas are the house speciality. *Closed Sun.*

Loriol du Comtat ✉ 84870

Château Talaud, D107, t 04 90 65 71 00, *www.chateautalaud.com* (€€€€–€€€). Fabulous *chambres d'hôtes* in an 18th-century castle, with five luxurious rooms, two apartments and a cottage in beautiful grounds. Attentive, friendly service from the Dutch owners, a breakfast fit for dukes and the elegant gardens to take tea or sip a cocktail in make it seem as if you are starring on your very own film set.

ⓘ **Carpentras >**
Hôtel-Dieu, Place Aristide Briand, t 04 90 63 00 78, www. carpentras-ventoux. com; open July and Aug Mon–Sat and Sun am; Sept–June Mon–Sat

Musée Comtadin-Duplessis
t 04 90 63 04 92; open Wed–Mon April–Sept 10–12 and 2–6; Oct–Mar 10–12 and 2–4; adm

d'Inguimbert (1735–73). This hospital is his monument, along with the important library he left to the town and the beginning of the collections in the **Musée Comtadin-Duplessis** on the ring road (234 Bd Albin Durand). Here are displayed artefacts and clutter from Carpentras' history, old views of the town, and 16th- and 17th-century paintings, many by local artists.

Between Carpentras and Mont Ventoux: The Gorges de la Nesque

Heading north for Mont Ventoux and Vaison-la-Romaine, you might consider a slight detour to the east, along the D974. Towards the village of **Bédoin**, a small resort below Mont Ventoux famous for its enormous forest, you will pass Carpentras' **aqueduct** – not Roman but a 17th-century work, impressive nevertheless. **Crillon-le-Brave**, just west, was the birthplace of Henri IV's companion-at-arms and has a belvedere with splendid views on to Mont Ventoux. **Caromb**, west of the D974 on the D55, is an attractive village that has kept parts of its medieval fortifications, as well as a surprisingly grand church, **Notre-Dame-et-St-Maurice**, with a wealth of Renaissance decoration inside.

Where to Stay and Eat in the Gorges de la Nesque

⭐ Hostellerie François Joseph >>

Crillon-le-Brave ✉ 84410

****Hostellerie de Crillon-le-Brave Provence**, Place de l'Eglise, **t** 04 90 65 61 61, *www.crillonlebrave.com* (€€€€€–€€€€). Sumptuous hotel in an old manor house, run by a Canadian infatuated with Provence. The views of Mont Ventoux are complemented by the hotel's guide to walks in the area. *Closed Dec–mid-Mar.*

Le Barroux ✉ 84330

***Hostellerie François Joseph**, Chemin des Rabassières, **t** 04 90 62 52 78, *www.hotel-francois-joseph.com* (€€€€–€€). Below the monastery, surrounded by flowerbeds and acres of woods and so quiet that guests awaken to birdsong. There's a pool, a small spa and a restaurant, and the bright rooms are equipped with TVs and mini-bars; many have kitchenettes. Bikes for hire. *Closed Easter.*

Le Four à Chaux, 2253 Av Charles de Gaulle, by crossroads for Caromb, **t** 04 90 62 40 10, *www.lefourachaux. com* (€€). Refined, traditional dishes. *Closed Mon–Wed.*

Château
t 04 90 62 35 21, *http://chateau-du-barroux.ifrance.com;* open July–Sept daily 10–1 and 3–7; June daily 2.30–7; Oct daily 2–6; April and May Sat and Sun 10–7; adm

From here the skyline is dominated by **Le Barroux**, a dramatically perched village built around a 13th-century **château** that belonged to the Seigneurs of Baux. Follow the signs in the village up to the lofty Benedictine monastery of **Ste-Madeleine**, set in a geometrical lavender garden, a fine example of Provençal Romanesque – built in the late 1970s. Come at 9.30am (10am on Sundays) to hear the 50 monks sing Gregorian chant, for an uncanny journey straight back to the days when Romanesque was spanking new.

Or take a tour through the centre of the Plateau de Vaucluse, on the **D942** almost as far as Sault, then return on the **D1**. Few ever take it, though those who don't miss the most spectacular scenery the Vaucluse has to offer: the dry, rugged **Gorges de la Nesque**, leading to Sault and the Plateau d'Albion (*see* p.251). **Monieux**, at the eastern end of the Gorges, is a strange and isolated village that seems to have grown out of the rocky cliffs. There are caves and underground streams in the neighbourhood; experiments with dyeing the water have suggested that one of the sources of the Fontaine-de-Vaucluse may be here.

Mont Ventoux and Around

You can pick it out from almost anywhere on the plains around Carpentras, a commanding presence on the northern horizon. Mont Ventoux, a huge, bald, humpbacked *massif* more than 18km across, is the northern boundary stone of Provence, and it has always loomed large in the Provençal consciousness. For the Celts, as for the peoples who came before them, it was a holy place, the Home of the Winds; excavations at its summit in the early 20th century brought to light hundreds of small terracotta trumpets, a sort of *ex voto* that has never been completely explained. Winds, in Provence, inevitably suggest the *mistral*, and as the source of that

Wine: Côtes-du-Ventoux

The vineyards of this little-known AOC region are situated on the lower slopes of Mont Ventoux. The area is known principally for its reds, which are similar in style to the Côtes-du-Rhone AOC. The best estates, such as the **Domaine des Anges**, make wines with a high proportion of syrah in the blend, giving them depth and structure.

A 15th-century glassworks, **Domaine de la Verrière**, at Goult, t 04 90 72 20 88, has been transformed into another of the area's best sources of wine. M. Maubert produces a wine of unusual concentration, full of broad, spicy flavours that complement the local dishes perfectly. The Perrin brothers, famous for producing one of the finest and most sought-after Châteauneuf-du-Pape wines at Château de Beaucastel, also make a very fine Côtes-du-Ventoux at their purpose-built winery on the outskirts of Orange, **La Vieille Ferme**, t 04 90 34 25 64, *www.lavieilleferme.com*.

chilling blast Mont Ventoux has always had a somewhat evil reputation among the people; medieval Christians sought to exorcize it, perhaps, with its string of simple chapels.

Mountain-climbers will find a special interest in Mont Ventoux, if only because the sport was invented here. Petrarch, that admirably modern soul, went up with his brother in 1336 – this, according to historian Jacob Burckhardt, was the first recorded instance of anyone doing such an odd thing for pleasure. The experience had an unexpected effect on the poet. Reading a passage from his *Confessions of St Augustine* at the summit, he was seized with a vision of the folly of his past life and resolved to return to Italy: '...and men go forth, and admire lofty mountains and broad seas, and roaring torrents, and the course of the stars, and forget their own selves in doing so.' For us the trip will be easier, if perhaps less profound; Edouard Daladier, the Carpentrassien who became French prime minister in the 1930s, had the D974 built to the top.

Malaucène and the Fountain of Groseau

The base for visiting the mountain is **Malaucène**, on the road from Carpentras to Vaison-la-Romaine. Piled under a little conical nib of a hill, its landmark is the enormous church-cum-fortress of **St-Michel-et-St-Pierre**, built in 1309 by Pope Clement V. From here, the D153 was the ancient route around Mont Ventoux, passing a pair of medieval chapels and a ruined defence tower around the village of **Beaumont-du-Ventoux**. Nowadays, the ancient route peters out into a hiking trail, the GR4.

The D974, into the heart of the *massif*, passes a pre-Celtic site dedicated not to wind, but water. **Notre-Dame-du-Groseau**, an unusual 11th-century octagonal chapel, marks the spot today. Originally, this was part of a large monastery, now completely disappeared. Pope Clement V used it as his summer home, and his escutcheon can be seen painted inside. But this was also a holy spot in remotest antiquity; the iron cross outside the chapel is planted on a stone believed to have been a Celtic altar. *Groseau* comes from Groselos, a Celtic god of springs; the object of

Notre-Dame-du-Groseau

the curé at Malaucène has the key

veneration is a short distance up the road, the **Source du Groseau**, pouring out of a cliff-face. The Romans, as at Fontaine-de-Vaucluse, channelled the spring into an aqueduct; fragments can be seen.

Further up the mountain, the almost permanent winds make themselves known and vegetation becomes more scarce. The D974's big day comes, almost every summer, when the Tour de France puffs over it; it was here that the English World Champion Tommy Simpson collapsed and died in 1967, and there is a memorial 1km from the summit. The top of Ventoux (6,200ft) is a gravelly wasteland, embellished with communications towers and a meteorological observatory. Coming down the eastern side of the mountain takes you into one of the backwaters of Provence, a land of shepherds, boar and *cèpes*. There are a few attractive villages: **Sault**, a UNESCO World Heritage site on its outcrop, surrounded by bucolic landscapes, forests and lavender fields, with a quirky **Musée Municipal** of fossils, village curios and archaeology (even a mummy); and, further north, two medieval *villages perchés*, **Aurel** and **Montbrun-les-Bains**. To the south of Sault, the lonely **Plateau d'Albion** takes its name (like the English Albion, the Alps and the Provençal village of Aups) from an ancient Indo-European root meaning 'white' – from the odd limestone mountains around it, that seem to be covered in snow. The landscape can be a bit eerie – much of this territory, around the village of **St-Christol**, has been taken over for a complex of nuclear missile bases.

Musée Municipal
t 04 90 64 02 30; open July and Aug Mon–Sat 3–6; call for other dates or group visits

Market Days around Mont Ventoux

Malaucène: Wed.
Sault: Wed.

Where to Stay and Eat around Mont Ventoux

(i) **Malaucène** ›
Place de la Mairie, t 04 90 65 22 59; open summer Mon–Sat; winter Mon–Thurs

(i) **Sault** ›
Av de la Promenade, t 04 90 64 01 21, www. saultenprovence.com; open July and Aug daily; May and June Mon–Sat and Sun am; Sept–Oct and Jan–April Mon–Sat; Nov and Dec Mon–Fri

Malaucène ✉ 84340

**L'Origan, Cour des Isnards, t 04 90 65 27 08 (€). A clean, shipshape hotel in the centre, with a restaurant serving dishes such as guinea fowl with morels. *Closed Mon and Nov–Feb.*

Hostellerie La Chevalerie, Place de l'Eglise, Les Remparts, t 04 90 65 11 19 (€€). A peaceful restaurant with terrace, by St-Michel-et-St-Pierre. *Closed Sun eve and Mon and most of Jan.*

Sault and Aurel ✉ 84390

***Hostellerie du Val de Sault, Route St-Trinit, Sault, t 04 90 64 01 41, www.valdesault.com (€€€€€–€€€€). A handsome hotel 2,494ft up and facing Mont Ventoux, with 11 rooms and five suites surrounded by trees and gardens; equipped with a swimming pool, a gym, a *terrain de pétanque*, a lavender spa and a good restaurant (€€€€–€€€) specializing in truffles in season. *Half-board in summer. Closed Nov–Mar.*

***Domaine des Tilleuls, Route du Mont Ventoux, t 04 90 65 22 31, www.hotel-domainedestilleuls.com (€€). A new hotel with spacious, sparsely decorated rooms and a large garden with a swimming pool. Private parking is available. A great option for families.

*Relais du Mont Ventoux, Aurel, t 04 90 64 00 62 (€€). A reasonably priced inn with plain, comfortable rooms and a restaurant (€€) with no surprises but some good vegetarian choices. *Closed mid-Nov–Mar.*

Les Dentelles de Montmirail

Montmirail's 'lace' is a small crown of dolomitic limestone mountains opposite Mont Ventoux, the other side of Malaucène. Eroded by the wind into a fantasy of thick columns and spikes, the peaks form an ever-changing pattern as you circle around them. This is superb walking country, and superb wine country.

Wine and Antiques

The ideal overview of Les Dentelles is along the D90 from Malaucène to Beaumes-de-Venise, passing by way of **Suzette**, a cluster of sun-bleached stone houses and a bar-pizzeria enjoying a dream-like vision of the mountains at their most fantastical. If you're in no hurry, steep semi-paved roads from Suzette plunge into the heart of the mountains for more of the same, towards **Séguret** to the west, or north to **Crestet**, a half-restored *village perché* with a castle, more fabulous views and an art centre.

The D90 takes you into Côtes-du-Rhône country (*see* box, opposite), beginning with **Beaumes-de-Venise**, the metropolis of the Dentelles, where worthies sit on the wall sunning themselves like fat cats. There's a ruined castle and a small archaeological museum. Don't expect any canals: 'Beaumes' comes from the Provençal word for cave, and the 'Venise' from a corruption of Comtat Venaissin – the papal county. North along the D7, the Romanesque chapel of **Notre-Dame-d'Aubune** overlooks the Comtat plain, its lofty bell-tower decorated with classical pilasters. A track leads up the **Côte Balméenne**, where terraces were settled by the Celto-Ligurians, Greeks, Romans and Saracens. Since the archaeologists had their way with it in the 1980s, the terraces have been replanted with olive, almond and fruit trees.

Vacqueyras, a dusty little crossroads devoted entirely to wine, has a byroad (the D233) up to **Montmirail**, a spa once famous for its purgative waters. It was sold off after the Second World War: a Greek shipping tycoon now owns the grand Victorian villa, while the rest of the spa is now a hotel (*see* p.254). A few kilometres north of Vacqueyras, **Gigondas**, like so many wine villages in the south, is much smaller than its fame: small and sweet, it overlooks the immaculate vineyards and is full of shops allowing you to *déguster* the eponymous red nectar. The château on top of the village has been turned into a modest outdoor sculpture garden.

The tourist offices sell maps of the paths through Les Dentelles: the GR4 passes nearby, and steep white roads lead back to Beaumes-de-Venise or to the **Col du Cayron** and **Lafare** for more lovely Dentelles scenery.

Sablet, north of Gigondas, is another pretty, hard-working wine village packed on a hill, with old covered lanes to explore. But most

Wine: Côtes-du-Rhône Sud

Wines called Côtes-du-Rhône originate in 263 *communes* within the 200km between Vienne and Avignon. Because of the diversity of growing conditions in such a vast area, from hot rocky plains to steep green slopes, the district is a crazy-quilt of local varieties. You may find any mix of 13 varieties of grapes in a bottle of southern Côtes-du-Rhône, but the dominant forces are grenache, which gives it tannin and its famous sturdy quality, cinsault, which counterbalances with its delicacy and finesse, and syrah, which contributes fragrance and ability to age.

The star of the Dentelles is Gigondas, its very name derived from 'joy', or *Jocunditas*, a holiday camp for Roman soldiers. Part of their delight, according to Pliny, was in the wine, the perfect match for pheasant, wild rabbit or truffles. If you are looking for red wines to keep, consider the Signature and Pavillon de Beaumirail labels, aged in oak barrels at the **Cave des Vignerons de Gigondas, t** 04 90 65 86 27, *www.cave-gigondas.fr*, responsible for 20 per cent of the total Gigondas production.

As usual, for the finest wines one has to go to the individual estates. Jean-Marc Autran, the young superstar of Gigondas, makes elegant Gigondas and rich Sablet at the **Domaine de Piaugier**, Sablet, **t** 04 90 46 96 49. The **Domaine Les Pallières**, in Gigondas, **t** 04 90 65 85 07, is run by the Brunier family. The **Domaine Les Goubert**, **t** 04 90 65 86 38, also in Gigondas, offers the dense Cuvée Florence and, more unusual for the Dentelles, a Sablet Blanc – a fine white wine from ancient clairette vines.

Vacqueyras, the minute region just to the south of Gigondas, produces sober and full-bodied wines; some of the finest used to be made by a Provençal-speaking Pole named Jocelyn Chudzikiewicz at the **Domaine Les Amouriers**, Les Garrigues, Sarrians, **t** 04 90 65 83 22. Chudzikiewicz died tragically aged 46 in 1997 in a motorbike accident; the estate is run on behalf of his heirs by Patrick Gras. Try the **Château de Montmirail**, in Vacqueyras, **t** 04 90 65 86 72, *www.chateau-de-montmirail.com*, a long-established family vineyard that also does a delightfully mellow Gigondas.

The small *appellation* of Beaumes-de-Venise produces good reds, but is rightly famous for its rich sweet white wine made from the muscat grape. The wine is made by partially fermenting very ripe grapes and arresting the fermentation by the addition of alcohol, which kills off the yeasts, leaving much of the sugar and giving the wine an extra potency. The locals drink it as an *apéritif*, not a dessert wine. The local co-operative makes a very good example.

The two leading estates are **Domaine de Durban, t** 04 90 62 94 26, *www.domainedurban.com*, which is owned by M. Leydier, and the Perrin brothers of **La Vieille Ferme, t** 04 90 34 25 64, *www. lavieilleferme.com*, on the outskirts of Orange. The Côtes-du-Rhône region experienced a very difficult 2002 vintage following the floods that devastated the area. Fortunately, 1998–2001 produced a string of good-to-great vintages, so there is no shortage of good wine from this area on the market.

of the passing tourists home in on **Séguret**, built on a terrace over the vine-striped Ouvèze plain. It bears the burden of being 'One of the Most Beautiful Villages in France' with a fair amount of grace: there's no room for cars, and none for more than a handful of artists and *santonniers*. Note the funny weathered faces on the 14th-century **Fontaine des Mascarons**. Séguret is a good base for hiking; there are two trails (GR4 and GR7) and one village track that passes through a gap in the Dentelles to the eastern side. The back road to Vaison-la-Romaine is steep but beautiful.

ⓘ **Beaumes-de-Venise ›***

Maison des Dentelles, Place du Marché, t 04 90 62 94 39, www. ot-beaumesdevenise. com; open Mon–Sat all year; also Cours Jean Jaurès; open same hours

Market Days in the Dentelles

Beaumes-de-Venise: Tues.

Where to Stay and Eat in the Dentelles

Beaumes-de-Venise ✉ 84190

Auberge St-Roch, Av Jules Ferry, t 04 90 65 08 21 (€). A quiet, old-fashioned inn with a modest restaurant (€€)

serving seafood and local dishes. *Restaurant closed Wed eve and Thurs.*

Vacqueyras ✉ 84190

***Hôtel Montmirail**, Château des Eaux, t 04 90 65 84 01, *www.hotel montmirail.com* (€€). A secluded hotel, once part of the spa (*see p.252*), with a pool, garden and restaurant. *Closed mid-Oct–mid-Mar.*

****Le Pradet**, Route de Vaison, t 04 90 65 81 00 (€€–€). A quiet new complex on the edge of the village.

***Hôtel-Restaurant Les Dentelles**, t 04 90 65 86 21, *www.les-dentelles.com* (€). Comfortable modern rooms. *Restaurant closed Sun eve and Mon in winter.*

Gigondas ✉ 84190

(i) **Gigondas** >
Rue du Portail,
t 04 90 65 85 46,
www.gigondas-dm.fr;
open daily all year

****Les Florets**, Route des Dentelles, 2km from town, t 04 90 65 85 01, *www.hotel-lesflorets.com* (€€€–€€). Simple, rustic rooms and a pleasant restaurant, offering peace and quiet in the middle of a vineyard. *Closed Jan–Mar. Restaurant closed Wed, plus Mon eve and Tues in winter.*

L'Oustalet, Place du Portail, t 04 90 65 85 30 (€€€). A good restaurant set in a neoclassical building. *Closed Mon in Oct–Mar, Sun eve, Tues eve and Wed eve in Nov–Feb.*

Violès ✉ 84150

(★) **Hostellerie**
Mas de Bouvau >

Hostellerie Mas de Bouvau, Route de Cairanne, t 04 90 70 94 08 (€). A

charming family-run hotel-restaurant among the vines, serving specialities from southeast France such as duck *confit, magret, foie gras*, pigeon and rabbit (€€). *Closed Sun eve, Mon and mid-Dec–Jan.*

La Farigoule, Le Plan de Dieu, t 04 90 70 91 78, *www.la-farigoule.com* (€). A pleasant old farmhouse offering bed and breakfast and bike hire. *Closed Nov–Mar.*

Séguret ✉ 84110

****Domaine de Cabasse**, on D23 towards Sablet, t 04 90 46 91 12, *www.domaine-de-cabasse.fr* (€€€). A hotel forming part of a Côtes-du-Rhône estate, with 14 comfortable rooms with terraces, a swimming pool and an excellent restaurant where you can enjoy truffle-based dishes during the season and an array of other rather extravagant dishes. *Closed Nov–Mar.*

La Table du Comtat, t 04 90 46 91 49, *http://perso.orange.fr/table.comtat* (€€€). A good restaurant in the heart of the village, well known for its refined cuisine, which includes *julienne de truffe en coque d'œuf. Closed Tues eve, Wed, Sun, and mid-Feb–mid-Mar and mid-Nov–mid-Dec.*

Le Mesclun, Rue des Poternes, t 04 90 46 93 43, *www.lemesclun.com* (€€€–€€). Local fare. *Closed Mon and Tues.*

Vaison-la-Romaine

Vaison, in all its 2,400 years, has never been able to make up its mind which side of the river Ouvèze it wanted to be on. Locals have always been wary of the river's mighty potential for destruction, and the town's peregrinations from bank to bank have left behind a host of monuments, including extensive Roman ruins. Such circumspection was proved justified in 1992 when, on the night of 22 September, the Ouvèze burst its banks and swept away houses, caravans, bridges and roads, drowning 30 people in one of the worst French floods of the century. The town's riverside is still being rebuilt, and the scars of the tragedy are yet to heal.

Yet, as the tourist office proclaims, the best way to support Vaison is to visit. The Roman ruins were untouched, and life goes on: Vaison is a pleasant and beautiful place and, despite the summer crowds, if you're interested in the Romans or the Middle Ages it's a mandatory stop. The **Vaison Festival** draws large crowds in July and August, when theatre groups, choirs and musicians from around the world perform.

History

Vaison-la-Romaine began on the heights south of the Ouvèze as a Celtic *oppidum*. During the late 2nd century BC, the Romans took control of it and refounded it as Vasio Vocontiorum, a typical colony on the gentler slopes to the north of the river. For an out-of-the-way site, Vasio prospered spectacularly for the following five centuries, an *urbs opulentissima* with a large number of wealthy villas and as many inhabitants as it has today.

Vaison survived the age of invasions better than many of its neighbours; church councils were held here in the 6th century, a time when the city could afford to begin its imposing cathedral. In the coming centuries, bishops ruled in Vaison as the city slowly declined. In perhaps the 8th century, the counts of Toulouse acquired the site of the old Celtic *oppidum* and built a castle on it. While they carried on a chronic quarrel with the bishops, most of the people were abandoning the Roman town for the freedom and safety of the heights, the beginnings of what is now the Haute-Ville. In the 14th century, Vaison fell into the hands of the Pope, along with the rest of the Comtat Venaissin, and did not become part of France until the Revolution.

In the 19th century, on the move once more, the Vaisonnais were abandoning the Haute-Ville for the riverbank. In 1840 the first excavations were undertaken in the Roman city. Yet Vaison had to wait for a local abbot, Chanoine Sautel, to do the job seriously. He dug from 1907 until 1955, financed mostly by a local businessman.

The Ruins

Vaison Ruins
t 04 90 36 50 00;
open April–Sept daily
9.30–6; Mar and Oct
daily 10–12.30 and 2–6;
Nov–Feb daily 10–12
and 2–5; adm also
includes cathedral
cloister

The canon uncovered almost 11 hectares of Roman Vaison's foundations, while the modern town grew up around the digs. There are two separate areas, the **Quartier de la Villasse** and the **Site Puymin**; their entrances are on either side of the central Place du Chanoine J. Sautel, by the tourist information pavilion.

Vaison's ruins are an argument for leaving the archaeologists alone; with everything sanitized, interspersed with gardens and playgrounds, there is the unmistakable air of an archaeological theme park. The Villasse is the smaller of the two areas; from the entrance, a Roman street takes you past the city's **baths** (the best parts are still hidden under Vaison's post office) and the **Maison au Buste d'Argent**, a truly posh villa with two *atria* and some mosaic floors. It has its own baths, as does the adjacent **Maison au Dauphin**; beyond this is a short stretch of a colonnaded street, a status embellishment in the most prosperous Roman towns. The Puymin quarter has more of the same: another villa, the **Maison**

des Messii, is near the entrance. Beyond that, however, is an *insula*, or block of flats for the common folk, as well as a large, partially excavated quadrangle called the **Portique de Pompée**, an enclosed public garden with statuary that was probably attached to a temple. On the opposite side of the *insula* is a largely ruined *nymphaeum*, or monumental fountain. From here you can walk uphill to the **theatre**, restored and used for concerts in the summer, and the **museum**, displaying the best finds from the excavations. You'll learn more about Roman Vaison here than from the bare foundations around it; there is a model of one of the villas as it may have looked. All the items a Roman museum ought to have are present: restored mosaics and fragments of wall paintings, some lead pipes, inscriptions, hairpins and bracelets, and of course statuary: municipal notables of Vaison, a wonderful monster *acroterion* (roof ornament) from a mausoleum, and a few marble gods and emperors – including a startling family portrait with the Emperor Hadrian completely naked and evidently proud of it, next to his demurely clothed empress Sabina, smiling wanly.

The Cathedral of Notre-Dame-de-Nazareth

The French, with their incurable adoration of anything Roman, neglect Vaison's real attraction, one of the most fascinating medieval monuments of the Midi. A treasure house of oddities, it is a reminder that there is more to the art and religion of the Middle Ages than meets the eye, and much of significance that is lost to us forever. It stands half a kilometre west of the ruins, on Avenue Jules Ferry.

The church was begun in the 6th century. Its apse is the oldest part; looking at it from the outside, you'll see where excavations have uncovered the dressed Roman stones and drums of columns that were recycled to serve as a foundation. The rest of the structure dates from a rebuilding that began in the 12th century, including sculptural decoration around the portals, cornices and bell-tower. The first clues to the mystery of this church can be seen near the top of the façade: a rectangular maze, and a triangular figure that may be a mystic representation of the Sun. Even with this, the exterior is subdued, and the muscular perfection of the columns and vaults inside comes as a surprise.

The 12th-century nave is Romanesque at its best, but still the eye is drawn down it to the magnificent, arcaded interior of the **apse**. There is nothing like this apse in France; it is a place to muse on time and fate – the last surviving work of Roman Provence, the wistful farewell of a civilization that can be heard across the centuries. Almost incredibly, the 6th-century marble **altar** is still present, carved in a beautiful wave-like pattern. Also here are the original bishop's throne, and benches set around the semicircle of the apse where the monks would sit: the earliest form of a choir, as in the churches of Ravenna.

In the medieval nave, some of the decoration is as provocative as that on the façade. At the rear, near a column that survives from the original basilica, you'll notice the figure of an unidentifiable 'hairy person', extending a hand in a gesture of benediction. Elaborate masons' marks are everywhere. Odd figures of the Evangelists embellish the squinches of the fine octagonal cupola; behind one of them, high up, on the second column on the right side of the nave, is what appears to be a little devil. You'll meet his big brother in the cloister.

Cloister
*open April–Sept
daily 10.30–12.30
and 2–6; adm*

Look around as you enter the **cloister**. Grinning over its ticket-booth is Vaison's most famous citizen – Old Nick himself, with horns and goatee, carved into the stone as large as life. This is not a personage one usually sees portrayed in cathedral cloisters, and no one has ever come up with an explanation for his presence here – one unlikely guess is that it's really Jesus, superimposed over a crescent moon. This is a small but graceful cloister from the 12th century, with finely carved capitals and architectural fragments displayed around the walls. And if you think the Devil and all the other curiosities were simply fanciful decoration, look up at the Latin verse inscription, running the entire length of the church's southern cornice:

> *I exhort you, brothers, to triumph over the party of Aquilon [the north], faithfully maintaining the rule of the cloister, for thus will you arrive at the south, in order that the divine triple fire shall not neglect to illuminate the quadrangular abode in such a way as to bring to life the arched stones, to the number of two times six. Peace to this house.*

The medieval Latin is in parts obscure enough for other interpretations to be possible, but these tend to be even stranger. The 12 stones seem to be pillars of the cloister, the 'quadrangular abode'. The rest is lost in arcane, erudite medieval mysticism, wrapped up with the architecture and unique embellishments, and undoubtedly with a monastic community that was up to something not entirely orthodox. Like most medieval secrets, this one will never be completely understood.

Chapelle St-Quenin

A bit of a climb to the north, on Avenue de St-Quenin, you can continue in this same vein of medieval peculiarity. St-Quenin, a chapel dedicated to a 6th-century bishop who became Vaison's patron saint, fooled people for centuries into thinking it a Roman building. Its apse, unique in France, is triangular instead of the usual semicircle, and crowned with a cornice that includes fragments from Roman buildings as well as primitive reliefs that may date from Merovingian times. It is difficult to ascribe any special significance to this odd form. Probably constructed in the 11th or 12th centuries, it may be simply an architectural experiment, typical of the creative freedom of the early Romanesque. On the front of the chapel is a Merovingian-era relief of two vine shoots emerging from a vase – a piece of early Christian symbolism that has become the symbol of Vaison.

The Haute-Ville

From Roman and modern Vaison, the medieval version of the town is a splendid sight atop its cliff, a honey-coloured skyline of stone houses under the castle of the counts of Toulouse. Almost abandoned at the turn of the last century, the Haute-Ville is becoming quite chic now, with restorations everywhere and more than a few artists' studios. You reach it by crossing the Ouvèze on a **Roman bridge**, still in good nick after 18 centuries of service (although it had to be repaired after the last floods; note the plaque, in Latin), then climb up to the gate of the 14th-century fortifications, next to the **Tour Beffroi**, the clock tower that is the most prominent sight of the Haute-Ville's silhouette. The cobbled streets and the shady **Place du Vieux-Marché**, with its fountain, are lovely; trails lead higher up to the 12th–14th-century **castle**, half ruined but offering a view.

Market Days in Vaison-la-Romaine

Vaison-la-Romaine: Tues, in the lower town; farmers' market Tues, Thurs, Sat in summer.

Where to Stay and Eat in Vaison-la-Romaine

Vaison-la-Romaine ✉ **84110**
Vaison has plenty of accommodation to go around, and in the crowded summer months you might end up here even if you would have preferred to be in one of the villages of Les Dentelles.

***Le Beffroi**, Rue de l'Evêché, Cité Médiévale, t 04 90 36 04 71, *www.le-beffroi.com* (€€€–€€). A hotel situated in a picturesque 16th-century house, representing a real bargain for its category. *Closed Feb–Mar.*

****La Bastide de Vaison**, Quartier Les Auries, west of town on D977, t 04 90 36 03 15, *www.hotel-labastide.fr.st* (€€). A modernized farmhouse with a pool.
La Fête en Provence, Place du Vieux-Marché, t 04 90 36 36 43, *www.hotellafete-provence.com* (€€). A nicely secluded hotel with a restaurant, which is open in winter only for guests who have booked.

****Le Burrhus**, 1 Place Montfort, t 04 90 36 00 11, *www.burrhus.com* (€€–€). A gorgeous hotel with minimalist but comfortable, pretty rooms with Art Deco touches and air-conditioning, and a shady terrace. It also hosts exhibitions. *Closed mid-Dec–mid-Jan.*
Le Brin d'Olivier, 4 Rue du Ventoux, t 04 90 28 74 79 (€€€–€€). A restaurant offering fresh and imaginative Provençal cuisine in which fresh herbs hold pride of place. *Closed Tues eve, Wed eve and Sun, plus first week Mar, first 2 weeks June, and one week Dec.*

ⓘ **Vaison-la-Romaine >**
Place du Chanoine J. Sautel, t 04 90 36 02 11, *www.vaison-la-romaine.com; open July and Aug daily; Sept–mid-Oct and April–June Mon–Sat and Sun am; mid-Oct–Mar Mon–Sat*

 Le Brin d'Olivier >>

The Provençal Alps

*The Côte d'Azur has an admirably
spacious back garden, rolling over
mountains and plateaux from the
Italian border, and covering the
better part of three départements.
It contains only two towns of any size,
Digne-les-Bains and Draguignan;
between them are plenty of wide
open spaces – landscapes on an
Arizonan scale, including a Grand
Canyon worthy of the name.*

*The stars of this area are, without
doubt, the spectacular mountains,
Italianate villages and frescoed
churches of the Alpes-Maritimes,
inland from Monaco and Nice.
Everything to the west is limestone,
eroded into fantastically shaped
mountains and deep gorges. Further
south the landscapes become gentler
and greener; you may find the
Provence you're looking for in the
amiable and relatively unspoiled
villages and wine country around
Draguignan.*

12

Don't miss

⭐ **Alpine heights
and wild flowers**
Parc National du
Mercantour **p.262**

⭐ **Prehistoric
engravings**
Vallée des Merveilles **p.266**

⭐ **The 'Sistine
Chapel' of the
Alpes-Maritimes**
Notre-Dame-des-
Fontaines **p.267**

⭐ **A mountain-
climbing train**
Train des Pignes **p.276**

⭐ **Natural wonder**
Grand Canyon du Verdon
p.279

See map overleaf

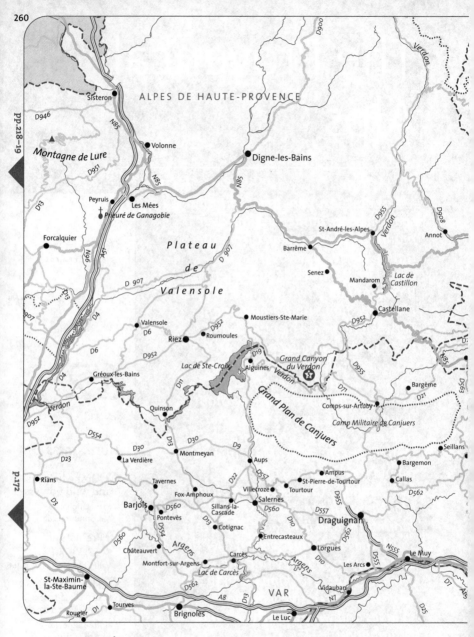

pp.218-19

p.172

Don't miss

⭐ Parc National du Mercantour **p.262**

⭐ Vallée des Merveilles **p.266**

⭐ Notre-Dame-des-Fontaines **p.267**

⭐ Train des Pignes, Var valley **p.276**

⭐ Grand Canyon du Verdon **p.279**

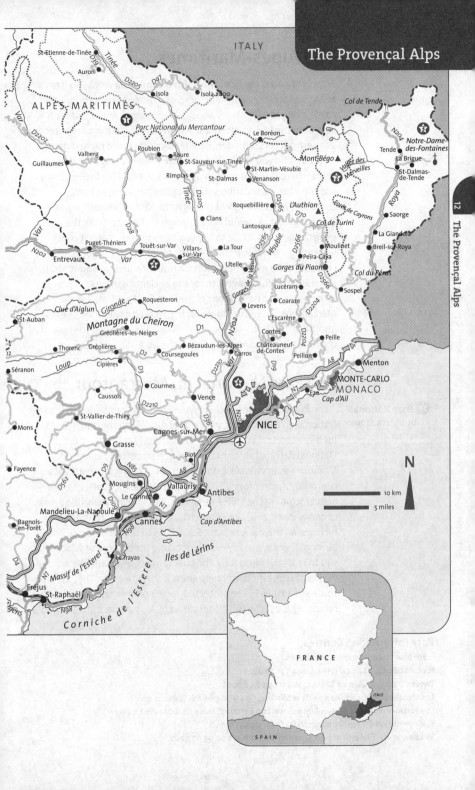

The Alpes-Maritimes

'*Lacet*' means shoelace, or a hairpin bend. It's a word you'll need to know if you try to drive up here, on Europe's worst mountain roads, designed for mules and never improved. When you see a sign announcing '20 *lacets* ahead', prepare for 10 minutes in second gear, encounters with demented lorry drivers, and ragged nerves.

So, what do you get for your trouble in this corrugated *département* where the Alps stretch down to the sea? For starters, these are real Alps – arrogant crystalline giants, that make their contempt felt as we crawl through the valleys beneath. Up in Switzerland, they would have enough altitude to make the geography books. Close to the sea, their numbers aren't over-whelming – but if you think 9,197ft Mont Bégo is a foothill, try climbing it. Bégo is a holy mountain, an Ararat or a Mount Meru, a prehistoric pilgrimage site for the ancient Ligurians.

The best parts have been set aside as the Parc National du Mercantour. But in the valleys of the Roya and the Tinée, there's another attraction – all those *lacets* will also take you to some of the finest Renaissance painting in the Midi.

The Parc National du Mercantour

⭐ Parc National du Mercantour

The highest regions of this *département* are contained in the Parc National du Mercantour, which stretches along the Italian border for more than 128km and joins with the adjacent Argentera National Park in Italy to make a unique preserve of alpine and Mediterranean wildlife. Established only in 1979, it consists of a central 'protected zone', a narrow strip of the most inaccessible areas, including the Vallée des Merveilles with its prehistoric rock carvings (*see* p.266), and a much larger 'peripheral zone' that includes all the villages from Sospel to St-Etienne-de-Tinée and beyond. There are many excellent hiking trails, some of which allow you to cross over into Italy. The park rangers, all local, have an excellent reputation for helpfulness and knowledge. They enforce some strict rules in the protected zone: no tents, dogs or fires, no motor vehicles (though all-terrain vehicles have recently been

Park Information Centres

See also *www.parc-mercantour.com*.

Nice: ✉ 06000, 23 Rue d'Italie, **t** 04 93 16 78 88.

Tende: ✉ 06430, Gare de St-Dalmas, **t** 04 93 04 67 00.

Les Mesches: ✉ 06430, Maison de la Minière, **t** 04 93 04 68 66. *Summer only.*

St-Martin-Vésubie: ✉ 06450, Rue Kellermann Serrurier, Place de la Mairie, **t** 04 93 03 23 15.

St-Sauveur-sur-Tinée: ✉ 06420, on D2205, **t** 04 93 02 01 63.

St-Etienne-de-Tinée: ✉ 06660, Quartier de l'Ardon, **t** 04 93 02 42 27.

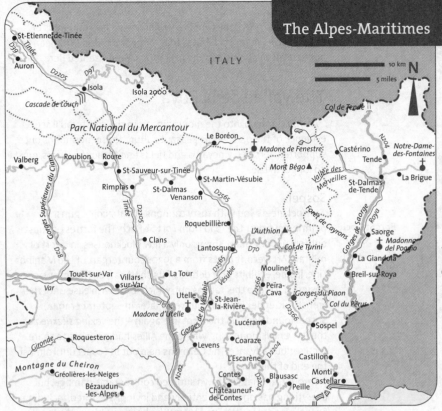

allowed on trails only, as an experiment), and no collecting of flowers, insects or anything else.

The most spectacular alpine fauna, and the sort you're most likely to see, are the birds of prey: golden eagles, falcons and vultures. A recent addition, reintroduced from the Balkans after becoming extinct here, is the mighty *gypaète barbu* (lammergeyer), a 'bearded' vulture with a bizarre face, orange-red feathers, black wings and a reputation for carrying off lambs and children. On the ground, there's the ubiquitous stoat or ermine, popping out of the snow in his white winter coat and looking entirely too cute to be made into royal coat linings. There's also his bulkier cousin, the marmot, and plenty of boars, foxes, *mouflons* (wild mountain sheep), chamois and, in the more inaccessible places, *bouquetins* (ibex). All of these have been rapidly increasing in number since the establishment of the park.

As for wild flowers, the symbol of the park is the spiky *Saxifrage multiflora*, one of 25 species found nowhere but here. Edelweiss exists in the park, but is as elusive as anywhere else. Beyond these exotic blooms, there is a tremendous wealth of plant life. Blue gentians and anemones are everywhere, as well as hundreds of other species, in microclimates that range from Mediterranean to alpine. Half the flowers found in France are represented here.

The Vallée de la Roya

As you climb up into the mountains from the coast, you'll see evidence of the prosperous peasant culture these mountains once supported. Terraced vineyards and fields line the lower slopes, most no longer in use.

Sospel

Fort St-Roch
*t 04 43 04 14 41;
open Tues–Sun
9.30–12.30 and 2–6*

Sospel greets you with rusty cannons and machine guns, pointing out over the road from **Fort St-Roch**. The fortress, almost entirely underground, shows only a few blockhouses, in a sort of military Art Deco; it dates from a 1930s counterpart of the Maginot Line. Inside, exhibits give details of its short career. The fort was designed to keep the Italians out, which it did with ease until the French surrender in 1940. Four years later, in September 1944, Sospel found itself on the front line again – the vexing *sitzkrieg* of the Provençal mountains, where the Allies had no effort to spare for a serious advance. The Germans held out in Sospel until almost the end of the war.

Through all that, the town suffered considerable damage, but everything has now been entirely, and lovingly, restored, including Sospel's landmark, the **Pont Vieux**, the base of which dates back to the 10th century. The tiny tower in the middle of the bridge was the toll on the salt road; in the Middle Ages, salt from the flats of Toulon and Hyères was taken by boat to Nice, and from there by convoys of mules to Piedmont and Lombardy.

The **Cathédrale St-Michel**, set in a handsome arcaded square, retains its original 12th-century bell-tower, but the rest has been Baroqued with charming tastelessness inside and out, including a wonderful circus-tent baldachin over the altar, dripping with gilt and tassels. A chapel to the left discreetly hides a fine *Annunciation* by Ludovico Brea, as well as another retable of the Virgin in a Gothic frame, possibly also by Brea or one of his followers. Don't miss a wander around the narrow winding streets of the rest of the old town, and another arcaded square, **Place St-Nicolas**, with a 15th-century fountain, on the other side of the bridge.

Breil-sur-Roya and Saorge

To the north, the D2204 is the best route into the Vallée de la Roya, with only a few dozen *lacets* and one mountain pass; the other route, following the D93 and the N204, is slightly shorter, but it passes two border crossings in and out of Italy.

Getting around the Vallée de la Roya

Of all the hinterlands of Provence, this is the region that is the most difficult to navigate by car, and ̀ɪ. most convenient for public transport.

One of the best ways to see the Vallée de la Roya is from that alpine rarity – a train. The railway line from Nice that runs to Cuneo in Italy offers spectacular scenery and serves L'Escarène, Sospel, Breil-sur-Roya, St-Dalmas-de-Tende and Tende. One train a day goes on to Turin. Don't miss the historic train carriages parked at Sospel station, including an old Orient-Express.

You can catch a special tourist train, the **Train des Merveilles**, from Nice to Tende, taking 1hr 45mins and leaving Nice at 9am, *www.tendemerveilles.com*, and there is also a **Train des Neiges Castérino** from Nice to St-Dalmas-de-Tende every Sun in the snowy season (Jan–Mar).

Sospel has daily **buses** to and from Menton, which take 20 minutes. There are regular bus services from Nice to Contes, L'Escarène and Lucéram, and a range of buses from Sospel into the smaller valleys (**Transports Rey, t** 04 93 04 01 24 or **Transports Collucini, t** 04 93 04 01 40).

Breil-sur-Roya, the first town in the French part of the valley, has two peculiar attractions: the unidentifiable black pseudo-turkeys who live in the river Roya under the bridge, and the 18th-century church of **Sancta-Maria-in-Albis**, which has some large cracks in its ill-formed walls that seem ready to bring the place down around the ears of the faithful. Inside there is another retable attributed to Brea, though it's not a very good one.

Further to the north, the village of **La Giandola** sits among the olive groves that once were the Vallée de la Roya's only resource, and beyond that you'll come to the **Gorges de Saorge**.

After the gorges, the village of **Saorge** is a truly magnificent sight with its neat and tidy rows of Italian slate-roofed, green-shuttered houses perched on a height like some remote Byzantine monastery and punctuated by church steeples with cupolas made of coloured tiles. Saorge guards the Roya valley, and the Piedmontese made it a key border stronghold. You won't see more than the ruins of their fort today, however – it was destroyed after a young commander named Bonaparte took it during the wars of the Revolution. The town suffered further during the Second World War, when its inhabitants were evacuated and forced to spend the duration in Antibes. Saorge is just as attractive from close up, an ancient border village with customs and a dialect all its own, a little bit Occitan and a little bit Ligurian Italian; instead of *rue* or *via* on the street signs, you'll see *caréra* or *chu* or *ciassa*. The streets – stairways more often than not – climb and dive and duck under arches.

The sights themselves require a kilometre's hike to the outskirts. There you'll find an 18th-century **Franciscan monastery**, in elegant Piedmontese Baroque, and beyond that the 11th-century chapel of the **Madonna del Poggio**, with some Renaissance frescoes, including a *Marriage of the Virgin*.

To the west of Saorge, you can penetrate into the southernmost corner of the Mercantour National Park, up the narrow D40 into the **Forêt de Cayrons** (or **Caïros**).

The Vallée des Merveilles

Before going any further, make sure you understand that the Roya is a cul-de-sac; there's no way out except by retracing your steps or continuing through the Tende tunnel to Cuneo, Italy. After Saorge, the mountains close in immediately, with the **Gorges de Bergue et de Paganin**; these end at the village of **St-Dalmas-de-Tende**, once the border post between France and Italy and now the gateway to the Vallée des Merveilles.

From about 1800 BC onwards, the Ligurian natives of these mountains began scratching pictures and symbols on the rocks here. They kept at it for 800 years, until more than 100,000 inscriptions decorated the valley: human figures, religious symbols (plenty of bulls, horns and serpents), weapons and tools. Most defy any conclusive interpretation – they are circles, spirals and ladders or chequerboard patterns of the kind found all over the Med (the Val Camonica in north Italy has even more carvings, from the same era). Why they were made is an open question; one very appealing hypothesis is that this valley, beneath Mont Bégo, was a holy place and a pilgrimage site, and that the carvings can be taken as *ex votos* made by the pilgrims.

The presence of these symbols has brought the valley some notoriety – superstition gave the surroundings place names such as **Cime du Diable** (Devil's Peak) and **Valmasque** (*masco*, mask, was an old local word for sorcerer). The first person to study the site systematically was an Englishman, Clarence Bicknell, in the early part of the 20th century. As the prime attraction of the Parc National du Mercantour, the valley gets its fair share of visitors these days. Besides the carvings, the landscape itself is worth the hike, including a score of mountain lakes, mostly above the treeline, all in the shadow of rugged, uncanny **Mont Bégo**, highest of the peaks around the Roya; the mountain's name, as far as anyone can tell, comes from an Etruscan god of storms.

Don't just wander up here like some fool tourist, looking for Neolithic etchings. Plan the trip out beforehand, with advice from the park information offices. They will probably recommend a guided tour; the symbols are plentiful, but inconspicuous and hard to find. Outside the summer months, many will be covered in snow. To tour the valley is *at least* a 20km round-trip trek from the *refuge* at **Les Mesches**, at the end of the road west from St-Dalmas. There are hotels in nearby **Castérino**, and *refuges* within the park if you want to stay over; make arrangements at the park office. Four-by-fours can also take you around (expensively) from St-Dalmas.

La Brigue and Notre-Dame-des-Fontaines

Vittorio Emanuele II, the last king of Piedmont-Sardinia and the first of unified Italy, may have been utterly useless at his job, but as a hunter few crowned heads could match him. When he arranged to give away the county of Nice in 1860, he stipulated only that the Upper Roya, above St-Dalmas-de-Tende, be left for him as a hunting reserve (to add to a few others he had, strung out across Italy, including the famous Isle of Montecristo). The few inhabitants had already voted (under French supervision) on union with France; suspiciously, 73 per cent of the electorate abstained. So this had to wait until 1947, when another plebiscite was held and the valley became France's latest territorial acquisition.

Tende, a dour, slate-roofed *bourg*, is the only town. No longer a dead end since the road tunnel through to Italy was built, it has become a busy place by local standards. It has the ruined **castle** of the Lascaris, long-time feudal lords of the Roya, and a late Gothic church, **Ste-Marie-des-Bois**, with a pretty sculpted Renaissance portal, and painted façade and ceiling. Don't miss its cemetery, built on steps for lack of space. On Avenue du 16 Septembre 1847, the **Musée des Merveilles** has copies and photos of the rock engravings, as well as ethnographic exhibits on life in the valley from prehistoric times up to the 18th century.

East of St-Dalmas-de-Tende, the D143 takes you into La Brigue, a minute region (partly in Italy) that grows apples and pears and raises trout. **La Brigue**, the tiny capital, has some fine paintings in its church of **St-Martin**, another late Gothic work of the 15th century: three altarpieces by Ludovico Brea and his followers, along with Italian paintings from the 17th and 18th centuries. The people who live here seem to have an elevated opinion of tourists, since the only ones who pass through have come a long way to see their paintings and, more importantly, those by Giovanni Canavesio at **Notre-Dame-des-Fontaines**, 4km from the village of **La Brigue**. The name comes from seven intermittent local springs, miniature versions of the Fontaine-de-Vaucluse (*see* p.240), gushing out of the rock or stopping according to pressure and the water table; these can still be seen, though on the Italian side of the border.

The Upper Roya may not have been much of an economic or strategic gain for France, but artistically it was a real prize – the country's total number of good Renaissance frescoes went up considerably. Giovanni Canavesio, from Piedmont, is not well known outside his own region, but he was a painter in the best north Italian Renaissance tradition, characterized by bright colours, exquisite, stylized draughtsmanship and an ability to put a genuine religious feeling into his frescoes that recalls Fra Angelico. His works in this rural chapel, done in the 1490s, include 26 large scenes of the *Passion of Christ* in the nave, and on one of the side walls a tremendous *Last Judgement* – a reminder that God wasn't joking: all the tortures of the damned are portrayed in intricate detail, as the devils sweep them into the Mouth of Hell. Around the

Musée des Merveilles
t 04 93 04 32 50, www. museemerveilles.com; open May–mid-Oct Wed–Mon 10–6.30; mid-Oct–April Wed–Mon 10–5; closed a few days in Mar and Nov; adm

 Notre-Dame-des-Fontaines

choir, on the triumphal arch, he painted scenes from the life of Mary, from the *Birth of Mary* to the *Presentation at the Temple*.

The frescoes in the choir itself are by Giovanni Baleison. Done in the 1470s, in a more old-fashioned style that still shows the influence of Byzantium, these include the *Four Evangelists* on the vaulted ceiling, the four *Doctors of the Church* (Ambrose, Jerome, Gregory and Augustine) under the arch, and scenes from the life of Mary, including an *Annunciation* and *Visit to the Tomb*.

Market Days in the Vallée de la Roya

Sospel: Thurs am; plus Sun am, farmers' market.

Breil: Tues; Sat am, farmers' market.

Tende: Wed; plus Tues, Sat and Sun am, farmers' market.

Where to Stay and Eat in the Vallée de la Roya

Sospel ✉ 06380

L'Auberge Provençale, Route du Col de Castillon, about 2km from town, **t 04 93 04 00 31, *www.auberge provencale.fr* (€€). An inn with a *terrasse* with a magnificent view over Sospel, and a restaurant. *Closed Tues and Wed mid-Nov–mid-Dec.*

Hôtel des Etrangers, 7 Bd de Verdun, **t 04 93 04 00 09, *www.sospel.net* (€€). Small hotel with a swimming pool. *Closed Nov–Feb.*

Domaine du Paraïs, off D2566 towards Moulinet at La Vasta Supérieure, **t** 04 93 04 15 78, *http://domaineduparais. monsite.wanadoo.fr/page7.html* (€€–€). A *chambres d'hôtes* outside Sospel (unfortunately you'll really need a car to get here), set in a villa that was taken over by officers during the Second World War and which has now been proudly restored by its owners. *Book ahead.*

Le Relais du Sel, 3 Bd de Verdun, **t** 04 93 04 00 43 (€€). The best place in town to eat, specializing in meat fondues. *Book. Closed Fri.*

Breil-sur-Roya ✉ 06540

***Castel du Roy, 146 Route de L'Aïgara, **t** 04 93 04 43 66, *www.*

castelduroy.com (€€). A modern, rather impersonal place spread out among different buildings close to the river, with a pool and a highly rated restaurant. *Closed Nov–Mar; restaurant closed lunch, and Tues and Wed.*

Le Roya, 3 Place Biancheri, **t 04 93 04 48 10 (€). A functional choice. *Open in winter only for pre-bookings.*

Saorge ✉ 06540

Le Bellevue, 5 Rue Louis Périssol, **t** 04 93 04 51 37 (€€). A restaurant with nice views. *Closed Mon eve and Tues out of season.*

Lou Pountin, 56 Rue Lt Jean Révelli, **t** 04 93 04 54 90 (€). Excellent pizzas. *Closed Mon–Thurs.*

La Brigue ✉ 06430

Le Mirval, 3 Rue Vincent Ferrier, at west end of village, **t 04 93 04 63 71, *www.lemirval.com* (€). The best of the three hotels here; some rooms have good views and the management can arrange trips (€€€) into the Vallée des Merveilles. *Closed Nov–Mar.*

Castérino ✉ 06430

If you're doing the Vallée des Merveilles on your own, it's most convenient to start from Castérino, a hamlet at the end of the D91.

*Les Mélèzes, **t** 04 93 04 95 95, *www. lesmelezes.fr* (€). Small but comfortable rooms and a good restaurant. *Closed mid-Nov–mid-Dec; restaurant closed Tues eve and Wed out of season.*

Santa Maria Maddalena, **t** 04 93 04 65 93, *www.casterino.com* (€). A *gîte d'étape* with restaurant; half-board is preferred in season. *Closed mid-Nov–Dec and April.*

ⓘ **Sospel** ›
19 Av Jean Médecin,
t 04 93 04 15 80, www.
sospel-tourisme.com;
open Mon–Sat
and Sun am

ⓘ **Tende**
Av du 16 Sept 1947,
t 04 93 04 73 71, www.
tendemerveilles.com;
open summer daily;
winter Mon–Sat
and Sun am

ⓘ **Breil-sur-
Roya** ›
Mairie, 17 Pl Biancheri,
t 04 93 04 99 76,
www.breil-sur-roya.fr;
open Mon–Fri
and Sat am

West of Sospel: The Paillon Valley

There is some painting here too, in the rugged mountains between Sospel and the valley of the Var. The Italian influence shows itself in another way – the road map looks like a plate of spaghetti. Lacking a mule, you'll need to return to Sospel to get out of the valley.

L'Escarène

The D2204 west will take you to L'Escarène, a lovely Italianate village that used to serve as a posting station between Turin and Nice. From the bridge you can see the houses overhanging the river, and you can visit the **Chapelle des Pénitents-Blancs**, with its spectacular rococo stucco decoration. There are some peculiar landscapes to the south of the village: stone quarries on the road to Nice have carved out a huge, nearly perfect ziggurat; the road is sometimes closed in the mornings for blasting. In the hills above, around **Blausasc**, 19th-century deforestation has left a lunar wasteland of bare rock.

Lucéram

North of L'Escarène, Lucéram is an old shoe of a village, well worn and a bit out at the toes. Full of arches and tunnels, like Saorge, it contains some remains of walls and towers on the mountainside, which make for a steep but pleasant excursion if you decide to circumnavigate them. The church of **Ste-Marguerite** is second only to Notre-Dame-des-Fontaines as an artistic attraction. Amidst the gaudy Baroque stucco of the interior, the altarpieces of the Nice school seem uncomfortably out of place. The best, with an innocence and spirituality matched by few other saintly portraits, is the *Retable de Ste-Marguerite* over the main altar, which has been attributed to Ludovico Brea. Marguerite, a martyr of Antioch, is another popular Provençal dragon-slayer, one who is often confused with St Martha (*see* p.123). Brea made her exceedingly lovely; the Tarasque-like demon at her feet never stood a chance.

The other retables around the church include saints Peter and Paul (with the keys and sword), St Claude, St Lawrence (with his grid-iron, upon which he was barbecued) and St Bernard, all by unknown 15th-century artists; Giovanni Baleison contributed a good one of St Anthony of Padua (1480) in the **Chapelle du Trésor**. It keeps company with a *trésor* of awful clutter: reliquaries, monstrances and statuettes, including a silver image containing relics of St Marguerite. Outside the church, **Chapelle St-Jean** was built by the Knights of St John – the Knights of Malta, who had a commandery here. Its beautiful exterior is painted to imitate precious marble (though the inside is full of electricity generators).

Getting around the Paillon Valley

All the villages in the Paillon are served by at least two **buses** a day from Nice.

If you have the time, there are some worthwhile digressions into the mountains around Lucéram, beginning just outside the village with two more chapels with frescoes by Giovanni Baleison, similar to his work at Notre-Dame-des-Fontaines: **St-Grat** (on the road towards L'Escarène) and **Notre-Dame-de-Bon-Cœur** (on the road for Coaraze); the sacristan in Lucéram has the keys for both. East of Lucéram, a half-hour climb up into the hills, there is a wild spot with a huge circular prehistoric wall, the site of a fortified village from the time of the Vallée des Merveilles inscriptions – a logical place for such a settlement, with a fine view of holy Mont Bégo.

North of Lucéram, the D21 and D2566 take you past **Peïra-Cava**, a resort for the French military and their families, to the **Forêt de Turini**, centred around a 4,987ft mountain pass, the **Col de Turini**, at the tip of three river valleys. Up above the pass are several old forts, near the summit of **L'Authion**, an eyrie that commands almost all the Alpes-Maritimes. These were one of the Germans' last redoubts in the war; signs of the battle are still evident, especially around the **Fort des Mille Fourches**, damaged, incredibly, by bombardment from the sea in 1945.

The Devil's Tail and Other Tales

A long tour on the D2566/D15 west from Lucéram (7km for the crow, 19 for you) will take you with some difficulty to **Coaraze**, a village that is a magnet for stories. One is its name, *Caude Rase* in medieval times, or the 'cut tail' of the Devil: the villagers back then somehow trapped Old Nick, who had to give up his tail like a lizard to get away. Coaraze has also attracted its share of artists lately; one has given the village centre a lizard mosaic to commemorate the event. Other artists, including Jean Cocteau, have contributed a number of colourful ceramic sundials around the village.

Another legend deals with the abandoned **Roccasparvière** village, a four-hour walk from Coaraze in the mountains. Queen Jeanne of Provence, the story goes, once took refuge from her enemies here. The plot differs in every version, but in most of them someone in the village kills Jeanne's twin sons and serves them up for dinner. '*Roc, méchant roc*,' Jeanne cursed. '*Un jour viendra où plus ne chantera ni poule ni coq*.' No chickens indeed are singing in Roccasparvière today, but spoilsport historians say it was because the village well dried up.

Another tortuous 10km south of here on the D15, **Contes** has its stories too. One fine day in 1508, the village was attacked by a horde of caterpillars. Apparently it was not the first time; the area

ⓘ Contes

Place Jean Allardi, **t** *04 93 79 13 99, www.ville-contes.fr; open Mon–Fri*

ⓘ Coaraze ››

7 Place Sainte-Catherine, **t** *04 93 79 37 47, office.de.tourisme. coaraze@tiscali.fr; open Mon, Tues, Thurs and Fri, plus Sat am*

ⓘ Lucéram ›

Place Adrien Barralis, **t** *04 93 79 46 50, www.luceram.com; open Tues–Sat*

Market Days in the Paillon Valley

Contes: Mon, Wed and Sun.
Lucéram: Christmas market.

Where to Stay and Eat in the Paillon Valley

In these mountains, so close to Nice and Monte-Carlo, food and accommodation are surprisingly basic and humble.

Lucéram ✉ 06440

Trois Vallées, Moulinet, **t 04 93 91 57 21, *troisvallees@wanadoo.fr* (€€). A handsome chalet in the woods at the top of Col de Turini, north of Lucéram, with 20 adequate rooms and a restaurant (€€) offering roast boar and more, plus great views.

La Bocca Fina, Place Adrien Barralis, **t** 04 93 79 51 54, *www.boccafina.net* (€€). Traditional cooking, served on a terrace. *Closed Wed, and Sun eve.*

Coaraze ✉ 06390

Coaraze, with its sundials and restored houses, seems to get more visitors than the other villages, perhaps because it has the most attractive mountain hideaway in the area.

L'Alivù, 816 Rte des Baisses, **t** 04 93 80 86 68, *www.alivu.com* (€€€–€€). *Gîte* run by a friendly woman, with rooms around a pretty pool with countryside views. Offers massage and a steam bath as well. Restaurant (€€). *Closed Nov–mid-Feb.*

has a colourful species the French call *chenilles processionnaires*, who enjoy a promenade in town every now and then. This time, the Contois had had enough; they called in the bishop of Nice, who brought inquisitors and exorcists, and made anathemas and proclamations until the caterpillars finally grew uncomfortable and went home. Such affairs were not uncommon, especially in old France. Animals, too, were considered subject to God's law; horses and dogs occasionally went on trial for their indiscretions when times were dull. Contes has another altarpiece in the Brea manner in its church, and down by the river a well-preserved forge with a water-powered hammer, near the communal olive oil press. Here, and in many villages in the mountains, oil presses are still in use.

The Valleys of the Vésubie and Tinée

The extensive valley of the river Vésubie is almost completely isolated from the regions to the east; from Lucéram the only ways across are the D21/D2566/D70 through the Col de Turini, or the miserable D2566/D73 directly over the mountains. There's an equally tortuous route from Contes, the D815/D19.

Levens to Lantosque

The Vésubie flows into the Var near **Levens**, a big walled village high on a small plain, with a big church and a scattering of small private art galleries. Beneath it, the main road up the valley, the D2565, follows the scenic **Gorges de la Vésubie**. From **St-Jean-la-Rivière**, at the end of the gorge, a winding 15km detour leads to

Getting around the Valleys of the Vésubie and Tinée

There are no **trains** in either the Vésubie or the Tinée valleys, and the **coach** service is sketchy.

St-Martin-Vésubie can be reached by **bus** from the *gare routière* in Nice (**Cars LA TRAM, t** 04 93 89 47 14); buses for St-Sauveur and St-Etienne in the Tinée also leave from here.

Roads in this area are as difficult as those to the east; service stations are few, so fill your tank whenever you get the opportunity.

the sanctuary of the **Madone d'Utelle**, one of the most popular pilgrimage sites in Provence, with a chapel full of naïve *ex votos* to *Notre-Dame-des-Miracles*, many from sailors, and a spectacular view as far as the sea. **Lantosque**, the next village up the valley from St-Jean, is a humble place that is regularly shaken by landslides and earthquakes. Lantosque was occupied by the Austrians in the Revolution; it's a joke in the other villages that you can always find someone in Lantosque named Otto.

St-Martin-Vésubie

At the top of the valley, St-Martin is the only town for a great distance in any direction, and a base for tackling the upper part of the Mercantour. It's as unaffectedly cute as a town can be, and once it was a spa of some repute. In the delightful and shady town square is an old fountain where the mineral waters used to flow, with inscriptions testifying to their 'organoleptic properties'.

The medieval centre is traversed by a lovely street (Rue du Docteur Cagnoli) with a mountain spring flowing down a narrow channel in the middle, as in a garden of the Alhambra. On this street you'll see an impressive Gothic mansion, the **Palais Gubernatis**, and the **parish church**, housing an altarpiece attributed to Brea and a polychrome wooden statue of the Virgin from the 14th century.

In the vicinity, **Venanson** is a beautiful village up in the mountains above St-Martin, with a small church full of frescoes by Giovanni Baleison. To the east, up into the Parc du Mercantour on the D94, the **Sanctuaire de la Madone de Fenestre** was an ancient holy site near the present Italian border; the name comes from a natural window in a nearby mountain peak. During the course of its long history the chapel has burned four times. In the Middle Ages the Templars held the site; they were massacred in the 14th century and their ghosts were often seen in the neighbourhood.

Hiking trails from here can take you on a very scenic route to the Vallée des Merveilles (*see* p.266). Another road from St-Martin, the D89, leads northwest up a valley between the peaks of **Mont Archas** and **Cime du Piagu** to the resort village of **Le Boréon**; this is a lovely area, with many hiking trails, a waterfall (near the village) and some mountain lakes near the Italian border.

The Valley of the Tinée

There's nothing splashy about the Tinée. People who love the Mercantour follow the slow D2205 along its length, from the N202 out of Nice up to the protected zone of the park. Skiers flock in winter to the modern resorts of Isola 2000 and Valberg. But outside their punctual visitations there is a sort of pious hush in this valley, which is serenely beautiful even by alpine standards. In the lower part of the valley, the scenery is as much indoors as out; prosperity during the 15th and 16th centuries allowed the villages of the lower Tinée to decorate their modest churches with fine Renaissance frescoes by artists of the Nice school.

The river flows into the Var with a climax at the **gorges**, across the mountains from Utelle. To the northeast, **La Tour** has frescoes from 1491 in its **Chapelle des Pénitents-Blancs**. Traditional subjects are represented: the *Passion* and a colourful *Last Judgement*, with Christ sitting on a rainbow and allegorical figures of the Seven Deadly Sins riding on fantastical animals, accompanying the damned to hell. The next paintings are at **Clans**, in two chapels just outside the village. **St-Antoine** offers more *Sins*, from an unknown, late 15th-century hand; they accompany some 20 rather peculiar scenes from the *Life of St Anthony* – cooking eggs and exorcising female demons. **St-Michel** has frescoes by an Italian named Andrea de Cella, *c.* 1515, including St Michael 'fishing for souls' – an odd conceit that goes back to the art of the Byzantine era. The **parish church** in the centre of the village has pictures too: surprisingly, a rare late medieval hunting scene. Next up the valley, there is a pleasant detour on the D2565 through **Valdeblore**, the only reasonable road through to the Vésubie. It begins at **Rimplas**, and the nearby **Chapelle de la Madeleine**, a conspicuous landmark occupying a gorgeous site overlooking the valley, and continues through **St-Dalmas**, where there is a large and sophisticated Romanesque church, the **Eglise de l'Invention de la Sainte-Croix**, with fragments of its original frescoes.

Continuing up the Tinée, the next stop is **St-Sauveur-sur-Tinée**, the throbbing metropolis of the valley, with its 496 souls. From here you can follow the Vionène valley west through the rugged and lovely villages of **Roure** and **Roubion**. The former, set amidst the biggest larch forest in Europe, has more painting: a Brea (attributed) altarpiece in the church of **St-Laurent**, and unusual frescoes of the lives of St Sebastian and St Bernard in the **chapel** outside the village. All these chapels outside villages, incidentally, are a regional peculiarity, set outside the gates as if to avert evil influences, and often dedicated to plague saints such as Sebastian. Roubion has a Sebastian chapel too, with another frescoed set of *Deadly Sins*.

Continuing in this direction, the next town is the modern ski resort of **Valberg**. There is alpine scenery in these parts, but little else; the best of it is in the long, lonely canyons stretching south off the D30/D28: the **Gorges Supérieures du Cians** and the **Gorges de Daluis**.

The uppermost part of the Tinée, following the D2205, runs through the northern half of the Parc du Mercantour, never more than a few kilometres from the Italian border. After St-Sauveur-sur-Tinée come the **Gorges de Valabres**, decorated with an EDF electric plant that somehow managed to sneak inside the park borders.

Isola, on the other side of the river, has two more appealing sights, both just off the D2205: a magnificently tall waterfall, the **Cascade de Louch**, and an impressive Romanesque **bell-tower**, the only survival from an abbey washed away by a flood 300 years ago. A good road takes you up to the Italian border and **Isola 2000**, a British-built, modern concrete ski resort that does good business because of its proximity to the coast. Everywhere else to the north is at ski level, and almost all the villages have learned to adapt their lives and habits to the seasonal invasions of ski-bunnies.

If you haven't yet had enough Renaissance frescoes, you may want to follow the Tinée to its source. In **Auron**, the 12th-century church of **St-Erige** has a sequence of paintings of that obscure Provençal saint, along with the Parisian St Denis, a stranger in these parts. **St-Etienne-de-Tinée** has two painted rural chapels: **St-Sébastien**, with a cycle of works by Canavesio and Baleison, in very bad shape, and the chapel of the **Couvent des Trinitaires**, where the subject is, of all things, the great naval victory of the Venetians and Spaniards over the Turks at Lepanto in 1571.

ⓘ **Levens** ››
*3 Placette de l'Olivier,
t 04 93 79 71 00, www.
levenstourisme.com;
open July and Aug
Tues–Sat and Sun am;
Sept–June Tues–Sat*

⭐ **La Vigneraie** ››

Market Days in the Valleys of the Vésubie and Tinée

Levens: Country show, first Sat in June.
St-Martin-Vésubie: Sat and Sun.

Where to Stay and Eat in the Valleys of the Vésubie and Tinée

In the mountains, look out for locally made liqueurs, an alpine speciality: *myrtille* (bilberry), pear or something called *genépi Meunier*, made from an alpine herb that is closely related to absinthe.

Levens ✉ 06670

★★La Vigneraie, 82, Route de St-Blaise, on Nice road south of village, t 04 93 79 77 60 (€). A very friendly *auberge* with comfortable rooms. Full board is a veritable bargain, and it would be madness not to take it at a hostelry that locals travel miles to visit for Sunday lunch in its restaurant (€€; *book early*). *Closed mid-Oct–mid-Feb.*

Lantosque ✉ 06450

★★★Hostellerie de l'Ancienne Gendarmerie, on riverbank, t 04 93 03 00 65, www.hotel-lantosque.com (€€). This hotel in a former police station occupies a pretty hillside site on the way up to the Parc du Mercantour, and has rooms looking on to the garden and a swimming pool. The restaurant (€€€) specializes in sea fish and *escargots. Closed Nov–Feb.*

① St-Martin-
Vésubie ›
Place Félix Faure,
t 04 93 03 21 28, www.
saintmartinvesubie.fr;
open summer daily,
winter Mon–Sat
and Sun am

St-Martin-Vésubie ✉ 06450

**La Bonne Auberge, Allée de Verdun, t 04 93 03 20 49, *www.labonne aubergeo6.fr* (€). A welcoming and pretty place with pleasant rooms and a cosy cellar restaurant (€€). *Closed mid-Nov–mid-Feb.*

Hôtel des Alpes, Place Félix Faure, t 04 93 03 21 06 (€). Modern hotel across the square from La Bonne Auberge.

Le Bella Vista, 1 Place St-Jean, Venanson, t 04 93 03 25 11 (€). A simple place outside St-Martin, with restaurant (€€). *Closed Mon in winter.*

La Treille, Rue du Docteur Cagnoli, t 04 93 03 30 85 (€€). The place to come for some of the best pizza this side of the border, baked in a proper pizza oven. Pasta and a few more ambitious dishes also crop up on the menu. *Closed Wed and Thurs in Dec and Jan.*

The Tinée Valley

Don't expect anything out of the ordinary in the little-visited Tinée valley: simple country inns with restaurants are the rule.

Auberge St-Jean, Clans ✉ 06420, t 04 93 02 90 21 (€). A simple inn with just two rooms. *Closed 2 weeks Feb and 2 weeks Sept.*

Chalet du Val de Blore, Valdeblore ✉ 06420, D2565, west of St-Dalmas, t 04 93 02 83 29 (€). Family hotel with 35 basic rooms in a modern chalet building, and a restaurant serving Niçois home cooking. In summer, a 7-night minimum stay. *Closed Nov.*

The Alpes de Haute-Provence North

Clearly we find ourselves in a place that is out of the ordinary. You need a strong character, and a little bit of soul.

Jean Giono

① Alpes de
Haute-Provence
*Maison des Alpes de
Haute-Provence,
Immeuble François
Mitterrand–BP 170,
✉ 04005 Digne-les-
Bains, t 04 92 31 57 29*

There is something of the Wild West in the *département* of Alpes de Haute-Provence, which comes complete with lofty plateaux and canyons; it even has a Grand Canyon of its own. Provence's wide open spaces are full of lavender fields and fresh air, and are a wonderful place to whitewater raft, hang-glide, horse-ride, climb or hike. The **Maison des Alpes de Haute-Provence** publishes some free and extremely useful practical guides to the region.

Villars-sur-Var to Entrevaux along the N202

The N202 is the east–west traffic chute, following the upper Var, and the only convenient way to get through the mountains north of Grasse. It isn't scenic, though the gravelly, impossibly blue Var makes a refreshing sight alongside; it may, however, be an antidote to claustrophobia after traversing too many gorges.

The trip begins with a local novelty – wine – at **Villars-sur-Var**. The centre of the only, tiny AOC wine region in the mountains, Villars was almost abandoned before the awarding of the *dénomination* in the 1970s. Production has vastly increased since then, and you'll occasionally see this variety of Côtes-de-Provence (*see* p.294) in trendy restaurants on the coast – perhaps more for its curiosity value than for anything else. The village **church** has a few Renaissance pieces: a retable of St John the Baptist and an Italian fresco of the *Annunciation*, both anonymous works from the early 16th century.

Getting around along the N202

Buses are so rare they aren't worth the trouble, but it can be fun seeing this region by riding the scenic, recently modernized **narrow-gauge rail line** from Nice to Digne, familiarly called the **Train des Pignes**. It follows the Var, and some trains stop at villages along the way: Villars-sur-Var, Puget-Théniers, Entrevaux and Annot. This is not the SNCF but a line called **Chemins de Fer de Provence** (in Digne, call **t** 04 92 31 01 58 for details; in Nice go to the Gare du Sud, 4bis Rue Alfred Binet; or check *www.trainprovence.com*). At weekends May–Oct, a **steam train** runs from Puget-Théniers to Annot.

⊕ **Train des Pignes** ∧

Next comes a postcard shot: **Touët-sur-Var**, seemingly pasted up on the side of a cliff, with much of its medieval defences intact. **Puget-Théniers**, the biggest village on this stretch of the Var, is more open and welcoming, a shady oasis after the stark mountain landscapes, where you may stop for lunch and look at more pictures. There are two genuine jewels among a number of altarpieces in the parish **church**: Antoine Ronzen's *Notre-Dame-du-Secours* and Mathieu d'Anvers' *Passion*, both done about 1525. A **monument** by Aristide Maillol in the town square commemorates Puget's pride: a local boy named Auguste Blanqui, who became a journalist and one of the leaders of the Paris Commune in 1870, for which he paid by spending 36 years in prison.

Under the sweeping twist of its cliffs, **Entrevaux** is the strategic key to the valley. There has been a fort of some kind here since Roman times, and its present incarnation is particularly impressive – the work of Louis XIV's celebrated engineer Sébastien Vauban, high above the village, complete with Second World War additions. At the time it was built, the French-Piedmontese border was only a few miles away (it is now the departmental boundary between Var and Alpes-Maritimes). The entrance is a fortified bridge, rebuilt by Vauban on medieval foundations.

Entrevaux cathedral
contact tourist office for opening hours and adm; guided tours available

Around the village, vestiges of its old garrison days can be seen: barracks and powder-houses, and an ancient drawbridge, still in working order, behind the 17th-century **cathedral**. There's a honeycomb of buildings and narrow alleys where people live; if you wander through the smelly damp alleys there are flowers high up in the windows, duvets thrown over the sills in the mornings. The serious part of the fort is a hard 15-minute climb if you're fit; take water, a sunhat, some historical imagination and some coins for the turnstile and you're on your own to explore the derelict tunnels and dungeons – once deliciously dangerous, now undergoing restoration to make them safe.

Musée de la Moto
t 04 93 79 12 70; open May–Oct daily 10–12.30 and 2–6; closed Nov–April

The landscape below, with the little Train des Pignes (*see* above), is as unlikely as an alpine train set. Try to get up there before 9am, when the first of the coaches are beginning to fit themselves in below. Harley fans will enjoy Entrevaux's **Musée de la Moto**, a collection of motorcycles from 1901 to 1967.

Market Days in the Var Valley

Puget-Théniers: Sun.
Entrevaux: Fri am.

ⓘ **Entrevaux >>**
Porte Royale du Pont-Levis, t 04 93 05 46 73, www.entrevaux.info; open mid-Jan–Nov daily; closed Dec–mid-Jan

ⓘ **Puget-Théniers >**
t 04 93 05 05 05, www.provence-val-dazur.com; open April–Nov daily; Dec–Mar Mon–Fri

Where to Stay and Eat in the Var Valley

Because it's the only good road across this region, the N202 has the best selection of places to stay and eat, including a few that are rather better than the average *routier*.

Touët-sur-Var ⊠ 06710

Restaurant des Chasseurs, t 04 93 05 71 11 (€€). Appreciative locals come here to enjoy fish and game; try the ravioli and the rabbit stew. There are also a few rooms (€€) to stay in.

Puget-Théniers ⊠ 06260

**Hôtel Alizé, RN 202, t 04 93 05 06 20 (€). Fifteen rooms but no restaurant. *Closed Christmas and New Year.*

Les Acacias, Le Planet, t 04 93 05 05 25 (€€). A great place to dine, featuring duck, pigeon and rabbit prepared in some imaginative ways. *Closed Wed.*

Entrevaux ⊠ 04320

**Hôtel-Restaurant Le Vauban, 4 Place Louis Moreau, t 04 93 05 42 40, *www.hotel-le-vauban.com* (€). The only hotel in Entrevaux, with a restaurant (€€). *Restaurant closed Sun eve and Mon except in mid-July–Aug.*

Mme Gaydon, t 04 93 05 06 91 (€). *Chambres d'hôtes* in a farm with lots of animals, and kitchenettes in the rooms, although breakfast is offered.

La Crêperie du Chevalier, Rue Basse, t 04 93 05 43 68 (€). Delicious crêpes. *Closed Nov–Jan.*

Le Pont-Levis, Place Louis Moreau, t 04 93 05 40 12 (€€). Good cuisine and a great view of the fort, village and valley. *Closed Fri and Dec.*

The *Clues* and the Esteron Valley

South of the Var is a grim and lonely region; you can see Nice and Cannes from the summit of the **Montagne du Cheiron** in its centre, but from here the Riviera beaches seem a world away. A *clue*, or more properly *cluse*, is a transverse valley, formed between the limestone folds of the mountains; here the name is given to the many narrow gorges that make life and communications in the area difficult. Local villages are humble and crumbling and few, and the roads across are winding and exasperating.

From Puget-Théniers, the D2211A/D17 takes you to **Roquesteron**, a fortified village divided into two parts (before 1860 one was Piedmontese, one French). West of the village, a bad road, the D10, leads off into the isolated **Clue d'Aiglun**, perhaps the most dramatic of the *clues*, with a big waterfall. On the other side of the mountains, the D2211A leads to **Briançonnet**, a spectral village with great views and bits of Roman inscriptions built into the old houses; beyond here is the **Clue de St-Auban**.

The more southerly route – which has a choice of roads running east–west, some of them conveniently reached from Vence or Nice – passes some lovely *villages perchés*: **Bézaudun-les-Alpes**, **Coursegoules**, **Gréolières** and **Cipières** (follow the D1/D8/D2 from Carros on the Var, to the north of Nice), all of which are starting to be colonized by people from the Riviera. Gréolières, under the Montagne du Cheiron, has an enormous ruined castle; from here you can follow the D603 into the **Gorges du Loup** towards Grasse, or take the D2/D802 on to the Cheiron and the new ski station of **Gréolières-les-Neiges**.

The Lac du Castillon and Mumbo Jumbo

After Entrevaux, the Var turns northwards, while the main road continues west, past the charming, modest mountain resort of **Annot** and the **Gorges du Galange**. Further west, the country becomes even stranger and lonelier; long monotonous stretches lull you to sleep until suddenly the road sinks into a wild gorge, or confronts a patch of striated mountains that look like gigantic *millefeuille* pastries tumbled over the landscape. Grey is the predominant colour, making a startling contrast with the opaque blue sheet of the **Lac de Castillon**, backed up behind the Barrage de Castillon, a mighty 292ft concrete dam begun in 1942 under the Vichy government, with a distinctly grim, wartime look about it. **St-André-les-Alpes**, on the north end of the lake, is France's hang-gliding capital. And what is that warped theme park on the west shore? Why, that's **Mandarom Shambhasalem**, the centre of Aumism, a fruitcake of a cult that half-bakes bits of every religion into its mix. You can visit most afternoons (take the road up from Castellane): the cult statues of the world's religious élite are enough to make the average *santon* look like a Michelangelo.

Castellane

Castellane, which lies a few kilometres to the south of the lake, has become the capital of the Grand Canyon and the base for visiting what must be considered one of the greatest natural wonders in the whole of Europe. The town is centred round a pretty square full of plane trees (the grilles surrounding the trees are have been designed in the shapes of plane leaves) where local people come to challenge one another at a game or two of *boules* and to hang out amiably, taking the air and shooting the breeze. But its edges are inundated with up-to-the-minute sports shops supplying slick whizz-gimmickry for any sport you could or couldn't conceive of (such as bungee-jumping).

The village also contains a pretty *mairie* and a **church**, where the 597ft ascent up Castellane's landmark square rock begins: you can either pick up the key for the chapel on top from outside the *curé*'s house, or else collect it on your way up from the last person coming down. Castellane's snappy motto, 'Napoleon stopped here. Why don't you?', comes from its spot on the **Route Napoléon**, the road that was taken by the emperor on his return from the island of Elba. These days it's a tourist trail starting from Napoleon's landing point at Golfe Juan and ending at his destination, Grenoble.

Market Days in Castellane

Castellane: Wed and Sat.

Where to Stay and Eat in Castellane

ⓘ Castellane >
Rue Nationale,
t 04 92 83 61 14,
www.castellane.org;
open daily; offers
guided tours

Castellane ✉ 04120

***Nouvel Hôtel du Commerce, Place de l'Eglise, t 04 92 83 61 00, *www. hotel-fradet.com* (€€). A friendly and comfortable choice. The restaurant serves a range of Provençal cuisine on a terrace. *Closed mid-Oct–mid-Mar; restaurant closed Tues, and Wed lunch.*

**Grand Canyon du Verdon, Falaise des Cavaliers, 14km east of village of Aiguines, t 04 94 76 91 31 (€€). A hotel with 15 rooms, 10 with balcony, and a glassed-in restaurant terrace looking down 984ft on to the Canyon. *Closed*

mid-Oct–Mar; restaurant closed Mon eve and Wed.

**Ma Petite Auberge, Bd de la République, t 04 92 83 62 06, *www. provence.guideweb.com/hotel/ ma-petite-auberge* (€€–€). Fifteen plain rooms and a restaurant (€€). *Closed Wed, Thurs out of season,Thurs lunch July and Aug, and Nov–Feb.*

**Hôtel La Forge, Place de l'Eglise, t 04 92 83 62 61, *http://pagesperso-orange.fr/forges/index-fichiers/ pages382.htm* (€). Reasonably priced option with a terrace from which to view the village, and a restaurant. *Closed mid-Dec–Jan; restaurant closed Fri eve and Sat except July and Aug.*

Moulin de la Salaou, Route des Gorges du Verdon, t 04 92 83 78 97, *www. moulin-salaou.com* (€). A 17th-century mill converted into a hotel with a restaurant (€€). Situated just outside the town, it has beautiful views and is very family-friendly. *Closed Nov–Mar.*

⭐ Grand Canyon du Verdon

The Grand Canyon du Verdon

The most surprising thing about the Grand Canyon du Verdon is that it was not 'discovered' until 1905. That the most spectacular canyon on the continent could be so overlooked speaks volumes about the French – their long-held aversion to nature, which they are now working so enthusiastically to correct, and the traditional disdain of Parisian authorities for the Midi. The locals always knew about it, of course; agriculturally useless and almost inaccessible, the 21km canyon had an evil reputation for centuries as a haunt of devils and 'wild men'. Even after a famous speleologist named Edouard-Alfred Martel brought it to the world's attention at the beginning of the 20th century, many Frenchmen weren't impressed. In the 1950s the government decided to flood the whole thing for another dam; when the plan was finally abandoned, it was for reasons of cost, not natural preservation.

The name 'Grand Canyon' was a modern idea. Like its Arizona counterpart it does put on a grand show: sheer limestone cliffs as much as half a kilometre apart, snaking back and forth to follow the meandering course of the Verdon; in many places there are vast panoramas down the length of it. There are roads along both sides, though not for the entire distance. Most of the best views are from the so-called **Corniche Sublime** (D71) on the southern side; if you want to explore the bottom, ask about trails and the best way to approach them (it's a long trek) at the tourist information office in Castellane.

The lands south of the canyon are some of the most desolate in France; you will find them either romantic or tiresome depending on your mood. But either mood will be definitely broken when columns of tanks and missile-carriers come rattling up the road. The army has appropriated almost all of this area, the **Grand Plan de Canjuers**, for manoeuvres and target practice; you'll see their base camp on the D955 towards Draguignan.

Directly west of the canyon, a less spectacular section of the Verdon has indeed been dammed up, forming the enormous **Lac de Ste-Croix**. There is yet another dam further downstream, and the next 40km of the river valley are underwater too: the **Gorges du Verdon**, in parts as good as the Grand Canyon, but sacrificed forever to the beaverish Paris planners. It's wild country on both sides, and access is limited since the roads are few. Beyond the dam, on the way to Manosque and the Luberon, **Gréoux-les-Bains**, with its above-average number of launderettes and poodles, is a favourite with the rheumatic set, who regularly treat their aching bones to a jolt of sulphurous, radioactive water at the baths. It is a clinical, eerie, hairdresser-smelling place, with New Age oddities on sale. This was a fashionable resort in the early 19th century, when Napoleon's tearaway sister Pauline Borghese dropped by, but that's about it. The village turns its back on the shabby castle, built in the 12th century by the Templars, which is occasionally used as a theatre and houses the tourist office.

Slightly further east on the banks of the Gorges du Verdon, **Quinson** has plenty of outdoor pursuits on offer, such as kayaking and hiking, as well as the Norman Foster-designed **Musée de la Préhistoire des Gorges du Verdon**, which claims to be the biggest of its kind in Europe. There are also reconstructed prehistoric huts nearby on the banks of the river.

Musée de la Préhistoire des Gorges du Verdon
t 04 92 74 09 59; www. museeprehistoire.com; open July and Aug daily 10–8; April–June and Sept Wed–Mon 10–7; Oct–15 Dec and Feb–Mar Wed-Mon 10–6; closed 16 Dec–Jan; adm

Riez and Moustiers

The **Plateau de Valensole**, north of the Verdon and the Lac de Ste-Croix, is a hot, dry plain of olive and almond trees, and one of the big lavender-growing areas of Provence – come in July to see it in full bloom. **Riez**, in the middle, is an old centre for lavender-distilling, now adapted to tourism. Ruined medieval houses have been restored, and artists and potters have moved in. It's pretty but bustling, a good place to dawdle in. Riez was an important Celtic religious site, though it isn't clear exactly which deity it honoured. Testimonies to later piety can be seen at the western edge of town, thought to have been the centre of Roman-era Riez: four standing columns of a **Roman temple** of Apollo, and a 6th-century **baptistry** that is one of the few surviving monuments in France from the Merovingian era. Octagonal, like most early Christian baptistries, it has eight recycled Roman columns and capitals; all the rest was heavily restored during the 19th century. Inside the medieval gates of the town are two pretty fountains that were recycled from Roman remains, and a number of modest palaces and chapels that recall the town's prosperity in the 16th to 18th centuries. Fourteen kilometres west of Riez, introspective, overlooked **Valensole** is an ancient village built over the ruins of its Roman predecessor.

Some 15km to the east on the D952, **Moustiers-Ste-Marie** gets all the attention, spectacularly hanging on the west cliffs of the Grand Canyon du Verdon. Like Castellane on the other side, it is a popular base for visiting the canyon, and gets busy in summer. The town will be familiar to anyone who haunts the museums of the Midi, as Moustiers in the old days was Provence's famous centre for painted ceramics. The blue and yellow faïences, usually painted with country scenes or floral designs, were often works of art in their own right; first popular in the time of Louis XIV, they were made here as late as the 1870s. Today, a large number of potters, some of them talented and some of them pretty awful, clutter the village streets, capitalizing on the perfect clay of the region (and on the tourists). You can compare their efforts with the originals at the **Musée de la Faïence**, a small collection on Place du Presbytère.

In the middle of the village is the deep-set 12th-century parish **church**, with a kink in it. Moustiers' other distinction, as everyone in Provence knows, is the **Cadeno de Moustié**, a 783ft chain suspended between the tops of two peaks overlooking the village. A knight of the local Blacas family, while a prisoner of the Saracens during the Crusades, made a vow to put it up if he ever saw home again; the star in the middle comes from his coat of arms. The original was stolen in the Wars of Religion and a replacement didn't appear until 1957. A climb up under the chain will take you to the **Chapelle Notre-Dame-de-Beauvoir**, where a notice piously requests that pilgrims do not write on the walls but inscribe their names on the heart of the Virgin instead.

Musée de la Faïence

t 04 92 74 61 64; open July and Aug Wed–Mon 9–12 and 2–7; April–June and Sept–Oct Wed–Mon 9–12 and 2–6; Nov–Mar Sat 9–12 and 2–6, Sun 9–12; school hols Mon and Wed–Fri 2–5; adm

(i) **Parc Naturel du Verdon**

t 04 92 74 68 00, www.parcduverdon.fr

(i) **Quinson**

Chapelle de la Rue St-Esprit, t 04 92 74 01 12, www.quinson.fr; open July and Aug daily; Sept–June Mon and Wed–Sat; has detailed lists of park activities

(i) **Riez**

4 Place de la Mairie, t 04 92 77 99 09, www.ville-riez.fr; open Mon–Sat and Sun am

(i) **Moustiers-Ste-Marie ›**

Maison de Lucie, Place de l'Eglise, t 04 92 74 67 84, www.moustiers.fr; open daily all year

(★) **La Bastide de Moustiers ›**

Market Days in the Grand Canyon

Riez: Wed and Sat.
Moustiers: Fri.

Where to Stay and Eat in the Grand Canyon

Moustiers-Ste-Marie ✉ 04360

★★★★**La Bastide de Moustiers**, just outside the village at La Grisolière, t 04 92 70 47 47, *www.bastide-moustiers.com* (€€€€€). Celebrity chef Alain Ducasse's 17th-century hotel, with 12 individually fashioned and comfortable rooms, a Jacuzzi, a swimming pool, a riding stable and more besides. The food is predominantly local, picked fresh from the kitchen garden, and innovative – herb and vegetable tart, then spit-roasted baron of lamb, followed by cherry *clafoutis* could be one memorable dinner. *Restaurant closed Jan, plus Mon, Tues and Wed in Feb.*

★★**Le Belvédère**, t 04 92 74 66 04 (€). An affordable option up in the village, with its own restaurant. *Closed Oct–April; restaurant closed mid-Dec–Feb.*

Les Santons, Place de l'Eglise, **t** 04 92 74 66 48, *www.lessantons.com* (€€€–€€). A restaurant with a gorgeous setting up at the top of the village; the standard of cooking matches the superlative views. *Book well in advance. Closed Mon eve and Jan.*

Also Worthy of Your Attention...

Digne means 'worthy', and one suspects a degree of deliberate etymological mutation in the gradual name change from the local Gaulish tribe, the Bodiontici, whose capital this was, to Roman Dinia, and finally to **Digne-les-Bains**. The capital of *département* 04 (Alpes de Haute-Provence), and the only city in a long stretch of mountains between Orange and Turin, over in Italy, Digne has a single thriving boulevard of cafés and touristic knick-knackery mixed with smart shoe shops, posh chocolates and bookshops. It has recently rediscovered its role as a spa, and holds a *Festival de Théâtre* in early July. In the town's minuscule medieval centre you can see the crumbling 15th-century **Cathédrale St-Jérôme**; this and its surrounding brightly painted houses stand shoulder-to-shoulder with some daring grey municipal buildings.

Out of town at 27 Av du Maréchal Juin is something unexpected: the **Fondation Alexandra David-Néel**, the former home of a remarkable Frenchwoman who settled here in her 'Himalayas in miniature' after a lifetime exploring in Tibet. Ms David-Néel called this house *Samten Dzong*, the 'castle of meditation', and Tibetan Buddhist monks attended her when she died here in 1969 at the age of 101. The Dalai Lama has since come twice to visit. There are exhibits of Tibetan art and culture, photographs and Tibetan crafts on sale. In summer, there are up to 40 people crammed into this tiny museum, so be prepared to wait in the garden. Staff will be happy to play the commentary in English if you ask.

At Place Paradis there is an old bunker in the hillside housing the **Musée de la Seconde Guerre Mondiale**, a museum about the last world war. At Parc St-Benoît, the **Musée Promenade**, which forms part of the Réserve Géologique de Haute-Provence, houses the largest geology collection in Europe, including an impressive wall

Fondation Alexandra David-Néel
t 04 92 31 32 38, www.alexandra-david-neel.org; guided tours daily 10, 2 and 3.30

Musée de la Seconde Guerre Mondiale
t 04 92 31 28 95; open July and Aug Mon–Thurs 2–6, Fri 2–5.30; mid-April–June and Sept–Oct Wed 2–5; closed Nov–mid-April

Musée Promenade
t 04 92 36 70 70; open July and Aug Mon–Fri 9–11 and 2–7, Sat and Sun 10.30–12.30 and 2–7; April–June and Sept–Oct Sat–Thurs 9–12 and 2–5.30, Fri 9–12 and 2–4.30; Nov–Mar Mon–Thurs 9–12 and 2–5.30, Fri 9–12 and 2–4.30; adm

ⓘ **Digne-les-Bains >**
Rond-Point du 11 Novembre, t 04 92 36 62 62, www.ot-dignelesbains.fr; open July–Aug daily; Sept–June Mon–Sat

★ **Hôtel de Provence >>**

Market Days in Digne-les-Bains

Digne-les-Bains: Wed and Sat.

Where to Stay and Eat in Digne-les-Bains

Digne-les-Bains ✉ 04000

****Le Grand Paris, 19 Bd Thiers, **t** 04 92 31 11 15, *www.hotel-grand-paris.com* (€€€– €€). A distinguished hotel set in a restored 17th-century monastery, with excellent restaurant (€€€). *Closed Dec–Feb; restaurant closed Mon lunch, Tues lunch and Wed lunch in winter.*

Hôtel de Provence, 17 Bd Thiers, **t 04 92 31 32 19, *www.hotel-alpes-provence. com* (€). A centrally located, typical, friendly little *pension de famille* with comfortable rooms. Renovated in 2008.

of ammonites. There is also a small collection of archaeological finds, which includes an altar with bull horns.

Follow Boulevard Gassendi to the eastern edge of town, passing the peculiar neoclassical **Grande Fontaine** (1829), and you will find Digne's former cathedral, **Notre-Dame-du-Bourg**, a large Lombard-style Romanesque building of the 12th century, complete with a bell-tower of that date, a deep-set Romanesque arch below a beautiful rose window, and fresco fragments.

The Alpes de Haute-Provence South

If you get off the motorway, the route across the Var from Grasse to Aix-en-Provence takes you through some charming villages, and some not so charming. Within an hour it can show you lush green landscapes, as well as lonely steel-grey plateaux. The greener parts are wine-growing country too, falling within the largest AOC region in France, Côtes-de-Provence.

From Fayence to Draguignan

This first leg of the journey is close enough to the coast to have become thoroughly colonized by the holiday-home set.

Fayence, a large village of moderate cuteness, has plenty of Englishmen and estate agents. Built on a steep hillside like Grasse, its road winds back and forth up to the centre, which is pleasant enough: there is a *mairie* perched on an arch over the main street, a forgotten 18th-century **church** and a view not to be missed from the **Tour de l'Horloge** at the very top of the village. Check the view you see against the ceramic panoramas painted and baked into tiles under your hands.

North of Fayence is some lovely, wild countryside; off the D37, **Roche Taillée** has a Roman aqueduct still in use, entirely carved out of the rock, along a steady descent of some 5km. Also from the D37, you'll see the towers of an impressive 17th-century castle, the **Château de Beauregard**, a private home. Further north, **Mons** is a beautiful and strange village of narrow streets overhung with arches. The language of its inhabitants still conserves some Ligurian Italian words; the people of Mons were totally wiped out in the Black Death of 1348, and colonists from the area around Genoa and Ventimiglia were brought in to replace them. There are a large numbers of **dolmens** in the area; some are inaccessibly located on the base of the Canjuers army camp, 2km away.

West of Fayence, the old farmhouses may now all be bijoux holiday homes, but the scenery is captivating; the main road, the D562 to Draguignan, is fine, but even better is the winding

Getting around the Alpes de Haute-Provence South

The main Provençal **railway** follows the motorway from Aix-en-Provence and Marseille to Cannes; for Draguignan you'll usually have to change at Les Arcs. Draguignan and Brignoles are well served by train.

Draguignan is also the hub for inter-village **buses**, though as always these are few and generally inconvenient. There are several buses daily to Grasse, stopping off at Bargemon, Seillans and Fayence along the way, and several daily travelling in the other direction, to Tourtour and Aups, with at best one or two to the other villages.

Driving in this southern half of the Provençal mountains is much less trouble than it is in the areas to the north and east; roads are better and service facilities are more common. You can take the A8 motorway straight across and miss everything, but the villages to the east and west of Draguignan offer some of the most delightful opportunities for casual touring in Provence; it's good **bicycling** country too.

There are two possible itineraries to consider: from Fayence (west of Grasse on the D562) to Le Muy, through the lovely villages along the D19 and D25 (the latter is the wine route); or from Draguignan, west on the D557, dipping into the mountains on the D77 for Aups, then the D22 for Sillans-la-Cascade and Cotignac, and westwards again (D32) to Fox-Amphoux or (D560) Barjols.

Orange Tree Galerie
www.theorangetree
galerie.com; open
Thurs–Sat 2.30–6.30

D19/D25, passing through three pretty villages. **Seillans**, with its cobbled streets leading up to the restored castle, has been occupied since the time of the Ligurians. It's one of the most beautiful villages in France and it's got a plaque to prove it. The village lives on flowers, and was the last home of Surrealist Max Ernst; visit the little **Orange Tree Galerie** on Route de Bargemon to see modern paintings and some Elisabeth Frink sculptures.

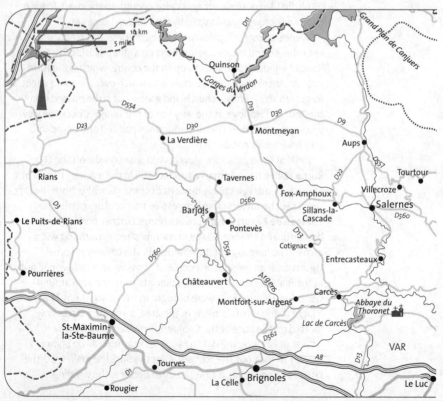

Bargemon, further west, is just as old; behind its medieval gates are fountains and a 15th-century church with a Flamboyant-Gothic portal and heads sculpted by Pierre Puget. It leapt to fame when the ubiquitous Posh and Becks acquired a holiday home there. From here you can take a detour north through the depressing Canjuers military zone to **Bargème**, the highest village in the Var (3,589ft), which is still encircled by its walls and ruined castle, although only a few people live there year-round to enjoy it.

Last before you reach Draguignan is **Callas**, which lies beneath a ruined castle. The D25 south of Callas, as far as Le Muy, is a beautiful drive through forests, with the **Gorges de Pennafort** and a waterfall along the way; it is also one of the best wine roads in the region, with a few places to stop and sample Côtes-de-Provence along the way (*see* p.294).

Draguignan

Draguignan gets a bad press, especially from the timid English: ugly, depraved, full of soldiers; avoid it if you can... Tough, sharp-edged Draguignan is not French so much as French Colonial. The army owns it – it's the biggest base in France – and its dusty, palm-shaded boulevards (laid out in 1849 by Baron Haussmann, *préfet* of

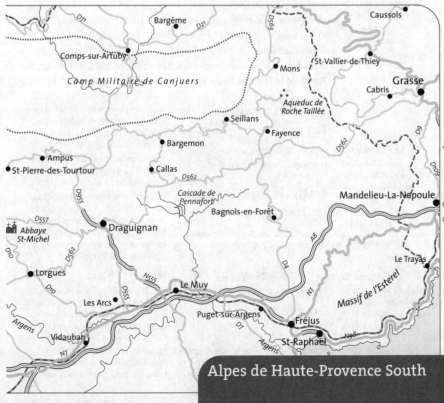

Alpes de Haute-Provence South

the Var, who treated the town to a trial run of his urban planning efforts in Paris) pass the national schools of artillery and military science. Draguignan's symbol is the *drac* – another Provençal dragon, chased out by an early bishop, though its fire-spitting image can still be seen everywhere. Draguignan could be Saigon or Algiers or Dakar, a cinematic fantasy in a wreath of Gauloises smoke, waiting for the Warner Bros cameras to capture Bogart, Lorre and Greenstreet conspiring in some tawdry nightclub.

Have your papers in order and try not to exceed the speed limits. Touring in Provence you'll be bound to pass through here, and it's a pleasant stop, really. The Saturday **market** is especially good, and there are a few things to see: the 17th-century **Tour de l'Horloge**, Draguignan's architectural pride; and a small **Musée Municipal** at 9 Rue de la République, with a picture gallery (including *Child Blowing a Soap Bubble*, by Rembrandt, a portrait by Camille Claudel, faïences from Moustiers and porcelain from China).

The Musée des Arts et Traditions Populaires offers an overview of everything that you'll never see in the real Provence any more – anything from mules to silk culture, along with reconstructions of scenes of country life. A pretty old merry-go-round with painted horses steals the show. There's an **American war cemetery** and memorial on Bd Kennedy, with a bronze map tracing the route of the approximately 150,000 men of the 7th army who disembarked in the south of France in the two weeks following D-Day.

Just outside town, on the D955 towards the Canyon du Verdon, is one of the biggest and most spectacular dolmens in Provence, the **Pierre de la Fée**; the table stone weighs 20 tonnes.

Musée Municipal
t 04 98 10 26 85;
open Mon 2–6, Tues–Sat
9–12 and 2–6

**Musée des Arts
et Traditions
Populaires**
15 Rue Joseph
Roumanille, t 04 94 47
05 72, www.dracenie.
com/museecollection.
htm; open Tues–Sat
10–12 and 2–6,
Sun 2–6; adm

(i) Fayence >
Place Léon Roux,
t 04 94 76 20 08, www.
paysdefayence.com;
open mid-June–mid-
Sept Mon–Sat and Sun
am; mid-Sept–mid-June
Mon–Sat

(i) Seillans >>
1 Rue du Valat, t 04 94
76 85 91, www.seillans-
var.com; open Tues–Fri,
Mon pm and Sat pm

 Moulin de la
Camandoule >

Market Days from Fayence to Draguignan

Fayence: Tues, Thurs and Sat.
Draguignan: Wed and Sat.

Festivals from Fayence to Draguignan

Callas: *Festival de Musique Ancienne*, late July, t 04 94 76 61 07.

Where to Stay and Eat from Fayence to Draguignan

Fayence ✉ 83440
***Moulin de la Camandoule, Chemin de Notre-Dame-des-Cyprès, t 04 94 76 00 84, www.camandoule.com (€€€). A lovely old olive-oil mill, restored by a British couple and including a garden, pool and restaurant. *Restaurant closed Jan.*

**Auberge de la Fontaine, Route de Fréjus, t 04 94 76 07 59 (€). A basic, family-run hotel and restaurant (€€).

Le Castellaras, Chemin Le Banegon, Route de Seillans, t 04 94 76 13 80, www.restaurant-castellaras.com (€€€). Refined, sunny cuisine such as courgette flowers and ratatouille, plus a great wine list. *Closed Tues.*

Seillans ✉ 83440
***Les Deux Rocs, Place Font-d'Amont, t 04 94 76 87 32, www.hoteldeuxrocs. com (€€€–€€). A highly recommended hotel where you're assured of a warm English-speaking welcome. There are 14 rooms and near-perfect food, including sublime desserts. It's a favourite among Americans. *Closed*

ⓘ Draguignan >

2 Av Lazare Carnot,
t 04 98 105 105,
www.dracenie.com;
open July and Aug
Mon–Sat and Sun am;
May–June and Sept
Mon–Sat; Oct–April
Mon–Fri and Sat am;
guided tours in summer
twice daily

Jan; restaurant closed Sun eve, Mon and Tues lunch; just Mon in summer.

Bargemon ✉ 83830

★★Auberge des Arcades, Av Pasteur, t 04 94 76 60 36 (€€). A noisy and slightly run-down but serviceable option with its own restaurant (€€€–€€). Closed Jan; restaurant closed Mon and Tues in winter.

Draguignan ✉ 83300

★★Le Col de l'Ange, Av de Tuttlingen, on D557 towards Lorgues, t 04 94 68

23 01, www.hotel-etoiles-ange-draguignan.federal-hotel.com (€€). The only really decent place in the area, situated outside of the town itself and offering clean and modern if somewhat characterless rooms. The view makes up for it. Restaurant closed Mon lunch.

Lou Galoubet, 23 Bd Jean Jaurès, t 04 94 68 08 50, www.lougaloubet.fr (€€€–€€). A restaurant serving a selection of good seafood dishes. Closed Sun eve, Tues eve and Wed, and mid-July–mid-Aug.

Villages of the Central Var

As you head west from Draguignan, you have two choices. If aesthetics are a bigger consideration than time, don't bother with the A8 motorway or the parallel road through Brignoles and St-Maximin-la-Ste-Baume; instead, take the D557 or D562 directly west for a leisurely tour through some of Provence's loveliest, most typical landscapes. Though this area gets its share of foreign and Parisian summer folk, it isn't quite chic – compared with similar but totally colonized places like the Luberon. But there's enough lavender and blowing cypresses, plenty of wine, and a dozen relentlessly charming villages that won't trouble you with any strenuous sightseeing.

From Lorgues to Aups

Lorgues is the first village, with an ensemble of 18th-century municipal decorations: a fountain, the huge, dignified church of **St-Martin**, and the inevitable avenue of plane trees – one of the longest and fairest in Provence. To the north, along the D10, you'll pass the **Abbaye St-Michel**, a recently refounded Russian Orthodox monastery; its handmade wooden chapel, a replica of a Russian church, may be visited. Further north, there are a number of pretty villages around the valley of the Nartuby: **Ampus**, **Tourtour**, over-restored but up on a height with views down to the sea, and **Villecroze**, with its vaulted lanes. At the edge of the Grand Plan de Canjuers, Villecroze is built up against a tufa cliff; there is an unusual park at the base of it, with a small waterfall and a cave-house that was dug into the rock in the 16th century.

Aups was a Ligurian settlement and a Roman town; its name comes from the same ancient root as 'Alps'. It has a reputation for being different; a monument in the town square records Aups' finest hour, when the citizens put up a doomed republican resistance to Louis-Napoléon's coup of 1851. The village is known in the region for its Thursday truffle market, held through the winter

Musée Simon Segal
t 04 94 70 01 95; open mid-June–mid-Sept daily 10–12 and 4–7; adm

months. The village **church** is oddly below surface level; the ground level around it was raised to avoid the frequent flooding of the old days. Aups, like the other villages, has not completely escaped Riviera modernism. The **Musée Simon Segal** on Avenue Albert Iᵉʳ, founded by an eponymous Russian artist, contains his and other 20th-century works.

Salernes, south of Aups, has been known for more than 200 years as a manufacturer of tiles – the small, hexagonal terracotta floor-tiles called *tomettes* that are as much a trademark of Provence as lavender. They still make them, and, in a day when French factory-made tiles all come in insipid beige, they are at a premium. Lately Salernes' factories and individual artisans have been expanding into coloured ceramics and pottery; there are a few shops in the village and factory showrooms on the outskirts. Despite such a workmanlike background, the village itself is rather drab, with a medieval fountain and a simple 13th-century church in the centre.

Further west, Sillans has lately been calling itself **Sillans-la-Cascade**, to draw attention to the 118ft waterfall just south of the village (it dries up in summer). Beyond that, **Fox-Amphoux** is worth a visit just to hear the locals pronounce the name; this minuscule, well-restored village of stepped medieval alleys sits on a defensible height. There is a ruined castle and, on the trail to the hamlet of **Amphoux**, an odd cave-chapel, **Notre-Dame-du-Secours**, hung with *ex votos*, many from sailors.

South of Salernes, **Entrecasteaux** is dominated by a 17th-century castle, completely restored in the 1970s by a Scotsman named McGarvie-Munn; visitors are admitted, but there's nothing to see and the fee is exorbitant. Further south, the artificial **Lac de Carcès** has been a favourite with fishermen since the dam was built in the 1930s. To the east are the biggest bauxite mines in France, which are playing hell with one of the most impressive medieval abbeys in Provence.

Abbaye du Thoronet

Abbaye du Thoronet
t 04 94 60 43 90; open April–Sept Mon–Sat 10–6.30, Sun 10–12 and 2–6.30; Oct–Mar Mon–Sat 10–1 and 2–5; adm

The Abbaye du Thoronet was the first Cistercian foundation in Provence, built on land donated by count Raymond Bérenger of Toulouse in 1136; the present buildings were begun about 1160. Like most Cistercian houses, it was in utter decay by the 15th century; and, like so many other medieval monuments in the Midi, it owes its restoration to Prosper Mérimée, Romantic novelist (writer of *Carmen*, among other works) and state inspector of historic monuments under Napoléon III. He chanced upon it in 1873, when most of the roof was gone, the galleries were overgrown with bushes and the refectory was inhabited by cows.

It often seems as if the restoration is still under way; you may find Thoronet full of props, scaffolding and concrete piers, as its keepers experiment desperately to save it from being shaken to pieces by the bauxite lorries rumbling past on the D79. The mines themselves (nearby, but screened by trees) have caused some subsidence, and cracks are opening in the walls. Nevertheless, this purest and plainest of the Cistercian 'Three Sisters' of Provence (along with Silvacane, p.228, and Sénanque, p.240) is worth a detour. In keeping with the stern austerity of Bernard of Clairvaux, it displays sophisticated Romanesque architecture stripped to its bare essentials, with no worldly splendour to distract a monkish mind, only grace of form and proportion.

The elegant stone **bell-tower** would have been forbidden in any other Cistercian house (to keep local barons from commandeering them for defence towers), but those in Provence got a special dispensation – thanks to the mistral, which would have blown a wooden one down with ease. There are no such compromises in the blank façade, but behind it is a marvellously elegant interior; note the slight point of the arches, a hint of the dawning Gothic – Thoronet was begun in the same year as France's first Gothic churches, in the north at St-Denis and Sens. The **cloister**, with its heavy arcades, is equally good, enclosing a delightful stone fountain-house. There's a **cellar** to visit, too, to see how the monks fared, and a modern **chapel** where people pray and visitors gawp and take photographs over the sign clearly requesting that they do not.

Domaine de l'Abbaye
t 04 94 73 87 36

If you like fine rosé wine, visit the nearby **Domaine de l'Abbaye**, where the wine-grower makes some of the best. His secret? Hand-picking the grapes by moonlight, when temperatures are cooler and the grapes avoid the shock of coming in from the hot sun into the cool of the *pressoir*. The grapes supposedly keep more of their strength, and the wine is bottled in a distinctive sky-blue bottle to protect it from the light.

Cotignac and Barjols

Cotignac is one of the cutest of the cute, a Sunday supplement-quality Provençal village where everything is just right, and every-one knows it. Almost half the town's 2,000 residents are British, so don't be surprised to hear English spoken. There are no sights, but one looming peculiarity: the tufa cliffs that hang dramatically over it. In former times these were hollowed out for wine cellars, stables or even habitations; today there are trails up to them for anyone who wants to explore. At the base of the cliffs there is a meadow where Cotignac holds its summer music festival.

Westwards on the D13/D560, the landscapes are delicious and drowsy; **Pontevès** will startle you awake again, with its castle in a remarkable setting atop a steep conical hill. Long the stronghold of the Pontevès family, feudal rulers of most of this region, the apparition loses some of its romantic charm after the climb up; there's nothing inside but a few houses, La Poste and a food shop.

Three kilometres further on, **Barjols** has little cuteness but much more character. This metropolis of 2,000 souls owes its existence to leather tanning, an important industry here for the last 300 years. There is still one shoe factory left, but Barjols is now little more than a market town, although it retains an urban and somewhat sombre air: elegant rectangular squares of the 18th century, and moss-covered **fountains** (there are 42 of them) similar to the ones in Aix, and *lavoirs* – hence its nickname 'the Tivoli of Provence'. To see Barjols at its best, come on 16–17 January, the feast of St Marcel (Marcellus, the 4th-century pope), whose gaudy relics, stolen in the Middle Ages from a Provençal monastery, can be seen in the 16th-century parish church. There'll be dancing and, equally unusual for Provence, the essentially pagan slaughter and roasting of an ox, accomplished to the sound of flutes and *tambourins*.

Market Days in the Central Var

Aups: Wed and Sat; truffle market Thurs am in winter.
Salernes: Wed am and Sun am.
Cotignac: Tues am; mid-June–mid-Sept farmers' market.
Barjols: Sat am.

Where to Stay and Eat in the Central Var

(i) **L'Auberge St-Pierre** >>

Lorgues ✉ 83510

Lorgues, 13km from Draguignan, is a pleasant place to stay if you happen to be passing through.

Bruno, Route de Vidauban, Campagne Mariette, t 04 94 85 93 93 (€€€€€–€€€). Three luxurious rooms and one suite at prices that extend into the ozone layer, in a very special old *mas* where the chef does wonderful things with truffles (€€€€). *Closed Sun eve and Mon out of season.*

Tourtour ✉ 83690

Easily the poshest of the villages in this region, Tourtour can also boast the most luxurious accommodation.

****Bastide de Tourtour**, Montée St-Denis, t 04 98 10 54 20, *www.bastidedetourtour.com* (€€€€€–€€€).

(i) **Salernes**
*Place Gabriel Péri,
t 04 94 70 69 02,
www.officetourisme-
salernes.fr; open
Mon–Sat and Sun am*

A modern Relais & Châteaux complex with a swimming pool, a tennis court and all the other amenities, including a highly reputed restaurant offering a blend of Provençal cooking and classic French cuisine. *Restaurant closed lunch Mon–Fri except July and Aug.*

***Le Mas des Collines**, Route de Villecroze, t 04 94 70 59 30 (€€€–€€). A charming little hotel offering tranquillity, air-conditioned rooms and a very pretty swimming pool overlooking the valley below Tourtour. *Half-board available. Closed Nov–April.*

***L'Auberge St-Pierre**, Route d'Ampus, St-Pierre de Tourtour, t 04 94 50 00 50, *www.guideprovence.com/hotel/saint-pierre* (€€). An up-to-date working farm built around a hotel 3km east of town, with exceptional rooms in an 18th-century house and a fine restaurant (€€€) with authentic Provençal food. Swimming pool, gym, tennis courts, and archery and fishing facilities. Just beware of the hostess when she's tired. *Closed mid-Oct–Mar; restaurant closed lunch except weekends.*

Les Chênes Verts, 2km from town on Route de Villecroze, t 04 94 70 55 06 (€€€€). A restaurant offering wonderful classical food featuring lobster, seafood, truffles and game in season. *Closed Tues, Wed and June.*

Sillans-la-Cascade ✉ 83690

Hôtel-Restaurant des Pins, on D32, t 04 94 04 63 26 (€). An extremely popular restaurant set in an old stone house, serving the likes of grilled meats with shrimps for starters and other good food (€€). It also has a few rooms, but you'll need to make your reservation way in advance during the summer. *Closed Wed, and Jan.*

Fox-Amphoux ✉ 83670

***Auberge du Vieux Fox**, Place de l'Eglise, t 04 94 80 71 69 (€€). One of the most pleasant village inns in the whole of Provence, with a delightful restaurant. *Restaurant closed mid-Oct–mid-Feb.*

Cotignac ✉ 83570

Maison Gonzagues, 9 Rue Léon Gérard, t 04 94 72 85 40, www. maison-gonzagues-cotignac.com (€€€). The only hotel in the town centre, set in a lovingly restored 18th-century *hôtel particulier* and run by a member of the local tourist office. Street parking is difficult here.

Les Trois Marches, 11 Cours Gambetta, t 04 94 04 65 99 (€€). A restaurant offering fresh, simple fare and attentive service in intimate surroundings. *Closed Jan and Feb.*

ⓘ Cotignac >>
Pont de la Cassole,
t 04 94 04 61 87; open
July and Aug Mon am,
Tues–Sat, and Sun am;
May–June and Sept
Tues–Sat; Oct–April
Tues–Fri and Sat am; has
lists of chambres d'hôtes
outside the village

ⓘ Barjols
Bd Grisolle, t 04 94 77
20 01, www.ville-barjols.fr;
open Tues–Sat

Along the Motorway: From Draguignan to Aix

With the Var's rocky coast, and the mountains behind it, the only easy route across the *département* is a narrow corridor through Brignoles and St-Maximin-la-Ste-Baume. The French have obligingly plonked a motorway across it, successor to the Via Aurelia and the St-Maximin pilgrims' route as the great high road of Provence.

Les Arcs and Le Luc

Picking up the D555 to the south of Draguignan, you'll pass through **Les Arcs**, a village of stepped streets, pink stone and ivy.

Next comes **Le Luc**, which is practically strangled by the motorway but is a game town nevertheless, with another steep medieval centre, a castle on top and a restored Romanesque church flanked by a 16th-century tower. To entertain the hordes of coast-bound tourists there's a **Musée Régional du Timbre**, housed in a 17th-century château on Place de la Convention, and another small museum in a 16th-century church, the **Musée Historique du Centre Var**, at 24 Rue Victor Hugo.

Musée Régional du Timbre
t 04 94 47 96 16, www.
lemuseedutimbre.com;
open Oct–Aug Mon and
Wed–Fri 2.30–5.30, Sat
and Sun 10–12 and
2.30–5.30; closed Sept

Musée Historique du Centre Var
t 04 94 60 70 12; open
June to mid-Oct
Mon–Sat 3–6; mid-
Oct–May by appt

Brignoles

The biggest date in Brignoles' history, perhaps, is 25 September 1973, when several thousand dead toads rained down from the sky – an event that does not seem to be commemorated in any way. Little else has ever happened here. This gritty but somehow likeable place earns its living mining bauxite. It has an attractive medieval centre, and a museum to remember.

Musée du Pays Brignolais

Musée du Pays Brignolais
t 04 94 69 45 18, www. museebrignolais.com; open April–Sept Wed–Sat 9–12 and 2.30–6, Sun 9–12 and 3–6; Oct–Mar Wed–Sat 10–12 and 2.30–5, Sun 10–12 and 3–5; adm

At the top of the old town at Place du Palais des Comtes de Provence, in a palace that was the summer residence of the counts of Provence, Brignoles' incredible curiosity shop has grown to fill the whole building since a local doctor began the collection in 1947. Over two floors packed with fossils, oil presses, cannonballs and roof tiles, you'll see things you never dreamed existed.

In the place of honour, near the entrance, is the original model of a great invention by Brignoles' own Joseph Lambot (1814–87): the steel-reinforced **concrete canoe**. Contemporary accounts on display suggest the thing floated, but the idea somehow never caught on. Lambot probably never collected a sou for his revolutionary new construction technique, since found to be better adapted to skyscrapers.

It's a hard act to follow, but just across the room is a provocative **sarcophagus**, dated *c.* AD 175–225, that is nothing less than the earliest Christian monument in France. Well sculpted and well preserved, the imagery is a remarkable testament to religious transition. The centre shows a familiar classical scene, a seated god receiving a soul into the underworld – but whether the god is Hades, Jesus or someone else remains a mystery. Also present are Jesus as the 'Good Shepherd', a figure that may be St Peter (fishing, figuratively, for souls), another that seems to be a deified Sun, and another early Christian symbol, an anchor. The sarcophagus is believed to be Greek, possibly made in Antioch or Smyrna; how it got here no one knows.

Nearby is a rare but badly worn Merovingian tombstone, and a part of the counts' palace, the **Chapel of St-Louis-d'Anjou**, a Provençal bishop who may be better known in California – the town of San Luis Obispo is named after him. The chapel houses a hoard of gaudy church clutter, with Louis' chasuble and rows of wax saints under glass. After that, you may inspect a reconstructed Provençal farm kitchen, and a reconstructed mine tunnel. Other prizes await on the second floor: a plywood model of Milan cathedral by a local madman, a stuffed weasel and large collections of owls and moths. Local painters are exhaustively represented: some of the finest works are 19th-century *ex votos* in the French tradition, with the Virgin Mary blessing people falling off wagons and out of windows. Even after all this, Gaston Huffman's *Allegory of Voluptuous Folly* takes the cake – a medieval conceit in a modern style, with a delicious lady in a little boat enjoying the caresses of a cigar-smoking pig.

Rue des Lanciers, the spine of old Brignoles, begins opposite the museum's front door, passing the 13th-century **Maison des Lanciers**, where the counts' guards stayed when visiting.

West of Brignoles

West of Brignoles, there are two sights of some interest off the main road, both of which you'll need to talk your way into: first the half-ruined **Abbaye de la Celle**, an ancient foundation (started in the 6th century) that made a reputation for itself due to the open licentiousness of its nuns, and which was dissolved in 1770; the buildings are now part of a farm. Second, also on a farm, off the D205 6km east of Tourves, is the **Chapelle de la Gayole**, an early Romanesque cemetery chapel in the shape of a Greek cross (built in 1029, though parts of it go back to the 700s).

St-Maximin-la-Ste-Baume

St-Maximin has always divided the views of its visitors. 'Considerable charm,' gushes one guidebook; 'another pretty Provençal village,' suggests another. Prosper Mérimée, back in 1834, had another view: 'St-Maximin is a miserable hole between Aix and Draguignan.' You can decide for yourself.

But once upon a time, the Miserable Hole was a goal for the pious from all over France. According to legend, the site was the burial place of the Magdalene and her companions St Maximin, the martyred first bishop of Aix, and St Sidonius. Their bodies, supposedly hidden from Saracen raiders in a crypt, disappeared and were conveniently 'rediscovered' in 1279 by the efforts of Charles II of Anjou, count of Provence. Inconveniently, the body of the Magdalen was already on display at the famous church of Vézelay, in Burgundy. Nevertheless, an ambitious basilica and abbey complex was begun, and eventually the pope was convinced or bribed into declaring St Maximin's relics the real McCoy. The pilgrim trade made St-Maximin into a town; among the visitors were several kings of France, the last being Louis XIV.

There were wild times during the Revolution; St-Maximin renamed itself 'Marathon', and was briefly under the command of Lucien Bonaparte, who was calling himself 'Brutus'. This most devoutly revolutionary of Bonapartes saved the basilica from a sacking. As the local legend tells it, an official from Paris came down to oversee its liquidation, but Brutus had him greeted with the 'Marseillaise', played all stops out on the church's great organ.

Basilique Ste-Marie-Madeleine

After its ramshackle, unfinished façade, on a desolate square decorated only by a faded Dubonnet sign, this basilica's interior seems like an apparition: it's the only significant Gothic building in Provence. Despite the prevailing gloom and the hosts of awful, neglected 18th- and 19th-century chapels and altars, it's worth a visit for the tall arches of the nave and the lovely apse, with its stained glass, which leave an impression of dignity and grace.

Wine: Côtes-de-Provence – *La Vie en Rose*

Half of all French rosés originate in the Republic's largest AOC region, the 18,000-hectare Côtes-de-Provence. The growing area stretches from St-Raphaël to Hyères, with separate patches around La Ciotat and Villars-sur-Var, and a wide swathe south and west of Aix-en-Provence. Based on grenache, mourvèdre, cinsault, tibouren, cabernet and syrah grapes, Côtes-de-Provence rosé is a dry, fruity, and elegant summer wine that doesn't have to worry about travelling well: more than enough eager oenophiles travel to it every holiday season. Unfortunately its price has travelled too, and there are no prizes for guessing which way. It is, however, possible to find good inexpensive alternatives, since some estates produce a *vin de pays*. This is often as good as wines with full *appellation contrôlée* status.

An excellent example is **Château d'Astros**, at Vidauban ①, t 04 94 99 73 00, *www.chateau.astros. com*, which produces a wonderful range of Vin de Pays des Maures: red, white and rosé. The property is run by M. Galliano. A visit to this grand rambling house and estate in the forest is great fun. One can also buy it draught – either supply your own containers or buy one from the owner.

Côtes-de-Provence reds (20 per cent of the production) are much finer today than the rough plonk Caesar issued to his legions, most notably the special *cuvées* put out by the better estates. The whites, of clairette and ugni blanc grapes, are scarcer still, and account for only five per cent of the AOC label. With 57 cooperatives and 350 private cellars, Côtes-de-Provence is easily sampled, especially along the signposted 400km Route des Vins, which you can pick up at Le Luc or Le Muy from the A8 or N7, or at Fréjus, Les Arcs and Puget-sur-Argens.

Two of the best-known producers are at Trets ②, on the D56 southwest of St-Maximin-la-Ste-Baume: **Château Ferry-Lacombe**, t 04 42 29 40 04, *www.ferrylacombe.com*, where the vines are planted on ancient Roman terraces (along with the pink stuff, you can find the excellent Cuvée Lou Cascaï); and the **Château Grand'Boise**, t 04 42 29 22 95, where the subtle red Cuvée Mazarine and a flowery blanc de blancs are grown amid a large forest.

Near Le Luc, Hervé Goudard's **Domaine St-Baillon**, on the N7 at Flassans-sur-Issole ③, t 04 94 69 74 60, mixes syrah and cabernet sauvignon to produce its truffle-scented Cuvée du Roudaï. Just under the cliffs of Montagne Ste-Victoire, **Domaine Richeaume**, at Puyloubier ④, t 04 42 66 31 27, in Provence's most modern and efficient *cave*, run by Sylvain Hoesch and producing along with rosés an interesting selection of red wines, one of pure syrah and another of pure cabernet sauvignon.

At La Londe-les-Maures ⑤ east of Hyères, **Domaines Ott**, Clos Mireille, Route de Brégançon, t 04 94 01 53 50, *www.domaines-ott.com*, offers one of the *appellation*'s top white wines, of ugni and semillon grapes aged in wooden barrels. The estate's top rosé, '*cœur de grains*', is one of the most sought-after wines in the region... and has a price to match.

A much higher percentage of red wine is produced in the cooler, drier Coteaux Varois, a region of 28 communes around Brignoles in the central Var, beginning a few miles north of the Bandol district east of La Ciotat and extending north as far as Tavernes. This old *vin de pays* has been elevated to the ranks of VDQS; all the vintners along the N7 and the other roads outside Brignoles hang out signs to lure you in.

You can try a good (and organic) Coteaux Varois at the **Domaine du Bas Deffens**, on the Cotignac road just east of Barjols ⑥. Or sample Coteaux Varois at **Château Thuerry**, set in a wooded landscape at Villecroze ⑦, t 04 94 70 63 02, *www.chateauthuerry.com*.

The original decoration is spare: coats of arms and effigies of Charles of Anjou and Queen Jeanne on some of its capitals. Among the later additions, the most impressive is the enormous, afore-mentioned **organ** with almost 3,000 pipes, all the work of one man, a Dominican monk named Isnard (1773). Another Dominican, Vincent Funel, was responsible for the lovely choir screen (1691).

To the left of the high altar, don't miss the retable of the *Passion of Christ* (1520) by an obscure Renaissance Fleming named Ronzen,

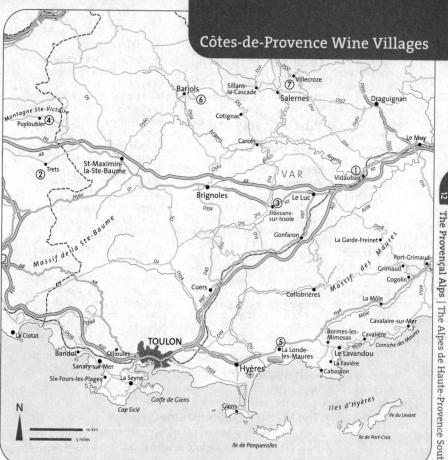

with 22 panels of the familiar scenes with some surprising backgrounds: the papal palace in Avignon, the Colosseum and Venice's Piazzetta San Marco. Stairs lead down to the **crypt**, a funeral vault from the 4th or 5th century AD, where the holy sarcophagi lie with a host of eerie reliquaries.

The Couvent Royal

The monastery attached to Ste-Marie-Madeleine was a 'royal' convent because the kings of France were its titular priors. After losing it in the Revolution, the Dominican Order bought back the monastery and church in 1859. Apparently St-Maximin proved too depressing even for Dominicans; they bolted for Toulouse in 1957, leaving the vast complex in a terrible state. Restorations have been going on fitfully since the 1960s.

The buildings include the imposing **hospice** from the 1750s (now the town hall), to the left of the basilica's façade; the rest, behind it, now houses an institute for cultural exchanges. The best

(i) **Brignoles >>**
Office Intercommunal de la Provence Verte, Carrefour de l'Europe, t *04 94 72 04 21, www.la-provence-verte.net/decouvrir/brignoles.php; open summer daily; winter Mon–Sat*

(★) **Le Logis du Guetteur >**

(i) **St-Maximin-la-Ste-Baume >>**
Hôtel de Ville, t *04 94 59 84 59, www.ot-stmaximin.provence verte.fr; open daily all year*

Market Days from Draguignan to Aix

Brignoles: Sat am, Av Foch.
St-Maximin-la-Ste-Baume: Wed.

Where to Stay and Eat: Draguignan to Aix

Les Arcs ✉ 83460

***Le Logis du Guetteur**, Place du Château, t 04 94 99 51 10, *www. logisduguetteur.com* (€€€€–€€€). An exceptional hotel-restaurant in a lavishly restored castle dating in parts from the 11th century, at the top of the old town. There's an attractive garden and a swimming pool, and some of the rooms have wonderful views. The restaurant serves ambitious *haute cuisine*, including stuffed sole and elaborate desserts. *Closed Feb.*

Brignoles ✉ 83170

**La Grillade au Feu de Bois, on N7 in village of Flassans-sur-Issole (✉ 83340), t 04 94 69 71 20, *www. lagrillade.com* (€€€–€€). A gracious and friendly farm hotel with 16 rooms and a restaurant serving admirable home cooking.

La Petite Marmite, Place Gabriel Péri, Montfort-sur-Argens, 6km north of Brignoles, t 04 94 59 55 06 (€€–€). A peaceful place for an intimate meal, with a handful of tables.

Saigon, Place St-Louis, t 04 94 59 14 51 (€€–€). A good Vietnamese restaurant. *Closed Wed.*

St-Maximin-la-Ste-Baume ✉ 83470

**Plaisance, 20 Place Malherbe, t 04 94 78 16 74, *www.plaisance-hotel.com* (€). The only decent place to stay if you are compelled to spend the night here, with pale orange shutters.

part is the **cloister**, with some cedars of Lebanon and a charming subtropical garden in the centre. One of the arcades is a Gothic original of 1295.

The Massif de la Ste-Baume

If you're heading towards Marseille or the coast from here, you might consider a detour into this small but remarkable patch of mountains. Rising as high as 3,199ft, and offering views over the sea and as far north as Mont Ventoux, the massif shelters a small forested plateau called the **Plan d'Aups**. This is a northern-style forest, including maple, beech and sycamore, as well as scores of species of wild flowers and other plants not often seen around the Mediterranean. They have remained in their primeval state because the *massif* is holy ground, the site of the **cave** (*Sainte-Baume*, or holy grotto) where, according to legend, the Magdalene spent the last years of her life as a hermit. The cave, furnished as a chapel, formed part of the pilgrimage to St-Maximin from the Middle Ages on, and can be seen today along the D80. Some monastic communities grew up around the site, and you can visit the 13th-century Cistercian **Abbaye de St-Pons**, near the loveliest part of the forests (the **Parc de St-Pons**). The St-Maximin tourist office has details of guided tours.

Beaches on
the Côte d'Azur

*If you fancy a day trip to a beach
during your stay in Provence, here is
a selection of the best, from Monaco
on the eastern end of the Côte to
Bandol and La Ciotat in the west.*

*On p.173 you can find a list of the
best beaches in the Marseille area.*

13

The beaches of the **eastern Riviera** are not renowned for their beauty. From Menton to Antibes the shore is rocky – beaches are shingle, or in some cases artificial pebble. The lack of sand is more than compensated for by the spectacular settings, however, backed by 200m cliffs, palm trees and some of the world's most expensive real estate. But purists should head as far as **Antibes**, where the sand starts in earnest. There are two public beaches in Antibes: the best lie out of the town centre, just before the cape. **Juan-les-Pins**, blessed with fine sand, is cursed with countless private beach clubs. Public beaches exist here – try further west towards **Golfe Juan**. **Cannes** has even more snooty beach clubs, but here, too, there is a public beach, in front of the Palais des Festivals. Further west towards **Mandelieu-La-Napoule** the beach is sandy, and free.

The **western Côte d'Azur** contains some of the most enticing beaches in France. From Cannes to St-Tropez the dramatic corniche road offers glimpses down to small sandy coves hiding between jagged rocks. This is above all a place to take your time, stopping where fancy dictates. The beaches of **St-Tropez** are actually 5km south of the town – Plage de Tahiti is the most infamous, Plage de Pampelonne the least spoiled. True aficionados head south to Plage de l'Escalet and round Cap Lardier to Gigaro. The footpath east of Gigaro takes you to a well-patronized nudist beach.

From St-Trop to Toulon the road climbs and falls along the Corniche des Maures. Some of the most revered beaches in Europe lie offshore – those on the **Ile de Porquerolles** have national park status and offer unrivalled sand (catch a ferry from Hyères). West of Toulon, **Sanary-sur-Mer** and **Bandol** have thin strips of beach, but these get very crowded in summer.

Best Beaches

Monaco Chic and sharp; safe swimming.
Beaulieu-sur-Mer (Plage des Fourmis) Backed by palms, view across to Cap Ferrat.
Villefranche-sur-Mer Fashionable, shingled and safe for children.
St-Jean-Cap-Ferrat (Plage du Passable) Views to Villefranche-sur-Mer.
Antibes Port and south of centre on the D2559.
Cannes Palais des Festivals and west to Mandelieu-La-Napoule.
St-Aygulf Long stretch of sand, lots of space, but crowded in summer.
Les Issambres As St-Aygulf.
Port Grimaud Long beach backing onto the Cité Lacustre, the waterside city by Spoerry
St-Tropez Plage de Tahiti, Plage de Pampelonne, Plage de l'Escalet.
Gigaro Long beach, a favourite with families.
Cavalaire-sur-Mer The long sandy beach of the bay, popular with families.
St-Clair Just outside Le Lavandou; views across to the islands.
Cap de Bregançon Wilder, more isolated coves at the eastern end of the Rade d'Hyères.
Ile de Porquerolles Plage de Notre-Dame, or any of the northern coastal beaches.
Ile du Levant Héliopolis, premier nudist beach.
Hyères Large town beach.
Bandol/Sanary/La Ciotat Thin beaches; crowded in summer, restful off-season.

Language

A working knowledge of French will make your holiday more enjoyable, but is hardly essential in the cities, where you can always find someone working in a travel office, bank, shop, hotel or restaurant who speaks at least rudimentary English.

Venturing into the less-travelled hinterlands may well require an effort to recall your school French; a small travel phrase book and English–French dictionary can come in handy.

Even if your French is brilliant, the soupy southern twang may throw you. Any word with a nasal *in* or *en* becomes something like *aing* (*vaing* for *vin*). The last vowel on many words that are silent in the north get to express themselves in the south (*encore* sounds something like *engcora*).

What remains the same as anywhere else in France is the level of politeness expected: use *monsieur, madame* or *mademoiselle* when speaking to everyone (and *garçon* in restaurants only if you add '*s'il vous plaît*'), from your first *bonjour* to your last *au revoir*.

See pp.58–62 for food, drink and menu vocabulary.

Pronunciation

Vowels

a, à, â between *a* in 'bat' and 'part'
é, er, ez at end of word as *a* in 'plate' but a bit shorter
e at end of word not pronounced
e at end of syllable or in one-syllable word pronounced weakly, like *er* in 'mother'
i as *ee* in 'bee'
o as *o* in 'pot'
ô as *o* in 'go'
u, û between *oo* in 'boot' and *ee* in 'bee'

Vowel Combinations

ai as *a* in 'plate'
aî as *e* in 'bet'
ail as *i* in 'kite'
au, eau as *o* in 'go'
ei as *e* in 'bet'
eu, œu as *er* in 'mother'
oi between *wa* in 'swam' and *u* in 'swum'
oy in middle of words as 'why'; otherwise as 'oi', above
ui as *wee* in 'twee'

Nasal Vowels

Vowels followed by an *n* or an *m* have a nasal sound.

an, en as *o* in 'pot' + nasal sound
ain, ein, in as *a* in 'bat' + nasal sound
on as *aw* in 'paw' + nasal sound
un as *u* in 'nut' + nasal sound

Consonants

Many French consonants are pronounced as in English, but there are some exceptions:
c followed by *e, i* or *y* and *ç* as *s* in 'sit'
c followed by *a, o* or *u* as *c* in 'cat'
g followed by *e, i* or *y* as *s* in 'pleasure'
gn as *ni* in 'opinion'
j as *s* in 'pleasure'
ll as *y* in 'yes'
qu as *k* in 'kite'
s between vowels as *z* in 'zebra'
s otherwise as *s* in 'sit'
w except in English words as *v* in 'vest'
x at end of word as *s* in 'sit'
x otherwise as *x* in 'six'

Stress

The stress usually falls on the last syllable except when the word ends with an unaccented *e*.

Vocabulary

The nouns in the list below are marked as either masculine *(m)* or feminine *(f)*.

If masculine, 'the' is *le*, or *l'* if the word begins with a vowel; and 'a' is *un*. 'Some' or 'any' is *du*. For example, *'A quelle heure part le train pour Montpellier?/Je voudrais un oreiller/du savon.'*

If feminine, 'the' is *la*, or *l'* if the word begins with a vowel; and 'a' is *une*. 'Some' or 'any' is *'de la'*. For example, *'Je cherche la sortie/une pharmacie/Je voudrais de l'aspirine.'*

If plural, 'the' is *les*, and 'some' or 'any' is *des*. For example, *'Où sont les toilettes/Est-ce que vous avez des cartes postales?'*

General

hello *bonjour*
good evening *bonsoir*
good night *bonne nuit*
goodbye *au revoir*
please *s'il vous plaît*
thank you (very much) *merci (beaucoup)*
yes *oui*
no *non*
good *bon (bonne)*
bad *mauvais*
excuse me *pardon, excusez-moi*

My name is... *Je m'appelle...*
What is your name? *Comment t'appelles-tu?* (informal), *Comment vous appelez-vous?* (formal)
How are you? *Comment allez-vous?*
Fine *Ça va bien*

I don't understand *Je ne comprends pas*
I don't know *Je ne sais pas*
Could you speak more slowly? *Pourriez-vous parler plus lentement?*
How do you say ... in French? *Comment dit-on ... en français?*
Can you help me? *Pourriez-vous m'aider?*
Help! *Au secours!*

WC *toilettes (fpl)*
men *hommes*
ladies *dames* or *femmes*
drinking water *eau potable*
non-drinking water *eau non potable*
doctor *médecin (m)*

hospital *hôpital (m)*
emergency room/A&E *salle des urgences (f)*
police station *commissariat de police (m)*
tourist information office *office de tourisme (m)*

Shopping and Sightseeing

Do you have...? *Est-ce que vous avez...?*
I would like... *Je voudrais...*
Where is/are...? *Où est/sont...?*
How much is it? *C'est combien?*
It's too expensive *C'est trop cher*
Do you have any change? *Avez-vous de la monnaie?*

entrance *entrée (f)*
exit *sortie (f)*
open *ouvert(e)*
closed *fermé(e)*
push *poussez*
pull *tirez*

bank *banque (f)*
money *argent (m)*
change *monnaie (f)*
credit card *carte de crédit (f)*
traveller's cheque *chèque de voyage (m)*
post office *la poste*
stamp *timbre (m)*
postcard *carte postale (f)*
public phone *cabine téléphonique (f)*

shop *magasin (m)*
central food market *halles (fpl)*
tobacconist *tabac (m)*
pharmacy *pharmacie (f)*
aspirin *aspirine (f)*
condoms *préservatifs (mpl)*
insect repellent *anti-insecte (m)*
sun cream *crème solaire (f)*
tampons *tampons hygiéniques (mpl)*

beach *plage (f)*
box office *bureau de location (m)*
museum *musée (m)*
sea *mer (f)*
theatre *théâtre (m)*

Transport

airport *aéroport (m)*
aeroplane *avion (m)*
go on foot *aller à pied*

bicycle *bicyclette (f) / vélo (m)*
mountain bike *vélo tout terrain, VTT (m)*
bus *autobus (m)*
bus stop *arrêt d'autobus (m)*
coach station *gare routière (f)*
railway station *gare (f)*
train *train (m)*
platform *quai (m)/voie (f)*
date-stamp machine *composteur (m)*
timetable *horaire (m)*
left-luggage locker *consigne automatique (f)*
car *voiture (f)*
taxi *taxi (m)*
underground/subway *métro (m)*
ticket office *guichet (m)*
ticket *billet (m)*
single to... *un aller (or aller simple) pour...*
return/round trip to... *un aller et retour pour...*

I want to go to... *Je voudrais aller à...*
When is the next...? *Quel est le prochain...?*
What time does the ... leave?
 A quelle heure part...?
From where does it leave? *D'où part-il?*
Do you stop at...? *Passez-vous par...?*

delayed *en retard*
on time *à l'heure*

Where is (the railway station)? *Où se trouve (la gare)?*
Is it far? *C'est loin?*
left *à gauche*
right *à droite*
straight on *tout droit*

Driving

breakdown *panne (f)*
car *voiture (f)*
danger *danger (m)*
diesel *gazole/gasoil (m)*
driver *chauffeur (m)*
entrance *entrée (f)*
exit *sortie (f)*
give way/yield *céder le passage*
hire *louer*
(international) driving licence *permis de conduire (international) (m)*
motorbike/moped *moto (f)/ vélomoteur (m)*
no parking *stationnement interdit*
petrol (unleaded) *essence (sans plomb) (m)*
road *route (f)*

This doesn't work *Ça ne marche pas*
Is the road good? *Est-ce que la route est bonne?*

Accommodation

single room *chambre pour une personne (f)*
twin room *chambre à deux lits (f)*
double room *chambre pour deux personnes (f)/chambre double (f)*
bed *lit (m)*
blanket *couverture (f)*
cot (child's bed) *lit d'enfant (m)*
pillow *oreiller (m)*
soap *savon (m)*
towel *serviette (f)*
booking *réservation (f)*
Do you have a room? *Avez-vous une chambre?*
I would like to book a room *Je voudrais réserver une chambre*

Months

January *janvier*
February *février*
March *mars*
April *avril*
May *mai*
June *juin*
July *juillet*
August *août*
September *septembre*
October *octobre*
November *novembre*
December *décembre*

Days

Monday *lundi*
Tuesday *mardi*
Wednesday *mercredi*
Thursday *jeudi*
Friday *vendredi*
Saturday *samedi*
Sunday *dimanche*

Time

What time is it? *Quelle heure est-il?*
month *mois (m)*
week *semaine (f)*
day *jour (m) / journée (f)*
morning *matin (m)*

14 Language

afternoon *après-midi (m or f)*
evening *soir (m)*
night *nuit (f)*
today *aujourd'hui*
yesterday *hier*
tomorrow *demain*
day before yesterday *avant-hier*
day after tomorrow *après-demain*

Numbers

one *un*
two *deux*
three *trois*
four *quatre*
five *cinq*
six *six*
seven *sept*
eight *huit*
nine *neuf*
ten *dix*
eleven *onze*
twelve *douze*

thirteen *treize*
fourteen *quatorze*
fifteen *quinze*
sixteen *seize*
seventeen *dix-sept*
eighteen *dix-huit*
nineteen *dix-neuf*
twenty *vingt*
twenty-one *vingt et un*
twenty-two *vingt-deux*
thirty *trente*
forty *quarante*
fifty *cinquante*
sixty *soixante*
seventy *soixante-dix*
seventy-one *soixante et onze*
eighty *quatre-vingts*
eighty-one *quatre-vingt-un*
ninety *quatre-vingt-dix*
hundred *cent*
two hundred *deux cents*
thousand *mille*

Glossary

abbaye abbey

ambulatory a passage behind the choir of a church, often with radiating chapels

anse cove

arrondissement a city district

auberge inn

aven natural well

bastide taller, more elaborate version of a *mas*, with balconies, wrought-ironwork, reliefs, etc; also a medieval new town, fortified and laid out in a grid

beffroi tower with a town's bell

borie dry-stone shepherd's hut with a corbelled roof

buffet d'eau in French gardens, a fountain built into a wall with water falling through levels of urns or basins

cabane simple weekend or holiday retreat, usually near the sea; a *cabane de gardian* is a thatched cowboy's abode in the Camargue

calanque narrow coastal creek, like a miniature fjord

capitelle the name for *borie* in Languedoc

cardo the main north–south street in a Roman *castrum* or town

caryatid column or pillar carved in the figure of a woman

castrum rectangular Roman army camp, which often grew into a permanent settlement

causse rocky, arid limestone plateau, north of Hérault and in the lower Languedoc

cave (wine) cellar

château mansion, manor house or castle

château fort castle

chemin path

chevet eastern end of a church, including the apse

cirque round natural depression created by erosion at the loop of a river

cloître cloister

clue rocky cleft or transverse valley

col mountain pass

commune in the Middle Ages, the government of a free town or city; today, the smallest unit of local government, encompassing a town or village

côte coast; on wine labels, *côtes*, *coteaux* and *costières* mean 'hills' or 'slopes'

cours wide main street, like an elongated main square

couvent convent or monastery

crèche Christmas crib with *santons*

donjon castle keep

écluse canal lock

église church

étang lagoon or swamp

Félibre member of the movement to bring back the use of the Provençal language

ferrade cattle branding

gardian a cowboy of the Camargue

garrigues irregular limestone hills pitted with caves, especially those north of Nîmes and Montpellier

gisant sculpted prone effigy on a tomb

gîte shelter

gîte d'étape basic shelter for walkers

grande randonnée (GR) long-distance hiking path

grau a narrowing, of a canyon or a river

halles covered market

hôtel particulier originally the town residence of the nobility; by the 18th century the word became more generally used for any large, private residence

hôtel de ville city hall

lavoir communal fountain, usually covered, for the washing of clothes

mairie town hall

manade a *gardian*'s farm in the Camargue

maquis Mediterranean scrub. Also used as a term for the French Resistance during the Second World War

marché market

mas a farmhouse and its outbuildings

mascaron ornamental mask, usually one carved on the keystone of an arch

modillon stone projecting from the cornice of a church, carved with a face or animal figure

motte hammock, or a raised area in a swamp

oppidum pre-Roman fortified settlement

parlement French juridical body, with members appointed by the king; by the late *ancien régime*, *parlements* exercised a great deal of influence over political affairs

pays region or village

pont bridge

porte gateway

predella small paintings beneath the main subject of a retable

presqu'île peninsula

puy hill

restanques vine or olive terraces

retable carved or painted altarpiece, often consisting of a number of scenes or sculpted ensembles

rez-de-chaussée (RC) ground floor (US first floor)

santon figure in a Christmas nativity scene, usually made of terracotta and dressed in 18th-century Provençal costume

source spring

tour tower

transi on a tomb, a relief of the decomposing cadaver

tympanum sculpted semicircular panel over a church door

vieille ville historic, old quarter of town

village perché hilltop village

Chronology

BC

c. **1,000,000** First human presence, near Menton; use of bone as a tool

c. **400,000** Discovery of fire, as at Terra Amata in Nice

c. **60,000** Neanderthal hunters on the Riviera and around Ganges

c. **40,000** Advent of *Homo sapiens*; invention of art

c. **8000** Invention of the bow

c. **3500** Development of Neolithic culture; first villages built

c. **2000** First metallurgy; copper and tin at Vence and Caussols

c. **1800–1000** Worship on Mont Bégo, at Tende, incisions made in the Vallée des Merveilles

c. **600** Greek traders found Marseille

c. **380** Celtic invasions in Provence

218 Hannibal and elephants pass through region on the way to Italy

125 Roman legions attack Celto-Ligurian tribes that threaten Marseille

122 Founding of Aquae Sextiae (Aix)

118 Founding of Narbonne and Provincia, the first Roman province in Gaul

102 Marius and his legionaries defeat the Teutones

49 Marius' nephew, Julius Caesar, punishes Marseille for supporting Pompey

14 Augustus defeats Ligurian tribes in the Alpes-Maritimes

AD

46 Arrival of the Boat of Bethany at Stes-Maries-de-la-Mer (trad.)

310 Emperor Maximilian captured at Marseille by son-in-law Constantine

314 Constantine calls Church Council at Arles

410 Honorat founds Lérins monastery

413 Visigoths conquer Languedoc

476 Formal end of Western Roman Empire

535 Provence and Languedoc ceded to the Franks

719 Arab invasions in Languedoc

737 Charles Martel defeats Arabs and crushes anti-Frank rebellions in Arles, Avignon and Marseille

759 Pépin the Short adds region to his Frankish empire

812 Canonization of St Guilhem, Languedoc's warrior saint

855 Creation of the kingdom of Provence for Charles the Bald

879 Duke Boson of Viennois proclaims himself king of Provence

c. **890** More Arab raids and invasions

924 Magyars (Hungarians) sack Nîmes

949 Conrad of Burgundy inherits Provence and divides it into four feudal counties

979 Count William defeats Saracens at La Garde-Freinet, proclaims himself marquis of Provence

1002 First written text in Occitan

1032 Death of Rudolph II, king of Burgundy and Provence; lands bequeathed to Holy Roman Emperor Conrad II

1095 Occitans join First Crusade under Raymond of St-Gilles, count of Toulouse and marquis of Provence; William of Aquitaine writes first troubadour poetry

1112 Marriage of Douce, duchess of Provence, with Raymond Bérenger III, count of Barcelona

1125 Provence divided between the houses of Barcelona and Toulouse

1176 Pierre Valdo of Lyon founds Waldensian (Vaudois) sect

1186 Counts of Provence make Aix their capital

1187 Discovery of relics of St Martha at Tarascon

1246 Charles I of Anjou weds Béatrice, heiress of Provence, beginning the Angevin dynasty

1248 Saint Louis embarks on Seventh Crusade from Aigues-Mortes

1266 Battle of Benevento gives Charles of Anjou the Kingdom of Naples

1274 Papacy acquires Comtat Venaissin

1280 Relics of Mary Magdalene 'discovered' at St-Maximin-la-Ste-Baume

1286 First meeting of the Etats de Provence

1295 The death of the 'last troubadour', Guiraut Riquier

1297 Francesco Grimaldi the Spiteful, merchant-prince of Genoa, conquers Monaco (but is forced to abandon it in 1301)

1303 Boniface VIII founds University of Avignon

1309 Papacy moves to Avignon

1327 Petrarch first sees Laura

1340s Sienese painters bring International Gothic style to Avignon

1348 Jeanne of Naples and Provence sells Avignon to the pope; the Black Death strikes the south

1349 Jews expelled from France and take refuge in the Comtat Venaissin

c. 1350 First paper mills in the Comtat Venaissin

1360s The *Grandes Compagnies* ravage the countryside

1362 Election of abbot of St-Victor as Pope Urban V

1363 The Grimaldis recover Monaco and hold it still

1377 Papacy returns to Rome

1380 Louis Ier d'Anjou adopted by Jeanne of Naples

1388 Regions of Nice, Barcelonnette and Puget-Théniers secede from Provence and join county of Savoy

1464 Founding of the Fair of Beaucaire

1481 Count of Provence leaves Provence to the king of France

1501 French create *Parlement* of Aix to oversee Provence

1524 Provence invaded by the imperial troops of Charles V

1525 Jews in the Comtat Venaissin compelled to wear yellow hats

1539 Edict of Villers-Cotterêts forces use of French as official language

1540 *Parlement* of Aix orders massacre of Waldensians in the Luberon

1559 Completion of the canal between the Durance and Salon

1562 Beginning of Wars of Religion: Protestant assembly at Mérindol

1577 First soap factory (Prunemoyr) founded in Marseille

1590–2 Carlo Emanuele of Savoy invades Provence

1598 Edict of Nantes ends the Wars of Religion

1603 Royal college founded at Aix

1639 Last meeting of the Etats de Provence before the Revolution

1646 Jews confined to ghettos

1680 Louis XIV enters rebellious Marseille

1685 Louis XIV revokes Edict of Nantes

1702–1704 The War of the Camisards

1720–21 100,000 die of plague, mostly in Marseille

1731 Principality of Orange incorporated into France

1752 Last Protestant persecutions

1779 Roman mausoleum and palace of the counts demolished at Aix

1784 Hot air balloon goes up in Marseille

1787 The Edict of Tolerance

1790 France divided into *départements*

1791 France annexes Comtat Venaissin

1792 Volunteers from Marseille sing 'La Marseillaise' on road to Paris

1793 Revolutionary tribunal in Marseille; Siege of Toulon makes Bonaparte famous

1795 Massacres in Marseille and Tarascon

1800 Marseille population around 100,000

1815 Napoleon escapes Elba and pops up again near Juan-les-Pins

1830 Revolution brings Louis-Philippe to power

1839 Inauguration of Marseille–Sète railroad; birth of Cézanne

1840–8 Prime Ministry of Guizot, Protestant liberal from Nîmes

1851 Louis-Napoléon's coup ends Second Republic; armed resistance in the south

1854 Founding of the Félibrige at the Château de Fontségugne

1859 Mistral publishes *Miréio*

1860 Plebiscite in county of Nice votes for union with France

1865 Silkworm industry destroyed by disease

1868–90 Phylloxera epidemic devastates vines

1869 Opening of Suez Canal brings boom times to Marseille

1888 Stephen Liégeard gives the Côte d'Azur its name

1888–90 Van Gogh in Provence

1900 Population reaches 500,000 in Marseille, 20 per cent of which is Italian

1904 Frédéric Mistral wins the Nobel Prize for Literature

1906 Colonial Exposition at Marseille

1928 Creation of the Camargue Regional Park

1930s Marcel Pagnol films his *Marius*, *Fanny* and *César* trilogy in Marseille

1939 Founding of the Cannes Film Festival

1942 Sinking of the fleet at Toulon

1943 Formation of the Maquis resistance cells

1944 American and French landings around St-Tropez; Provence liberated in two weeks

1945 Creation of the Institut d'Etudes Occitanes

1962 Independence of Algeria: tens of thousands of French North Africans (*pieds-noirs*) settle in the south

1965 Last silk-weaving company closed

1966 Steelworks founded at Fos-sur-Mer

1970 Completion of Paris–Lyon–Marseille *autoroute*

1982 Regional governments created

1992 30 die in Vaison-la-Romaine floods

1995 The election of Jacques Chirac as president ends 14 years of socialist presidency

2001 End of compulsory national service

2002 January: euro replaces franc as national currency

16

Chronology

Further Reading

Ardagh, John, *France In the New Century: Portrait of a Changing Society* (Penguin, 2000). One of Penguin's informative paperback series on contemporary Europe.

Barr, Alfred, *Henri Matisse: his Art and his Public* (Museum of Modern Art, New York, 1951).

Bishop, Morris, *Petrarch and His World* (Chatto & Windus, 1964).

Bonner, Anthony, *Songs of the Troubadours* (Allen & Unwin, 1973). An introduction to the life and times of the troubadours, with translations of best-known verses.

Cézanne, Paul, *Letters* (London, 1941).

Cook, Theodore A., *Old Provence* (London, 1905). A classic traveller's account of the region, out of print and hard to find.

Daudet, Alphonse, *Letters from my Windmill* (Penguin, 1982). Bittersweet 19th-century tales of Midi nostalgia by Van Gogh's favourite novelist.

Drinkwater Carol, *The Olive Farm* (Abacus, 2001). A lyrical account of the restoration of an old olive farm and integration into a Provençal community by a former British TV actress.

Dumas, Alexandre, *The Count of Monte Cristo*, many editions. Romantic fantastical tale of revenge, much of it set in Marseille and the Château d'If.

Durrell, Lawrence, *The Avignon Quintet* (Faber, 1974–85). Lush wartime sagas that take place in Avignon and around.

Fitzgerald, F. Scott, *Tender is the Night*, many editions. 1920s Riviera decadence based on personal research.

Ford, Ford Madox, *Provence: From Minstrels to the Machine* (Allen & Unwin, 1935). A lyrical pre-war view of the region.

Fortescue, Winifred, *Perfume from Provence* (1935). Poor, intolerable Lady Fortescue's misadventures with the garlicky peasants near Nice.

Giono, Jean, *To the Slaughterhouse, Two Riders of the Storm* (Peter Owen, 1988). Giono is a major 20th-century novelist of Provence, whose deep pessimism contrasts with the sunnier views of his contemporary, Pagnol.

Goldring, Douglas, *The South of France* (Macdonald, 1952). Travels and comments by another English resident.

Gramont, Sanche de, *The French: Portrait of a People* (Putnam, New York, 1969). One of the funnier attempts at the favourite French pastime: national self-analysis.

Hugo, Victor, *Les Misérables*, many editions. Injustice among the galley-slaves and basis for the hit musical.

Ladurie, Emmanuel Leroi, *Love, Death and Money in the Pays d'Oc* (Scolar, 1982). An analysis of a Provençal folk tale, resulting in a history book, novel and literary essay rolled into one.

Larrabeiti, Michael de, *The Provençal Tales* (Pavilion, 1988). Troubadours' tales, legends and stories told by shepherds around the camp fire.

Mayle, Peter, *A Year in Provence, Toujours Provence* and *Encore Provence* (Penguin, 2001). The entertaining bestsellers on ex-pat life in the Luberon.

Mistral, Frédéric, *Miréio* and *Poème de la Rhône*, epic poems by the Nobel prize-winning Félibre, widely available in French or Provençal.

More, Carey and Julian, *A Taste of Provence* (Pavilion, 1987). Father and daughter team up to evoke the countryside and gastronomy of Provence in words and photographs.

Morris, Edwin T., *Fragrance: The Story of Perfume from Cleopatra to Chanel* (Charles Scribner & Sons, 1984). A fascinating overview of the history of one of the world's oldest industries.

Pagnol, Marcel, *Jean de Florette* and *Manon of the Springs, The Days were too Short* (Picador, 1960). Autobiographical works by Provence's most beloved writer.

Petrarch, Francesco, *Songs and Sonnets from Laura's Lifetime* (Anvil Press, 1985).

Pope Hennessy, James, *Aspects of Provence* (Penguin, 1952). A fussy but lyrical view of the region in the 1940s and '50s.

Smollett, Tobias, *Travels through France and Italy* (London, 1776). The irrepressible, grouchy Tobias 'Smellfungus' makes modern travel writing look like advertising copy.

Stendhal, *Travels through the South of France* (London, 1971). Impressions by the great 19th-century French novelist.

Süskind, Patrick, *Perfume* (Penguin, 1989). Thrilling and fragrant murder in the 18th-century perfume industry in Grasse. Now also a film.

Valery, Marie-Françoise, *Gardens of Provence and the Côte d'Azur* (Taschen, 2001). A beautifully illustrated look at the varied gardens of southern France.

Van Gogh, Vincent, *Collected Letters of Vincent Van Gogh* (New York, 1978). Correspondence by the tormented genius.

Vergé, Roger, *Cuisine of the Sun* (London, 1979). The owner of the Moulin de Mougins tells some of his secrets of *nouvelle* Provençal cooking.

Whitfield, Sarah, *Fauvism* (Thames and Hudson, 1991). A good introduction to the movement that changed art history.

Worwood, Valerie, *Aromantics* (Pan, 1987). An amusing look at aromatherapy.

Wylie, L., *Village in the Vaucluse* (Harvard University Press, 1971). The third edition of a very readable sociologist's classic based on the village of Roussillon.

Young, Daniel, *Made in Marseille* (HarperCollins, 2002). A lavishly illustrated celebration of Marseille's hearty cuisine.

Zeldin, Theodore, *France 1845–1945* (Oxford University Press, 1980). Five well-written volumes on all aspects of the period.

Index

Main page references are in **bold**. Page references to maps are in *italics*.

abbeys
Celle 293
Montmajour 142–3
Prieuré de Carluc 228–9
Prieuré de Ganagobie 220–1
Psalmody 159
St-Gilles 33–4, **166–8**
St-Michel 287
St-Michel-de-Frigolet 120
St-Pons 296
St-Victor 186–7
Sénanque 240
Silvacane 228
Thoronet 288–9
Troglodytique Saint-Romain
de l'Aiguille 129
Abd ar-Rahman 23
Abstractionism 37
accommodation 75–80
bed and breakfast 76–7
camping 78
gîtes d'étape 77
gîtes de France 77–8
hotels 75–6
self-catering 77–8
useful phrases 301
youth hostels 77
see also under individual
places
Aigues-Mortes 169–70
aïoli 53
airlines 69–70
Aix-en-Provence *172*, **201–13**,
202–3, *213*
art and architecture 32–8
Atelier Cézanne 210
bars 213
Bibliothèque Méjanes 211
Cathédrale Saint-Sauveur
208–9
Cité du Livre 211
clubs 213
Cours Mirabeau 205–6
eating out 212
entertainment 212–13
festivals 211
Fondation St-John Perse 211

Aix-en-Provence (*cont'd*)
Fondation Vasarely 210
Fontaine d'Eau Chaude 205
Fontaine du Roi René 205
history 201, 204–5
Hôtel Boyer d'Eguilles 207
Hôtel Maurel de Pontevès
205
Hôtel de Ville 208
La Rotonde 205
Les Deux Garçons 205
markets 211
Monument Joseph Sec 210
museums
Granet 206–7
Histoire Naturelle 207
Paul Arbaud 206
Tapisseries 210
Vieil Aix 208
nightlife 212–13
Palais de Justice 207
Pavillon de Vendôme 210
Place d'Albertas 207
Place de l'Hôtel de Ville 208
Place des Prêcheurs 207
Place St-Honoré 207
Quartier Mazarin 205
St-Esprit 207
St-Jean-de-Malte 206
Ste-Marie-Madeleine 207–8
shopping 211
Tour de l'Horloge 208
tourist information 211
Vieil Aix 207–8
where to stay 211–12
Albaron **160**, *161*
Albigensian Crusade 25, 126
Alpes de Haute-Provence
North *260–1*, **275–83**
Castellane 278–9
clues 277–8
Digne-les-Bains 282–3
Entrevaux 276–7
Esteron valley 277–8
Grand Canyon du Verdon
279–80, 281–2
Moustiers-Ste-Marie 281–2

Alpes de Haute-Provence
North (*cont'd*)
Plateau de Valensole 280
Riez 280–1
tourist information 275
Villars-sur-Var 275
Alpes de Haute-Provence
South *260–1*, **283–96**,
284–5
Abbaye du Thoronet 288–9
Bargemon **285**, 287
Brignoles 33, **291–2**, 296
Draguignan 32, **285–7**
Fayence **283**, 286
getting around 284
Massif de la Ste-Baume 296
St-Maximin-la-Ste-Baume
293–6
Seillans **284**, 286–7
Var 287–91
Alpes-Maritimes *260–1*,
262–75, *263*
Breil-sur-Roya **265**, 268
flora and fauna 263–4
La Brigue 267–8
L'Escarène 269
Lucéram **269–70**, *271*
Merveilles valley 266, *267*
Paillon valley 268–71
Parc National du Mercantour
225, **262–4**
Roya valley **264–5**, 268
St-Martin-Vésubie **272**, 275
Saorge **265**, 268
Sospel **264**, 268
Tinée valley 273–5
Vésubie valley **271–2**, 274–5
Alpilles *132*, 137–44
Amphoux 288
Ampus 287
Annot 278
Ansouis 226
Antibes 298
Antoninus Pius, Emperor 22
apéritifs 55
Apt 230–2

Aqueduc de Roquefavour
    215–16
Arab invasions 23
Arles **144–57**, *146*
    Alyscamps 153
    Arènes 148–9
    art and architecture 32, 33, 38
    Boulevard des Lices 149
    Cryptoportiqes 151
    eating out 157
    entertainment 157
    festivals 155
    getting to and around 145
    history 23, 144–5, 147
    Hôtel de Castellane-Laval 151
    Hôtel de Ville 151
    Jardin d'Eté 149
    Jardin d'Hiver 149
    markets 155
    museums
        Arlaten 151–2
        Arles et de la Provence
            Antiques 154–5
        Réattu 152–3
    nightlife 157
    Place du Forum 152
    Place de la République 149
    St-Honorat 153
    St-Trophime 149–51
    shopping 155–6
    Théâtre Antique 149
    Thermes de Constantin 152
    tourist information 155
    where to stay 156–7
aromatherapy 46
art and architecture **32–8**
    churches 33
    Cubism 37, 38
    Dark Ages 33
    époque classique 34–5
    Fauves 37
    Gallo-Roman 32
    Gothic 34
    Napoleonic era 35–6
    prehistoric 32, 192, 266
    Renaissance 34
    Romanesque 33–4
ATMs 68
Augustus, Emperor 22
Aumism 278
Aups 287–8
Aurel 251
Auron 274
Avignon **100–16**, *102–3*
    art and architecture 33, 34
    Cimetière St-Véran 113
    Couvent des Cordeliers 113
    eating out 115–16

Avignon (*cont'd*)
    Eglise des Carmes 113
    entertainment 116
    festivals 114
    getting to and around 101
    history 100–1, 104–5
    Hôtel des Monnaies 108
    Hôtel de Villeneuve-
        Martignan 111
    Ile de la Barthelasse 105–6
    Lambert Collection 112
    Les Halles 113
    Librairie Roumanille 111
    Livrée de Ceccano 112
    Maison aux Ballons 111
    markets 114
    museums
        Angladon 112
        Calvet 111–12
        Lapidaire 112
        Louis Vouland 111
        Mont de Piété 112
        Petit Palais 108–10
        Requien 112
        Théodore Aubanel 113
    nightlife 116
    Notre-Dame-des-Doms 108
    Palais des Papes 105, **106–8**
    Palais du Roure 111
    Place des Carmes 113
    Place de l'Horloge 110
    Place Pie 113
    Pont St-Bénezet 105
    Quartier de la Balance 111
    Quartier des Fusteries 111
    Rocher des Doms 105, **108**
    Rue des Teinturiers 113
    Rue du Vieux-Sextier 113
    St-Agricol 111
    Ste-Claire 113
    St-Didier 112
    St-Pierre 113
    shopping 114
    synagogue 113
    where to stay 114–15

Babylonian Captivity 26, 43, 104
Baleison, Giovanni 34
Bandol 298
banks 68–9, 85
Banon 222
barbarian invasions 22–3
Barben, château 200
Barbentane **119–20**, 121
Barcelona counts 24–5
Bargème 285
Bargemon **285**, 287
Barjols 290

Baroncelli-Javon, Folco de,
    Marquis 164
Baux-de-Provence **137–40**, 143
beaches 87
    Côte d'Azur 298
    Plage de l'Espiguette 170
    Plage de Beauduc 161
    Plage Gaston Deferre 191
    Plage de Piémanson 161
Beaucaire 126–8
Beaumes-de-Venise **252**, 253–4
Beaumont-du-Ventoux 250
Beaurecueil **214**, 216
Beauregard, Chateau 283
bed and breakfast 76–7
Bédoin 27, 248
beer 55
Benedict of Aniane 23–4
Benedict XII, Pope 43
Benedict XIII, Pope 104–5
Bergue et de Paganin gorge
    266
Bézaudun-les-Alpes 277
bicycles 74–5
Black Death 26
Blausasc 269
Bois des Rièges 161
Boniface VIII, Pope 100–1
Bonnieux **234**, 235–6
bories 32, 239
bouillabaisse 53
Boulbon 120
bourride 53
Brayer, Yves 138
Breil-sur-Roya **265**, 268
Briançonnet 277
Brignoles 33, **291–2**, 296
bullfighting 48–9, 86
Buoux **234**, 236
buses and coaches 71–2, 73
Byrrh 55

Cabassols 214
Cabriès 216
Cadarache 222
Cadenet **227**, 230
Cadeno de Moustié 281
Caesar, Julius 22, 179
calanques 87, 174–5
    Callelongue 191
    eating out 194–6
    En-Vau 174
    Figuerolles 173
    Goudes 191
    Mont Rose 191
    Morgiou 192
    Port-Miou 174
    Samena 191

calanques (cont'd)
Sormiou 192
Sugiton 192
calendar of events 65–6
Callas 285
festival 286
Callelongue 191
Calment, Jeanne 144
Camargue 132, 158–70
Aigues-Mortes 169–70
Albaron 160, 161
Bois des Rièges 161
Digue de la Mer 161
Domaine de Méjanes 160
Domaine de la Palissade 161
Etang de Grande Palun 161
Etang de Vaccarès 160–1
flora and fauna 160
gardians 159
getting to and around 159
history 158–9
Le Grau-du-Roi 170
Marais de la Grande Mar 160
Mas du Pont de Rousty 160
Musée Camarguais 160
Petite Camargue 166
Pont de Gau 164
Port Camargue 170
Psalmody 159
St-Gilles 33–4, 166–8
Saintes-Maries-de-la-Mer
161–5
Salin-de-Giraud 160–1
salt pans 169
sports and activities 165, 170
where to stay and eat 161,
165, 168
camping 78
Canal de Caronte 198
Canavesio, Giovanni 34
Cannes 298
canoeing 86
Cap Canaille 174
Cap Couronne 197
Cap Croisette 191
Carluc 228–9
Caromb 248
Carpentras 245–8
Cathédrale St-Siffrein 246
getting to and around 246
Hôtel-Dieu 247–8
markets 246, 248
Musée Comtadin-Duplessis
248
Palais de Justice 246
Passage Boyer 246
Place de l'Hôtel-de-Ville 247
Porte Juive 246

Carpentras (cont'd)
Porte d'Orange 245
Secret Cathedral 247
synagogue 247
Triumphal Arch 247
Carro 197
Carry-le-Rouet 197, 200
cars 72, 73–4
Carthaginians 21
Cascade de Louch 274
Cassis 172, 174–6
Castellane 278–9
Castellet 32, 141
Castérino 266, 268
Catalans 24–5, 27
Cathars 25, 26, 126
Cathédrale d'Images 140
Cavaillon 236–7
cave art 192, 266
caves
Cosquer 192
Fées 142
Thouzon 243
Celle, abbey 293
Celts 21, 32, 206
Céreste 228
Cézanne, Paul 37–8, 197, 205,
207
Atelier Cézanne (Aix) 210
Route Cézanne 213
Chaîne de l'Estaque 196–201
chambres d'hôtes 76–7
Chapelle Notre-Dame-de-
Beauvoir 281
Charlemagne, Emperor 23
Charles of Anjou 25–6, 180
Charles III 26
Charles Martel 23
Charles V, Emperor 26
Charles XII 26
Châteauneuf-du-Pape 96–8
Châteaurenard 120–1, 122
châteaux
Barben 200
Beauregard 283
Gordes 238–9, 242
If 192
La Tour d'Aigues 226, 229
Le Barroux 249
Lourmarin 227, 229–30
Sabran 226
Sauvan 221
Vauvenargues 214–15,
216
cheeses 54
children 83
chocolate 98, 215
Christianity 22

churches
architecture 33
opening hours 85
Cians gorge 274
Cimbri 21
Cime du Diable 266
Cime du Piagu 272
cinema 43–4
Cipières 277
Cistercians 24
Clans 273
Clement V, Pope 26, 43, 99, 101
Clement VII, Pope 104
climate 64
clothing sizes 82
clues 277–8
coaches and buses 71–2, 73
Coaraze 270, 271
coffee 54
Col du Cayron 252
Col de Turini 270
Col de la Vayède 140
Colorado 232
Combe de Lourmarin 234
Comtat Venaissin 25–6, 242
Constantine, Emperor 22
consulates 66–7
Contes 270–1
conversion tables 82
Corniche des Crêtes 174
Corniche Sublime 279
Cornillon-Confoux 199
Corot, Camille 36
Cosquer, Henri 192
Côte d'Azur 298
Côte Balméenne 252
Coteaux d'Aix-en-Provence 215
Coteaux des Baux-en-Provence
139
Côtes-du-Rhône Sud 253
Côtes-du-Luberon 234
Côtes-de-Provence 294, 295
Côtes-du-Ventoux 250
Cotignac 289, 290, 291
country calendar 40–1
Courbet, Gustave 36
Coursegoules 277
Coustellet 240
Crau 132, 157–8
crèches 184
credit cards 68–9
Crestet 252
Crillon-le-Brave 248, 249
crime 29, 83
Croix de Provence 214
Crusades 24, 169
Cubism 37, 38
Cucuron 226–7

customs formalities 67
cybercafés 84, 193
cycling 74–5

Dabisse-Les Mées 223
Daluis gorge 274
daube 53
Daudet, Alphonse 46–7, 122–3, 124–5, 138
  Moulin de Daudet 141
Daumier, Honoré 36, 189
Dauphin 222
David, Jacques-Louis 35
Deferre, Gaston 181
Dentelles de Montmirail 252–4
Derain, André 37
dialling codes 82
Digne-les-Bains 282–3
Digue de la Mer 161
disabled travellers 67–8
diving 87
dolmens 20, 32, 283
  Pierre de la Fée 286
Domaine de la Citadelle 235
Domaine de Méjanes 160
Domaine de la Palissade 161
Domitius Ahenobarbus 21
Drac 126
Draguignan 32, 285–7
drinks 54–5
drugs 83
Dufy, Raoul 37
Duparc, Françoise 189
Durance valley 220–3
duty-free allowances 67

Eguilles 216
EHIC cards 68
electricity 83
embassies 66–7, 82
emergencies 82, 84
En-Vau 174
Entrecasteaux 288
Entremont 215
Entrevaux 276–7
environmental issues 83–4
époque classique 34–5
Ernaginum 140–1
essential oils 46
Estaque coast 196–201
Esteron valley 277–8
Etang de Berre 196–201
Etang de Grande Palun 161
Etang de Vaccarès 160–1
Etruscans 21
Eurostar 70
exchange rates 68
Expressionism 37

Eygalières 140
Eyguières 200

Fabre, Jean-Henri 95
Falaises du Soubeyran 174
Fauves 37
Fayence 283, 286
Félibrige 28, 41–2
fermes auberges 77
ferries 72
festivals 64–6
  Aix-en-Provence 211
  Arles 155
  Avignon 114
  Callas 286
  Cassis 175
  Châteauneuf-du-Pape 97
  La Ciotat 175
  Marseille 193
  Roussillon 242
  Saintes-Maries-de-la-Mer 164–5
  Tarascon 125
  Vaison-la-Romaine 254–5
Figuerolles 173
films 43–4
fires 83–4
First World War 28
fishing 86
flora and fauna
  Alpes-Maritimes 263–4
  Camargue 160
Fontaine-de-Vaucluse 240–2
Fontvieille 141, 143–4
food and drink 52–62
  aïoli 53
  apéritifs 55
  bouillabaisse 53
  bourride 53
  cheeses 54
  chocolate 98, 215
  daube 53
  drinks 54–5
  menu reader 58–62
  picnic food 54
  Provençal cuisine 52–4
  restaurants 56–7, 83
    see also under individual places
  snacks 54
  tripe 53
  vegetables 54
  vegetarians 57
  see also markets; wine
football 181–2
Forcalquier 221, 223
forest fires 83–4
Forêt de Cayrons 265

Forêt de Turini 270
Forêt de Venasque 244
Fort de Buoux 234
Fort des Mille Fourches 270
Fort St-Roch 264
Fos-sur-Mer 198
Fox-Amphoux 288, 291
Fragonard, Jean-Honoré 35
Franks 23
French rule 25–6
Frioul 192–3
Fry, Varian 183

Galange gorge 278
Gallo-Roman art and architecture 32
Gallo-Roman winery 129
Ganagobie 33, 220–1
Garagai 214
Gardanne 216
gardians 159
Gigondas 252, 254
Giono, Jean 46–7, 222
Giovannetti, Matteo 34
Girondins 27
gîtes d'étape 77
gîtes de France 77–8
Glanum 22, 135
Golfe Juan 298
Gordes 32, 238–9, 242
gorges
  Bergue et de Paganin 266
  Daluis 274
  Galange 278
  Nesque 249
  Pennafort 285
  Saorge 265
  Supérieures du Cians 274
  Valabres 274
  Verdon 280
  Vésubie 271
Gothic art and architecture 34
Goudes 191
Grambois 226
Grand Canyon du Verdon 279–80, 281–2
Grand Plan de Canjuers 280
Grandes Compagnies 26
Granet, François-Marius 35–6
Grans 199
Great Schism 104
Greeks 21
Gregory IX, Pope 137–8
Gregory XI, Pope 104
Gréolières 277
Gréolières-les-Neiges 278
Gréoux-les-Bains 280
Grotte Cosquer 192

Grotte des Fées 142
Grottes de Thouzon 243
Guigou, Paul 36–7
Guizot, François 28

health 68, 84
Henry IV 27
herbal tea 55
hire cars 74, 177
history 20–30
    barbarian invasions 22–3
    French rule 25–6
    Middle Ages 23–5
    post-war era 29–30
    prehistory 20–1, 32
    Revolution 27–8, 180–1
    Romans 21–2, 32
    Wars of Religion 26–7
    World Wars 28–9
horse-riding 86
hot chocolate 54
hotels 75–6
    see also under individual
        places
Hungarians 23
Hypogeum of Castellet 32, 141

Ile de Porquerolles 298
Ile Verte 173
Iles du Frioul 192–3
Innocent VI, Pope 118
insurance 68
International Gothic 34
Internet access 84, 193
Isola 274
Isola 2000 274
Istres 198

Jacobins 27
Jeanne, Queen 26
Jews 183, 237
John XXII, Pope 43, 104
    tomb 108
Jou, Louis 139
Joucas 233
Jouques 216
Juan-les-Pins 298
July Monarchy 28

kayaking 86

La Bastide-des-Jourdans 229
La Brigue 267–8
La Ciotat 172–3, 175–6
La Giandola 265
La Montagnette 119–20
La Palette 215
La Tour 273

La Tour d'Aigues, château 226, 229
La Turbie 21
Lac de Carcès 288
Lac du Castillon 49, 278
Lac de Ste-Croix 280
Lacoste 235
Lafare 252
Lagnel, Jean-Louis 184
Lançon-Provence 199
language 299–302
    menu reader 58–62
    Occitan 28, 29, 41
Lantosque 272, 274
Laurana, Francesco 34
L'Authion 270
lavender 46
Le Barroux 249
Le Boréon 272
Le Corbusier 38, 190
Le Grau-du-Roi 170
Le Luc 291
Le Pen, Jean-Marie 29–30
Le Tholonet 213, 216
Le Thor 243
Le Vieux Mas 124–5
Les Arcs 291, 296
Les Baux-de-Provence 137–40, 143
Les Bornes Milliaires 129
Les Dentelles de Montmirail 252–4
Les Mées 220, 223
Les Mesches 266
L'Escarène 269
L'Estaque 197
Levens 271, 274
L'Harmas 95
Ligurians 20
Limans 222
Lirac 99
L'Isle-sur-la-Sorgue 243, 245
Lorgues 287, 290
Loriol du Comtat 248
Louis IX (Saint Louis) 169
Louis XI 26
Louis XIV 27, 180
Louis-Philippe 28
Lourmarin 227, 229–30
Luberon 223–37, 224–5
    Abbaye de Silvacane 228
    Apt 230–2
    Cadenet 227, 230
    Cavaillon 236–7
    getting to and around 224
    Lacoste 235
    Lourmarin 227, 229–30
    Ménerbes 235, 236

Luberon (cont'd)
    Pays d'Aigues 225–7
    Petit Luberon 234–6
Lucéram 269–70, 271

Madone de Fenestre 272
Madone d'Utelle 272
Maillane 121–2
Malaucène 250, 251
Mandarom Shambhasalem 278
Mandelieu-La-Napoule 298
Mane 221
Manosque 222, 223
Marais de la Grande Mar 160
marc 55
Marguerite, Saint 269
Marignane 197
Marius, general 21, 201, 204, 214
markets 54, 85
    Aigues-Mortes 170
    Aix-en-Provence 211
    Apt 231
    Arles 155
    Aups 290
    Avignon 114
    Barjols 290
    Beaucaire 128
    Beaumes-de-Venise 253
    Bonnieux 235
    Breil 268
    Brignoles 296
    Cadenet 229
    Carpentras 246, 248
    Carry-le-Rouet 200
    Cassis 175
    Contes 271
    Cotignac 290
    Coustellet 242
    Cucuron 229
    Digne-les-Bains 282
    Draguignan 286
    Entrevaux 277
    Fayence 286
    Fontvieille 143
    Gordes 242
    La Ciotat 175
    La Tour d'Aigues 229
    Lacoste 235
    Le Thor 245
    Levens 274
    L'Isle-sur-la-Sorgue 245
    Lourmarin 229
    Lucéram 271
    Marseille 182, 193
    Martigues 200
    Moustiers-Ste-Marie 281–2
    Oppède-le-Vieux 235
    Orange 96

markets (*cont'd*)
Pernes-les-Fontaines 245
Pertuis 229
Puget-Théniers 277
Riez 281
Roussillon 233
St-Gilles 168
St-Martin-Vésubie 274
St-Maximin-la-Ste-Baume 296
St-Rémy-de-Provence 136
Saintes-Maries-de-la-Mer 164
Salernes 290
Salon-de-Provence 200
Sospel 268
Tarascon 125
Tende 268
Vaison-la-Romaine 258
Villeneuve lez Avignon 119
Marseille *172*, **176–96**, *178*
Abbaye St-Victor 186–7
Ancienne-Major 186
Anse des Auffres 191
Anse des Catalans 191
Anse de la Fausse Monnaie 191
Anse de Maldormé 191
art and architecture 32–8
Bar de la Marine 186
bars 196
botanical garden 191
Café Parisien 184
calanques 191–2
Cathédrale de la Nouvelle Major 185
Centre Bourse 182
Château Borély 191
Château d'If 192
Château Talabot 191
cinemas 196
classical music 196
clubs 196
Corniche J.F. Kennedy 190–1
Cors Belsunce 188
Cours Julien 188
eating out 194–6
entertainment 196
festivals 193
fish market 182
Fort Dt-Nicolas 187
Galerie des Transports 188
getting to and around 177
Grobet-Labadié 189
history 179–82
Hôtel de Cabre 184
Hôtel de Ville 184
Internet access 193
Jardin des Vestiges 182

Marseille (*cont'd*)
La Canebière 188–9
La Criée 186
Le Panier 183–6
Maison Diamantée 184
Marché des Capucins 188
markets 182, 193
Mazargues 190
Montagne de Marseilleveyre 190
Montée des Accoules 184
museums
  Archéologie Méditerranéenne 185
  Art Contemporain 191
  Arts Africain, Océanien et Amérindien 185
  Beaux-Arts 189
  Cantini 186
  Docks Romains 184
  Faïence 191
  Histoire de Marseille 182
  Histoire Naturelle 189
  Marine et de l'Economie de Marseille 182
  Mode 183
  Vieux Marseille 184
music hall 188
nightlife 196
Noailles station 188
Notre-Dame-de-la-Garde 187–8
observatory 189
Opéra 186
orientation 179
Palais de la Bourse 182–3
Palais Longchamp 189
Palais du Pharo 187
Parc Borély 191
Place de Lenche 184
Place du Mazeau 184
Place Notre-Dame-du-Mont 188
Plage Gaston Deferre 191
Porte d'Aix 188–9
post office 193
public gardens 189
Quai de Rive Neuve 186
Rue des Trois Rois 188
Sainte-Anne 191
St-Jean 182
St-Nicolas 182
sanctuary of Roquepertuse 185
shopping 193
sports and activities 193–4
theatre 196
tourist information 193

Marseille (*cont'd*)
unité d'habitation 190
Vieille-Charité 184–5
Vieux Port 182–3
where to stay 194
zoo 189
Marseilleveyre 191
Martigues **197–8**, 200
Martini, Simone 34
Mas Gallo Romain des Tourelles 129
Mas du Pont de Rousty 160
Massif de la Ste-Baume 296
Matisse, Henri 37
Maubec 235
Maurice of Nassau 92
Maximin, Saint 293
Mayle, Peter 223, 235
Méjean 197
Ménerbes 235, **236**
menu reader 58–62
Mercantour National Park 225, **262–4**
Mérindol 227–8
Merveilles valley 266, 267
Middle Ages 23–5
Mimet 216
mineral water 55
Mirabeau, Count 205
Miramas 198
Miramas-le-Vieux 198
mistral 64
Mistral, Frédéric 28, **41–2**, 138, 164
  Maillane museum 120–1
  tomb 121
monasteries *see* abbeys
money 68–9
Monieux 249
Mons 283
Mont Archas 272
Mont Bégo 262, **266**
Mont Rose 191
Mont Ventoux *238*, 249–51
Montagne du Cheiron 277
Montagne de Cordes 142
Montagne Ste-Victoire 204, **213–14**
Montbrun-les-Bains 251
Montfort, Simon de 25, 126
Montfuron 229
Monticelli, Adolphe 36, 189
Montmajour, abbey 142–3
Montmirail 252
Morgiou 192
Motorail 72
Moulin de Daudet 141
Mourre Nègre 229

Moustiers-Ste-Marie 281–2
Muret, battle of 25
Murs 233
museum opening hours 85

Nantes, Edict of 27
Napoleon Bonaparte 28
Napoleonic era art and archi-
    tecture 35–6
National Front 29–30
national holidays 84
Neanderthals 20
Neolithic civilization 20
Nesque gorge 249
Niolon 197
Nostradamus 199, 200
Notre-Dame-de-Beauvoir 281
Notre-Dame-de-Bon Coeur 270
Notre-Dame-des-Fontaines
    267–8
Notre-Dame-du-Groseau 250–1
Noves 121, 122
nuclear industry 84

Observatoire de Haute-
    Provence 221–2
Occitania 20, 23, 28
    language 28, 29, 41
ochre mining 232–3
Op Art 38
opening hours 85
    banks 69, 85
    public holidays 84
Oppède-le-Vieux 235, 236
Oppedette 222
oppidum 20–1
    Entremont 215
Orange 32, 91–6
    Arc de Triomphe 94–5
    Cathedral 94
    history 91–2
    markets 96
    Musée Municipal 93–4
    Palais du Vin 95
    Rue Victor Hugo 94
    St-Eutrope 94
    Théâtre Antique 92–3
    where to stay and eat 96
Ostrogoths 23

Pagnol, Marcel 43–4
Paillon valley 268–71
Palette 215
papacy 26, 42–3, 100–1, 104
Parc du Mugel 173
Parc National du Mercantour
    225, 262–4
Parc de St-Pons 296

parlements 26–7, 204
passports 66
pastis 55
Pavillon de la Reine Jeanne 140
Pays d'Aigues 225–7
Peïra-Cava 270
Pennafort gorge 285
Pépin the Short 23
Pernes-les-Fontaines 33, 244,
    245
Pertuis 225–6, 227
pétanque 87, 173
Peter II of Aragon 25
Petit Luberon 234–6
Petite Camargue 166
Petite Crau 120–2
Pétrarque 241
Petrobrusians 25
petrol 73–4
Peyruis 220
pharmacists 84
Philip Augustus 25
Phoenicians 21
Picasso, Pablo 38, 214–15
    grave 215
picnic food 54
Pierre de la Fée 286
pilgrimages 24, 163
Plage de Beauduc 161
Plage de l'Espiguette 170
Plage Gaston Deferre 191
Plage de Piémanson 161
plagues 26, 27
Plaine de la Crau 132, 157–8
Plan d'Aups 296
Plateau d'Albion 251
Plateau de Valensole 280
Plateau de Vaucluse 237–42
police 83
politics 29–30
Pomégues 192
Pont Flavien 199
Pont de Gau 164
Pont Julien 233
Pontevès 289–90
Porquerolles 298
Port Camargue 170
Port du Frioul 192–3
Port-Miou 174
Port-Pin 174
post offices 85
Pourrières 214
prehistory 20–1
    art and architecture 32, 192,
        266
Prieuré de Carluc 228–9
Prieuré de Ganagobie 220–1
Protestants 27

Protis 179
Psalmody, abbey 159
public holidays 84
Puget, Pierre 35, 189
Puget-Théniers 276, 277
Punic Wars 21, 179
Puyloubier 214, 216
Puyricard 215

Quarton, Enguerrand 34
Quinson 280

racism 85
railways 70–1, 73
    Eurostar 70
    Motorail 72
    des Pignes 276
    TGV 30, 70–1
rainfall 64
Ratonneau 192–3
Raymond Bérenger V 25
Raymond VI 25
refuges 77
Reillanne 228
religion
    Cathars 25, 26
    Christianity 22
    Petrobrusians 25
    Protestants 27
    Wars of Religion 26–7
Renaissance 34
René the Good 26, 123–4, 204
restaurants 56–7, 83
    menu reader 58–62
    see also under individual
        places
Revolution 27–8, 180–1
Rhône 90, 91–130
    Alpilles 132, 137–44
    Arles 144–57, 146
    Avignon 100–16, 102–3
    Beaucaire 126–8
    Camargue 132, 158–70
    Châteauneuf-du-Pape 96–8
    Crau 132, 157–8
    La Montagnette 119–20
    Les Baux-de-Provence
        137–40, 143
    Orange 32, 91–6
    Petite Crau 120–2
    St-Rémy-de-Provence 132–6
    Tarascon 122–6
    wine 97, 99, 253
Richelieu, Cardinal 27
Riez 280–1
Rigaud, Hyacinthe 35
Rimplas 273
Robert, Hubert 35

Roccasparvière 270
Roche Taillée 283
Romanesque art and architecture 33–4
Romans 21–2, 32
Roquefavour 216
Roquemaure **98–9**, 100
Roquesteron 277
Roubion 273
Roure 273
Roussillon 47–8, **233**
  festival 242
Route des Crêtes 174
Roya valley **264–5**, 268
Rustrel 232

Sables de Roussillon 232
Sablet 252
Sabran, château 226
Sade, Marquis de 235
Saignon 229
sailing 87
St-André-les-Alpes 278
St-Antoine 273
St-Antonin-sur-Bayon 214
Sainte-Baume 99
St-Blaise 32, **198**
St-Chamas 198–9
St-Christol 251
St-Dalmas 273
St-Dalmas-de-Tende 266
St-Donat 220
St-Etienne-de-Tinée 274
St-Gilles 33–4, **166–8**
St-Grat 270
St-Jean-la-Rivière 271–2
St-Laurent-des-Arbes 99
St-Martin-de-Crau 158
St-Martin-Vésubie **272**, 275
Saintes-Maries-de-la-Mer 161–5
St-Maximin-la-Ste-Baume 293–6
St-Michel 273
St-Michel, abbey 287
St-Michel-de-Frigolet, abbey 120
St-Pantaléon 239–40
St-Pons, abbey 296
St-Rémy-de-Provence 132–6
Saint-Romain de l'Aiguille 129
St-Saturnin-lès-Apt **232**, 233
St-Sauveur-sur-Tinée 273
St-Tropez 298
St-Victor, abbey 186–7
Salernes 288
Salin-de-Giraud 160–1
Salon-de-Provence 199–201
salt pans 169

Samena 191
Sanary-sur-Mer 298
Sanctuaire de la Madone de Fenestre 272
santons 184
Saorge **265**, 268
Sault 251
Sausset-les-Pins 197
Sauvan, château 221
School of Arles 33
School of Avignon 34
Seaquarium 170
Sec, Joseph 210
Second Empire 28
Second Punic War 21
Second Republic 28
Second World War 29
Séguret 252, **253**, 254
Seillans **284**, 286–7
self-catering accommodation 77–8
Sénanque, abbey 240
Sérignan-du-Comtat 95
shoe sizes 82
shopping 85–6
  Aix-en-Provence 211
  Arles 155–6
  Avignon 114
  conversion tables 82
  duty-free allowances 67
  Marseille 193
  opening hours 85
  useful phrases 300
Sillans-la-Cascade **288**, 291
Silvacane, abbey 228
Simiane-la-Rotonde 222
skiing 87, 274
Smollett, Tobias 87
snacks 54
soft drinks 55
Sophia-Antipolis 29
Sorgue river 240, 243
Sormiou 192
Sospel **264**, 268
Source du Groseau 251
Souterrain du Rove 197
special-interest holidays 78–80
speed limits 74
sports and activities 86–7
  Camargue 165, 170
  Marseille 193–4
Stein, Gertrude 49
Sugiton 192
Suzette 252
Sylvester II, Pope 42

Tapie, Bernard 30, 182
Tarascon 122–6

Tarasque 125
Tartarin 122, 124–5
Tautavel Man 20
Tavel **99**, 100
tea 54–5
telephones 87–8
  dialling codes 82
  emergencies 82
temperature chart 64
Tende 267
Teutones 21, 22, 204
textile industry 27
TGV 30, 70–1
thalassothérapie 87
Third Republic 28
Thoronet, abbey 288–9
  Marys legend 161–2
tiles 288
time 82, 88
  useful phrases 301–2
Tinée valley 273–5
tipping 88
toilets 88
Touët-sur-Var **276**, 277
tour operators 78–80
tourist information 66
Tourtour **287**, 290
trains *see* railways
travel
  airlines 69–70
  bicycles 74–5
  cars 72, 73–4
  coaches and buses 71–2, 73
  disabled travellers 67–8
  ferries 72
  insurance 68
  trains 70–1, 73
    Eurostar 70
    Motorail 72
    des Pignes 276
    TGV 30, 70–1
  useful phrases 300–1
  when to go 64
Trémaïé 140
tripe 53
Troglodytique Saint-Romain de l'Aiguille 129
Trophime, Saint 153
troubadours 24, **44–5**

Vacqueyras **252**, 254
Vaison-la-Romaine 22, **254–8**
  castle 258
  Cathedral of Notre-Dame-de-Nazareth 256–7
  Chapelle St-Quentin 257–8
  eating out 258
  festivals 254–5

Vaison-la-Romaine (cont'd)
Haute-Ville 258
history 255
markets 258
Place du Vieux-Marché 258
Roman ruins 255–6, 258
Tour Beffroi 258
where to stay 258
Val d'Enfer 140
Valabres gorge 274
Valberg 274
Valdeblore 273
Vallabrègues 130
Vallée des Merveilles 266, 267
Vallée de la Roya **264–5**, 268
Valmasque 266
Van Dongen, Kees 37
Van Gogh, Vincent 37, 134–5, 147–8
museum 133
Var 287–91
Vasarély, Victor 38
Vaucluse *218–19*, 237–58
Abbaye de Sénanque 240
Carpentras 245–8
Comtat Venaissin 25–6, **242**
Fontaine-de-Vaucluse 240–2
Gordes **238–9**, 242
Le Thor 243
Les Dentelles de Montmirail 252–4
L'Isle-sur-la-Sorgue **243**, 245
Malaucène **250**, 251
Mont Ventoux *238*, 249–51
Pernes-les-Fontaines **244**, 245
Plateau d'Albion 251
Plateau de Vaucluse 237–42

Vaison-la-Romaine 22, **254–8**
Venasque **244**, 245
Village des Bories 239
Vaugines 227
Vauvenargues **214–15**, 216
vegetables 54
vegetarians 57
Venanson 272
Venasque **244**, 245
Véran, Saint 240
Verdon gorge 280
Verdun, Treaty of 24
Vernègues 200
Vernet, Claude-Joseph 35
Vésubie gorge 271
Vésubie valley **271–2**, 274–5
Via Domitia 129
Vichy government 29
Vidal, Peire 45
Village des Bories 239
Village in the Vaucluse 47
Villars-sur-Var 275
Villecroze 287
Villeneuve lez Avignon 116–19
Abbaye St-André 118
Chartreuse du Val Bénédiction 117–18
Collégiale Notre-Dame 117
eating out 119
Fort St-André 118
Livrée de la Thurroye 117
markets 119
Musée Pierre-de-Luxembourg 117
Tour des Masques 118
Tour Philippe-le-Bel 116
where to stay 119

Villers-Cotterêts, Edict of 26
Violès 254
Viollet-le-Duc 36
visas 66
Visigoths 23
Vitrolles 229
Vlaminck, Maurice 37

walking 75
Wars of Religion 26–7
watersports 87
weather 64
White Terror 28
William of Orange 92
wine **55–6**
Cassis 175
Châteauneuf-du-Pape 97
Coteaux d'Aix-en-Provence 215
Coteaux des Baux-en-Provence 139
Côtes-de-Provence 294, *295*
Côtes-du-Luberon 234
Côtes-du-Rhône Sud 253
Côtes-du-Ventoux 250
Gallo-Roman winery 129
La Palette 215
Lirac 99
Tavel 99
Villars-sur-Var 275
World Wars 28–9
Wylie, Laurence 47

youth hostels 77

Ziem, Félix 198
zoo 189

About the Updater

Jacqueline Chnéour is a freelance translator and researcher. Brought up in Paris and Nice, she moved to England in 1979 to follow a dream, and has lived in London ever since. She has updated or consulted on Cadogan's guides to French-speaking countries for the past 12 years.

First American edition published in 2009 by

CADOGAN GUIDES USA
An imprint of Interlink Publishing Group, Inc.
46 Crosby Street, Northampton, Massachusetts 01060
www.interlinkbooks.com
www.interlinkbooks.com/cadoganguides

Text copyright © Dana Facaros and Michael Pauls 1996, 2000, 2002, 2004, 2009
Copyright © New Holland Publishers (UK) Ltd, 2009

Cover photographs: © Jupiter Images
Photo essay photographs: © Alys Tomlinson, except p.6 (b) © Yann Guichaoua/PCL, p.12 © Chris Warren/
    PCL and p.16 © Gail Mooney/CORBIS
Maps © Cadogan Guides, drawn by Maidenhead Cartographic Services Ltd
Cover design: Jason Hopper
Photo essay design: Sarah Rianhard-Gardner
Editor: Linda McQueen
Proofreading: Elspeth Anderson
Indexing: Isobel McLean

Printed and bound in Italy by Legoprint
Library of Congress Cataloging-in-Publication Data available

ISBN: 978-1-56656-760-2

Provence touring atlas

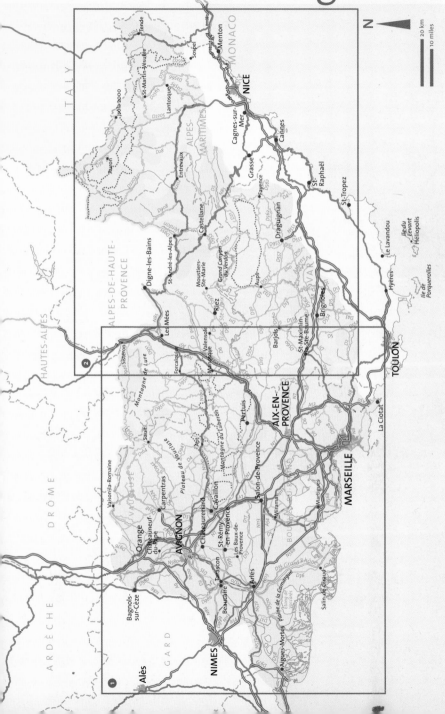

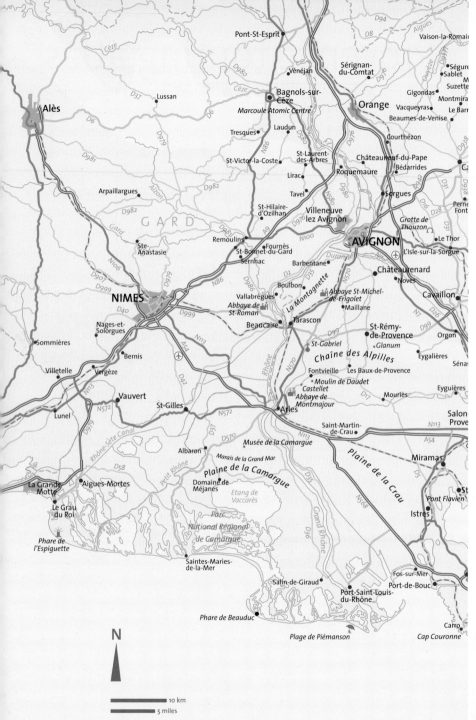

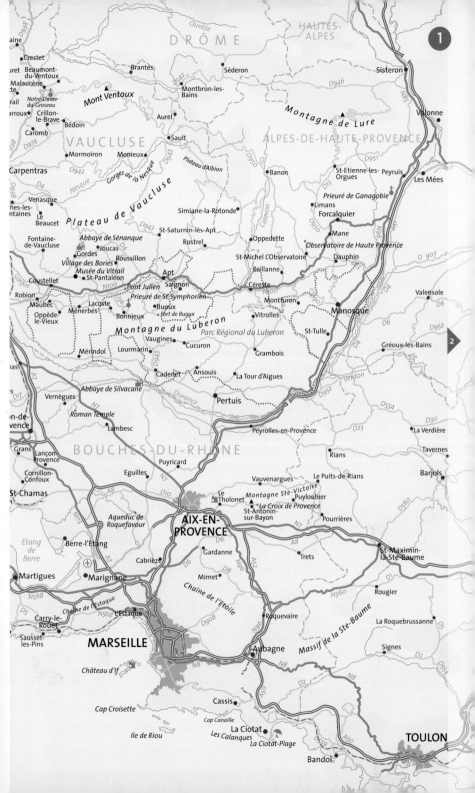

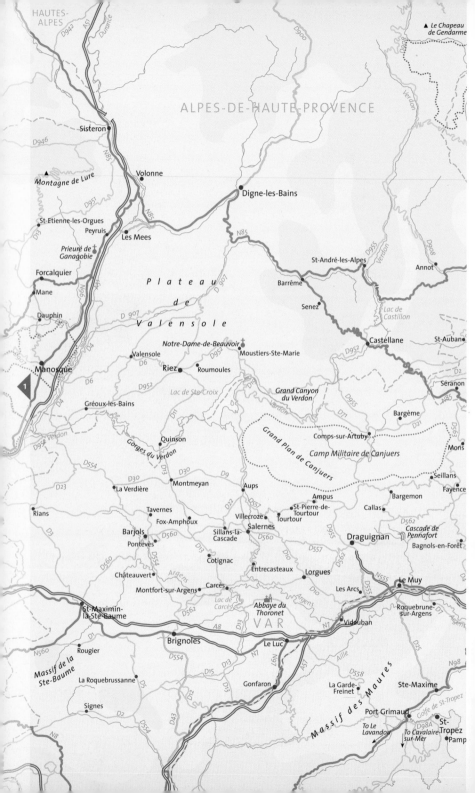

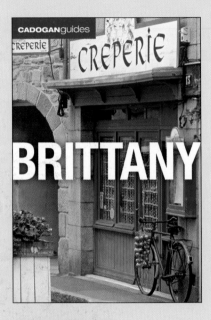
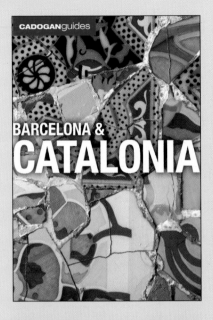

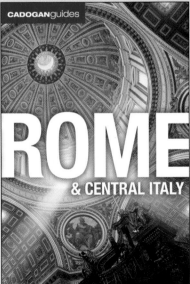

there can only be one guide

'A balance of infectious enthusiasm and solid practicality.'

Michael Palin

CADOGANguides

Buying a property

'An in-depth look at buying and living... everything from employment law to etiquet
Ideal Home Magazine

Buying a Property Bulgaria • *Buying a Property* Croatia • *Buying a Property* Cyprus • *Buying a Property* France • *Buying a Property* Greece • *Buying a Property* Ireland • *Buying a Property* Italy • *Buying a Property* Turkey